CLOSING TIME

JOE QUEENAN

CLOSING TIME

A Memoir

VIKING

VIKING
Published by the Penguin Group
Penguin Group (USA) Inc., 375 Hudson Street,
New York, New York 10014, U.S.A.
Penguin Group (Canada), 90 Eglinton Avenue East, Suite 700, Toronto,
Ontario, Canada M4P 2Y3 (a division of Pearson Penguin Canada Inc.)
Penguin Books Ltd, 80 Strand, London WC2R 0RL, England
Penguin Ireland, 25 St Stephen's Green, Dublin 2, Ireland
(a division of Penguin Books Ltd)
Penguin Books Australia Ltd, 250 Camberwell Road, Camberwell,
Victoria 3124, Australia (a division of Pearson Australia Group Pty Ltd)
Penguin Books India Pvt Ltd, 11 Community Centre,
Panchsheel Park, New Delhi–110 017, India
Penguin Group (NZ), 67 Apollo Drive, Rosedale, North Shore 0632,
New Zealand (a division of Pearson New Zealand Ltd)
Penguin Books (South Africa) (Pty) Ltd, 24 Sturdee Avenue,
Rosebank, Johannesburg 2196, South Africa

Penguin Books Ltd, Registered Offices: 80 Strand, London WC2R 0RL, England

First published in 2009 by Viking Penguin, a member of Penguin Group (USA) Inc.

1 2 3 4 5 6 7 8 9 10

LIBRARY OF CONGRESS CATALOGING-IN-PUBLICATION DATA
Queenan, Joe.
Closing time : a memoir / Joe Queenan.
p. cm.
ISBN 978-0-670-02063-8
1. Queenan, Joe. 2. Queenan, Joe—Childhood and youth. 3. Queenan, Joe—Family.
4. Working class—Pennsylvania—Philadelphia—Biography. 5. Fathers and sons—
Pennsylvania—Philadelphia. 6. Family violence—Pennsylvania—Philadelphia.
7. Philadelphia (Pa.)—Biography. 8. Forgiveness—Case studies. 9. Social mobility—
United States—Case studies. 10. Authors, American—Biography. I. Title.
CT275.Q44A3 2009
974.8'11043092—dc22
[B]   2008034567

Printed in the United States of America
Set in Minion
Designed by Francesca Belanger

To Ree, Eileen, and Mary Ann

Some are Born to sweet delight,
Some are Born to Endless Night.

—William Blake
  Auguries of Innocence

Contents

Chapter 1. **The Man on the Roof**

When a father dies, it is customary to forage through stored memories to conjure up an image that bathes him in the most heroic light. A single memory from my childhood eclipses all others. One Thursday night when I was thirteen years old, my father was standing alone in the kitchen of our Philadelphia row home, downing one of the ghastly local brews he'd long fancied. He was talking to himself, delivering some variation on his stock "O tempora, O mores" peroration, deploring the latest indignities that vested interests had imposed on the working man. The engulfing darkness of the civil rights movement, the demise of the Big Bands, and the collapse of Holy Mother Church as a viable institution were his other standard themes. We never knew whether he thought that the rest of us were listening attentively or were merely indulging him. Though the truth is, he never really required much in the way of an audience; often, when he entered the Ciceronian mode, he was content to declaim to an empty room.

That night, something unexpected interrupted his jeremiad. Hearing tiny steps approaching, he looked up and realized that the swinging door connecting the dining room to the kitchen was about to smash my five-year-old sister in the face. The bottom of the door was solid wood—thick but innocuous—but the pane above it was a taut sheet of rippled glass. This was the section that would have struck my sister right around eye level.

Mary Ann, his third daughter and fourth child, was chubby and angelic, the only member of the family everyone liked. She was, the rest of us contended, though she furiously denied it, a beneficiary of the Final Child Syndrome: Even parents who cannot stomach their firstborn children, deeming them conspirators in the massacre of their dreams, are reasonably indulgent toward, or at least oblivious to, the last one.

This forbearance may derive from a sense of mutual relief that the pro-creative ordeal has finally run its course, or perhaps the capacity for rage has simply exhausted itself. But Mary Ann had another ace up her sleeve: She was fabulously cute. This being the case, the idea of seeing her face scarred forever was unthinkable.

Reaching out to shield his daughter from injury, my father grasped the edge of the door just as it was closing. In doing so, he trapped two of his fingers in the space between the jamb and the frame. The door swung shut; we heard him scream. His fingers were horribly mangled; it seemed at first that he might lose one. Suffering greatly, and making no secret of it, he was taken to the emergency room at nearby Germantown Hospital. We did not own a car at the time, as we were going through one of our fallow economic periods, and in any case my mother had never learned to drive. Next door to us lived a man my father always called Tex because he was tall, fat, blustery, and not terribly quick on the draw, though he was not actually from Texas. I suppose it was Tex who provided transport. My father's mutilated fingers got patched up; he was given some painkillers; he returned home in great pain. He had been drinking heavily before he caught his fingers in the door, and he was certainly drinking heavily afterward.

At the time, my father was employed as a truck driver for a com-pany called Bachman Pretzels. His job was to deliver boxes of potato chips, pretzels, and other savory snacks to supermarkets and grocery stores all over the Delaware Valley. The job didn't pay well and wasn't leading anywhere, but it was better than the ones he had held recently, and much better than the ones he would have later. His salary, which amounted to slightly more than the minimum wage, was not enough to support a family of six, which is why my mother, after a sixteen-year hiatus, would soon return to the workforce, corralling a job as a credit manager at the hospital where my father had been treated. This was the hospital where I had been born thirteen years earlier, the year the Reds invaded South Korea.

Every workday, my father would rise at six in the morning, shave, dress, then grab a trolley and two buses to the company warehouse several miles away. There he would load his truck and set out on his travels. His route was picturesque and varied, though not especially glamorous. A good number of his accounts were the wholesome, reliable A&P supermarkets that could then be found on half the street corners in America. He also serviced a number of tiny, not especially profitable independent grocery stores in South Philadelphia and several of the cavernous Center City automats operated by the Horn & Hardart company, an iconic chain that was once ubiquitous but is now forgotten. His job was to replace packages that had been sold since his last visit, remove merchandise that had passed its expiration date, and use guile, subterfuge, charm, or whatever delicate forms of intimidation he could muster to persuade his clients to give exotic new products a try. One of these cutting-edge novelties was the now-famous cheese curl, an audacious midcentury innovation whose triumph over entrenched municipal resistance to anything "hoity-toity" was by no means a foregone conclusion at the time.

The supermarkets he visited each week were in run-down North Philadelphia neighborhoods where it was inadvisable to linger after nightfall and not an especially good idea to loiter during the day. The grocery stores were mostly in featureless south Jersey hamlets or drab though not especially dangerous neighborhoods in Trenton. His only swanky accounts were the Union League of Philadelphia—a private club, founded in 1862 by local swells, that occupied a stately brownstone on historic Broad Street—and the spiffy downtown headquarters of the Philadelphia Savings Fund Society, which at that time was the second-tallest building in the city. Back then, a city edict—or perhaps merely a time-honored tradition—decreed that no building could stand taller than the peak of the surprisingly ritzy hat crowning William Penn's head atop Philadelphia's anachronistic yet oddly beautiful City Hall.

This may have been because the city fathers feared that if Philadelphia ever forswore its conservative Quaker roots and developed a skyline, it would turn into New York. Philadelphians were both contemptuous and jealous of New Yorkers; they hated them personally but envied them their storied metropolis. Philadelphians believed that New York was a great city whose inhabitants had done nothing to deserve it. They resented New York's lycanthropic relationship with the rest of the country, feasting as it did on the fresh victims who poured off the buses at the Port Authority each day, siphoning off all the talented, energetic young people who, had they stayed home in the hinterland, might have made cities like Philadelphia and Pittsburgh and Baltimore more like New York. This was an attitude that would become more pronounced later, when New Yorkers, against all odds, would become even less likable. But by that time, the City of Brotherly Love would have its own skyline.

There was no question of my father's taking off work the day after his mishap, no matter what the condition of his hand. He, and his family with him, inhabited a Darwinian universe: If you didn't work, you didn't get paid. If you repeatedly didn't work, you got fired. He could not afford to lose his job, because we had only recently escaped from a housing project into a halfway-decent neighborhood and now found ourselves slowly, somewhat astonishingly, experiencing an economic rebound. My father, who dropped out of high school in ninth grade, had gone through long periods when he could not find any work whatsoever, and he always had trouble holding jobs for any length of time. Though he would argue otherwise, this was mostly his fault: Cantering home jauntily after his first day on any new job, with a smile on his face and a spring in his step suggesting that he had just had tea with the Elector of Saxony, he would describe his superiors and coworkers as princes among men who were prepared to give you the very shirt off their back even though they had only just made your acquaintance. They would continue to be described as shirt-doffing stalwarts for several weeks, their salt-of-the-earth qualities sedulously catalogued every night, their stature growing to Olympian proportions with each passing hour. But one day, perhaps a month after taking the job, he would have words with his boss, or cross swords with a colleague, or say the wrong thing to a customer, and the next thing we knew, he would be out on the street, cursing the day his *confreres*, now unmasked as degenerates, and his ignoble superiors, no longer the lights in the piazza, were born. There can be no doubt that he liked the people he met at his new jobs; it was just that he never liked them for long.

Sometimes, after paterfamilias's latest regurgitation into the ranks of the unemployed, we would come home from school and find him storming around the kitchen, having a few beers, working himself into a lather. In these instances, he would sullenly inform us that he had been "laid off." This well-traveled euphemism, a family delight, implied that he had been purged from the workforce through no fault of his own but because of unforeseen financial reverses compelling his employer to dismiss a handful of sacrificial lambs and/or black sheep. Such reverses always had something to do with the perfidious Dwight D. Eisenhower and the reptilian Richard Milhous Nixon, who seemed to take a personal interest in seeing to it that working-class people went to bed hungry. This was a situation that persisted even when Eisenhower and Nixon were no longer in office, suggesting that they had now taken to tormenting the proletariat purely as a hobby.

My father must have liked his job at the pretzel company much more than his other jobs, because he actually held on to it for a while—about three years, a very long stretch for one of such a refractory disposition. He enjoyed the job because he got to drive a nice-sized truck, which made him feel like a big deal, like he was his own boss. Sometimes he would bring the truck home for the night, and if we saw that he was not too tired or too obviously soused, we would beg him to take us out for a spin. When he was not in a black mood, he would oblige us, loading us into the back of the truck and thundering off into traffic, sending us careening back and forth between the unforgiving metal walls of the vehicle, all of us very merry indeed. The luckiest one among us—usually me—got to stand in the deep well on the right side of the truck, with the heavy sliding door pulled all the way back, allowing air to get in. If I was not careful, I could have easily tumbled out into the street and been flattened by oncoming cars. But I was careful—I was born careful—and these outings were rollicking good fun. Anyway, back in the Paleocene 1950s, when being fond of one's children had not yet come into vogue, poor people didn't seem to mind all that much if one of their offspring went flying out into traffic, as everyone had spares.

The day after my father's accident, he roused me out of bed early in the morning and said he would need me to go out on the truck with him, as it would be impossible for him to open and close doors with his hand in that condition. He would not be able to write anything in his order book, nor to ferry the boxes of pretzels and potato chips from the truck into the stores. He would not even be able to steer the vehicle. So my older sister Agnes Marie—always known as "Ree"—took a note to Mother Superior's office saying that I had the flu, and off we went.

This was not the first time he had allowed me to play hooky, nor the last, but it was the one childhood escapade I would remember most vividly. The whole day was a miracle, from start to finish, which would not have been the case had anyone at the warehouse noticed the condition of his hand and suggested that he should not be driving as, even if the truck was well insured, the authorities would probably take a dim view of such extravagant interstate vehicular hijinks. Somehow, by dint of stealth and cunning, we managed to sneak out of the building without anybody being the wiser, and before you could say "Jack Robinson," we were scooting across the Betsy Ross Bridge to south Jersey.

It was clear that my father was still in pain, lots of it, but he didn't mope or grumble. Whenever he needed to change lanes or make a sharp turn, he would tell me to jump up off the pretzel can I was perched on, stand directly to his right, and ease the steering wheel around in the prescribed direction. It was first-class lunacy, careening around the highways the way we did that day. We could have been killed out there on the open roads, but we weren't; he could have had his license taken away, but he didn't. Neither of us would ever forget the bracing drama and high adventure of it all. We were making the best of a bad situation. We were rising to the occasion. We were staring down misfortune. We were the types of men—or, in my case, boys—upon whose like the world would not soon look again. My father was proud of me that day, proud in a way he had rarely been before. I was his confederate, his partner in crime. Gallivanting around the Delaware Valley with his fingers in ribbons and my untested hands at the helm was more daring and heroic than anything any of my playmates' fathers had ever done or ever would do. And I was right there beside him, riding shotgun.

Before we returned to the warehouse that day, we stopped off at the Latimer Deli in downtown Philadelphia for a hamburger with a side of fries and a vanilla milkshake the size of Vesuvius. This would never cease to be my favorite meal, not even when I was all grown up and could order anything I pleased, because every time I had a burger with fries and a milkshake I would remember the day my father was the bravest man in the whole wide world. Returning home in triumph that evening, I felt, for perhaps the first time in my life, that God had put me in a situation where my father not only loved me but actually needed me.

For years, I'd believed that if I prayed hard every night and was very patient, He Who Knew All and Saw All would eventually come through for me. God, in my opinion, was not cruel; He was merely otherwise engaged. So when my father died one balmy December evening thirty-four years later, the day we went out on the truck together was the one I chose to remember him by. He was the man who drove the pretzel truck with a single hand, his other hand wreathed in bandages, because he did not want to lose his job and see his children go hungry. He was the man who would do anything for his family.

Days like that were rare. My father got broken when he was young, and he never got fixed. He may have wanted to be a good father, a good husband, a good man, but he was not cut out for the job. He liked to drink, but unlike some men who liked to drink, it was the only thing he liked to do. Among our relatives, he had a reputation as a happy-go-lucky fellow who, once he got a few beers in him, would turn into the life of the party. He was not the life of our party. Most of the time he was already dead drunk when he came home from work, spoiling for a fight with whoever crossed him first. When the fancy struck him, and he was not too tired, he would take off his belt and beat us. Other times he would announce impending beatings, only to explain that, as he was too tuckered out to administer a whipping that day, we'd have to reschedule. He had gotten it into his head that these stays of execution were in some way merciful, perhaps even appreciated.

By the time I started getting worked over by a man five times my size, beating children was going out of style in this great nation. By "beating" I refer not to generic spanking but to the ritualistic act of stripping your offspring and whipping them across the buttocks and thighs with a thick leather belt so that they scream and plead and bleed and stay marked for days and wish both you and they were dead. By the 1950s—the age of the progressive, though some said overly permissive, Dr. Benjamin Spock—even the reflexively barbarous poor were beginning to realize that inflicting severe, humiliating punishment on one's children was inadvisable, if only because those same children might grow up to be large, muscular barbarians who would one day return home and inflict severe, humiliating punishment on their parents.

As was so often the case, my father trailed far behind the pedagogical curve in this sphere of human relations. At some point in his life, he had decided that if he could not cast a shadow over the world, he would cast one over his family. And so he did. He beat us often and he beat us savagely. He beat us individually and he beat us together. The worst beatings were when he got spectacularly bombed, came unmoored from reality, and grasped the belt by the wrong end. Then the metal flange would wrap around my thighs and flail against my penis and testicles. It was no use protesting that the punishment was not being meted out in strict accordance with Marquess of Queensberry rules, as this would only make him more angry, and the normal level of rage he routinely, effortlessly attained was bad enough. He could go from zero to sixty in a hurry.

Years later, I verified—through discreet inquiries—that none of my close friends was ever subjected to such a reign of terror. At the time, I had no way of knowing this: As youngsters, we were not aware of what went on inside our classmates' homes, and these issues did not come up in conversation. Recreational mistreatment of children merely seemed like something expected of fathers, a prerogative of sorts, as working-men needed to let off steam at the end of a long, hard day. We knew that some of our friends' parents were drunks, and that at least one of them had to be carted off to the loony bin from time to time to get his noggin reconditioned. But our friends did not live in fear of their fathers, nor did they want them out of the picture. We did.

I never forgave my father for the way he treated us. I never fell prey to the *tout comprendre c'est tout pardonner* slant on dysfunction, the notion that if you assembled all the pertinent data about a malefactor's childhood and reviewed it dispassionately, you would come to understand the forces that had shaped him and assign the blame, or at least a good portion of it, elsewhere. This put the victim in a position where absolution, previously an act of charity, was now deemed morally compulsory.

Manufacturing excuses for my father's behavior was a family industry. For as long as I could remember, an army of back-porch barristers—his sisters, cousins, aunts, even a couple of commiserating brothers-in-law—stood ready to cite chapter and verse to explain away his misdeeds, positioning his cruelty in a context that made him seem far less culpable. One, his father had been beastly to him, abusive in the generically horrific way that Irish males often are to their sons. Two, he had grown up during the Great Depression, when poor people literally peddled apples on street corners and many a night the entire Delaware Valley went to bed hungry because there was no food in the larder, and perhaps not even a morsel of stale bread left in the entire tristate area, because rats the size of ocelots had already gotten to it. Three, he had undergone a series of heartbreaking wartime experiences, with both his parents dying in their midfifties while he was just a few hours away, standing guard over Italian prisoners of war at Fort Knox. Four, despite being only a few hours away at Fort Knox, from which the harmless Eyeties in his custody were not terribly likely to escape, he was denied a pass to attend either parent's funeral, and his volcanic response to that rebuff—deserting his post at a time when going AWOL was punishable by death, and getting into an ill-advised slugging match with a pack of MPs back in Philadelphia—landed him in a military prison in Georgia. There he languished for three years, from 1944 until 1947, a slender young northerner of the Irish-Catholic persuasion in a prison manned by beefy, middle-aged men of the Johnny Reb persuasion.

Mitigating Circumstance Number 5 was that he had never finished high school, even though he was far brighter and considerably more gifted than most people who did. Six, he was a fine-looking chap who was emotionally traumatized by losing his hair in his early thirties. Frankly, I never understood how that one made it onto the list, but it kept popping up anyway. Seven, he never recovered from the 1958 recession, which cost him the only white-collar job he ever had. Eight, he never recovered from the disgrace of losing our house in 1959, as a result of losing his job, as a result of the 1958 recession, a disaster for which Dwight D. Eisenhower was personally responsible.

Nine—and this was the real haymaker—he had been shot in the head at age twelve, when a friend accidentally fired off his father's service revolver and the bullet ricocheted off the kitchen ceiling and into his skull, where it remained until a grizzled army surgeon motored all the way down from West Point to excise it, as it was lodged so close to the brain that no jerkwater Delaware Valley sawbones would dare take a crack at it. The surgeon, legend had it, thereupon inserted a metal plate in the back of his head; legend also had it that the plate was still there. If this was true, and we had no reason to believe it was not, it was the sort of H. P. Lovecraft development that in and of itself might account for my father's explosive, unpredictable behavior.

Justification Number 10, as if all that preceded it were not enough, was that his baby sister Betty had died under mysterious circumstances when he was still a small child himself, and this tragedy had haunted him for the rest of his life. The circumstances were murky; he may have been playing with matches, then run away and hidden in a neighbor's house while his two-year-old sister burned to a crisp, but there were also suggestions that the luckless toddler had tripped and fallen down the stairs while he was supposed to be babysitting. No one could ever say for sure how Betty perished, only that she did, and that he was in some way responsible. Speaking for myself, I always felt that the infant sibling's death should have taken the top spot on this cavalcade of rationalizations, but within the family, it was the metal plate in the head that occupied pride of place. Little Betty's death might explain why he was depressed. The bullet in the head explained why he was crazy.

Given this phenomenal *curriculum vitae miserabilis*, there was no point in our bellyaching about a handful of character-molding flayings here and there, or a few nights going to bed without a proper meal, or my sister and I being left to fend for ourselves out on the street in a raging blizzard when she was eight and I was six while he was somewhere nice and toasty getting juiced to the gills, and while his wife was giving birth to his fourth child, or having no food in the house and three cavities and a manic-depressive mother who had been missing in action since Shrove Tuesday. No matter how sorry you might feel for yourself initially, you would eventually pull up short and come to your senses, realizing that you couldn't outpoint an opponent holding as many high cards as him. He was tough in the self-vindicatory clinches; no one in the history of urban misfortune had ever experienced more setbacks, emotional trauma, and all-purpose injustice than our very own Quaker City Jean Valjean.

On the positive side, it was nice to know that his antipathy toward us wasn't personal; he had simply suffered through so many calamities that the only way he knew how to respond to adversity was to brutalize those closest to him. Happily, his preference for victims shorter than forty-eight inches kept my mother out of the line of fire. Like many Irish-Catholic men of his generation, he would never dream of raising his hand to his wife, not only because he feared that it would have brought down the curtain on their marriage, but because men like him had an unwholesome reverence for their spouses, viewing them as domestic stand-ins for the Virgin Mary, with the one notable difference that, unlike the Madonna, they also cooked and cleaned. My mother was not a Madonna; she was an emotionally inert woman who had injudiciously brought four children into the world with no clear idea of how henceforth to proceed. While my father was skinning us alive with his trusty old belt, she would entomb herself in her bedroom, surrounded by newspapers she never seemed to learn anything from, pretending not to hear what was going on downstairs. But the walls were not thick and the sound must have carried, if not into her conscience, at least into her cochleae.

Armed with this abundant exculpatory material, my sister Ree and I tried to construct an elaborate moral apparatus that would exonerate our father of his misdeeds. My younger sister Eileen, three years my junior and far and away the smartest member of the family, was having none of it; compassion was not her long suit. Ree and I were less vindictive, less intransigent, less bright. The way we assessed the situation, to admit that Dad was the person he appeared to be was to concede that his cruelty was deliberate. This was unthinkable. Instead, we decided that violence was a bent he could not control, but that through medication or a confidence-boosting job that would reverse the emasculation he had undergone after losing his house, or perhaps simply through good, old-fashioned divine intervention, everything would one day work out for the best.

I was not above concocting my own theories that even the tiniest amount of alcohol could interact with his metal plate, generating a chemical chain reaction that instantaneously triggered impossibly subtle psychoneural responses and impelled this otherwise lovable man to knock his kids around the room and tear the fixtures out of the walls. This sent the reassuring message that our troubles were essentially mineral in origin; it was all the result of some weird electromagnetic process that made it impossible for him to function properly. Like Ree, I derived solace from these daft theories, if only because they conferred upon our oppressor an aura of tragic romance and mystery, which were hard to come by in that part of Philadelphia.

This being our mind-set, we began sifting through the data to prepare an *amicus curiae* brief should he ever be hauled before the authorities and asked to explain his passion for brutalizing the prepubescent set. We did this because for the longest time we still loved him and refused to accept that he was beyond redemption. But we also did it because no one wants to spend the rest of his life reviling a person who once viewed his birth as a blessing. We did not believe that he did the things he did because he was evil. We believed that he did them because he was damaged goods. That, at least, was the approach Ree and I adopted; Eileen felt otherwise. She had him sized up early.

For years, Ree and I reasoned that if our father would only stop drinking, he would immediately reemerge, frog-prince style, as the most wondrous of God's creations, the very flower of Christian manhood. When we were small, when we did not yet wish him ill, we used to chat among ourselves about how affectionate and funny he could be when he was not drinking, when, like Henry Jekyll, he truly was a capital fellow. My mother, who never seemed especially fond of the man she ultimately spent thirty years living with, would thereupon remind us that if the good side of his personality had ever existed, it would never have allowed the dark side to take over. It was a valid point, but as we enjoyed his company more than she ever had—he took us to the movies, he played Monopoly with us, he let us take days off from school—we did not want to hear it. We were still too young and guileless to understand why he drank with such implacable fury, much less to understand that Henry Jekyll and Edward Hyde were one and the same person, that Jekyll had indeed created Hyde.

As a child, hamstrung by the sense of guilt that all Catholics are born with, as if it were a side effect of the obstetric procedure, I often wondered if it was something we had done, or said, that made him beat us. He would regularly tell us that we would never amount to "a pimple on an elephant's rear end," as if the repetition of this prophesy would ensure that it came true, or aggrandize the size of the pimple he himself had amounted to. Our mistreatment, both verbal and physical, was baffling, for we were excellent students, devout Catholics, attentive, respectful progeny, and had long been in possession of solid documentary evidence that we were not vermin.

Primitive home movie cameras came into fashion in the early 1960s, and my uncle Jerry, always the first one on the block to be seduced by voluptuous new technologies, immediately went out and bought one. We were by far his favorite subjects, as we were, by common consent, remarkably well behaved, by no means moody or withdrawn, fun to be around. Whenever our families would convene, Uncle Jerry would haul out his equipment, set up the projector and screen, and present grainy footage of my sisters and I frolicking in the bouncy, rambunctious fashion that was our calling card. Even my father, who generally disapproved of anything we did that did not involve him, seemed amused by our antics. I only wish we had worked up the nerve to add a bit of commentary to these films, to help him better understand what should have been apparent to the naked eye. "See! We're not ingrates," we might have informed him. "We're not failures. We're not pimples on an elephant's rear end. We're your children."

There can be no denying that my father possessed what my mother always referred to as "good qualities." This was only to be expected, for while it was true that she had on their honeymoon night tactlessly informed him that she did not love him and had married him for practical reasons (she did not want to end up an old maid, two paychecks were better than one), he must have had a number of redeeming features when they met or else she would not have taken the ring he offered and spent the next three decades in his company. He did have many redeeming features, but they were mostly in the realm of intellect, not emotion. He had a great deal of personal charm, which enabled him to constantly land new jobs he would subsequently lose when the charm wore off. He had a highly developed sense of humor and knew how to spin a yarn. Strangers were invariably seduced by his wit, at least for a while; he was, by turns, mordant, puckish, irreverent. He had a smile that could melt the iciest heart, a treasure he did not bequeath to me. A charter member of an ethnic group one sage described as "a race of gregarious strangers," he was typical of first-generation Irish-American males: monstrous to their progeny, sweetness and light to everyone else.

He had very good taste in motion pictures and even better taste in literature. His preferences ranged from heavyweights like Ernest Hemingway and F. Scott Fitzgerald to solid middlebrow authors like A. J. Cronin, John O'Hara, and Edwin O'Connor. He had read all the Sherlock Holmes mysteries, much of Shakespeare, and many books about Abraham Lincoln. He sometimes read twaddle (Erle Stanley Gardner), but he never read trash (Mickey Spillane). He belonged to a class that had once flourished: the working-class autodidact who reads good books because he understands that good books lift mankind out of the slime. This species is now extinct, wiped out by television or despair. Working-class people today do not read good books; they read offal churned out by churls, nitwits, and swine, if they read at all.

Even in his worst moments, my father never resembled the simpletons who masquerade as blue-collar heroes on television; in the darkest of times he never talked like Archie Bunker, the malignant sow dreamed up by West Coast millionaires as a mechanism for sneering at people who have to work for a living. Unlike TV's prefab proletariat, self-congratulatory buffoons all, my father could tell you why Julius Caesar crossed the Rubicon, why Richard III killed the little princes, why Hannibal dragged his elephants over the Alps, and why one should think twice before venturing out onto the English moors at night. Hemmed in by ignorant men, he was not himself ignorant.

Nor was he vulgar, at least not in public. He was, in his finest moments, the best the working class had to offer. He was ceaselessly in the process of educating himself, not because he thought it might advance his career—he had no career—but because reading was a way to escape to a better world. This is the same conclusion I reached when I was young, poor, lacking in prospects. While some people, to borrow an insight from C. S. Lewis, read to know that they are not alone, the poor read to know that they are not condemned. It is often said that children are the wealth of the poor. This was not my experience. But books are without question the wealth of the poor's children. Books are a guiding light out of the underworld, a secret passageway, an escape hatch. To the affluent, books are ornaments. To the poor, books are siege weapons.

My father's attributes, laudable though they might be, did not alter the fact that once he took on the role of a parent, he had wandered out of his depth. By the time I was thirteen or so, I understood that whatever relationship I would have with my father in later years, it was going to be a salvage operation. I was going to get only one father in this life, and if this one was not up to the mark, then I would just have to pretend he was, to convince myself that his heroic performance in driving the truck with shredded fingers was the sort of thing he could do every day of the week, if only he wanted to.

Later, when I had a family of my own, I would sometimes backtrack and reassess pivotal events, not from the perspective of a child but from that of a father. When I was still an infant, my father bought a set of Lionel electric trains and wrapped them around the Christmas tree. My mother later assured me that both father and son were enraptured by the trains, though for obvious reasons I have no memory of this. One night when I was around five, a hurricane hit town, our basement flooded, and the train set was destroyed. My memory of the trains is not of watching them chug their way round and round the Christmas tree but of playing with the rusty tracks and the corroded, water-damaged engine all year round, using them as substitutes for toys. My father never replaced the train set, because he interpreted the flood as an act of God, and once God had destroyed the trains, it would have been foolhardy—and perhaps even blasphemous—to try to undo the damage, let alone buy another set. And so he pouted, like an even less mature Achilles.

When I was eight, my father lost the only white-collar job he ever had, and with it our house, so we were forced to move into a housing project. The rusted trains came with us, corroded symbols of Paradise Lost, hanging around for years as an unmistakable memento of inadequacy and bad luck. One Sunday night, my uncle Jim stopped by the housing project on an unexpected visit. Uncle Jim, a prosperous sort, was laden with precious cargo that evening: In his hands he held a nifty set of American Flyer trains that my cousin Jimmy, now in college, no longer played with. Sleek, less ostentatiously "classic" than Lionels, American Flyer trains had a breezy, suburban feel to them, evoking little of the romance of the rails one automatically associated with their more famous competitors. But they were electric trains, and that beat no electric trains hands down.

One can readily imagine my excitement when I tore open the boxes containing the trains that evening. Clearing off the dining room table, my father, my uncle, and I hurriedly set up the track and attached the transformer. Then, slipping into the role of the gracious hostess, a role she was rarely called upon to fill, my mother told me to go out and buy some pound cake and cookies for our visitors. There were no stores in the housing project; the nearest grocery was a good fifteen-minute walk. I raced off with one of my sisters, then raced back. By the time we returned, my father had jacked up the transformer to full speed and sent the entire set of trains hurtling off the table onto the harsh linoleum floor. Some of the cars were merely chipped and scratched, certainly not damaged beyond repair. But the engine was kaput.

I suppose I cried that night; I suppose my father beat me, as he always beat me when I cried, because crying was not manly, and my misfortune paled by comparison with what he had endured in the Great Depression, when little kids would have cut off their right arms to have a set of busted, rusted electric trains to play with. My misfortune did pale by comparison with what he had endured in the Great Depression. But it was misfortune all the same. In theory, that engine could have been taken to the shop and repaired, or replaced with another engine, but that, I would come to realize, is not the way things work when the poor are involved. When things get broken in a poor person's house, they get chucked out into the backyard or tossed into the basement or thrown into the trash. But they never get taken to the repair shop, because the very concept of "repair" attests to a confidence in the universe that poor people never actually feel.

Various incidents from my youth haunt me still: beatings, lies, gruesome dental experiences, hijacked piggy banks, being sent to bed on an empty stomach. But the saga of the electric trains abides with me, not because of what it did to a child but because of what it did to a man. My father went through his entire life expecting a flood to destroy the Lionel trains he had slaved away to purchase for his newborn son. He went through life convinced that if he ever got a chance to redeem himself in the eyes of his family, the good money said he would screw that up, too. He went through life believing that when the clouds did part and good fortune, on one of its pitifully infrequent visits to our neighborhood, did shine upon him, it would simply provide him with yet another opportunity to make a fool of himself in front of his wife, his children, and his brother-in-law, who had always looked down on him anyway. Yet tellingly, like so many Irish-American men, he had an amazing ability to make his victims feel sorry for him, for when I think back on my locomotively sabotaged childhood, I do not feel sorry for myself, but I still feel sorry for him.

When I was small, I did not hate my father in the way I would hate him later. I did not wish he were dead; I simply wished he were elsewhere. One of the epochal vignettes from that era was the day my father, his younger brother Johnny, and my uncle Jerry clambered up a ladder onto Jerry's roof to do some repairs and then got so drunk they were afraid to come back down. For no very good reason, they had gone up there to do some retiling and spread a little paint around and perhaps mend the outside of the chimney. My father was useless around tools; he could not hammer a nail, smooth a plane, replace a window, cut a lawn.

My uncle Jerry was slightly less hapless, though he thought otherwise: He once replaced a lighting fixture without setting the house on fire and ever afterward thought this put him in the same weight class as Thomas Edison. The third member of this unlikely crew was Uncle Johnny, who had recently been paroled from the slammer and emancipated for one of his brief but eventful forays into normal society. Having served as a mechanic in the Navy during the war and having mastered all sorts of skills while in prison, Uncle Johnny was actually quite the craftsman. When he was not drunk.

It was boiling hot that afternoon, and the three of them started hitting the sauce pretty early, periodically asking us to fetch them fresh supplies. We were more than happy to provide this livery service, carrying bottle after bottle up to the men on the roof. My uncle Jerry drank only two brands of beer: Miller High Life, the beer that had, by reputation, made Milwaukee famous, and Carling Black Label, the beer that manifestly had not. My father, who always invested foods and beverages with precisely calibrated socioeconomic values, did not care for either of these brands: He thought their hifalutin names sounded Republican. He refused to drink anything other than Ortlieb's or Schmidt's, locally brewed swill so vile, so flat, you had to pour a shaker of salt inside to conjure up even a wan simulacrum of a foamy head. But that day up on the roof, he was perfectly content to guzzle my uncle's Carling Black Label, because he was so lightheaded and happy, he'd completely forgotten about Republicans.

By the time the sun started to disappear, my father and my two uncles were three sheets to the wind, too plastered to make the perilous return trip down the ladder. They had no choice but to sit on the roof until they got their sea legs about them and felt steady enough to descend. That evening was one of the seraphic moments in my childhood. The lads seemed to be having a swell time of it up there, and the noncombatants—children, sisters, wives—were having an equally wonderful time down below. My father was up on the roof drinking, which was a potentially fatal activity. But none of us was hoping that he would fall and smash his skull and die without getting to remind us, one last time, that no matter how hard we tried, we would never amount to a pimple on an elephant's rear end. We simply wanted him to stay up there, ever so slightly removed from his family, quaffing his beer, harming no one. We wanted him to stay right where he was, up on that sloping roof in Havertown, Pennsylvania, until the cows came home. We wanted him to stay up on that roof forever.

Chapter 2. **Sin City**

In the milieu I grew up in, pivotal events were associated with a particular street or parish, rather than a specific day, month, or year.

"Your mother got a reputation for being flighty because of Wendle Street," a chiding relative would report. What transpired on Wendle Street would go unexplained, as would the meaning of the word "flighty."

"You look like you're from Fifth and Gybyp" was a popular insult.

"Father Whearty got in trouble with the archdiocese, so they shipped him out to Our Lady of Victory" was the sort of unsubstantiated assertion my father loved to make, adorning a quip with the mantle of theory.

"Was I born in Holy Child or Holy Angels?" I would ask my parents, ignorant of the yawning socioeconomic gap that divided the two parishes.

Dates were irrelevant in such an environment, because everything anyone needed to know was contained in this otherwise inscrutable semiotic code. "Your father started his heavy drinking on Russell Street, but it didn't get really bad until you moved to Saint Bridget's," my aunt Cassie would confide. Within its context, this was as exactingly precise as saying "The Spanish Armada was destroyed on August 5, 1588." These were Irish-Catholic hieroglyphics that, however mystifying to the uninitiated, made perfect sense to us. The entire city was gerrymandered into parishes whose very names served as code words for distinct economic classes.

"They live in Saint Ambrose's." (*They're loaded.*)

"They moved up to Saint Cecilia's." (*They think they're better than us.*)

"They live in Saint Matthew's." (*They think they're a lot better than us.*)

"They never got out of Saint Ed's." (*Those poor bastards are still living down there with the spear-chuckers.*)

This penchant for describing all urban phenomena in narrow diocesan terms sometimes defied logic. When, at age sixteen, I introduced a new friend to my mother, she asked if his house on the 4800 block of Franklin Street was located in Holy Child parish or the Church of the Incarnation. His name was Weiss; he was a lion of Judah; until that moment, he had no idea that he was living in an invisible city over which a Catholic zoning board held sway, surreptitiously reconfiguring municipal boundaries without any of the Jews, Baptists, Seventh-Day Adventists, or atheists being any the wiser.

Every family I associated with during my childhood could trace its rise or fall to a single apocalyptic event, terrible in its grandeur, seismic in its ramifications. It might be one pregnancy too many, or a job that got away, or a car crash, or the munificence of a wayfaring stranger bubbling up from an economic class of whose existence we had previously only heard unsubstantiated rumors. The watershed moment in our history occurred in 1958, when my father lost his job as an "expeditor" at a company called Proctor & Schwartz. The firm was revered the length and breadth of the nation for its sturdy Mary Proctor appliances, which included a line of staggeringly reliable toasters. An expeditor was the Triple A equivalent of a draftsman, a blue-collar acolyte poised hopefully on the cusp of the white-collar world yet still constrained by the fetters of the proletariat. Handy to have around but hardly indispensable, my father spent his entire tenure at the company living in fear of being laid off. His Waterloo occurred during an economic downturn brought on, at least in his version of events, by heartless Republican policies devised with no other purpose than to smash the dreams of the workingman.

At the time, we were living on Russell Street in a North Philadelphia parish called Saint Veronica's. It was Saint Veronica who captured the imprint of Christ's face on her veil as the Son of God was dragging himself through the backstreets of Jerusalem on his way to Golgotha; she was one of those star-crossed holy women who, unlike Saint Agnes or

Saint Joan of Arc, did not become famous by doing something overtly theatrical, like spontaneously growing hair all over her body to demoralize potential rapists or assuming command of the armies of France at the age of seventeen. She was merely someone who happened to be in the right place at the right time. It helped that she came equipped for emergencies.

After my father's unexpected expectoration into the ranks of the unemployed, we could no longer pay our bills and were forced to abandon our winsome home and move into a housing project in a neighborhood no one we knew was even vaguely familiar with. Though the Schuylkill Falls Housing Project—always referred to as the East Falls Housing Project because no one could spell "Schuylkill"—was only about six miles away from Russell Street, the psychological distance was Saharan. Everyone—relatives, friends, neighbors, creditors—knew that we were not moving there out of choice but because we had been banished from the lower middle class. We were slipping further down an economic ladder on which we had no more than a tenuous foothold to begin with. We were going into exile.

Storm clouds had been gathering on the horizon for some time before the day of our *hegira* officially arrived. One Friday night, I was watching a popular television program called *The Adventures of Rin Tin Tin* with my older sister. The central dramatic figure in the program was a diligent and resourceful German shepherd stationed at a frontier outpost in the Old West who, by dint of his prodigious tracking skills, quietly evolved into the nemesis of the depraved Apache, the bloodthirsty Kiowa, and the legendarily inhospitable Comanche. Unexpectedly, as we were marveling at Rin Tin Tin's latest ingenious solution to some sagebrush conundrum, the doorbell rang. My mother answered, and a few seconds later two burly men in trench coats entered the living room, unplugged the television, and lugged it out of the house. I was eight at the time, my sister sixteen months older. My two younger sisters, five and one, were upstairs sleeping. Prior to this event, no one had explained the concept of property repossession to us, so we had no idea why or by what right the men had taken the television away. Luckily for them, my father was not home that evening, for had he been (or so we believed at the time), he would have fought tooth and nail to prevent the repo Gestapo from filching our TV set, or at the very least delayed them long enough to let us see the end of the show. But he was not there, as not being places where he ought to have been was standard operating procedure.

This was not the only sign that something was amiss. On Saturday mornings, we would often be jolted awake by the sound of a mammoth wooden cart—more like a gigantic wheelbarrow—being hauled up the street to our front door by a squat, powerful man belonging to an ethnic group with which we had had no previous social congress. I think he may have been Lebanese. The cart was laden to overflowing with quality foodstuffs purchased at Neubauer's Market, a mildly upscale emporium of the type that my parents never patronized, as they had rarely been in the chips and viewed the purchase of pricy foods as evidence of "snootiness," at that time a grave ethnic transgression. The merchandise had been paid for by my aunt Addie, an eccentric figure cloaked in copious mystery, whose own snootiness was indulged, if not encouraged. Strictly speaking, Aunt Addie was not my aunt, nor my father's; she was some sort of cousin. But in those days, any benevolent, gray-haired spinster eternally poised to loosen her purse strings was known as an aunt. These women were rarely lookers.

Aunt Addie (short for Adelaide) had slaved away her entire life in downtown Philadelphia, in some midlevel secretarial capacity. She was famous hither and yon for attending daily mass at nearby Old Saint Joseph's Church, the longest-standing Catholic house of worship in the city and one of the most venerable in all of English-speaking America, before reporting for work. As daily mass included Saturdays and Sundays, this obsession demanded an immense commitment of time and energy on her part, given that she lived miles away from downtown Philadelphia, nowhere near the church, and was completely dependent on public transportation.

It was said by some that my aunt Addie had narrowly missed crossing the Atlantic on the *Titanic* in April 1912, that her taxi had been delayed or her train halted at the junction or her steamer trunk mislaid, but this was unlikely. People back then liked to tart up their otherwise humdrum biographies with apocryphal tales of narrow escapes from epic nautical disasters or chance encounters with shadowy associates of Buffalo Bill or John Dillinger or Quanah Parker. Aunt Addie was gruff but generous and had doted on my father since his youth, deeming him a victim rather than a victimizer, an ill-starred will-o'-the-wisp who never got the breaks. His marriage was one of the breaks he had not gotten. My mother and Aunt Addie never got along; my mother, in her opinion, was the one responsible for my father's failure—something about Wendle Street, thinking she was better than him, flightiness.

One day, the magic wheelbarrow rolled up for the very last time, and a week or so later we were turfed out into the street. Because we had vacated our house under ignominious circumstances, we never went back to visit our friends in the old neighborhood. I never saw my playmates again, though I remember their names to this day: Jackie Purnell and Charlie Lebencki. Little else about the neighborhood has stayed with me, only that my third-grade teacher was the first rich person I ever met, a scioness who was determined to give back to the community, in the way that only the children of the rich can.

The assumption that Miss Needham was rich was predicated on two facts that could not be gainsaid: She had the same last name as the founder of a nationwide trucking firm, and she was breathtakingly pretty. If she were not rich, so the common wisdom went, then her decision to take a job as a poorly paid elementary school teacher—and to do so in a working-class neighborhood—made no sense, as her brains and her matinee-idol looks should have enabled her to do much better for herself elsewhere. She was teaching because she could afford to teach; she was dawdling in the precincts of the proletariat to make some kind of point to her parents. That settled it, then: She was rich. This was my introduction to the concept of noblesse oblige. Noblesse oblige or not, she was an outstanding teacher.

One other memory from those years stands out. There were two slovenly but merry drunks named the Parker brothers who lived around the corner on Tioga Street, one of those evocative names that urbanites used to confer on highways and byways, thoroughfares and streets, back in the days when people still thought cities were beautiful. The Parker brothers lived right next door to a reclusive barfly rumored by neighborhood children to be a witch. Both houses were falling apart at the seams. Juvenile necromancy was the first casualty of our relocation; the housing project, hampered by both its recent nativity and its terse, brutalist style, lacked the shabbiness, architectural nuance, and sense of faded grandeur needed to support the illusion that witchcraft was afoot at the local level.

Ever afterward, 1959 was referred to as "the year we lost the house." Losing the house signified not only defeat and humiliation but a rupture with a putatively arcadian past. Decades later, when I went back to visit Russell Street, I was startled to come upon a tiny, standard-issue two-story row house with a three-step front stoop, a vest-pocket garden in the back, and no garage, located in a grubby, charm-free district that had disintegrated into a slum just a few years after we left it. The way my parents always talked about this repository of shattered dreams, it was as if we had been evicted from Versailles or Eden itself.

My father, as usual, blamed Dwight D. Eisenhower for this catastrophe, insisting that if the bland, passionless Ike had spent less time lollygagging around the fairways and more time at the economy's helm, misfortune would have eluded us. He reviled Ike with a virulence that very nearly surpassed human understanding, given that our thirty-fourth president, both then and now, struck most people as an affable fuddy-duddy, an amiable duffer, a harmless old coot. But perhaps I did not know all the particulars.

Our more prosperous aunts, uncles, and in-laws—most of them on my mother's side of the family—laid the blame for our displacement into the public-housing wilderness directly at my father's feet. Notwithstanding the fact that the nation had been hit hard by the 1958 recession, they believed that a more resourceful man would have figured out a way to shield his family from the disgrace of going on pubic assistance and being deported to a housing project. I have always believed that my father's ruinous drinking and brutality toward his children dates from this event. But my mother insists that he was already hitting the hard stuff when she met him, that he was always a willful, irresponsible sort, and that losing the house was probably inevitable, given his flaccid moral character. These assertions may be true, and if so, they certainly call into question her decision to marry him. Still, I have no recollection of his being monstrously cruel to us before he lost his house. To the contrary, I have vivid memories of adoring him.

Eight years old at the time we pulled up stakes, I had no idea what a housing project was, nor what living in one symbolized. I knew that it meant changing schools and leaving my friends behind, and I suppose I had some hazy notion that our relocation was less than voluntary. My parents, especially my mother, were initially successful in convincing us that our present situation was little more than an inconvenience, and an evanescent one at that. The family was not dying; it was merely convalescing, so we should all just buck up. One of my mother's most impressive traits was her ability to give reality an on-the-spot overhaul, dissembling here, fantasizing there, in the process making our misfortune seem not only tolerable but almost appetizing. She prided herself on having shrewdly managed to secure us lodgings in a new, reasonably safe housing project in northwestern Philadelphia and not in the dreaded Tasker or Wilson Park Homes all the way down in South Philadelphia, where, presumably, those children lucky enough to escape abduction by white slavers would be ripped to shreds by ravenous curs. Forty-seven years later, as we were motoring past one of the wretched, far-flung South Philly slime pits we had fortuitously sidestepped, she would reflect with tremendous pride on our narrow escape from the terrors that lay in store south of Market Street.

"No matter how bad things got," she said, beaming, "at least we kept you kids out of South Philadelphia."

And what was so horrible about South Philly? Italians lived there.

The East Falls Housing Project had originally been designated as living quarters for soldiers returning from the Second World War. Functional structures never intended to be permanent residences, they were meant to serve as inexpensive, temporary housing for cash-strapped war vets until they could get back on their feet. However, by the time we showed up, housing projects had already begun to assume a different function, serving as unofficial dumping grounds for luckless white trash, Negro fugitives from the Dixie diaspora, divorcees, alkies, lollapaloozas, con artists, bad actors, lunatics, perennial screwups, stage-door Johnnies, black sheep, abject failures, and women of easy virtue. Increasingly, the assumption was that when you moved to the project, you stayed there; it was society's version of a called strike three. As far as your old friends were concerned, when you pitched camp in a housing project, you might as well have relocated to Quito or Mombasa or Dar es Salaam. You had been cast out into the darkness, and that was probably where you belonged.

Buffaloed by parental guile, my sisters and I were at first seduced by the cheesy glamour of public housing. It helped that our new living quarters did not reek of coal, as the house on Russell Street had. We even convinced ourselves that *our* project was superior to one about a mile away, because even though the Abbottsford Homes were in a nicer location and boasted a slightly classier clientele, the buildings themselves were dreary redbrick affairs with ugly green doors and microscopic windows. By contrast, the units in *our* housing project sported commodious plate-glass windows that filled the living room and second-story bedrooms with sunlight. Moreover, *our* housing project snaked its way up a hill, and right at its apex sat our house, at 4575 Merrick Road, just a few hundred yards from the mighty Schuylkill River, creating a fleeting illusion of grandeur.

The project was divided into two sections: a pair of looming fifteen-story apartment buildings planted on opposing hills, and roughly three hundred house-type objects. Our house was one of the many two-story, flat-roofed, three-bedroom structures, which were identical save for a colorful strip of cardboard inserted inside the rippled piece of transparent glass that gazed out from each living room. This was perhaps a design gambit to make the homes look perky, or at the very least less interchangeable. There were yellow strips and red strips and blue strips and green strips. There were no unusual colors; magenta and teal and chartreuse and ochre, if they even existed at the time, had not yet won the hearts of the American public. As far as I know, no one ever tried to remove the strips or replace them with some other color or pattern, though doing so would not have been very difficult. Everything about the units was maladroitly cute; for all intents and purposes, we were living in a Lego village. It was shiny and amusing and peppy and not at all demeaning—at least from the point of view of us children. But the cumulative effect on adults must have been to make them feel juvenile. They had lost their livelihoods; they had lost their homes; they had not behaved with the competence expected of adults; so now they must live in dollhouses.

The high-rises did not look juvenile; they looked foreboding and, in the fullness of time, as they steadily became more and more unsafe, bleak. They had been built in the mid-1950s, with four apartment units sharing a common elevator on each floor; four elevator banks served roughly sixty units apiece. Only later did the powers that be realize that this architectural scheme made policing the buildings impossible, because each elevator bank could easily be controlled by criminals. In due course, the high-rises became nesting grounds for drug dealers.

The apartment buildings were quite tall for their time and entirely out of character with the surrounding district, which consisted of block after block of two-story row homes. The high-rises had balconies on each floor, but after a number of mishaps, the authorities blanketed the façades of each building with industrial fencing. This could not help but reinforce the notion that residents were living in a penitentiary; the buildings looked like gigantic hamster cages. At the time they were built, the high-rises won several architectural awards, though I never found out from whom. Probably the Stasi.

Across the river, on a hill overlooking the Schuylkill, stood a set of luxurious edifices known as the Presidential Apartments. These were inhabited by prosperous people we never saw or met, as we had no reason to cross the river. Our twin high-rises quickly acquired the nickname the Vice Presidential Apartments, while the project as a whole was dubbed Sin City by better-fixed residents of the surrounding community. Apparently, this struck them as funny. Years later, I met a girl who had moved into the Vice Presidential Apartments three or four years after we put East Falls behind us. By then, the project was not only depressing but dangerous. Still, it was not as dangerous as the neighborhood Marguerite had grown up in; it was actually a step up. Once we spent an entire day in her apartment while her mother was at work. She was the first girl I ever loved, but that did not make this return trip any more nostalgic. It is natural to believe that love or hope or one of the other life-affirming emotions is capable of resanctifying a desecrated space, a place haunted by bad memories. But this did not happen here.

Many years later, the Clinton administration offered the City of Philadelphia a substantial chunk of money to rehabilitate the housing project. The city asked for dynamite instead. It blew up the apartments, razed the homes, and after many delays erected pert little town houses in their place. I visited the town houses one day and stood on the spot where our house had been and then on the approximate site of the high-rise where Marguerite and I had spent that memorable afternoon. I hoped that the residents of the cute little town houses would be happy there, that they would maintain their homes, that they would never take their good fortune for granted. Otherwise, a few years hence, it might be time for more dynamite.

East Falls—the entire neighborhood, and not just the housing project that bore that name—was an anomaly in that all the economic classes save for the spectacularly wealthy dwelt within its confines, though not contiguously. There were poor people, working-class people, middle-class people, and rich people all living within easy walking distance of one another. This was most unusual, since Philadelphia neighborhoods tended to be demographically monochromatic, demarcated along strict economic and racial lines. North Philadelphia, once teeming with poor Irish immigrants, was by the late 1950s teeming with poor black people. Lower-class white people lived in sullen neighborhoods called Kensington, Port Richmond, and Fishtown, which prided themselves on their ethnic purity and fealty to traditional values, as if that made their cheerless, claustrophobic streets any less grubby. Middle-class white people lived in the near-Northeast, middle-class Jews a bit farther north. Italians of all classes—including Angelo Bruno, head of the local Mafia—kept to themselves down in South Philly, minding their own business inside tiny, well-maintained row homes. Well-heeled Wasps who had not fled the city for the patrician Main Line lived in sprightly apartments ringing Rittenhouse Square. The few bohemian types

Philadelphia could scare up pitched camp a few blocks south. The more generic Wasps lived in the city's leafy northwest corner, in communities with plummy names like Mount Airy and Chestnut Hill. Truly rich people, by and large, did not live in Philadelphia.

The housing project itself abutted a working-class district consisting of small, unassuming houses undulating patiently up two adjacent streets: Calumet and Stanton. The residents of these streets never forgave the city fathers for sticking public housing right next to them, reasoning that people who did not own their own houses were not likely to maintain them and that poorly maintained houses were likely to attract an even worse class of poor people. The project, they complained, with intense passion but to no discernible effect, would eventually become a slum, thereby imperiling the nondescript but nonetheless flourishing community that adjoined it.

This is exactly what happened; this is what always came to pass back in that era, when central planning committees were forever concocting ingenious new schemes to make working-class people turn homicidal. Tellingly, as soon as we escaped from the project and moved into a middle-class community, we were pressured by our new friends into making the same fatuous statements about poor black people that were once made about us. Black people bred like rabbits and lived like pigs. Black people all drove Cadillacs. Black people all cashed multiple welfare checks. Black people spent the entire day devising cunning schemes to rip off the federal government. The proof of their astounding duplicity and ingenuity was that they got to live rent-free in glamorous locales like Cabrini-Green and Watts and North Philly and Bedford-Stuyvesant. Their perfidy knew no bounds. We knew, firsthand, that none of this was true, especially the part about the Cadillacs, but we acted as if it were. There was no point in graduating into the middle class unless you got to spit on the class you had just left behind.

A few blocks away from the meek community on Calumet and Stanton streets was a more prestigious neighborhood where the streets had enchanting names like Vaux and Ainslie and Indian Queen Lane. Indian Queen Lane was my favorite, the sort of street name that manages to be evocative without sounding synthetic, the kind of thing we never hear anymore. Indian Queen Lane—which also meandered diligently up a steep hill, another anomaly in the generally horizontal City of Brotherly Love—was home to a small theater company that was forever putting on corking amateur productions of plays like *You Can't Take It with You* and *Charley's Aunt*. The theater stood no more than a half mile from the project. But I never set foot in it, nor did anyone else in my family. It was a mite too genteel for the Queenan family.

A short pace up the road sat Warden Drive, a prosperous enclave whose tree-lined streets bristled with tasteful, well-appointed Tudor-style homes. It was a refined, understatedly twee community where one sensed the engulfing presence of thatched roofs, even though they were not there. For many years, Arlen Specter, Philadelphia's much-admired district attorney, a member of the Warren Commission (which investigated John F. Kennedy's assassination and was thought by many to have muffed the assignment), and later a powerful, mildly independent-minded Republican senator, made his home there. A few times as an adult I ran into Specter on the Metroliner heading to Washington, and we reminisced about the old neighborhood. Though our recollections did not mesh seamlessly, I acted as if they did, adhering to that inexplicable stricture mandating that working-class people behave deferentially toward the rich and the powerful, not out of fear or respect or even envy but because no one wants to make a scene. This may also derive from a classwide belief that when the wealthy are making an honest effort to stay awake while you are speaking, the least you can do is be civil.

Perched at the very top of Warden Drive stood the modest little house where Grace Kelly had grown up. Several times in the middle of a surprise blizzard, my father and I trudged up to the Kelly residence, which stood directly across the street from a public park, and shoveled the snow off their path. I was amazed at how slender and unostentatious the building was, given the clan's international fame and fabulous wealth; in this sense it resembled Graceland or the *Mona Lisa*, both of which are much smaller than first-time visitors to Memphis or Paris expect them to be. Though we never met any members of the family— patriarch John B. Kelly was already getting along in years; Grace had long since blown town, first for Hollywood, then for the bright lights of Monaco; and Olympic champion playboy son John B. Junior never seemed to do anything but row crew—we felt honored to clear the snow from the sidewalks of Philadelphia's most storied Irish family.

John B. Kelly Jr. was a beloved figure among the Irish, and for much the same reason as was John Kennedy: To all appearances, he did not have a job, at least not a real one, which to people like my father was a dream come true. "Work is the curse of the drinking man," he used to joke, pilfering a line from Oscar Wilde, but he wasn't joking. It was as if the entire Irish-American population of Philadelphia was able to derive vicarious pleasure from John B. Jr.'s life of ease, even though they themselves had to go out and sling hash, scrub toilets, and mop floors. This affection was rooted in the belief that an ethnic group hadn't really arrived (or, in Kelly's case, made a splash) until they had sons—nay, scions—who didn't have to work for a living. Or, if they did, worked only on advisory committees and blue-ribbon commissions. Kelly's father, by contrast, had a reputation as a hard-ass who'd made his money in the brick business. My father maintained that the bricks used to build the housing project were supplied by Kelly's outfit, conferring upon us an even more intimate mythic rapport.

Usually, once we'd gotten the shoveling out of the way, the staff would bring us hot chocolate and cookies. They were not great tippers; perhaps they felt that the sheer honor of servicing the sidewalks of our ethnic group's most cherished icons was adequate recompense for our efforts. They were probably right, though the reason I never bought a snowblower as an adult, the reason I always loved shoveling snow, was that it elicited atypically warm memories of my father. It had nothing to do with Grace Kelly.

When I was a child, I always thought of Warden Drive, and especially the Kelly house, as breathtakingly classy, but I never dreamed of living in places like that, because my parents nourished only plausible dreams. "Don't get your hopes up, because you'll only be disappointed" was their credo. This was a philosophy that contaminated the cumulative psyche of the city, breeding an attitude that kept fans from even dreaming about triumphs on the playing fields, because dreams were better left undreamt; at least that way, they wouldn't get smashed. It is hardly a surprise that the statue of Rocky Balboa outside the Spectrum arena in South Philadelphia dwarfs the statue of Julius Erving. Erving is a flesh-and-blood superstar whose career was perhaps something of a disappointment to the locals, as he brought home only one championship. Rocky, in sharp comparison, is the hometown hero, the valiant underdog who never fails to come through in the clutch, the working stiff whose rough-and-tumble demeanor and can-do attitude captures the gritty blue-collar ethos of the city, most of whose season-ticket holders live in the suburbs and work in front of LCD screens. Rocky, however, does not exist, and Sylvester Stallone grew up in Silver Spring, Maryland. Curiously, in the original *Rocky,* the only film in the long-running series that comes close to being believable, Rocky finishes second.

It took a long time for me to overcome this predisposition toward tamping down expectations. As an adult, living in New York, a state that had no emotional connection with my youth, it would give me great pleasure to drive past beautiful homes and park the car for a few minutes, purely to admire their grace and elegance. It wasn't necessary for me to live in them, or even have enough money to live in them; I could derive joy from the mere fact that they existed. A beautiful house, I had come to appreciate, made everyone who looked at it feel better, while an ugly house could drag down people's spirits for the next hundred years. But as a child, I never wasted any time gazing at rich people's homes. If I wasn't going to live in them, what was the point of looking at them?

The entrance to the East Falls Housing Project was no more than a couple hundred yards north of the Schuylkill River, which flowed straight through the city. The Schuylkill was neither a raging cataract nor a mythical waterway, and while it is true that the river was the preferred setting for many paintings by Thomas Eakins, the greatest artist America has ever produced, few Americans are aware of this. Despite this lack of epic stature, the river was reasonably wide, with plenty of open space on either bank where people could picnic, fish, frolic with their children, or sit back and watch the world go by. It was a feature of the landscape that had the power to console and inspire; it was lovely, it was accessible, and it was free.

My family never went down to the Schuylkill. We never went on picnics. We never set up a folding table and sat out playing cards or checkers. And we certainly never watched the regatta teams row past. The river was off-limits to us. The official party line was that it wasn't safe for children to go down to the river by themselves, because the area was poorly traveled and rampaging Negro gangs from North Philadelphia were known to pounce on defenseless tykes and beat them to a pulp. As for the prospect of a picnic, that would never have occurred to anyone in my family or just about anyone in my neighborhood. Poor white people didn't go on picnics; the bucolic fête was the province of the bourgeoisie or otiose Negroes. Poor white people stayed inside and watched sports and drank beer and terrorized their kids. All the years that we lived in the project, all the years that we lived just a few hundred yards away from a placid, slow-moving river that could have provided a respite from our unhappiness, we simply ignored it.

One summer morning not long after we moved to East Falls, my father woke me early. He said he was headed downtown to apply for unemployment compensation and wanted me to come along. I did not know what unemployment compensation was—it took me a long time to understand the protocol involved in losing a job—but the prospect of embarking on an adventure with my dad was thrilling. What I did not realize when he issued the invitation, however, was that we would not be taking the bus, the subway, or the trolley car downtown that morning, because we had no cash on hand. Not one thin dime. Not one red cent. Not even one wooden nickel. Nothing. Instead, we would be making our way on foot. Children have a distorted concept of size and space, so in my memory the distance between our home and downtown Philadelphia was easily fifteen to twenty miles, a Herculean undertaking for a youngster, as we would also be making the return trip on foot. This made the outing immeasurably less appealing.

Life in those days, for the Queenans at least, was a trail of automotive tears. Not having a car in the age of the Thunderbird was a tremendous humiliation for a grown man. It was bad enough not having a television or a telephone, but those were minor inconveniences. Having no car left us at the mercy of the dreaded Philadelphia Transportation Authority and its fleet of unreliable, herky-jerky buses, subways, and trolleys, most of them going places we did not wish to visit. No car meant no trips to the country, no trips to the seashore, no trips to visit those few relatives we did not wish to see impaled on sharp sticks. Not once in his life did my father own a new car or anything resembling one. For most of my childhood, we did not have a car, and on the rare occasions when we did scrape together enough cash to buy one, it would turn out to be some wheezing bomb that keeled over and died within a few weeks. To the best of my knowledge, my father also never flew on a plane or found himself in a position to order room service. The late twentieth century had a lot to offer working-class people, but he missed out on all of it.

Carless, cashless, we hoofed it downtown that day. Though there were several routes we could have taken, he opted to walk straight down Ridge Avenue, straight through his old childhood haunts, straight through the heart of the North Philadelphia ghetto. My father was not especially fond of Negroes; like most white people we knew, his idea of race relations was to stay as far away from black people as possible. But he was adamant in his refusal to surrender this hallowed terrain to these tetchy intruders. To him, traipsing through a slum was a way of abolishing reality, a way of insisting that the past was still the present and always would be. It was an attitude he maintained until the end of his life, when he would breathlessly tell me about his latest excursion to an unappetizing neighborhood his ethnic group had deserted two generations earlier. To him the phrases "Eighth and York" and "Strawberry Mansion" forever evoked the glory of days long past. Such glories were not apparent to the uninitiated. Our trek through the urban wilderness scared me speechless; I didn't know anything about black people except that they weren't all that fond of white people. Throughout that forced march down Ridge Avenue, I kept my eyes down, my face forward. And I walked double-time; I wanted to make sure we were out of North Philly before nightfall.

Many years later, on a visit home, I took a long, relaxing walk along the river. I was forty-seven yet had never once strolled any great distance along the Schuylkill. My feelings toward the city of my birth would always be mixed. One part of me loved to revisit a municipality whose charms had generally eluded me when I was growing up; but sometimes, particularly when I would hear the chillingly pedestrian Philadelphia accent, I felt as if I had never moved away to New York, as if my adult life had never happened. This return visit was a particularly illuminating experience. Casting my mind back, viewing events through the eyes of a nine-year-old, I remembered the distance between the housing project and Center City Philadelphia as Bunyanesque, a veritable death march. But now, after all those years, I discovered that the total distance was only about six miles, that it was no more than a sixty-minute hike from the foot of the Art Museum to the project entrance. Kelly Drive, named after Grace's sculling sibling, was now a tree-lined urban paradise for joggers and bicyclists. This was a revelation. When my father dragged me downtown to sign up for public assistance thirty-seven years ear-lier, he made a point of marching through a slum, where we were not wanted, rather than along the banks of the river, where we might have enjoyed ourselves. He preferred to wallow in melancholy urban nostal-gia rather than avail himself of Mother Nature's restorative powers; he would rather sift through the ashes of the past than take delight in the present. The river, the bushes, the flowers, the trees—none of it meant anything to him. The river had not been part of his childhood, so it could never be part of his adulthood.

What accounted for this attitude? He was poor. Libertarians, self-made men, and sage pundits believe that money can make any problem disappear, that if one merely put enough cash into the hands of the poor, they would draw on the prodigious reserves of wisdom and enterprise they'd been clandestinely stockpiling for so many years and make all the right choices needed to turn their lives around. School vouchers are the most obvious example of such thinking; who, after all, is better posi-tioned to make Solomonic decisions about her child's education than a sixteen-year-old mother of three? Adherents to this school of thought have difficulty grasping that poverty is as much a state of mind as an economic condition, a pathology that encourages the poor to make bad decisions. Ravished emotionally, not widely liked, rarely chipper in disposition, the poor early on develop a knack for making bad situations worse. Their folly is thereupon used as an additional indictment of their character. Poverty becomes a self-fulfilling prophecy: It may not be your fault that you were born poor, but somewhere along the way you've certainly mastered the art of behaving like a poor person. You are shiftless. You are self-destructive. You are foolish. Now, go away.

One of my earliest memories of the project was being dispatched into the streets to gather up cigarette butts for my father. If the butts were long enough, he would smoke the remains; if they were not, we would rip them open, pour the contents into a jar, and use the remnants to roll fresh cigarettes, using a handy, inexpensive device manufactured and sold by some enterprising tobacco company. This was the ragpicker phase of my youth, though I did not know it at the time. I thoroughly enjoyed these foraging expeditions, as I thought I was being useful to my father and also in some way creative. I did not yet fully realize how straitened our circumstances had become.

There were plenty of hints. While we were living on Russell Street, my father's job at Proctor & Schwartz had been a reasonably well-paid position, with clear possibilities for advancement. But after he got laid off, he would never work in an office again. Instead, he labored at menial, low-paying jobs with no future whatsoever. He moved furniture. He worked as a security guard. He logged time in a factory or two. He manned a lunch wagon. And, of course, he drove a pretzel truck.

None of these jobs ever lasted very long; he would get tired of them, grow despondent, start missing work, get himself fired. Then we would be back on relief. Things around the house would start to disappear: The TV would get hocked to a pawnshop, then the radio, then the clock radio. He unloaded these items not to buy food but to buy liquor. Because he liked to drink in taprooms, and because my mother would not allow him to bring whiskey into the house, the money never lasted very long. We hated to see him start drinking, because as soon he opened that first bottle of beer we realized that he had already given up on the day. As time went by, he started throwing in the towel earlier and earlier. He was only in his middle thirties, but he knew that he was already playing out the string. In an oft-heard idiom of the era, which described many adult males of our acquaintance, he'd had it.

The section of the project we lived in was organized in a peculiar, modular fashion. On each of a series of adjacent cul-de-sacs, a row of four attached maisonettes sat perpendicular to the street, with another four units facing them across a narrow pathway. At the end of each path stood a twelve-foot-high fence topped with barbed wire, sealing off the railroad tracks plied by local commuter trains. On the other side of the tracks, up a steep hill, sat a middle-class development of top-notch two-story, redbrick houses that were always referred to as the New Homes. They, too, were sealed off by barbed wire. Because of this wrong-side-of-the-tracks arrangement, which may have been inadvertent but probably wasn't, we could catch glimpses of the good fortune and respectability that lay just outside our reach merely by turning our eyes north.

Proximity to mild affluence did little to inspire us, for even though the New Homes were less than fifty yards away, as the crow flies, we were not crows. To reach them, we would have had to walk all the way to the back of the project, where the barbed-wire fence ran out, then hack our way through a "jungle" teeming with weeds that never got tended, then make our way up a narrow road with no sidewalks, and finally climb up a steep hill to arrive at a neighborhood we had no business being in. I never visited the New Homes until forty years after we'd left the project, and when I did, I still felt that I did not belong there.

The houses we lived in were designed in an unconventional way, fusing intimacy with anonymity, despite the fact that behind each home stood a virtually identical unit. In fact, the houses were grafted together jigsaw-style, with the kitchens of the rear units jutting out into the living rooms of the front units and vice versa, and the bedrooms interlacing in an identical pattern. At the end of each block, a four-foot-high chain-link fence separated the eight units on one cul-de-sac from the eight units on either side. This largely cosmetic barrier discouraged fraternization between people living in adjacent cul-de-sacs. In fact, it discouraged any intercourse whatsoever with the people who lived just a few feet away on the other side of the walls. Due to this socially prophylactic layout, we could hear the people whose living quarters intersected ours, but we never actually saw them. They were our neighbors, but then again they were not our neighbors. They lived right next door to us, but we never felt that they lived right next door to us. It was as if the walls were swarming with gigantic squirrels.

The gimcrack architecture and weird, arbitrary boundaries disconnected and desensitized everyone. One day, a little girl living directly behind us set herself on fire while playing with matches. This was in the early sixties, an era when children still wore flammable pajamas and often perished in them. The firemen were summoned, but the child could not be saved. The rest of us could see some sort of creature lying on a blanket on the ground beside the house when we came home from school. Her father and brother, who may have been Amish, or Hasidim, or even prototypes of hippies, were standing there weeping. Another person, the mother, was charred but extant. To the best of my knowledge, she survived, though I may be mistaken, for, from our perspective, the fire was the end of their story. Despite their physical proximity, these people were complete strangers. We never knew their names. We never spoke to them. We never found out what happened to them after their little girl died.

Years later, I asked my mother if she or any of the other neighbors had gone around the corner to console these ill-fated exotics after their child incinerated herself. Were there flowers, pastries, mass cards, commiseration?

"No," she replied.

"Why not?" I asked.

"We didn't know them," she replied.

"What do you mean, we didn't know them?"

"We didn't know them," she reiterated, and that was the end of that.

Just months before this conversation, when my best friend's ten-year-old son died after his heart stopped in a swimming pool in Mount Laurel, New Jersey, everyone in the community grieved; it seemed as if the earth itself cried out in anguish at his demise. This was not the case in the project. We did not know the parents of the dead child. They did not know us. A foolish youngster had set her pajamas on fire and died. The earth did not cry out in anguish.

All but the most perceptive children find poverty incomprehensible, because poverty is idiotic. Further confusing the issue is the fact that poverty comes in several distinct varieties. From the start, my sisters and I had trouble figuring out which brand of indigence we were experiencing. We knew that we were not black, a tremendous relief to us all, and we knew that we were not poor in the way the Okies or the starving children of Armenia were. Mostly, what we endured was intermittent deprivation—poverty, yes, but not abject destitution. Sometimes we had little to eat, a few times nothing. One Friday evening, Ree and I stayed up until midnight, gnawing on raw spaghetti noodles, waiting for my father to come home with his paycheck and perhaps something tasty to nibble on. Eventually, we gave up and went to bed. It was the first time he failed us in this way, but it would not be the last.

Poverty, conceptually as well as viscerally, suffers from a mythology concocted by those who were never poor. Poverty goes far beyond not having money or food. Poverty means that when you do have money and food, the money gets spent unwisely and the food is not nutritious. Poverty is not simply a matter of being unable to buy certain things; it's about buying the wrong things, or the things that nobody else wants. It's about off-brand shoes, off-brand underwear, off-brand socks, off-brand ice cream, off-brand appliances, off-brand roach killer. It's about sneakers that fall apart the third time you drive to the basket, shoes held together with adhesive tape, shirts that start out as XLs but end up as Mediums the first time they're laundered. It's about socks that aren't worth mending, jeans that aren't worth patching, appliances that aren't worth fixing, cookies whose packages bear a vague resemblance to Fig Newtons and Lorna Doones but prove upon closer inspection to be Smack Dibbers or Chunk Fiddles. It's about buying FBR when everyone else is buying RCA, about settling for a $3.95 Val-Tex when everyone else is buying a $12.95 Ban-Lon. It's about wearing shirts with labels that deliberately obscure the miniaturized words MADE IN PAKISTAN because everyone else is wearing shirts whose labels proudly proclaim MADE IN THE U.S.A. It's about always eating in and eating badly, never eating out and well. It's about bad diets, bad teeth, bad feet, bad playgrounds, bad parents, bad housing, bad attitudes.

Poverty is a tumor it takes a lifetime to excise, because poverty is lodged deep inside the brain in a dark corner where the once-poor don't want to look. Poverty is a lifestyle, a philosophy, a modus vivendi, an agglomeration of bad habits, which is why nobody who has ever been poor physically ever stops being poor emotionally. The once-poor simply become masters of disguise, listening patiently while other people lament problems they cannot imagine having, trying to keep a straight face while someone talks about low self-esteem resulting from a relationship with an emotionally distant parent or the trauma of realizing that Kristin, wait-listed by Dartmouth, will probably have to swallow her pride and go to Middlebury. But every night before they go to bed, the once-poor empty their pockets and count their change, never quite believing that they are no longer paupers.

The poverty my family experienced was grinding, dull, and monotonous—the traditional one-size-fits-all, no-frills variety. We did not have enough food. We rarely ate fresh fruits or vegetables; everything came out of a can. We had crummy toys. Our appliances were always going on the fritz, because my father tended to buy dud lookalikes "on time" at twice the normal retail price. We wore hand-me-down clothes and shoes that did not fit; we never had money for anything stylish. We did not have a car. We did not have a telephone. We did not go on vacations, as my father never held a job long enough to earn time off. When my sisters did get whisked away one time to a summer camp operated by the Catholic Charities, they came back two nights later scared speechless by the hoodlums who made up much of the camp's population. They also returned with their hair swarming with lice. Last but not least, there was the matter of our macabre dental care. One afternoon, my mother, at the ripe old age of thirty-nine, waltzed in and casually announced that she had just had all her teeth pulled. They'd been acting up lately and were far too much trouble to tend to on a daily basis, she explained; a nice set of dentures would make things easier on everyone. I had suspected for some time that my father was not quite right in the head; now it seemed that the affliction was spreading.

Did the moral injustice of poverty ever occur to us? Yes, but it was not something we could dwell on at the time. While we were living in the housing project, we were far too busy worrying about our father to worry about bias in the social order. Not until years and years later would it ever occur to any of us that the deck was stacked against members of our class, that whatever adults may have done to wreck their lives, it was unfair for their children to begin life with their chances for success preemptively sabotaged. In this sense, poverty is not so much cruel as unsportsmanlike. Those who despise the poor, Calvinist types who unfailingly point to wantonly self-destructive behavior as a sign of the underclass's moral and intellectual inferiority, do not understand that poor people behave stupidly because poverty is a finishing school where children learn how to be stupid. Growing up poor teaches young people to buy clothing that shrinks, appliances that break, furniture that disintegrates, food that provides no nutrition—and, if possible, to overpay for it. If a young person born in a housing project in the United States of America grows up to be stupid, self-destructive, or evil, this should come as no surprise to anyone. They have studied at the feet of the masters.

I did not start thinking these thoughts until I went to college and was exposed to provocative class-warfare theories promulgated by sensitive chaps from Bryn Mawr. As a child, the thought of blaming society for our tribulations would never have crossed my mind. The responsibility lay with my father. He was the one who couldn't hold a job. He was the one who drank up our money. He was the one who beat us. True, the inequity of our daily existence confused us. We were the smartest children in our classes, usually by a wide margin. We had a flair and a creativity that was lacking in most of our peers, interchangeable drones destined for low-level administrative duties with Blue Cross of Pennsylvania or the Naval Supply Depot. We were well-scrubbed, well-groomed, and dressed as well as it was possible for our cash-strapped mother to dress us. We were easy to get along with, never got into trouble. Our teachers liked us, encouraged us, perhaps even admired us, constantly reassuring us that we would all do well in life if we would merely lay our troubles at the feet of the Lord and be patient until He took them up.

It was all well and good to tell us that better times lay ahead, that a heaping pot of gold lay somewhere at the end of the rainbow. But this did not help us in the existential moment. In the existential moment, we wondered why we were living in a housing project, the penniless offspring of a vicious, violent drunk. Why did other kids get to go home to safe neighborhoods and warm houses and delicious meals and parents who enjoyed their company; children whose births were planned events, a dream fulfilled, not the haphazard by-product of adherence to a scientifically unreliable insemination schedule? Why didn't we get fancy clothes and trips to the seashore and a backyard with flowers and a swimming pool and a car? Whose idea of a childhood was this?

Because of my mother's hoi polloi–shunning temperament, we never felt the slightest sense of solidarity with our class. If anything, we despised them. We were like haughty survivors of a shipwreck floating aimlessly in a lifeboat: The only thing we had in common with the other passengers was that we did not want to drown, and if we did have to drown, we would prefer to do so with a better class of misfits. But at some level we were baffled by our situation, unable to position ourselves in a precise historical context. We certainly did not feel that we were part of a heroic struggle the way people did in the 1930s, when everyone pulled together and made common cause. But we also never considered ourselves participants in the economic explosion of the 1950s. Quite to the contrary, we felt that we had been remanded to the sidelines. The U.S. economy was undergoing a stupendous boom when we were young, transforming what had been a sleeping giant into the mightiest industrial colossus the world has ever known. But we were not profiting from it. To this day, when I am asked about growing up in the fifties and sixties, I mechanically confirm that it was an era of immense wealth and social mobility, which in fact it was. But in talking about the fifties as most Americans experienced them, I might as well be discussing Maori dining rituals.

Our fifties family life bore no resemblance to the world of Lucy and Ricky Ricardo or Ward and June Cleaver. Ward did not beat his children with the buckle of his leather belt. Ricky did not drink boilermakers all night while his family went hungry. Lucy did not suffer from manic depression. June could cook. When anyone asked about the fifties, a world we knew only in retrospect, at a distance, we would respond like a recuperating coma victim who devours reams of disintegrating old newspapers to get caught up on everything he missed during the seventeen years he was out cold after that I-beam flattened him. We responded in terms people could understand, providing essential, plausible details about a bygone era as if we ourselves had actually participated in it. We were like Yankee utility players who got traded to the Senators in April of the year the Bronx Bombers entered the Pantheon of the Immortals.

"Didn't you play on the '27 Yankees?" people would later ask.

"Well, sort of."

As a family, we had lived through the fifties, but only in the narrow chronological sense. My father, who rarely spoke to anyone without at some point demanding, "How much wood could a woodchuck chuck if a woodchuck could chuck wood?" or warning them, "Don't take any wooden nickels," an exhortation he never bothered to explain, also used to endlessly repeat a nonsensical rhyme:

> As I was walking down the stair,
> I met a man who wasn't there.
> He wasn't there again today,
> I wish that man would go away.

That was my family to a tee. We were there and we were not there. We were in the fifties but not of it. And though I would not come to fully understand this, or even think about it, until many years afterward, a great many other people were not of it, either: Things were infinitely worse for black people living south of the Mason-Dixon Line, who were being raped and lynched and generally treated like animals while the rest of the country was chuckling at the latest pickle Lucille Ball had gotten herself into. The idea that the mythical 1950s encompassed an entire nation is cretinous. But this is a country that has never been in any danger of running out of cretins.

No afterglow accompanies these experiences. Nothing good ever came out of living in that project. One might argue that the degrading experience of poverty taught me to be ambitious and self-sufficient, but it would be more accurate to say that it taught me to be ruthless and cruel, indifferent to other people's feelings, particularly if I was writing about them. I never had any warm memories of the project; it gave me nothing, it taught me nothing. The rich old men who run Hollywood have long been smitten by the romance of indigence, zealously manufacturing life-affirming cultural pornography that appeals to middle-class people who quite fancy the poor but only in an innocuous celluloid incarnation. Up close and personal, the poor are less appealing: They wear bad clothes and use bad language and do bad things, and have guns. They make excellent fodder for films but even better fodder for cannons. They are fascinating when seen from a distance, less fascinating when they move in next door. They make unsatisfactory dining companions; they are too busy being desperate to be idiosyncratic or clever. My sisters and I understood this perfectly. We knew that there was nothing poetic or ennobling about our plight. We could not understand why we had been subjected to it. We were the odd men out, and we did not know why.

Throughout those long years of mandated misfortune, I felt, perhaps with the genetically transmitted aloofness of my mother, that our predicament was a momentary aberration that had been visited upon us due to a mix-up in paperwork down at the Municipal Building. Soon it would be all sorted out and we would be restored to our rightful place in the social firmament. This exemplifies mankind's ability to unearth wheat among chaff, diamonds amid rust. For even though we were living in the proverbial "run-down neighborhood," infested with creeps, lushes, petty criminals, the functionally insane, women of ill repute, and a wide swath of social misfits who fell under the general rubric of "fuckheads," my parents, and my mother in particular, never stopped reminding us that things could have been worse.

They were right. None of us ever got stabbed, shot, or raped while we lived in the project. We never experienced the devastating horrors that black urbanites were subjected to in subsequent years in the public housing developments of America's worst neighborhoods, because we never had to deal on a daily basis with violent crime. Our poverty was economic, spiritual, and psychological, but we were never in fear for our lives. We were never as badly off as the children in Cabrini-Green or Compton or North Philadelphia. We were simply badly off.

Other housing projects—those situated in the epicenter of the urban wilderness—would have been worse, certainly from an aesthetic perspective, as they were isolated, completely cut off from parks or rivers or creeks, and far more dangerous. But this was hardly cause for jubilation. We never went to the parks or the rivers or creeks near our home; they were entirely outside our range of experience, as were swimming pools, ice-skating rinks, arboretums, zoos, aquariums, and museums. None of us ever learned to swim or ice-skate; the idea of mastering these skills never occurred to us. We were poor, and as poverty ground us down, we began to acquire the self-flagellatory skills at which the poor are so adept.

My parents never understood that just because things could be worse, that didn't mean things weren't already bad. For even though my sisters and I were unsophisticated, impressionable children, we were not imbeciles, and it soon became apparent to us that there was something down-market about our new living arrangements. One indication was the fact that we had to walk a considerable distance to reach the closest grocery store, which meant we were never allowed to go shopping alone at night. Back in Saint Veronica's, there had been stores of one sort or another on every other corner. Not here. The owners of the nearest grocery kept a ferocious Great Dane in the backyard, locked behind a fence, frothing and glaring, where everyone could see him. We assumed that this display of canine menace was intended to deter shoplifters living in the adjacent project. One day the dog attacked a beautiful young girl who worked in the grocery, ravaging her face beyond repair. There was some sort of out-of-court settlement, but none of us ever felt comfortable entering that store after that, nor, presumably, did she. It was a cautionary tale for potential thieves. I lived in East Falls for four years and never once went into that store without reconnoitering to make sure the Great Dane was locked up in the yard.

The only retail activity in the project itself was an illicit operation run by a family of extravagantly uncharismatic albinos, who sold candy, batteries, lightbulbs, cigarettes, and sundries out of their living room. People who could not afford a pack of twenty cigarettes could instead buy individual smokes from these most unlikely of merchants. The albinos overcharged for everything, making them the target of immense antipathy in the community, but two cigarettes were better than none, so customers learned to grin and bear it. My father would sometimes send me over to buy a couple of cigarettes from them, thereby introducing me both to the underground economy and to a world where nicotine served as a vaccine against reality.

I went to school with the two albino children, neither of whom could be called sugar plums. No one seemed to like them, not other children, not their teachers, not even the nuns. At the time, I could not understand why they did not make more of an effort to be cordial toward their classmates, but in later years I would see the glaring faults in my logic. These were poor albinos, the children of unemployed adult albinos, condemned to life in a housing project, where they had been abandoned to the tender mercies of the children of the poor. It's hard to see how being nice could have helped.

After a while, my sisters and I began to suspect that there was something disreputable about our situation, because no one who lived outside the project ever invited us over to play with them. I lived in the project from 1959 until 1963 and never once stepped inside the home of anyone from outside it. Perhaps my classmates' parents feared that kids from the project would heist their jewelry or geld the schnauzer or dismantle the plumbing and sell the fixtures to Roscoe the Fence. Whatever the official explanation, we now sensed that we were persona non grata.

My family literally had no money when we arrived in the project; we were on what was then called public assistance, or, as it was more commonly known, relief. "Relief" was a surgically precise term in that era, though it would later be replaced by the coy euphemism "welfare." Being on relief was mildly shameful for women and children, but it was an out-and-out disgrace for able-bodied men. It meant that you were so devoid of basic human dignity that you literally had to beg the government for money. This strongly suggested that you were a bum, a perception reinforced by the routine involved in obtaining the federal government's monthly food allowances. In the days before food stamps were invented, people on welfare were given vouchers for use at designated supermarkets. The vouchers could not be used to purchase fair-traded brand goods; they could be used to acquire only baking supplies. Every month or so, we would exchange these vouchers for allotments of flour, sugar, canned egg yolks, and powdered milk. The powder could be mixed with water to make a clotted beverage that tasted like calamine lotion; the egg yolks gave off a disgusting odor not unlike that of rotting eggs; sometimes, if the containers had ruptured, the flour and cornmeal were already playing host to bugs festering jubilantly inside.

The supermarket stored the baking supplies in metal compartments directly beneath the fruit and vegetables, creating a jarring juxtaposition of the immanent and the potential. The flour, cornmeal, and milk came in generic brown cardboard boxes, so as we trooped out of the store shoppers who were not on welfare could see that we were. As we had no car and the establishment could not be reached on foot, my father had to ask a neighbor to drive him to pick up our monthly supply of ingredients that served little more than a decorative function in our home. Sometimes he would bring us along, thereby allowing us to share in the humiliation of being viewed as "pikers." All the while we would cast envious glances at the Cheerios and Wheaties beckoning to us from the nearby shelves; all the while we could feel the contemptuous stares of the staff.

For the Queenan family, these shopping excursions were pointless, as my mother possessed neither the talent nor the inclination to bake bread, muffins, cookies, or cakes. Before she met my father, she worked as a secretary at the Navy Yard at the southern tip of the city. Unlike her husband, who had not finished ninth grade, she had a high school diploma and considerable white-collar experience. She was the product of a slightly loftier economic class and a better neighborhood than he was; her own father was a baker, employed by a venerable Philadelphia bread company, whereas my father's father was a common laborer. She had worked hard to rise above the circumstances into which she was born, evincing a ladylike aplomb that was otherwise in short supply in the project. She never dressed especially well, as our financial situation prohibited it, but she spoke well; she was never vulgar or profane and never displayed any emotion in public. She was blue-collar in neither temperament nor demeanor, and she never would be.

Ditching her job when she married my father was the biggest mistake of her life, a self-engineered calamity she would never cease to regret. Marriageable, presentable males were in short supply after the war, so, to use her terminology, she "grabbed the first guy off the boat." She then proceeded to have four children, not because it was her lifelong dream to raise a family but because children were what married people had. Large families were a Catholic tradition in that era; children were the unavoidable by-products of cohabitation; any effort to frustrate the natural procreative process assured one of an eternity in Hell. Compliantly, my parents adhered to the Church-mandated birth-control method known as "rhythm," a jerkwater procedure that did not so much prevent conception as reduce its likelihood by 13.6 percent. Had she been born a few decades later, by which point the Church had started to look the other way whenever the issue of recreational sex was raised, she might never have given birth. Procreation, parenting, anything involving nurturing, was a burr under her saddle; even when we were adults, she did not hesitate to remind us that being a mother was a job she never felt cut out for.

"I could never play with you kids like that," she would remark in her detached way as she watching me rolling around on the floor with my infant son and daughter, tickling them till their fat little cheeks turned red. She would monitor this otherwise heartwarming scene like a spectator watching a sport whose rules she neither understood nor had any great interest in learning. Then she would add, "I never wanted children."

It was an undiplomatic thing to say, but she said it anyway. It wasn't that she recoiled at the sight of her four children; it was simply that they were never the be-all and end-all of her existence. Children were the result of sharing a bed with a man one did not love. Children were not gifts from above but retribution from below. This she did not ever say in so many words, but this was what was strongly implied.

Cooking was another punitive consequence of marriage, but this was one indignity to which she refused to succumb. Never seeking to be a housewife, much less a mother, she drew a line in the sand and refused to acquire the skills needed to succeed in this sphere of domestic activity. My father, though generally a menace in the kitchen, was not completely inept; in a pinch, he could fry an egg, grill a steak, open a can of soup. Of course, if he was under the influence, things could go woefully awry. Once, after he got roaring drunk while my mother was in the hospital, he served the four of us heaping plates of spaghetti dripping with catsup he had warmed up in a saucepan. We nibbled at the periphery of the pasta but no farther, as the meal was really quite revolting. He then threw a fit when we tried to explain—know-it-all ingrates that we were—that while catsup and tomato sauce were undeniably cousins, they were not in fact interchangeable.

Though my mother was more knowledgeable and better trained than he, her approach to cooking was uncompromisingly castigatory. Preparing dinner was a Kafkaesque ritual in which a rib roast or a sextet of pork chops were reprimanded for crimes of which they were wholly innocent. She took no joy from cooking; to her it was more like a vendetta. She did not prepare food; she chastised it. This was not because she explicitly wished to punish her family; her attitude was more in the interests of self-preservation. If she had ever learned how to convert the ingredients we gathered up each month into bread or cake or muffins, it would signify that our descent into the ranks of the underclass was complete. Happily for her, she never did, remaining the least enthusiastic, least resourceful cook I have ever met. Her nearly supernatural incompetence in the kitchen was her badge of honor.

In American mythology, these humiliating trips to the supermarket are the moment when the penniless child makes a solemn oath that when he grows up he will never go hungry, that he will construct a globe-spanning commercial empire and spend days on end sipping champagne on his well-appointed yacht, instructing Simcox to fetch Lydia and Gwyneth so they can play Chabrier duets on the pianoforte. But poor people do not dream in color. Poor children do not dream of Croesian wealth, triumph, vindication, or revenge. They dream of Cheerios.

Chapter 3. **The Predicament**

Three things kept us going through these wilderness years: the Catholic Church, the generosity of the few relatives who did not abandon us in our time of need, and the public library. In recent times, it has become fashionable to attack the Church, as if everything would be going along swimmingly if the atheists were in charge. These attacks are often mouthed by celebrity heathens who are oblivious to the role the Church has long played in preventing the unfortunate from being swallowed up by the abyss. The Catholic Church kept my family afloat, partly through periodic infusions of cash, partly through the inspiration that pageantry-laden rituals can provide, but mostly through the superb education we received from the nuns who taught at Saint Bridget's Elementary School.

Laughable to some, dysfunctional to others, mysterious to virtually everyone, nuns are in reality exactly what they seem: angels of mercy who have sacrificed their lives in the service of God and humanity. It was the nuns who taught us to read and write, the nuns who taught us the principal export of Bolivia, the nuns who explained the significance of the Dred Scott decision. It was the nuns, not the priests, who pointed the way out of the darkness; the nuns who made it clear that if you were born poor and you didn't want to stay poor, you'd better know the principal export of Bolivia. When we were hungry children, wearing tatty clothes, living in a crummy neighborhood, the only way we could make ourselves feel special was by excelling at school. So we studied hard, and we excelled.

The physical structure of Saint Bridget's church was fraught with symbolism, though I may not have realized it as a child. One day decades later, with light snow blanketing the City of Brotherly Love, I decided to take a sentimental journey back to the neighborhoods I knew so well as a youth. Driving through a shabby district of North Philadelphia, I noticed the church of Saint Edward the Confessor rearing up in the distance. This was the house of worship that stood just fifty yards from the house where my aunt Marge and uncle Charlie had once lived. I had forgotten how colossal Saint Edward's was; it took up an entire city block. Back in olden days, when immigrants alighted from the trolley late at night, returning from brutal, poorly paid jobs that slowly broke them into pieces, the sight of those looming temples must have seemed exhilarating. Ordinary people built these parishes, they could remind themselves; immigrants built these parishes. And when immigrants caught a glimpse of those spires thrusting heavenward from what amounted to their very own neighborhood cathedral, they must have taken enormous comfort from the spectacle, knowing that, at long last, after another murderous day in the sweatshops, they were home. To working-class Catholics, Saint Edward's wasn't a church. It was a fortress. And Saint Bridget's, blessed with the additional advantage of sitting on the side of a hill, played exactly the same role.

If I have any criticism of the Church during this dispiriting period, and admittedly it is but a quibble, it concerns the clumsy way charity was sometimes dispensed. Every few months, the nuns would ask children who were not poor to bring in cans of food to be distributed to the families of those who were. When the cans arrived, the labels would be peeled off to prevent the needy from grabbing the most desirable products and leaving behind the items no one wanted. A few days later, our parents would be ushered in to select a dozen cans without knowing what each one contained.

Several times when my father was out of work, my mother and I rendezvoused in the lunchroom and loaded up. For the next couple of weeks, she would boil some potatoes and toast some bread, then take out the can opener and peel open one of the donated objects. Whatever she found inside would constitute the main portion of our evening meal. If we were lucky, the contents might be pork and beans or spaghetti and meatballs. But more often than not, donors had bequeathed us canned asparagus, canned lima beans, or canned creamed corn. All of these, from the child's point of view, were vile. Not until I was in my twenties did I learn that asparagus was a delicacy, not a repellent vegetable cultivated with the deliberate objective of taunting the poor. Creamed corn, by contrast, was a mushy perversion of the noble culture of maize bequeathed to the white man by the Indians, and lima beans I shall forever view as the handicraft of Beelzebub.

A mixture of astonishment and horror flooded across our faces the night my mother pried open a labelless can, only to discover a cluster of artichoke hearts within. We had no idea what artichokes were or what man or beast could possibly eat them, much less what kind of person thought that donating canned artichoke hearts to the needy was apt to lift their spirits. When people with no direct experience of poverty try to conceptualize it, they mentally array gaudy images of rats and defective space heaters and .38 slugs embedded in the walls. They never think of canned artichoke hearts, because people who have never been poor understand only the economic components of deprivation, not the symbolism that colors everything. When your father is an unemployed alcoholic and your mother has four children she can't feed and may not even love, and there is no car and no TV and no telephone and no prospects, finding out that a stranger has donated a can of artichoke hearts to the cause is not likely to fill a child's heart with joy. What's next? A wheel of Camembert? A few strands of reindeer kidneys? Or perhaps next time the gentry will send along some cast-off top hats, ascots, and monocles so the starving kids can dress up as P. G. Wodehouse characters.

The second thing that sustained us as a family was the affection—not to mention the occasional infusion of cash—supplied by a handful of concerned relatives. Our relations were divided into two groups: those who came to see us during the four years we lived in the project and those who did not. The relatives who did the most to ease our pain through this doleful interregnum were my uncle Jerry, married to my dad's sister Catherine, and my uncle Charlie, wed to Aunt Marge, another of those gentle, much-admired "aunts" who were actually my father's cousins. Jerry and Charlie were the most important men in my life in those years, the father figures who provided inspiration at a time when I was losing interest in growing up to be anything like my father. Both were charismatic, somewhat eccentric men who did not have conventional nine-to-five jobs and whose influence on me was so powerful and enduring that it probably made it impossible for me to ever work at a conventional job, either.

My uncle Jerry was a salesman employed by the Philadelphia Gas & Electric Company. He worked hard, feared communism, hated taxes, and viewed Richard Nixon as a minor deity, even when Whittier College's most celebrated alumnus was still only vice president. Uncle Jerry was the only Republican in the family; had he immigrated to Philadelphia from Ulan Bator, he could not have been more culturally estranged from the rest of us. Physically, he was a remarkable-looking man, though not in any positive sense. He had been blighted from birth by *Good Soldier Schweik* hair, bristly spikes that stuck up in the air even when he was submerged beneath the waves of the Atlantic. It was hair that made you look fat even if you were thin, hair that made you look old even if you were young. German in ancestry, he seemed determined to evoke an ethnic stereotype associated with another continent and another century, at a time that many German Americans were trying to play down their Aryan roots. With his pugnacious cheeks and prominent snout, he could easily have passed for a Prussian sergeant-at-arms delivering humiliating terms of surrender to Napoleon III at Sedan.

When the sixties arrived, an era when even the most conservative older men started experimenting with their appearance in a misguided attempt to look fashionable, Uncle Jerry refused to budge, unwilling to temper his lifelong commitment to the anachronistic. I suspect that his hatred of the hippies who would come along a few years later stemmed less from disdain for their excrescent politics and debauched sexual practices than from resentment of their fabulous hair—all those ponytails and floppy British bangs. If there is such a thing as follicular predetermination, whereby an adult's overall orientation in life is dictated by his hair, then my uncle's fate was sealed early; with a look like that, he had no choice but to be a Republican.

Uncle Jerry was forever gadding about in a mammoth Oldsmobile or Buick convertible; he liked people to think he was loaded. He played billiards and he played pool; coming from upstate New York as he did, he said "pop" instead of "soda" and referred to me and my sisters as "pretty good coconuts." He loved to play shuffleboard and he didn't care who knew it. He also liked to banter with strangers, sometimes parking his car, dismounting, and crossing the street to congratulate a quartet of Negro ditchdiggers on their exemplary earth-removal skills. He would stand at the edge of the ditch with a perfectly ridiculous smile on his face and say, "Hey. That's a pretty nice ditch you're digging." To a child, such behavior was unspeakably audacious, as children were taught at an early date to speak only when spoken to, and maybe not even then. The ability to initiate conversations with complete strangers was one of the things I loved about my uncle; he seemed to be on a first-name basis with everyone he came into contact with: bus drivers, waiters, grease monkeys, cops. What's more, this promiscuous chumminess sometimes crossed racial lines.

Uncle Jerry was a man much given to dotty theories. He had convinced himself that the finest pizza in the tristate area was to be found in a flyspeck dive called Charlie's, which was located in a run-down part of Trenton, New Jersey. We would later discover that Trenton consisted entirely of an intricate series of intersecting run-down neighborhoods; no one alive could ever recall a time when the state capital was anything less than forlorn. We suspected that, even when George Washington surprised the redcoats and their Hessian minions on Christmas night in 1776, Trenton had already fallen on hard times. Of these facts Uncle Jerry was ignorant, perhaps willfully. Many evenings, he would motor all the way across Philadelphia, scoop us up in his fancy car, and drive an additional thirty miles to Trenton just so we could chow down in his favorite pizzeria. He had been dining at Charlie's since the late forties, when he first moseyed south from upstate New York, where good pizza was not to be found, and rented an apartment in a pokey little town called Morrisville, just across the Delaware River from Trenton.

To get to Trenton, you had to drive straight up Route 1 past a huge illuminated sign affixed to the bridge spanning the Delaware. The sign read TRENTON MAKES, THE WORLD TAKES. Nobody had any idea what this cryptic, almost goofy, assertion meant, and nobody seemed to care. Thirty-five years later, riding the train to Philadelphia from New York with my mother, I would ask if she could explain the sign. She could not; Garden State pontine lore was never her forte. Overhearing our conversation, a conductor told us that the sign had originally read WHAT TRENTON MAKES, THE WORLD TAKES but that the word WHAT had tumbled into the river years ago. The WHAT in the sign referred to Bayer aspirin, which had been manufactured in the Greater Trenton area for many years. The conductor maintained that the sign had dropped into the Delaware during the Second World War when Bayer, a German company, was taken over by the U.S. government. This was almost certainly not true. Nobody visiting Trenton ever seemed to draw any connection between the sign and the company, and the Bayer people must have wanted to keep it that way, for the WHAT, if it existed, never got dredged up and the sign remained as it was, preening incoherently in its incandescent inanity.

The way Uncle Jerry talked about Charlie's, you would have thought it was a pasha's feast, a cross between the Savoy Grill and La Tour d'Argent. In reality, it was just another pizza joint, a dank, malodorous hole-in-the-wall where the delights on offer were no better and no worse than the pizza we could have bought right down the street on any street corner in Philadelphia. Still, we didn't fuss about his quirky tastes; it was a free meal and a carefree outing. These jaunts into the heart of central Jersey darkness weren't about cuisine; they were about diplomatically giving us a day pass from the stockade, but doing so in a way that would not make my father feel insulted. Pizza had nothing to do with it.

Uncle Jerry was the only person in my family who dared to wear a fedora. His came complete with a chic, blood-red feather in the headband, and he wore it in a non-ironic fashion. He was from upstate New York, way up near the Canadian border, and irony never got there. His fedoras, needless to say, were natty; the nattiness of them was the stuff of legend. Men in natty fedoras were cut from a different cloth than ditchdiggers and pretzel-truck drivers; unlike them, Uncle Jerry did not have to report to an office or a store or a factory or a ditch every morning. Men in natty fedoras simply got into their cars, put the pedal to the metal, and hit the open road.

Occasionally, on Saturdays, Jerry would take me out on his sales calls. He did this because he liked my company—his adopted son,

Jerry Jr., was still an infant—but also because he and his wife understood how important it was to get my sisters and me away from my father and the project, if only for an afternoon. They knew that things were going downhill; they knew about the ruinous drinking; they almost certainly knew about the beatings. These outings were my uncle's way of tossing us a lifeline.

As soon as we arrived at the target destination, he would park the car, turn on the radio, and leave me sitting there while he went inside to sell gas and electric. Immediately, I would turn off the music—piffle like "How Much Is That Doggie in the Window?"—and read my comic books. I was particularly fond of Batman, who, though he possessed no superpowers as such, was not a man to be trifled with; moreover, like my third-grade teacher back at Saint Veronica's, he was a benevolent plutocrat who was committed to giving back to the community. I did not hate or even envy the rich when I was young, because I never knew any rich people personally; my only exposure to the upper classes was Miss Needham and Bruce Wayne, who both seemed absolutely peachy. Eventually, Uncle Jerry would return to the car and tear open a paper bag filled with industrial-strength salami-on-rye sandwiches. Salami was an unbelievably exotic food in the 1950s, and after overcoming my initial distress at its piquant taste, I soon became a lifelong devotee. Rye bread was something I had never tasted at home, not only because it was more expensive than white bread but because my father viewed esoteric items like rye and caraway seeds as deeply suspicious, perhaps even a menace to the republic.

For a public-utilities salesman, Uncle Jerry had an awful lot of panache. He drank foreign-sounding beers at a time when such beverages were almost impossible to find in the Keystone State. He played canasta. He played pinochle. On a few occasions, he may even have tried his hand at Mille Bornes. He taught me how to play chess, using the most unusual chessmen I have ever seen: dueling caballeros. I can no longer recall whether he had purchased the chess set on a trip to Mexico itself or picked it up at some curiosity shop in the States, but the chessmen made a lasting impression on me. One army was beige and brown, the other crimson and white. The bodies were hand-carved wood, and the heads were made of hard plastic, though I did not know this at the time; I imagined they had been crafted from mother-of-pearl by artisans named Antonio de Chavez y de Cusipata and Ignacio Gonzalez-Portilla. The pawns had what looked like pointy little beanies on top, while the knights resembled horses, but all the other pieces sported fancy head-dresses that looked emphatically Castilian. The lone exception was the rooks, bold-as-brass roués decked out in raffish sombreros. My uncle, a so-so chess player, had a hard time telling the pieces apart, and I rapidly progressed to the point where I could capitalize on his miscues and beat him without any trouble. This may have been because of all those fancy Milwaukee beers he was downing, or maybe he was merely taking a dive to make me feel better about living in a housing project.

All this was joyously strange and wonderful. I started playing chess at the age of nine not because the game interested me, which it did not then and does not now, but because I had fallen in love with those daz-zling little chess pieces. Just as my mother would adorn the walls of our house with inexpensive paintings of show horses cantering off into the sunset or of well-heeled Victorian women sipping afternoon tea, I felt that each time I played chess with my uncle, I was transported to another time and place where everything was classy and lacquered and shiny and expensive. This may not have been Mexico, but at least it was not East Falls.

My uncle Jerry and aunt Catherine (always known as Cassie) were extraordinarily generous to us while we were living in the proj-ect. They were also riotously entertaining. Fights were their forte; the more witnesses, the better. They argued here, they argued there; they did not stand on ceremony, they had no sense of occasion; the possibil-ity of being reproved for waging war in an inappropriate setting would never have occurred to them. They argued in living rooms, in dining rooms, in basements, in attics. They argued in movie theaters, in pizza parlors, in parking lots, in doctors' offices. They argued in Buicks, in Chevys, in Oldsmobiles, in Pontiacs; they argued with the roof up and the roof down. They once took my sister Ree and I to Dunkirk, New York, an all-day drive from Philadelphia, and argued nonstop for 422 miles.

They argued on the beach, on the boardwalk, on the patio, on the front lawn. You never had to wait for them to take the gloves off, because they never put the gloves on. For as long as I could remember, my aunt and uncle were always feuding, and by the looks of things, they enjoyed every second of it. Sometimes they argued about household matters. My uncle fancied himself a bit of a handyman, which was considerably more of a handyman than he was, and consequently their house was filled with doors that did not quite shut, windows that did not quite lock, and drapes that did not quite billow, as if he had made all his purchases at Monsieur Inept, a down-market hardware emporium specializing in prevandalized household fixtures. But mostly they argued about politics. Aunt Cassie was a Kennedy Democrat, Uncle Jerry a dyed-in-the-wool Republican, and their donnybrooks regarding the talents and merits of one Richard Milhous Nixon were the stuff of legend. Uncle Jerry never stopped insisting that JFK was a scoundrel; Aunt Cassie steadfastly maintained that Nixon was a tightwad, a liar, a Gloomy Gus, and an all-around son of a bitch. History has proven both of them correct.

Although these arguments often attained a level of vitriol no child would have expected from a married couple—my parents did not scream at each other, preferring to conduct their lifelong war in proxy skirmishes featuring alcohol (him) or abdication of the conversational prerogative for weeks at a time (her)—there was something comical about my aunt and uncle's squabbles. Whenever she was losing an argument, which she often was, she would resort to the tried-and-true taunt "Go ahead, Schwartz, go shit in your hat and pull it down over your ears."

This was shockingly coarse language for a woman in that era and that social milieu; my mother never cursed, rarely mouthing anything earthier than "that dirty so-and-so," and my father never tolerated profanity of any sort in our house. He would throw a fit if someone merely said "Geez," contending, perhaps speciously, that this was the blasphemous diminutive of "Jesus." He felt so strongly about swearing that when he did fly off the handle, he would substitute the term "G.D." for "goddamn," as if such declamatory shorthand mitigated the impiety of the expletive. As for the villainous execration "motherfucker," just to think about it in his presence was to run the risk of on-the-spot disembowelment.

Despite these sensitivities, he took no umbrage at his sister's indelicacy; like many men who smile at the maledictions of irate women who have never learned to swear properly, he actually found it rather charming. What made Cassie's trademark epithet so memorable was that it was the only crude remark that ever passed through her lips; it was the trick pitch she fell back on in the bottom of the ninth when she desperately needed an out. Whenever those two would come visit, I would sit on the edge of my seat waiting for the main event to get under way, the knockdown, drag-out slugfest that always involved Nixon and JFK and always ended with Aunt Cassie sneering, "Go ahead, Schwartz, go shit in your hat and pull it down over your ears." Though employed in a profane, secular setting, these words were as solemn, ritualistic, sacrosanct, and inevitable as the exhortation "Ite, missa est" with which priests signaled that Holy Mass had come to an end. Once Aunt Cassie told her husband to go shit in his hat and pull it down over his ears, we all knew it was time to go up to Trenton for pizza.

A generation older than my parents, my uncle Charlie shared many of Jerry's traits. They were both German American, a genuine rarity in our closed Hibernian circle. They both made their own hours. They both liked to spread their money around. They both smoked like chimneys. They were both fond of women, and not just their wives. Neither took any lip from anyone. Each, in his way, was larger than life.

Uncle Charlie, like Jerry, did not have a regular job. By day he worked in some unspecified capacity for the local Democratic Party, making sure that on Election Day the right people voted and the wrong people didn't. By night he worked as an entertainer, or what was called a saloon singer. He was a self-taught musician who played a gorgeous midnight-blue tenor guitar. It was a Gibson, the top of the line. The tenor guitar, now obsolete, had only four strings, and while chords could be played on it—in an emergency—it gave off a shrill, tinny sound and was generally played as a solo instrument, the guitarist plunking out a melody while another guitarist or a pianist lent background support. Uncle Charlie, for whatever reason, had always flown solo. Like many musicians of that era, he had started out playing the ukulele before switching over to a less whimsical, less robustly Polynesian instrument. He could not read music, had no great gifts as a singer, and, ultimately, I came to realize, wasn't much of a finger-picker. Guitarists short on talent usually played a six- or twelve-string guitar, because these instruments were easily mastered and, if thumped upon with sufficient verve, could produce just enough of a din to create the illusion that the person playing them knew what he was doing. This was especially true if he was performing in a bar filled with comatose lushes and loudmouthed floozies who were already three sheets to the wind.

Loading up his beautiful instrument, Uncle Charlie would saunter off to various North Philadelphia watering holes in the early evening and spend the next few hours croaking out adamant, demonstrative, but not terribly lyrical renditions of "Yellow Bird" and "On a Slow Boat to China," accompanying himself feebly on that majestic Gibson. He was the sort of person who, though he could not actually sing, had learned how to "put a song over" by dint of moxie and flair. All the time he was bulldozing his way through a number, he would be chomping on a cigar. It was never a cigar in the humidor-stored sense of the word but, rather, a stinking old tree trunk that made the entire room smell like a trough. It was clear from the way the audience applauded that Charlie was a tremendously popular fellow, probably more because of his political connections and the cash he could spread around on Election Day than because of his musicianship or taste in cigars.

I got to see my uncle perform several times when I was young and was impressed by his stage presence, if not his craft. Warbling "Alexander's Ragtime Band" or "Beyond the Blue Horizon" while puffing on a stinking cigar was an amazing feat, yet somehow he was equal to the task. "Puffing" is probably not the accurate term to describe the procedure; like most serious cigar smokers of that era, he would physically munch on his cigar the whole time it was entrenched in his mouth. I now believe that one of the reasons men chewed on their cigars that way, ripping them to shreds and drowning them in saliva, was to prevent other men from stealing them. My uncle Charlie was the first man I ever met who was invested with the undeniable moral authority to smoke a cigar. When I grew up, when imported cigars became ludicrously fashionable among men of suspect manliness, the act of smoking a cigar took on a ritualistic, fetishistic aura. Preposterous striplings would gather furtively in fancy tobacco shoppes, check the inventory in their padlocked humidors, and discuss Nicaraguan wrapper quality with similarly silly men, who themselves would wax poetic about long-dead masters of the hand-rolled Cohiba, men whose remains were now interred in unmarked graves in Havana or Managua. These *sigaristas* had somehow confused tobacconists with notary publics, vainly hoping that the establishments themselves would certify a virility no one would otherwise believe they possessed.

Uncle Charlie, by contrast, simply smoked his stogie; and then when he was done, he started smoking another one. Fortunate to live in an era when cigar smoking was still viewed as a vice rather than a symbol of eccentricity, he didn't need to go to any fancy emporium to enjoy his cigar, and he certainly didn't need any company while he was demolishing his lungs. He could sit there and wreck them all by himself.

Early on, Uncle Charlie had taken a liking to me. This may have been because he was not on the same wavelength as his own son, a good-looking hotshot who drove a shiny red convertible and would one day carve out a fine career for himself as a banker. Cousin Bobby had a snazzy crew cut, a seraglio of ravishing girlfriends, and a passion for Johnny Mathis records—at the time, the very height of sophistication, particularly in our down-at-the-heels environment. Bobby had almost certainly patterned his personality after Ricky Nelson, the charismatic star of *Ozzie and Harriet,* and we all worshipped him. He gave us money for treats, sometimes took us for a spin around the block with the hood of his convertible down, and always acted pleased to see us. But he didn't usually hang around that long; whenever we came to visit, he would abruptly vaporize into the night for an assignation with one of his fetching inamoratas. He was a high-powered go-getter who was going places his father had never been, and his father knew it.

This being the case, it was not surprising that Uncle Charlie liked having me around. He could see that I was fascinated by his ability to generate cash without having to report to a place of business or punch a clock or inform anyone of his movements. To say nothing of the fact that he took no guff—it was not in his nature. My father did take guff, quite a bit of it. One day when we returned from a foray on his pretzel truck, his boss, a short, wiry grump who was more than a few years his senior, stalked out of his office and excoriated him right in front of me. I am not sure what my father's offense was that day, but I could see that he was ashamed to be chastised in front of his son by a middle-aged beanpole he could have decked with one punch. Even as a kid, I knew that his boss's behavior was beyond the pale; it was the sort of gratuitous cruelty that permeates the workplace in this country, one colossal job-creating machine in which millions of Americans start their own businesses every year because they cannot stomach even one more day of abuse from their superiors. This way, they can run their own operations and mistreat their underlings, who will then run off to start their own businesses.

You didn't need to have much on the ball to see that my uncles were supplanting my father as my heroes. They were independent, they were flashy, they made their own hours, they had yet to meet any crap they were prepared to take. Whippersnapper-protégé that I was, I got into the habit of asking them tons of questions, not because I cared all that much about the answers but because it enabled them to assume the enviable role of the wise old patriarch, sagaciously explaining to a callow youth who was who and what was what. After which they always bought me soda pop.

One Saturday, Uncle Charlie rounded me up to help out with his undefined duties as a ward heeler. We spent the morning stuffing hundreds of envelopes with fliers beseeching voters to get out and support the Democratic ticket. Then, after lunch, we delivered the envelopes to houses throughout his neighborhood. My uncle smoked cigars all day, bought me some ice cream, and then, at the end of the afternoon, rewarded me with a few bucks for my efforts. I told him that I would put the money toward the purchase of a jet-black English racer that I'd had my eye on for some time. About a year earlier, I had purchased a used bike at the Salvation Army for $12 with cash I had saved up from birthdays and my confirmation, but the vehicle was a dud whose steering wheel would never stay in place, causing me to regularly go flying off in all directions. To work my way back to the house after a spin around the project, I had to pedal past a playground teeming with inclement white trash, so relying on a bicycle with a defective steering wheel was a bad idea. The bike I'd been dreaming about was going to set me back $33, though I never really expected to make that purchase, because as soon as I had $33 amassed—a princely sum that was probably half what my father was earning each week back then—I knew he would requisition it for some dubious emergency, like stocking up on blended whiskey in case the state of Tennessee got nuked by the Russians. My father was the Internal Revenue Service writ small; he was the physical embodiment of all those tax-and-spend Democratic legislatures that Republicans have always reviled, in that he made it pointless to work hard, because the money was only going to end up getting confiscated by lazy sons of bitches who had their own ideas about how to spend your hard-earned cash. He, like them, was a master at demoralizing the workforce.

Two Saturdays after the outing with Uncle Charlie, my mother dispatched a search party and told me to come home immediately, as a fantastic surprise awaited me. I could not imagine what this surprise could be, but as surprises were in short supply back then, I ran home as fast as my little legs could carry me. When I nipped through the front door, my uncle Charlie was kneeling on the living room floor, clutching a wrench, putting the final touches on the assembly of a magnificent jet-black English racer. The bicycle had been manufactured by a German company called Hermes, after the god of speed, though, technically, he was also the deity responsible for watching over anyone involved in shady financial transactions. No matter how long I lived, no matter how radiantly fortune shone upon me later in life, I never got a better present. I rode that bicycle every single afternoon until the day I went to college. I rode it up hills, down hills, past gangs of hoodlums, through gangs of hoodlums. I loved that bicycle the way a mother loves a son. More, in the case of my mother. It was the only toy I ever owned that I took care of: I washed it, I waxed it, I polished it, I adored it. That bicycle symbolized triumph; that bicycle symbolized escape. I never forgot that afternoon, and I never forgot my uncle Charlie. He was a man who had cash burning a hole in his pocket, and men who had cash burning holes in their pockets could make little boys' dreams come true.

In theory, he could have made little girls' dreams come true as well, but this did not come to pass that day. Forty years later, when I was reliving the events of that unforgettable afternoon at a family gathering, my younger sister Eileen, in her inimitably direct fashion, told me what it felt like to sit there and watch me take possession of that bicycle while she and my two other sisters slowly came to the realization that there would be no bikes for the girls, no dolls for the girls, nothing whatsoever for the girls, as they were not the apples of their uncle's eye. I had not previously examined that day from their perspective, enthralled as I was by my own good fortune. But my good fortune was not theirs, and none of them would ever forget it.

Uncle Charlie and Uncle Jerry treated us just swell, as did their wives. Cassie became my sister Ree's surrogate mother and inseparable companion, while Charlie's bride, the serene, loving, and long-suffering Aunt Marge, dutifully adopted the role of the grandmother none of us ever had. My grandparents, immigrants from Ireland, were all dead before I was born, and for a time I thought I had missed out on something. Then I heard stories about how the men liked to knock around their kids, and I decided I was better off without them. Aunt Marge and Uncle Charlie would do just fine.

There were a few other relatives who occasionally stopped by East Falls for short visits, perhaps because they preferred our company to that of their children. My uncle Jim, a foulmouthed, chain-smoking insurance salesman, and his wife, Mary, my mother's nicotine-drenched older sister, who also swore like a sailor, lived in Drexel Hill, a modestly affluent suburb just outside the city limits. The very words "Drexel" and "Hill" evoked a grandeur and an aura of poshness that would have been unattainable for Irish Americans a generation earlier. The Burkes, however, were not posh.

Mary and Jim didn't go overboard on their trips to the project— they popped in perhaps once a year—but from time to time they would invite me for overnight trips to their house, where Jim would exhume his trusty old tape recorder so we could listen to the entire fourth quarter of the Philadelphia Eagles' triumph over the Green Bay Packers in the 1960 NFL championship game. The game ended with the immortal linebacker Chuck Bednarik (who played all sixty minutes, as he was also the Eagles' center) wrestling the Packers' star running back, Jim Taylor, to the ground on the eight-yard line and pinioning him there. "You can get up now, Jim," the neolithic Bednarik is reported to have said to the likable Taylor as the final gun went off. "This fucking game is over." It was the last championship the Eagles ever won.

I liked Uncle Jim and loved being around my aunt Mary, because she was volcanically crude, one of the few women I have ever met who *did* know how to swear. Every third person she talked about was a "son of a bitch," which quickly grew to be one of my favorite expressions, as Chuck Bednarik used it and my dad did not. Mary's son, who would eventually go into the same line of work as his dad, was the first bona fide halefellow-well-met to enter my life. Endowed from childhood with the gift of gab, this silver-tongued sharpie buttonholed me at a family gathering when I was twelve and smooth-talked me into buying a life insurance policy. My mother, appalled when she got wind of this, made him cancel the policy. From my point of view, falling prey to Little Jim's ethical slovenliness was a small price to pay for his dad's company, as every year Jim senior would take me to an Eagles game at venerable Franklin Field on the University of Pennsylvania campus in West Philadelphia. Eagles tickets were hard to get and did not come cheap, as is true to this day.

Usually the game was a dud, as Jim did not care to waste his best tickets on a kid who was still wet behind the ears, though I did once get to see the Eagles' fleet-footed wide receiver Ben Hawkins score three touchdowns against the hapless New Orleans Saints. Hawkins was famous for refusing to do up his chin strap, and though he was never much of a receiver, his renegade idiosyncrasies played well with Philadelphia's blue-collar fans, who imagined that in the gridiron melee of the mind, they too would enter the fray with their chin straps dangling impudently. At the time, the Eagles used to shuttle three quarterbacks in and out of the game. One couldn't pass (Jack Concannon), one couldn't run (Norm Snead), and one couldn't play (King Hill). Be that as it may, King Hill was quite a hit with the fans, because he had crafted himself a superb nickname, as had King Corcoran, the star of an upstate minor-league ball club called the Pottstown Firebirds, who kept trying to make the Eagles' squad, but always got cut in preseason. The young men who attended Eagles games in that era, the slightly paunchy ones who were just starting to go to seed, were never delusional enough to imagine that they could have played in the NFL. But suiting up for a third-rate squad like the Pottstown Firebirds—a blue-collar outfit filled with lunch-pail Vercingetorixes like themselves—did not seem entirely outside the range of possibility. I saw King Hill play once, but only for a few downs before he got yanked back to the sidelines, and never saw King Corcoran at all. The reign of the Kings was short.

Jerry and Cassie and Mary and Jim were the relatives who kept us treading water as we struggled through what we hoped was only a temporary reversal of fortune. They would usually break open their wallets during their visits and were always generous on birthdays and at Christmas. They knew better than to bring over hand-me-downs, as we were already pretty well set in that department. But there was an entirely different type of relative out there, mostly on my mother's side of the family. These were the ones who did not come to see us, the ones who thought they were better than us. Foremost among them was Uncle George, the husband of my mother's older sister Nora, and a figure of mythological primness and Caledonian parsimoniousness. He came to visit us only once in the four years we lived in East Falls, and said nothing. He spent the whole visit in a state of apprehensive self-quarantine, cowering inside a disintegrating armchair over on the far side of the room, as if he feared that he might contract dengue fever if he came too near us. He made no attempt to disguise how much he hated being there, but at the same time he looked a bit frightened, fearing perhaps that a quartet of hungry but determined children might machete loose one of his legs and cook it up in an impromptu fondue.

Irish American himself, arriving in the world with no more advantages than my parents, Uncle George felt that my father was a wastrel; that my mother had married beneath her station, and that because she had married beneath her station, she had gotten what she deserved. For many years, he worked in a reasonably important position for the Radio Corporation of America in a New Jersey office complex directly across the Delaware from his home, which was located in a mildly upscale Philadelphia neighborhood called Mayfair. This was an impressive achievement, given that he had all the charm of a culvert. Upon retirement, he moved to Florida, where he lived until a squadron of harpies came to claim his soul. He and his wife, Nora, never had any children. Good thing, too. Uncle George resembled the prissy grump—also named George—who was the child-loathing neighbor in the popular TV program *Dennis the Menace*. But whereas George Wilson was a harmless old fussbudget, George Aitkin was a prick. I could understand his despising my father, but why us? We hadn't done anything to offend him. We hadn't squandered any opportunities for advancement. We hadn't married beneath our station. We were only 11, 9, 6, 1½.

Most of our other relatives fell into the same general category. They rarely visited, and when they did come, they didn't stay. The lone exception was my mother's younger sister Cecilia and her husband, Bill. Like my father, Bill had lost his job—as a typewriter salesman, of all things—when he got caught in an economic downdraft and was forced to take refuge in a housing project. Luckily for the Tierneys, the Hill Creek Housing Project was a much classier operation and was miles and miles away in that up-and-coming, semisuburban district called the Great Northeast. Even though their puffin-scale house was cramped and dark and ugly as sin and was much gloomier than the starter hovel we lived in, there was no gainsaying its chic address on Adams Avenue. Uncle Bill, who died of lung cancer in his early forties, was a lovely man with a quick, mordant sense of humor. He never lorded it over us. Aunt Celie, on the other hand, never let my mother forget that she was living in a project demonstrably inferior to the one the Tierney family called home. My mother said that this behavior, while reprehensible, was understandable, as it was "only human nature." We later found out that my mother had strong-armed her beautiful, vivacious, spectacularly popular younger sister and erstwhile roommate into quitting high school a year early and taking a job, thereby denying Celie the opportunity to be the prom queen, the belle of the ball, the girl most likely to succeed. My mother did this, so the story went, because she needed to clear the decks in order to marry my father. Aunt Celie, forced to finish high school by night, never forgave her.

The third beacon of light throughout these dark times was the public library, and particularly the bookmobile that came around every Friday night. The bookmobile, a sort of cultural bread truck, was filled with materials that enabled us to travel to foreign lands in our minds. Card-holders were allowed to borrow five books at a time, though I would have much preferred to borrow ten, because even at an early age I understood that if I wanted to grow up to have a dainty little Colonial home with a white picket fence and a collie, I'd better read a lot of books. I read books about the Greeks, the Romans, the Vikings, the Moors. I taught myself the causes of the French and Indian War, the latitude and longitude of Timbuktu, the composition of the Spartan phalanx, the philosophical underpinnings of the bicameral legislative system. I taught myself who Sennacherib was, what he was famous for, and how the reign of Ashurbanipal fit into the grand scheme of things, dead certain that this information might one day come in handy.

I was never jealous of rich people when I was young, because I didn't know any. Poor people tend to resent those in the economic stratum directly above them, so I grew up ferociously jealous of the lower middle class, a group that rarely attracts such ire. I grew up wishing that I lived in the slatternly houses adjacent to the project, not the stately mansions that lined prestigious Lincoln Drive, several miles down the road. I was never jealous of children who went to private school, because I was unaware that they even existed. Not until I read *A Separate Peace* in high school did I find out that there were prep schools out there loaded with bashful psychopaths who liked nothing better than to push one another out of trees. We all had a great laugh when our teachers assigned us these coming-of-age tearjerkers; from our perspective, the more boys named Phineas who got pushed out of trees, the better. We had not made a separate peace; we had not even been invited to the war. We could identify with the characters in *David Copperfield* and *Oliver*

Twist. But why would any of us care about someone named Phineas? Much less Holden.

Later on, I would have similar feelings about misty-eyed films like *Dead Poets Society* and *The Emperor's Club:* When I was young, Dead Poets Society boys were as far removed from my experience as the ancient Medes. What the rich were, what the rich hankered after, none of it had anything to do with me. I did not want a yacht or a Mercedes or a chance to participate in the regatta. I did not want to accompany pert debutantes to the cotillion. I did not want to attend the Hackley School or Wankworth Academy or become a master of the *poignard.* I wanted a pair of shoes. I wanted a pair of shiny black Cuban-heel slip-ons that I could wear when I served Sunday Mass, rather than the high-top Converse sneakers I usually wore, to the consternation of the assembled faithful. I did not want to look rich. I wanted to stop looking poor.

By the time we had been living in the project for a couple of years, my father had come to accept that he would never again have a desk job, that his life from this point on would be a daisy chain of minimum-wage stints as a truck driver, a security guard, a deliveryman. One year he went through thirteen jobs, none of which suited him. We did not understand why he could not hold a job, or would not, only that he did not. He would get fired for calling in sick when he was actually drunk, or he would quit because he wanted to stay home and get drunk. Sometimes he quit because he hated the work, sometimes because he hated the commute, sometimes because someone looked at him the wrong way.

From this point on, he drank at every opportunity and beat us whenever the mood took him. His skills with the belt proceeded apace; his wrist maintained a supple quality long after the first bloom of youth had faded. He terrorized us by day, and kept us awake at night. Sometimes he would be quite a sporting fellow for entire days; sometimes he would be a pig for weeks. Slowly we began to get it through our heads that nothing we did could ever please him, that to him our mere presence was a reminder of all those dreams that had gone up in smoke. We were proof of his poor judgment, his wasted opportunities, his forfeit life. He had given hostages to fortune, and fortune had now come to collect. To him, we were nothing more than leeches, millstones, saboteurs. We did not bring him joy. We brought him bills.

I did not hate living in the project anywhere near as much as I hated living under my father's roof. I could have tolerated hunger and poverty and having to wear sneakers instead of shoes and never going to the seashore if only my father had not acted as if my nativity was his funeral. When I grew up, I never felt that surviving poverty was any great achievement or that no longer being poor would in and of itself guarantee a person's happiness. But not having to live under my father's roof would. Poverty is bad, but some things are worse.

Music, for example, particularly the popular tunes of the Great Depression era, whose baleful legacy hung over our lives forever. From the moment my sisters and I were old enough to study history, we realized that the teeth-rattling, awe-inspiring, incontestably heroic poverty of the Great Depression had us whipped. Depression-era penury was the V.S.O.P. of adversity; our breezy I Like Ike–era indigence paled by comparison. We didn't have murderous bootleggers or armies of paupers marching on Washington or distraught plutocrats leaping out of skyscrapers, nor were we forced to experience the trauma caused by the overnight collapse of the global financial system. Our poverty lacked the epic, mythic, death-defying quality of the poverty in *The Grapes of Wrath;* it gave off a fetid, bargain-basement aroma. It was Brand X mendicancy.

One thing that made the Great Depression so special was the sound track. The story ran something like this: At the very darkest moment in the history of the republic, Glenn Miller, Benny Goodman, Harry James, the Dorsey Brothers, and yes, perhaps even Duke Ellington and Count Basie, swooped down from the heavens and administered the kiss of life to a stricken nation, their foot-stomping swing helping a catatonic race scratch and claw its way out of the crypt. It was the credo of my family that the Big Bands in general, and one bandleader in particular, had single-handedly rescued American society from the asphyxiating gloom of the 1930s.

My father was a mystic who had somehow conflated the teachings of Jesus Christ with the string arrangements of Lawrence Welk. In the

1950s and 1960s, Welk hosted a very popular television program that aired on Saturday nights at 8:30 p.m. Welk was a bellicosely corny German-American accordionist who had recorded a handful of minor hits in the 1930s. He hailed from Strasburg, North Dakota, but talked as if he came from the Danzig Corridor. He wore repellent baby blue suits, loved to cut the rug with plump, ungainly octogenarian audience members, and cultivated an atmosphere of wholesome fatuousness on his show, furnished in large measure by barbershop quartets sporting pasted-on handlebar mustaches and fresh-faced songbirds preening in flouncy petticoats. No expense was spared in an effort to evoke an innocent, bygone, small-town America that not even Welk himself, who made his home in Los Angeles, could honestly have believed had ever existed.

Unlike Ellington and Basie, geniuses who helmed virtuosic jazz-based ensembles, Welk was a calculating schmaltzmeister who compelled gifted musicians to play as if they were not gifted, to crank out the same bland, assembly-line numbers, cryogenically frozen in mothballed arrangements, over and over again. Because my father forced us to watch the program every Saturday night, as part of a rigid cultural-indoctrination program that closely resembled those invented by the communists he professed to despise, my sisters and I developed a special bloodlust toward Welk and his putatively merry "Champagne Music" makers. Notwithstanding his lofty taste in films and literature, my father had the same haphazard, intermittently crummy taste in music as everyone else of his generation, and no one was more objectionable than Lawrence Welk. Forcing us to listen to this tripe was a Procrustean form of child abuse, suffused as it was with a subtext of intergenerational reprisal. Veteran bozos like Guy Lombardo, Louis Prima and Mel Tormé had had their moment, we felt, and now it was time for them to get off the stage and let somebody else step into the spotlight. But my dad felt otherwise.

Ex-cons often complain that the worst thing about prison is the noise; in the domestic detention center my father had constructed, the worst thing was the music. As a child, I placed music in an emphatically punitive context: Dad's cueing up a record on the turntable, whether it was Welk or Bing Crosby or Mitch Miller and his insufferable bouncing

sing-along dots, was merely another way of being cruel to us. A neuras-
thenic sappiness saturated the tunes of that era: "How much is that doggie in the window?" "Hey mambo, mambo *italiano*." "What did Della
wear, boy, what did Della wear? She wore a brand-new jersey, she wore
a brand-new jersey." The tunes spewing out of our tinny little radio
were flatulent, juvenile, nauseating. We were not only suffering from
deprivation and contempt; we were being driven around the bend by a
man whose suzerainty over the infrastructure of entertainment in our
household was absolute.

The off-brand music fell into a special category. My father was forever
coming home with the "generic" version of a current hit; the voice gasping from inside the portable stereo was never Dean Martin singing "Non
Dimenticar" on a Warner Brothers LP but Dino Martino warbling "Te
Adoro" on an album put out by Vinodyne Records. It was never Frank
Sinatra singing "Come Fly with Me" on Reprise; it was Fred Sinerosa
squawking his way through "You, Me, and That Sulky Old Moon" on
Voxogroove. The record that most stands out in memory was a horror
called *Movie Themes Go Mambo!* or something to that effect. This was
a cheese-ball compendium of fully orchestrated samba, tango, rhumba,
and bossa nova versions of the themes from *Gone with the Wind, My
Fair Lady, Ben-Hur, Roman Holiday, The Bridge on the River Kwai,* and
High Noon, as performed by Lex Rabinowitz and the Van Nuys Strings
or the Rancho Mirage Festival Orchestra or some pickup ensemble of
that general ilk. My father would play this chilling record at ear-piercing
volume at all hours of the day and night; our only hope was that enraged
neighbors might one day break down the doors and rip him to shreds,
knowing full well that no jury in the land would ever convict them. This
is the unreported side of poverty: It's not just rats in the basement or
cockroaches in the bathtub or alkies in the bedroom or drug dealers in
the hallway. It's a linen closet filled with scratched LPs called *Sal & Edna
Sing Steve & Eydie* and *Blame the Theme from* Exodus *on the Bossa Nova!*

After we had been living in the project a year or two, we began to suspect that our father was a lost cause. But somewhere along the line, we
started to realize that there were other things wrong with him. Maybe

the old tin plate in his skull was acting up. For example, he got into the habit of coming into the bathroom to relieve himself when we were taking baths, a gross violation of privacy for which my sisters never forgave him. He sometimes slept in my bed, sometimes in the spare bed in the room my sisters shared. He never explained why, and no one cared to guess. He grabbed me by the testicles a few times in a ham-fisted effort to explain "the birds and the bees." I did not like this one bit. This kind of unpredictable behavior went on for years while my mother diligently worked her way through that pile of newspapers down the hall.

Seeking to impersonate a happy family, he would sometimes take us along on one of his little outings. These would usually start out as attempts to mend fences but almost always ended badly, because deep inside he did not really enjoy our company, finding children overly judgmental when confronted by substance abuse. He would often recruit us for missions that were inappropriate for small children, dragging us into depressing, amoral, or emotionally insalubrious environments. He would bring us along when he went to visit his brother in prison. Or he would take us to saloons to see old cronies or to trade anecdotes with bartenders of edifying perspicacity and Shavian wit.

I spent a lot of time in saloons as a boy. My father would sometimes treat me and my older sister to a movie, covering our eyes with his hands during the risqué sequences, then stop off at a nearby taproom for a few belts. We were usually not allowed to sit at the bar, as this sort of thing didn't sit well with bartenders or even with some of the patrons. Instead, he would plant us in the plush leather booths that ringed these establishments and bring us one ginger ale after another while he slowly got soused. When we were quite young, we thought such excursions a lark, because we could plunge our fingers down into the upholstery and excavate loose change that had tumbled out of someone's pockets and into these crevices. But as we grew older it was much less diverting to sit there for hours on end, watching our father slowly transform himself from a well-spoken gentleman into a brute spoiling for a fight. It was also less fun because nobody—not even a kid—wants to sit for three hours straight drinking thirteen glasses of ginger ale.

On occasion, a tippler might buy us a soda, using this as a pretext to slide into the booth and chat with us, at least until my father shooed him away. When we asked who these men were and why he had given them the brush-off, he would simply say that they were "odd." They *were* odd, but so was he; nobody else we knew brought their kids into gin mills and exposed them to public drunkenness and the oddity of strangers, then acted as if this type of outing was normal.

My father had a powerful sense of social obligation. He made a fetish out of visiting his uncle Joe, a cadaverous Irishman who seemed to have been in the process of dying, without making much headway, since the Japs seized Manchuria. Uncle Joe lived in one of those heartrending two-story redbrick houses on a pygmy-sized street in a part of Phila-delphia where at night the entire neighborhood would hunker down on their front stoops and guzzle sickening concoctions devised by local brewers to whom quality and taste were alien concepts.

My mother refused to live down there; the boozy camaraderie and claustrophobia of those grim, taut thoroughfares felt to her like an eth-nic straitjacket. This, I later suspected, was the origin of the Wendle Street folktale. My mother thought she was too good to live in a dump like this, a glorified ghetto teeming with coarse men in stained under-shirts and brassy women who wore revealing shorts and skintight pedal pushers. Years later, communities like this, now on life support, would be resuscitated by artists flooding in from the suburbs, urban pioneers who found something positively thrilling about rolling up their sleeves, yanking out their trowels, and gussying up the dilapidated homes of the chain-smoking, lunch pail–toting, salt-of-the-earth proletariat and then selling them for three times their value to attorneys.

Many a Sunday morning, my father and I would make the long trip by bus, bus, and trolley to Uncle Joe's home on Mutter Street, where we would spend an hour or so watching him die. Uncle Joe was perpetually lying in state in a bed upstairs, doing his level best to get this thing over with, but he was never quite able to close the deal. For all I know, he may still be alive today, rasping and wheezing and bitching about the cupidity of the transit workers' union and the villainy of Negroes, at the ripe old age of 128. Though the truth is, he was never much of a conversationalist, at least not by the time I met him. He had an impenetrable brogue and seemed content to listen to guests bellyache about some miscarriage of justice or offense to common decency, then nod his head in agreement. I am not even sure how he was related to us, only that he had exactly the same name as my father and me. He didn't seem to get much out of our visits, and even though other relatives said that I emitted a certain elfin charm as a child, I got the definite impression that it was wasted on him.

Uncle Joe's bedroom was suffused with an aroma of vomit, cirrhosis, nicotine, immigration, and failure. There was a brass spittoon at the side of the bed into which Uncle Joe would spew mucus or blood or other unsavory bodily fluids. My father used the elegant term "cuspidor" to describe this object; this was my first exposure to the world of euphemism, where the unspeakably disgusting could alchemically be transformed into something markedly less repugnant merely by a slight shift in terminology. But I never thought of that spew-drenched receptacle as a cuspidor. To me, it was a spittoon. The thing I most clearly recall about those Sunday morning visits was that while other kids were going to the movie theater to see *101 Dalmatians,* we were going to an in-house oncology ward to watch a relative twice removed by marriage try to die. This was my father's idea of fun.

The evidence that he was going off the deep end steadily mounted. One of our favorite games as children was to trap bumblebees in tubby glass jars that had previously contained apple butter. The object was to tilt the jar toward the target as it nestled on a flower, delicately twist off the cap, and then catch the insect before the already incarcerated bees realized that the lid was open, that the moment for a jailbreak was propitious. The object was also to avoid getting stung. We kept records of how many bees we apprehended; George Lang, a boy who lived two doors down from my home, was the uncontested king of the bee catchers, having snared eighty honeybees and twenty-three bumblebees in a single day. George had been the only Zorro on the block until I showed up. After stumbling upon each other clad in black hats and black capes and black masks one afternoon—each of us straddling a sawed-off broom handle and lashing the crisp autumn air with our lariats, each of us absolutely convinced that we were the reincarnation of the fox, so cunning and free, who made the sign of the Z—George clippity-clopped off and hung up his Zorro outfit forever. I never knew why; I was perfectly willing to be Zorro on Monday, Wednesday, and Friday, and let George handle the champion-of-the-peons duties the rest of the week, but for whatever the reason, my new playmate abdicated the post without a fight.

Whenever we were out on our foraging expeditions, we made sure to punch holes in the jar lid so the bees would not suffocate, though we usually only kept them under lock and key overnight before releasing them. There was a widespread belief among my social set that bees could remember their captors' identities and might unexpectedly return at some later juncture to wreak vengeance. So when we cut the bees loose, we took care to do it a few blocks away, theorizing that they would never be able to find their way back to our cul-de-sac, as they would now be too disoriented. We believed that while bees could remember human faces, they were completely stumped by road signs and house numbers. Our skills in the apian sector were limited.

We never tried to catch wasps, as it was rumored that these creatures could communicate with one another, that a trapped wasp could call in an air strike against his jailers from inside the bottle. It was further believed that consecutive wasp stings inevitably resulted in death. I have no idea who taught us this strange hobby or the improbable entomological theories that came with it, but it was a great deal of fun, especially for George Lang, who needed tons of diversions to take his mind off the fact that his father was locked away in the nuthouse and that his days as Zorro were over.

One day I came home to find that my bees had been drowned. So had my sisters'. My father, spectacularly juiced, explained that he had filled the jars with water on the erroneous assumption that bees required oxygen to live—and what better source of oxygen than water? It was nerve-wracking when he would do screwy, or what Philadelphians called "whifty," things like this: A drunk we could handle, a bully we could at least get a read on, but a screwball was beyond our frame of reference.

One winter night when we were particularly hard up for money, my father told me to put on my coat and hat, as we were going off to visit the rectory. When things got really bad, he would sally forth and put the squeeze on some gullible parish priest for a few bucks to tide him over until his ship came in. These debts, I am certain, were never repaid. On the evening in question, we were ushered into a small office at the rectory and joined by a stone-faced young cleric. After the obligatory social niceties about the weather and the price of eggs, my father explained that he was between jobs and short of cash. He said that he had a bunch of children and no food in the house and we were running low on heating fuel. All this was true, though I am not sure the priest believed him. I was still very young at the time, barely old enough to understand that having to ask a priest for money was humiliating, even more so if the priest was half your age, was better educated, and made no effort to disguise his contempt. I was also old enough to understand that the priest was reluctant to hand over any cash whatsoever, that the whole situation made him uncomfortable, that he gave in only because spreading a bit of cash around was the sole diplomatic way to get rid of us. But I was not old enough or sophisticated enough to know that my father saw me not so much as a colleague or a confederate in this caper, but as a prop, that without my heart-melting presence, the priest would have sent him away empty-handed.

The priest forked over $20, a not-inconsiderable sum at the time. We thanked him and poured ourselves back into the night. It was too late to shop for food—grocery stores closed early—but it was not too late to visit a taproom. We wandered into a typically sepulchral watering hole, where my father ordered a whiskey with a beer chaser. The bartender brought me a ginger ale. Money was handed over, but when the change came back, I noticed that there was only about $12 left. My, these were certainly expensive drinks. I later came to understand that my father had been running a tab. He ordered another whiskey and another beer chaser while I had a second ginger ale and a bag of pretzels. He did not talk to me much when he was drinking like this; he chatted with the bartender or other patrons, usually about politics. It was universally agreed in such establishments that Republicans were the satraps of Lucifer, but there wasn't much room for the conversation to expand in any exciting new direction, because nobody from the Republican Party ever came in to advance any countervailing arguments.

After another round of drinks, my father turned to me and said, "How much money did the priest give us?"

"Twenty dollars," I replied.

He shook his head and smiled in the way he always did when he was going to treat me like a nitwit. "No, not twenty dollars," he explained with a civility I found unsettling, for the way his jaw now set sent out an unmistakable signal that I was skating on thin ice. "He gave us *fifteen* dollars: one ten-dollar bill and one five-dollar bill. Can you remember that when your mother asks?"

"Yes," I said, since there was no possibility of saying no. Even though lying was a sin and suborning a child to perjury an even more serious one, my father had decided exactly how this was going to play out.

"So how much did he give us?"

"Fifteen dollars."

"In what denominations?"

"One ten and one five."

He returned to his drinking. There was more powwowing, then more drinking. As was always the case on these bizarre outings, I was being marinated with a beverage I was rapidly tiring of. We must have been gone from the house for two hours now, perhaps more. He had another drink, bought a round for one of his engaging associates. The bartender fiddled with the cash lying on the bar. A few more bills disappeared.

Again my father turned to interrogate me. "How much money did the priest give me?" he asked.

"Fifteen dollars," I replied.

Again that granitelike set to his jaw. "No, not fifteen dollars," he corrected me. "Ten dollars. He gave me ten dollars. Can you remember that?"

I could. I could also remember "five dollars," which is what he had me tell my mother we had been given at the rectory when we finally got home late that night. She did not believe him, of course; he was a pitiful liar. Notwithstanding years of practice and innumerable occasions to hone his skills, he never got any better at lying as he grew older. He was not aware of this; like most drunks, he felt that attention to detail—the texture of the furniture, the ambience in the room, the pallor of the cleric's cheeks—made his lies seem more believable, when in fact they rendered his falsehoods ever more insulting. Though dissembling was never where his true talents lay, he went to his grave believing he was one of the most gifted liars in the history of North American duplicity.

I remember that incident in particular because it was the first time I felt that it was ethically permissible for me to lose respect for my father. Until he enlisted me as a coconspirator in this boozy escapade, his drinking was something he kept at arm's length. He got laid off from work, he got drunk, he hit us, he got drunker, we went to bed and prayed that he would stop drinking. But now he had forced me to lie to my mother, to corroborate a story that could not possibly be true. He was a liar; now I was a liar, too.

The next day, I told my mother the truth, and at some point she must have confronted him, registering disbelief that he would sink so low as to strong-arm a child into backing up his transparent deceptions. Though she didn't need me to catch him in one of his lies—it was not as if his misdeeds were under review by some international tribunal based in the Hague—he knew that I had come clean, which made me a squealer, which was far worse than being a drunk, because God would forgive a drunk but he would never forgive a rat. As usual, a pretext was invented to work me over with the belt, as if one were needed. All in all, that trip to the rectory turned into quite an adventure: He got bombed, I got beaten, a permanent breach opened between us, a priest got stiffed out of twenty bucks, and my sisters, as usual, went to bed hungry. The only thing I got out of the deal was a half-dozen ginger ales. And I wasn't even thirsty.

American folklore stipulates that those who rise above their humble circumstances do so because of an indomitable will to succeed, coupled with the good fortune to inhabit a country that rewards industry. That's one way of looking at it. Here's another: Poor people who succeed do so because they are born with talents that other poor people do not possess, because they are cunning enough to capitalize on these talents, and/or because they are either born lucky or develop a lucky streak pretty damn quick. If you are born poor and stupid, you're going to need to be very lucky. If you are poor and stupid and ugly, you are going to need to be even luckier. If you are poor and stupid and ugly and a member of an ethnic group that America purports to admire but secretly abhors, then you might as well skip the preliminaries and get yourself started on a life of crime at the earliest possible opportunity. Why bother standing on ceremony?

Most things in life come down to the luck of the draw. Line up ten poor people. Nine of them won't make it. One, maybe two, will. It might as well be you, third pauper from the left. It will help if you are born with chutzpah and personality or are capable of unleashing a stupefying amount of violence on complete strangers in a short period of time with little concern for the consequences. But even that may not be enough. Everyone who is saved is saved because someone tossed him or her a lifeline or, in my case, numerous lifelines. It may be a parent, it may be an employer, it may be a teacher, it may be a priest, it may be a boxing instructor, it may even be a parole officer. But, as the events of Good Friday make abundantly clear, no one is saved all by himself. Alumni of the slums succeed either because someone is reaching down from above or because someone keeps pushing hard from below. Or, in the ideal situation, both.

By the time I was ten, I recognized that my sisters and I were trapped. It was pointless to try running away; we would only be sent to institutions or foster homes, and we knew what they were like. It was useless begging relatives to intercede; they would dutifully report our grievances to my father, perhaps even gently upbraid him, and he would then rip the skin off our hides as soon as they were gone. It was futile to try reporting my father to the authorities, because there was nothing to report. He got drunk every night, he terrorized us, he hit us with belts, he made us feel useless. But, lacking top-flight data, we assumed that most parents did the same things back then, at least in that social setting. He did not mutilate us or put out his cigarettes on our flesh or hit us with metal objects; our lives were not threatened, merely ruined. This was not a job for social services; it was an internal affair. One of his favorite movies was *Gaslight*, in which a serpentine aristocrat (Charles

Boyer), operating behind closed doors—far from the scrutiny of friends and well-wishers—methodically drives his innocent wife (Ingrid Bergman) mad, all the while passing himself off as the wronged party, the long-suffering victim of her all-consuming dementia, the man more sinned against than sinning. Our lives were lit by gaslight.

The predicament I found myself in was clear. My dad was a drunk, his dad was a drunk, his dad had probably been a drunk, and unless I played my cards right, I was going to end up a drunk, too. This was not shaping up as an idyllic childhood. The same held true for my sisters. We had landed in a perilous situation and our survival was by no means assured. We were going to need outside help, lots of it. I knew this to be a fact. I also knew that if I did not get a break, I was going to be crushed beneath the wheel like so many others who started out poor. If I did not get a break, I was going to be trapped in the underclass forever, where the cuisine would be execrable and the sculling would be at an absolute minimum. If I did not get a break, I was going to end up exactly like my father, a miserable, deranged, booze-soaked failure.

Perhaps it was time to bring God into the picture.

Chapter 4. *Domine, Non Sum Dignus*

Around the age of five, I announced to all and sundry that when I grew up, I intended to be a man of the cloth. To underscore the seriousness of my intentions, I commandeered a pudgy little fruit cup, a cracked dessert plate, and a frayed tablecloth from the kitchen and erected a makeshift altar atop my bedroom dresser. Soon after, I added a crucifix, a Bible requisitioned from my parents' bedroom, and a pair of candlesticks. Then, to further the illusion that I was a cleric in training, I fashioned a flimsy version of the garment known as the chasuble, using a sheet my mother had dyed more crimson than the blood of Saint Bartholomew, the first of Christ's twelve apostles to be flayed alive. In Armenia, no less.

Somewhere along the line, I added a colorful armband known as a maniple, though in all honesty I could never see the point in draping this extraneous object over my arm, as it made it much more difficult to distribute what passed for Holy Communion in my compact inner sanctum. Decked out in my liturgical finery, I began saying mass in the privacy of my bedroom, using cherry Kool-Aid as a substitute for the wine I would pretend to transubstantiate into Christ's blood, with stale bread serving as the prosaic foodstuff I would simulate transmuting into His Most Precious flesh. All these I would mix together in my fruit-cup chalice. I conducted most of the service in a tot's simulacrum of Latin, an idiom I learned to mimic by repeating pithy phrases I had heard in church: "Confiteor deo, omnipotente," "Tantum ergo sacramentum," "Requiescat in pace," that sort of thing.

On occasion, I would invite my sister Ree into this jerry-rigged tabernacle to evaluate my growing expertise in the field of prepubescent Christian alchemy. But because she had already detected a reasonably direct link between the Church's obsession with retribution and my father's brutality, she was not terribly interested. Not wishing to be accused of impiety—a lynching offense in our house—she soft-pedaled her burgeoning alienation from the faith whenever she was in his presence. To me, though, her feelings were clear. She was going off organized religion early.

How I knew that I wanted to be a priest at such a tender age is beyond me. Today, this unoccasioned pronunciamento seems more like a clever gambit designed to temper my father's rage by shielding myself behind the aegis of the supernatural, rather than a practical objective. A stripling unversed in the ways of the world, I perhaps believed at the time that if God were truly all-seeing and all-knowing and was actually keeping a meticulous record of all human transgressions, He would eventually corner my father in a dark alley somewhere and see to it that he got what was coming to him.

I was initially attracted to the Church because of the theatrics. I loved the smell of incense, the euphony of such phrases as "Domine, non sum dignus," "Kyrie Eleison," and "Venite adoremus." I reveled in the pomp, the circumstance, the costumes, the paraphernalia. A glimpse of a jewel-encrusted chalice took my breath away, and I could bend strangers' ears for hours regarding the majesty of even the most commonplace monstrance. As for the ravishing beauty of the ciborium—be still, my heart. Even as a child, I was smitten by the prospect of gaining admission to the world's oldest, largest secret-handshake society, the non-Wasp, non-homoerotic version of Skull and Bones. It was all so far removed from the dreary predictability of the communities I grew up in. In those neighborhoods, in that city, in that era, pronouncing words like "Septuagesima" was as close to bona fide glamour as any of us were ever likely to get. Quakers didn't even get that far.

Years later, when I felt sufficiently emancipated from the Catholic Church to attend the occasional Episcopalian, Presbyterian, or Lutheran service, I was astonished at how drab and businesslike they were. Filing into church back in the days of the Latin Vulgate, when the entire building reeked of incense, and the priests rained down fire and brimstone on the iniquitous, and one of the more gifted nuns hauled her weary bones up into the organ loft and got cracking on the keyboard, was like flying down to Mardi Gras or going to the circus. By comparison, attending a

Protestant religious service was like going to a supper-club performance of *State Fair*.

Revisiting my childhood today, I am amazed at how quickly I accelerated from daydreaming about a garden-variety clerical career to actively laying the groundwork for canonization. Even as a child, I had no trouble grasping the fundamental selling point of Christianity: Life is awful, so get it over with as quickly as possible. Don't waste your time on all that rigmarole of becoming an ordained priest; proceed directly to sainthood. In olden times, before bureaucracy stripped the Catholic Church of its panache, it was possible to wander in right off the street and become a saint without having to endure any of the irksome preliminaries. Saint Francis of Assisi, before becoming a titan in Church history, worked in retail. Many future saints started out as peasants. Saint Martin of Tours, from whom I inherited my middle name—a Celtic favorite—was beatified after slicing his cloak in half and handing the chunkier portion to an unidentified beggar. This ensured him an eternity of peaceful slumber nestling in the bosom of the Lord. As Saint Martin at the time was a Roman centurion—and thus, a pagan who had no previous affiliation with the Church—there is some reason to suspect that his canonization may have been a contrived public-relations stunt designed to woo the lares and penates set.

Cast one's thoughts all the way back to the first century and it quickly becomes apparent that Christ's entourage was but a motley assortment of fishermen, masons, scribes, and general dogsbodies with no prior training in the sacerdotal arts. They were chosen because they were brave, resourceful, or charismatic; some because they could get things done (Saint Peter), some because they could inspire others to do so (Saint Paul). Church history abounds with tales of ordinary people who became saints without any formal tutelage, without having to submit to even the most cursory peer review. Of course, this was back in the days when Christianity was still a sect dominated by plucky amateurs.

As has been widely documented elsewhere, the easiest way to become a saint was to be murdered for one's beliefs. Precociously self-destructive, I began contemplating martyrdom at an early date, when someone—a nun, a relative—told me the story of Saint John Bosco, who was ripped to pieces by infidels or Jews (the details were hazy) while carrying the concealed Sacred Host on his person. This took place at some point in the reign of Valerian, when municipal transportation of the Eucharist demanded a good deal of finesse and subterfuge, and go-getting Christian tykes were often recruited as mules. Bosco's refusal to fork over the Most Precious Host to the marauding swine, even upon pain of death, earned him almost immediate canonization, and because he was one of the very few saints who had breathed his last while still in grade school, I unhesitatingly adopted him as my role model. Other boys wanted to grow up to strike out Willie Mays on a 3-2 heater in the bottom of the ninth just like Robin Roberts, the Phillies' ace right-hander; I wanted to get torn to shreds by roving heathens a full decade before reaching adulthood. It was in homage to Bosco that I selected John as my confirmation name when, at age twelve, I underwent the rite officially welcoming me into the Church. (Until they have been confirmed in a splendid, first-class ritual requiring the mediation of a bishop, Catholic children are merely considered trainee soldiers of Christ, not the real thing.)

The advantage of worshipping a saint like Saint John Bosco was that, because he had been butchered while still a teen and would thus remain the exact same age until the Last Judgment—when he would be reunited with the missing portions of his body—he could conceivably appear to me, an aspiring martyr, in my dreams and show me the sanguinary ropes; whereas if I tried to emulate one of the twelve Apostles, all of whom died as adults, I might have to wait several more decades—perhaps as many as seven—before getting the opportunity to earn my eternal reward. In the interest of full disclosure, there is also some reason to believe that I selected Saint John Bosco as my patron saint because I was dazzled by the cloak-and-dagger elements surrounding his demise.

Years later, I found out that the child saint I had admired and envied for so many years was in fact Saint Tarcisius; Saint John Bosco lived in a completely different historical period and is the patron saint of something else entirely. From that point onward, whenever I was fed what sounded like a tall liturgical tale—such as Saint Isaac Jogues's receiving a special papal dispensation to serve Holy Mass with the festering stumps that were all that remained of his fingers after the fiendish

Iroquois munched them clean off—I would retreat to my upstairs sanctuary and verify the facts in *The Lives of the Saints* just to make sure
that I was not being led on yet another wild-goose chase by some overly
imaginative nun or misinformed relative. The story about Saint Isaac
Jogues and the Iroquois, as luck would have it, is true.

My self-propulsion toward martyrdom got its biggest boost when,
at the age of nine, I came into contact with the Maryknoll Fathers, a
religious order that specialized in facilitating early departures from this
vale of tears. The Maryknolls, officially the Catholic Foreign Mission
Society of America, had been founded in 1911 as a missionary organization consisting of men who were not afraid to roll up their sleeves and
get their hands dirty while toiling in unappealing foreign climes. Later,
they would be joined by an order of Maryknoll nuns, who displayed a
similarly cheerful orientation toward harsh manual labor and prema-
ture self-extinction. Maryknolls were tillers of soil, reapers of wheat,
millers of soy: adept at building, damming, milking, farming, and mid-
wiving goats. They also pulled teeth.

Maryknolls were anything but intellectual, certainly nothing like
the dashing, cerebral Jesuits. They seemed to go out of their way to
trumpet their anti-intellectual disposition, to the point of maintaining
a subdivision of clerical helpmates called brothers, devout but oafish
handyman types whose principal qualification for the job seemed to be
that they didn't have much on the ball. Still a youngster, but certainly
not a sap, I had misgivings about what kind of a future I could expect in
such an intellectually emaciated environment. Because I was bright and
clever and curious—I had read a tot's version of *The Iliad* twice by the
age of eight—the Maryknolls did not seem like a religious order whose
values would neatly dovetail with mine.

Had things turned out differently, had it had been possible for me
to enter a Jesuit seminary after grade school, I am sure I would have
become a Jesuit priest and today would be a very smug, very self-
satisfied, stupefyingly reactionary prelate, perhaps even a ranking
member of Opus Dei or some other stealthy ecclesiastical cabal. But the
Jesuits did not accept candidates for the seminary until they had finished college, nor did most of the other orders. Only the Vincentians

or the Dominicans—I forget which—ran a preparatory seminary for high school boys. Unfortunately, this formative institution was way out in the Midwest somewhere, and I had no desire to travel such a great distance from my mother, my sisters, and my friends. Nor did I have any burning ambition to abide among hayseeds. But I was desperate for status, freedom, and liberation from financial anxiety, and I wanted to get out of my father's house in the worst way. So I began laying smooth the path for entering the Maryknoll Junior Seminary immediately after graduating from eighth grade.

No sooner had I expressed interest in joining the order than I began to receive regular Sunday visits from a well-turned-out, easygoing young priest who served as a sort of celestial recruiting officer. Much like college athletic programs, which dispatch duplicitous alumni, treacherous scouts, and ethically malleable assistant coaches all over the nation to pressure talented young athletes into attending this or that school, the Maryknolls stayed in close contact with me throughout my grade-school days, constantly checking in to make sure that my vocation was intact, my zeal undiminished. The priest, to my great surprise, was actually quite bright.

Sometimes I would be invited out to Maryknoll headquarters, way over on the other side of Philadelphia, where I would spend the afternoon learning more about what awaited me after ordination. There wasn't much to learn: The Maryknolls built hospitals, operated farms, fed the poor, healed the sick. They were comfortable around water buffaloes and handy with yaks. They occasionally got themselves abducted and beheaded by communists masquerading as agricultural reformers. Their monthly magazine always featured photographs of sturdy young priests and hearty campesinos joining joists and mending roofs and planting yams and establishing a solid irrigational infrastructure, facilitating the cultivation of land in areas of the Third World where such marvels had previously seemed inconceivable. The priests also sometimes harvested papayas. The magazine, to its credit, did not downplay the decapitation angle, often running stories with titles such as "The Boyish Priest Who Was Beheaded" and "Priest Among Head Hunters." The junior seminary was named after the French cleric Theophile Venard, who got his head chopped off by Indochinese heathens in 1861. None of this can-do, shoulder-to-the-wheel, plow-that-broke-the-plains roustabouting held any appeal for me, but if feigning passion for a career in manual labor was the price I had to pay to get out of my father's house, I would pay it. If things didn't work out in the seminary, I'd cross that bridge when I came to it.

Reassessing events now, it is amazing that I ever had any interest in entering the seminary, because the priests I came into contact with when I was growing up, almost without exception, possessed little personal magnetism, did not appear to enjoy their work, gave no appearance of being especially devout, and generally made poor role models for a trainee paragon of virtue. They did have nice cars, though: Buicks, Oldsmobiles, Caddies. The first of these clerics was Father Cartin, the Methuselahan, carbuncular pastor of Saint Bridget's church, where I served as an altar boy from the fifth to the seventh grade while living in the housing project. Saint Bridget's was a stately edifice that sat halfway up a gently sloping hill; from a distance it looked like a vest-pocket cathedral, though on the inside it had more the feel of an economy-sized mausoleum.

This was not an inappropriate environment, given the physical condition of the pastor. Much like my father's perennially expiring uncle Joe, Father Cartin had been waging a decades-long delaying action against some kind of pulmonary disease, spewing his malignant breath everywhere, persistently threatening to kick the bucket without ever actually getting around to doing so. Rumor had it that he began wasting away midway through Roosevelt's second term and kept wheezing toward the finish line straight through the Truman, Eisenhower, and Kennedy administrations. Yet, for some reason, he was incapable of putting the finishing touches on the job. Some parishioners thought he was deliberately prolonging the agony, fearing the earth-shattering reforms his brash young replacement would put in place once he was gone. Because of his infirmity, age, and overall lack of pep, it took him about an hour to say mass, easily twenty-five minutes more than most priests required. He spent the entire service staggering around the inner sanctuary, groaning and moaning, drooling all over the patens and cruets—not to mention his cassock and chasuble—and those of us who served as altar boys always gave him a wide berth, as we expected him to keel over and die any second and did not want to be in the line of fire when he did. But he never died, at least not while I was on the premises.

His nominal protégé, the dashing, good-looking Father Griffin, was one of those flashy young priests who became hideously fashionable in the sixties—flippant and irreverent, just one of the guys, forever astounding the congregation with his wisecrack-laced sermons. Father Griffin, who seemed to have derived his Hotshot of the Hieratic persona from a controversial early-sixties film called *The Hoodlum Priest,* which lionized an inner-city padre who actively sought out, and indeed seemed to prefer, the company of society's offal. Father Griffin also scandalized the devout by conducting Holy Mass in twelve minutes flat. Seemingly working from the premise that mass was an empty, mind-numbing ritual, he rocketed through the Introit, the Kyrie, and the Agnus Dei as if he had an urgent noon meeting at the UN Security Council. His philosophy was unequivocal: The faithful were obligated to attend Sunday Mass, yes, but there was no reason they had to suffer through it. With his snap services, Father Griffin, in the view of older parishioners, made a mockery of the most important ritual in Catholicism.

A child reactionary, I was perhaps the only young person in the congregation who shared Father Cartin's opinion about his heir apparent, and I ceaselessly implored God—during our twice-daily private colloquies—to delay the old priest's demise until a more suitable replacement could be found. To my mind, rituals were important, even empty ones: twenty-one-gun salutes, thirty seconds of silence, heartfelt renditions of "Far Above Cayuga's Waters"—all these ceremonies had to be taken seriously. Father Griffin must have known that his Chinese-fire-drill masses were offensive to older parishioners, but he did not care. He was a likable chap, the hipster in the Roman collar, a bit of a cutup with the altar boys. But I think he was in the wrong line of work.

Monsignor Collis, who presided over the parish my family moved to when I was thirteen, was a fat, blustery racist. He had a lilting brogue, a touch of the poet, and the gift of gab, but like many Irish-American clergymen, he was narrow-minded and pompous, and his heart was dead. We did not know this at the time we started renting the house directly across the street from Saint Benedict's church. When my mother announced that we were moving out of the housing project and shinnying up the economic ladder to West Oak Lane, a congenial district where my uncle Jerry and aunt Cassie lived, we were ecstatic. We would now be renting a two-story, three-bedroom house with an enclosed porch, from which we could gaze out on bustling Chelten Avenue. There was a small garden in the back and a storage shed attached to the rear of the house. There was also a bar in the otherwise dank and gloomy basement, with silhouettes of naughty dancing girls wriggling across the front panel. My father vowed to have the racy silhouettes removed, but he never did, rarely venturing into the basement except on those occasions when he took issue with municipal parking ordinances, ripped a traffic sign out of the sidewalk, and stored it downstairs. We could not imagine who our predecessors were or why they would have abandoned this august abode, assuming as we did that tenants wealthy enough to afford their very own subterranean lounge must be descendants of the Medicis.

We were even more ecstatic when we found out that Saint Benedict's was a space-age facility with pink walls and modernist stained-glass windows and plenty of direct sunlight, and not a caliginous tomb like Saint Bridget's, where even weddings took on the aura of funerals. The best news of all was that Saint Benedict's had a monsignor as its pastor. Monsignors ranked just below bishops in Church hierarchy but far above ordinary parish priests. This meant that Saint Benedict's was a parish the archdiocese took seriously. To have a monsignor running the show was a clear sign of class, sophistication, money. The Queenans were finally getting somewhere.

Where we were getting, in fact, was into a once-prosperous neighborhood that was going downhill fast. Blacks were moving in; whites were moving out; for-sale signs were popping up everywhere. Spurred on by the federally subsidized highway system that made flight to the suburbs not only feasible but enticing, middle-class white people dumped their houses at fire-sale prices and hightailed it to racially segregated suburbs all over south Jersey. Overnight, huge tracts of North and West Philadelphia turned into slums as white people made a mad dash for the exits, fleeing the African-American onslaught the way the Romans had once fled the Huns. There was never any chance for integration to work in Philadelphia, the city that wouldn't let Jackie Robinson rent a hotel room when he made his major-league debut. Inflamed by the populist thug Frank Rizzo, a feared, inept police commissioner who then became a feared, incompetent mayor, white people acted as if their black neighbors were savages. Once in control, Rizzo gleefully harvested the seeds of discord he had planted years earlier when he begged the federal government to send him Sherman tanks to help quell urban discord fueled by "outside agitators," meddlers, commies. This approach set the overall civic tone for the next two decades. The city imploded in the twinkling of an eye; it never recovered from the urban holocaust of the sixties. Tellingly, the no-nonsense "savior" idolized by so many whites, including my father, was the man who was ultimately responsible for the Caucasian stampede out of town. No one seemed to notice the irony.

Soon after we moved to West Oak Lane in 1963, I met a boy named Mike Craig. He was the first black person I ever knew personally; before we moved to West Oak Lane, I had never been inside a black person's house. Mike and I became fast friends; we played football together, we played pinochle together, we started a rock band together, we attended the same high school and college; we would not lose contact until we were twenty-six, when I moved to New York City.

One day during our junior year in college, a few of us were sitting around discussing pertinent issues of state in the way upperclassmen so often will. At some point, the conversation turned to the subject of the white man's burden, specifically the young white man's burden: whether earnest, unbiased young white people should be held accountable for centuries of racial abuse for which they in no way felt responsible. Mike then told an amazing story. A few days before my family moved into Saint Benedict's parish, Monsignor Collis, who bore a strong resemblance to a vindictive leprechaun, visited the fourth, seventh, and eighth grades and implored the students to be extra hospitable to the Queenans, because we were the first white people to move into the neighborhood in three years. Each of the classes contained a handful of black students, who were obliged to sit through this spiel. The monsignor did not seem to notice them, much less care. Nearly a half-century after that little pep talk, Monsignor Collis is long dead and forgotten, while the congregation that worships at Saint Benedict's consists almost entirely of African Americans, devout servants of the Lord who inhabit a neighborhood where a white face has been a rarity for decades. The monsignor's dream that my family's arrival might portend a sea change in the parish's fortunes did not come to pass; the ethnic renaissance our advent seemed to announce was a mirage.

The students and nuns at Saint Benedict's were extraordinarily nice to us, but not even the most glowing accounts of their hospitality could attract the fresh Caucasian blood needed to stem the onrushing ebony tide, and within four years the neighborhood was down for the count. To paraphrase Debussy's comment about Wagner's music, the arrival of the Queenans may have seemed like a glorious sunrise, but in fact it was a bittersweet sunset. If a rapidly deteriorating white neighborhood couldn't attract anyone more upmarket than the Queenans, it was probably time to throw in the towel.

Throughout my childhood, I believed that having a vocation in and of itself set me head and shoulders above my fellow students, who rarely spoke of their career plans. The nuns encouraged this swelled-head attitude, taking pains to inquire about my latest visit to Maryknoll headquarters and doing so within earshot of my classmates. It was as if they were looking forward to my being martyred, or at least tortured; and if they continued to laud my virtues in public the way they did, in front of classmates who had no dreams of one day joining the Curia, they might succeed in getting me dispatched into the arms of the creator before I even started high school. No one, myself included, seemed to realize that there was an unhealthy side to my aspirations, that unlike my peers, who derived their vocational inspiration from real-life firemen and nurses, I drew most of my inspiration from people who had been dead for two thousand years and had not breathed their last under agreeable circumstances.

It is remarkable that I even considered pursuing a career in the liturgical sector, given my father's efforts to undermine my faith. But it is pointless to hate Christ merely because of Christians, and, in any case, my dealings with God usually went directly through His son, the saints, and my guardian angel, not through the Church itself. Bypassing intermediaries and making direct contact with Almighty God was a tactic I learned from my father. More a stay-at-home mystic than a devout churchgoer, he gave the impression that his relationship with God was a personal one and, indeed, that the two were rather chummy. He did not require the mediating force of the Church to commune with the Almighty; he went straight to the source.

For a long time he had been an ardent communicant, attending Sunday Mass and trooping in for weekly confession just like everyone else, but this did not prevent him from criticizing our parish priests for doctrinal lapses or for delivering intellectually threadbare sermons. He often told us that if his life had turned out differently, he would have happily become a Trappist monk, an unusual career choice for one who was so gabby by nature and so disinclined to stay in one place for any length of time. His churchgoing habits tailed off considerably after a grizzled missionary, on sabbatical from the fields of the Lord, heard his confession and told him he was a worthless drunk and a bully who ought to be ashamed of the way he treated his family. At least this is what my mother reported, though she may have tidied up the language here and there; my father later disclosed that his confessor had specifically referred to him as a son of a bitch. Because the priest who had rebuked him was a missionary, my father henceforth took a dislike to all those who toiled in foreign climes and then, upon their return to their native shores, acted as if their privations gave them carte blanche to pull rank on the hapless laity.

Up until then, he had been all in favor of my becoming a Maryknoll, because he, like most people, viewed missionaries as heirs to the martyrs: rough-and-tumble types infused with a Cagneyesque swagger, as opposed to diocesan priests, who were scorned as fussy bureaucrats, lazy sticks-in-the-mud, and sometimes prima donnas. Now his attitude changed. A confederate-to-be of the man who had chastised him, I now morphed into a symbol of missionary haughtiness on whom he could vent his rage. The way he sized things up, the missionary had been guilty of the sin of pride, for charity vaunteth not itself and pride goeth before a fall. Thus, once again, through no fault of my own, I had been sucker-punched by the One True Church, finding out the hard way that being devout and selfless and even cultivating an aura of personal sanctity were no match for physical size. So out came the belt.

One day my father decided to take matters of faith into his own hands, jettisoning the weekly sabbath-honoring duties mandated for all Catholics and installing a direct, personal pipeline to the creator. Now, whenever he got juiced to the gills, he would command his family to assemble after dinner and participate in the excruciating ritual of "saying the rosary." Alcohol and Catholicism are a deadly combination, so what should have been a simple act of devotion—a humble ritual that had enabled believers to survive centuries of persecution in nests of vipers as far-flung as Ireland, Mexico, and China—he transmuted into a punitive ceremony.

Every night after dinner, he would herd the family into the living room, where we were ordered to kneel down and haul out our rosary beads. My mother, because of her arthritic knees, was allowed to sit in an armchair, but the rest of us had to take our places on the floor. My father and my sisters would usually prop themselves up against the sofa or one of the armchairs, but I always tried to kneel up straight—perhaps a bit too theatrically—a few feet away from the chairs, thereby demonstrating the intensity of my devotion to the Church Militant. But I think my father assumed that I did it to upstage him and remind him that he was getting old, which gave him yet another reason to wish he had a different son, or no son at all.

A normal family could say the rosary in about fifteen minutes. But for us, once alcohol got added to the equation, the allotted time could double, and even triple, due to extended pauses for bathetic sermonizing on my father's part. The main portion of the rosary consisted of five sets of ten Hail Marys, each preceded by a brief recapitulation of a famous "mystery" from scripture. These mysteries—more like anecdotes—were divided into three categories: the Sorrowful, the Joyful, and the Glorious. (The Church would later add an off-brand set of mysteries called the Luminous.) Technically speaking, we were not obliged to repeat the same mysteries every night, but since my father had a soft spot for the Sorrow-ful tales, which hewed more closely to his worldview than the Joyful or Glorious ones, there tended to be much more discussion of crucifixion and flagellation than of angels popping through the window to make sur-prise announcements of impending pregnancies to flummoxed virgins. Many nights, he would ask me to lead the family in prayer. In doing so, I would try to work my way through the rosary as quickly as possible with-out appearing irreverent, because my sisters, who had no professional religious aspirations, loathed this sundown charade. But I dared not go too fast, or he would accuse me of sacrilege or blasphemy, and there would be no living with him for days.

Reaching the end of each decade of Hail Marys, I would dutifully note that Christ had been turned over to Pontius Pilate, or that the angel Gabriel had engaged the Virgin Mary in conversation, or that the Paraclete had descended amid tongues of fire—to the consterna-tion of the Sadducees, who, unlike the Pharisees and the Levites, never seemed prepared for these spur-of-the-moment conflagrations—and if my father was sufficiently marinated, he might allow me to continue unobstructed. But when he was still vaguely sentient, or when he was in a particularly belligerent mood, he would halt the recitation to deliver one of his own micro-homilies, cautioning us to reflect more carefully on the deeper meaning of this or that mystery. This was an opportunity to accuse us of simply going through the motions, or of being insuf-ficiently contemptuous of the mealymouthed weasel Pontius Pilate, or of failing to express an appropriate level of horror at Christ's torments, especially the part where the iron spikes got driven into His Most Pre-cious hands. He always spoke as if Christ's crucifixion was a recent event, perhaps even a local one.

In retribution for perceived callousness, he would make us retrace our steps and repeat the last decade, this time more obsequiously. Sometimes he would burst into tears, not unlike the child who sees the same movie a hundred times but always acts surprised when Bambi's mother takes one for the team. Every time he knelt down to say the rosary, he seemed to do so in the expectation that this time around Pilate might let Christ off with a warning. It suggested, in our minds, that the dirt-cheap horse piss my father guzzled by the case might not be the mild stimulant we took it to be but an out-and-out hallucinogen.

On nights when he got totally pulverized, he would forget where we were and accuse me of skipping a mystery, of trying to take a shortcut. This was sometimes true; on the few occasions when I did manage to condense the total number of Hail Marys, my sisters would smile with wry complicity at these blows against the empire. But in the end, these were feeble acts of sedition, similar to the exploits of the French Resistance, whose operatives would occasionally blow up a train or assassinate a Gestapo officer to annoy the Nazis, realizing that it was unlikely to have much effect on the outcome of the war.

In the fall and winter, it made no difference to us when we engaged in this despised ritual; the sun had already gone down by suppertime, and it was not as if we were going out to play again that day, so we might as well grin and bear it. But once daylight saving time arrived, when the sun dallied, there was still a sliver of time left to squeeze in a few innings of baseball after dinner, provided we said the rosary early enough. Here, with the choreographed malice that is the hallmark of the Irish American, my father would fuss around in the kitchen, delaying the post-prandial ceremony while he quaffed a few more beers. The rest of us would sit in the living room, watching the day slip away, as he careened around the kitchen in a stupor. By the time we got around to saying the rosary, there would be barely enough time for two innings of baseball and only then if we did not linger over Christ's long-running feud with the Pharisees or the complicity of the Jews in His execution. But on all too many occasions, my father did have a few extra comments to slip in regarding Jesus or Mary Magdalene or the Holy Ghost's unpredictable comings and goings, as the booze rendered him even more garrulous and even more sententious, and by the time he was done, the sun would have gone to bed for the day and any chance of playtime was over.

This family obligation did not end until I was fifteen, when one night he keeled over, landed flat on his face, broke his eyeglasses, and passed out. We all found this quite hilarious. For years, my youngest sister, Mary Ann, would reenact the scene, always making sure to remove her own eyeglasses first. We left him there, facedown, all night, hoping that he might suffocate on his own vomit. Alas, luck was not with us. After that incident, he was too embarrassed to ask us to say the rosary ever again. He had disgraced himself in the eyes of the Lord, and the Lord was unlikely to forget it.

Miraculously, these twilight burlesques did not rattle my faith in the Church, nor did they undercut my desire to be a priest. This is because I had no trouble distinguishing between the One True Faith and the parody sect my father had devised for his personal use. It was famously said, by a Jesuit, of course, that if the Church could have a child for seven years, it would have the child forever. This was certainly true in my case: Repudiating the Church would be tantamount to deserting my ethnic group, acting as if everything that happened in my childhood was false and irrelevant and stupid. There was never any chance of my falling prey to that kind of revisionism, no possibility of abjuring my faith or forgetting where I came from. Moreover, I didn't want to grow up to be like everybody else, as I truly believed that Catholicism—particularly taking into account the pageantry, the spectacle, the iconography, the props, and even the aromas—had all the other religions beat hands down. To me, as to most Catholics of that era, other religions were polenta.

My first direct involvement in official Church ritual occurred when I was ten years old. A hoot and a holler up the road from the housing project stood Ravenhill Academy, the ritzy private school where Grace Kelly received her top-of-the-line education and, presumably, replaced her Philadelphia accent with something more plummy. Ravenhill was run by a mysterious order of nuns based, so the story went, in the Philippines. The Religious of the Assumption had actually started out in France, but their numbers included quite a few Filipinos, which is how the rumor of a Manila connection reached my ears. They wore phantasmagoric maroon and yellow habits, but instead of concealing their heads inside starched lampshades the way most nuns did, they topped off the ensemble with headdresses that looked like top-quality dishcloths. The Filipino nuns were giggly and bouncy and spoke preposterous English. At that point in my life, they were the most exotic people I had ever met, challenged for visual glitz only by the Mummers. Until our paths crossed, I had no idea that people with dark skins were even allowed to be Brides of Christ.

One day toward the end of fifth grade, Mother Superior waddled into our classroom at Saint Bridget's seeking volunteers to serve mass for the nuns at Ravenhill during the summer. This was an unusual request, because altar boys were typically not allowed to serve mass until they were in seventh grade. For reasons that later became clear, no one in the upper grades had put in dibs for the assignment. So I nabbed it. Paradise, as Christ once put it, was a mansion filled with many rooms, and accepting this assignment was my chance to get in on the ground floor.

No sooner had I signed on the dotted line than the downside of the enterprise manifested itself. Masses were served at 7:00 a.m. and 8:30 a.m. every day of the week save Sunday, when the services were held somewhat later. This meant that I had to go to bed every night at eight o'clock in order to get up in time to serve mass the following morning. It meant that the summer was wrecked. It meant no late-evening baseball, no tag, no foraging for bumblebees, no masquerading as Zorro. I had been hoodwinked. I had been had.

Ravenhill Academy was about a mile from my home, but to get there, I had to walk all the way to the back of the project; tiptoe across a vast, deserted, overgrown plot known as the Jungle; then walk on the shoulder of an out-of-the-way road up to the private school. The road had no sidewalk on either side; it was mostly used as a truck bypass. The nuns would not have permitted me to take this assignment, nor would my parents have agreed to it, unless I was accompanied by another boy. By custom, if not by edict, two altar boys were needed to serve mass: one to hold the cruets, the other to pour ablutions over the priest's fingers, but mostly to provide visual symmetry for the congregation. In a pinch, you could get away with a single altar boy, but only in an emergency, as the sight of one adolescent serving mass all by himself looked unprofessional. And so Jackie Godman was recruited for the assignment.

Jackie Godman lived directly across the path from my house. His mother was a smidgen plump, with a smushed-in face that gave her the appearance of a charwoman in a Dickens novel, hemmed in by a phalanx of wee nippers who refused to part with a precious morsel of information for less than a guinea. Jackie's father was an intense American Indian. He had long black hair and piercing eyes, and did not say much, but every so often the screen door would burst open and Jackie would come rocketing out into the front yard with his father in hot pursuit, usually with a belt flailing. In our family, this sort of behavior was viewed as poor form, as the Irish-Catholic code of conduct stipulated that children should always be beaten in private, and beaten mercilessly, but preferably with the windows closed, if only to keep up appearances. It was an unassailable tenet of our family credo that no matter how bad our father's behavior was, other children's fathers were worse. Especially stupid goddamn Indians.

Whenever Mr. Godman would explode out of his house and chase Jackie down the street, my father would quip that our neighbor was "on the warpath." We never knew what tribe Mr. Godman belonged to, nor what he did for a living, though it was bruited about that he, like most Indians of that era, worked as a steeplejack. This was because Indians, as everyone knew, had no fear of heights, since heights did not exist in pre-Columbian culture. None of us ever knew if the ethnic myths we were ceaselessly retailed were true, but as adults invariably coated them with a patina of plausibility, gullible children generally accepted them as gospel truth.

Jackie was the only one of my friends who I knew for a fact was beaten by his father. He, on the other hand, never found out what transpired inside my home, as I deemed the whole subject too shameful to discuss. Though we were friends for years, we never talked about our fathers, not even to compare how much we disliked them. I have no idea what we talked about back then. Nor do I recall what byzantine arguments I marshaled to hornswoggle him into a summer of diocesan penal servitude. Unlike me, Jackie had no clerical aspirations; why he became an altar boy in the first place was never made clear. He was not a cerebral sort, not a reader, nor terribly communicative. But he was sturdy and reliable, and somehow I managed to talk him into getting up every morning for three months straight an hour before sunrise to serve mass for the nuns who had taught Grace Kelly all the things that the daughter of a construction tycoon needed to know in order to pass herself off as a femme fatale Cary Grant simply could not live without—thereby punching her ticket out of Philadelphia. I also suspect that we were enticed by the very elegance of the institution, which made such a sharp contrast with the banality and obviousness of the housing project. Or at least I was.

By the time I grew up, few parents would have allowed their children to make a daybreak pilgrimage on a deserted road, no matter how majestic the enterprise. But people didn't think that way back then. School House Lane was not entirely untraveled in the morning; there were always a few delivery trucks whizzing by. My father made me swear that I would walk up the side of the road facing traffic, because to do otherwise was to invite death. But Jackie and I decided that if we walked up that side of the road, it would be impossible to get rides from passing truckers. Though we had been warned not to accept lifts from strangers, we ignored this counsel, because the road was steep, because the truckers we met seemed to be salt-of-the-earth types, and because little boys only fear danger they can see.

The principal structure at Ravenhill Academy was an imperious gray brick building that sat a hundred yards or so back from the road. In my memories, it resembles Salisbury Cathedral, sulking there in indolent repose, reticent, confident, fully cognizant of its all-encompassing, quasi-arcadian magnificence. It was ringed by lovely, manicured grounds, speckled with trees and flowers; but we never roamed around the property, because we had no interest in scenery and felt uncomfortable in places where we did not fit in. Inside the main structure was a beautiful chapel where we served two masses every morning. The chapel may have been neo-Gothic or postmedieval or Romanesque; it looked like something you would see in Europe.

The chapel bells I recall in much greater detail. Up until then, I had attended services where the altar boys were equipped with tiny silver bells that had a single clapper inside. These bells emitted a tinny, noncommittal sound, as if a telephone were ringing three rooms down the hall. But the ponderous objects we found waiting for us on the altar steps at Ravenhill Academy were chunky, eye-catching chimes the size of teakettles. They were massive and blaring and imbued with a just-add-water orientalism I found intoxicating. The elaborate devices had four separate compartments, each filled with a cluster of ringers that, when rattled, suggested that the czar was arriving with a retinue of 350 sleighs. Years after the fact, I cannot remember one single thing about the priests who served mass each morning, nor what beatitudes the chapel's stained-glass windows may have depicted, but I have never forgotten those amazing bells. They were wonderful playthings, and I loved to make them sing out, having always been a sucker for affordable exoticism, particularly at the municipal level. Whenever I rattled those chimes, I felt transported to Samarkand or Constantinople or Oz.

The best thing about that summer at Ravenhill Academy was breakfast. Every morning after the first service, one of the diminutive Filipino nuns would scurry into the sacristy to bring us a tray containing orange juice, raisin toast, and coffee. Children did not drink coffee in those days—I am not sure they do now—but once I overcame my initial disgust at the acrid taste, I drained those urns to the dregs. After the second mass, another pint-sized nun would appear with a second tray, overflowing with pancakes, sausage, and bacon, or eggs, scrapple, and home fries, or some kind of delicious pastry, always accompanied by more coffee and more orange juice. Breakfasts at home mostly consisted of off-brand cornflakes. These were the best breakfasts I have ever tasted, rivaled only by a few crack-of-dawn, belt-loosening repasts in Limerick and Kilkenny. It is impossible to put into words how much those meals meant to us. They made it easier to go to bed in the early evening, easier to drag ourselves out of bed in the dead of night. They gave us something to look forward to every day. They made us feel like princes.

One morning halfway through August, one of the little nuns told us that we did not need to come serve mass the following morning. We could sleep late, kick back, relax. It was our only day off that summer, and I am sure we enjoyed the respite. That night my aunt Rita, who had a reputation as a gossip, phoned my mother, two years her junior. Aunt Rita was occasionally sent to reasonably priced, well-maintained institutions to recuperate from seasonal nervous breakdowns that were, apparently, the high point of her marriage. My mother always referred to her as "high-strung," but the smart money said she was crazy. She was married to the dullest man in the history of *Homo erectus,* a postman said to have achieved the only perfect entry-exam score in the history of the United States Post Office, even though everyone knew that he was the sole author of this rumor.

The Lynches, whose dour, roly-poly son no one liked, rarely visited the housing project, so if Rita was taking time to call my mother, it was probably to stir up trouble. We did not have a phone most of the time we lived in the project; if relatives needed to reach us, they would call the Dengels' house next door. Because of this, the Dengels always knew what my mother referred to as "all our business."

My sisters and I viewed the Dengels as ambulatory fossils, though they were probably only in their fifties at the time. Even by the standards of marked-down humanity that flourished in the project, they looked a trifle shopworn. Mr. Dengel was a short, stubby, serious man with a stooped back, who wore his trousers up around his chest like an unhappy dwarf treading water in a pair of 46-long waders. He drove a puke-green Studebaker, the first unapologetically hideous car I can ever recall seeing on the streets of Philadelphia. He himself was uncompromisingly ugly; he looked like Richard Nixon's Scandinavian cousin Blingen the Troll.

His wife was a chain-smoker who used to perch her jumbo-sized buttocks against a rail at the foot of our cul-de-sac and run her mouth all day long. I never saw Mrs. Dengel wear a dress; she always left the house cosseted in a loose shift called a muumuu. For all intents and purposes, she spent her entire adult life lounging in her pajamas. My mother did not approve of her, as she was vulgar and a smoker and forever had her hair up in curlers and talked like Lauren Bacall. My father liked her well enough but always maintained that the childless Dengels were closet gentry, the kinds of well-heeled individuals who did not have to live in a housing project but did so because they were cheap. Mr. Dengel's not having a job reinforced this perception.

Anyone who could support himself without going to work every day my father suspected of being closet gentry, a sponger who sucked at the public's copious teat. The Dengels lived next to us for four years, and we were never once in their house, nor they in ours. They did not care much for children. This was during the Sputnik era, when America was terrified that the Russians might catch us off guard during the World Series or the season opener of *The Honeymooners* and drop the H-bomb. The Dengels looked kind of foreign, as he, in particular, was quite the hatchet face and she was no bathing beauty herself. A lot of people in our cul-de-sac thought the Dengels were communist spies, though why they would have gone underground to gather information about losers like us was anybody's guess.

Whatever their relationship with the Soviets, the Dengels did have a phone, and, so long as we did not overdo it, they would allow us to receive calls in case of an emergency. The night of my unexpected furlough from Ravenhill Academy, Aunt Rita called to get all the details about that morning's service, having heard on the radio that the new archbishop had celebrated mass there. And so he had, assisted by a pair of eighth-graders handpicked for this most blessed event. When my mother told me this, I refused to believe it. Or let us say that, while I had no trouble believing that the priests at Saint Bridget's had stabbed us in the back, I would not accept that the sweet little Filipino nuns were complicit in such treachery. They knew that I had my heart set on being a priest; they knew that my life was short on surprises; they knew how much a once-in-a-lifetime chance to serve mass for the archbishop would have meant to me.

When Jackie and I resumed our duties the next day, I asked the tiniest, youngest nun about the service the day before. Her English was impenetrable; she had no idea why we had been given the day off; she did not understand the question; it was not her fault. We had no way of finding out whose fault it was. It was all some sort of mix-up; lines had gotten crossed somewhere; these things happened. As usual, she brought us juice and coffee and raisin toast after the early mass, then a hearty breakfast after the later service. We left without eating that day, and perhaps even the next day. We were angry, humiliated, disappointed, ashamed. We would have loved to vent our fury on someone, but it was hard to hold a grudge against these cherubic creatures in their divine little costumes, and those breakfast banquets were unimaginably tasty; so by the end of the week we had lost our nerve, swallowed our pride, and gone back to enjoying our early-morning smorgasbords. After all, we adored the little nuns, and they adored us.

It would be nice to say that we never ate breakfast again after realizing that we had been betrayed, or that the meals never tasted half as good. But this was not the case. Poor people have dignity, but not much of it, least of all children. We continued to serve mass at Ravenhill Academy every day for the next three weeks. We dutifully honored our commitment. Then the summer came to an end, and we returned to school. I never went back to Ravenhill Academy, and I doubt that Jackie Godman ever did, either. The wonderful little nun, as always, brought us breakfast that final day, and, as always, we ate it. But when we left that morning, we did not say thank you and we did not say goodbye. At the very beginning of the summer, our parents had warned us about accepting treats from strangers. And now we had learned our lesson.

From the time I was small, I kept my eyes peeled for role models I could substitute for my unsatisfactory father. They did not have to be breathing. One day when I was five years old, I stumbled upon a curious object in my parents' bedroom. It was a wooden-and-glass box with a silver crucifix poised atop it and pint-sized candleholders squatting on either side. On the front was a glass viewing screen, through which, by rotating a lever, I could gaze at colorful images of the fourteen Stations of the Cross, imprinted on a sheet of cloth. Here was Christ arraigned before Pontius Pilate. Here was Christ on the road to Calvary. Here was Christ having nails driven into His hands by executioners who looked almost blasé, as if they were civil servants punching the clock.

The box had tiny hinges on the back, which I soon pried open. Out spilled a cornucopia of religious paraphernalia: oil, water, cotton swabs, a prayer book, a silver plate. Rifling through this unexpected haul of swag, I unearthed a gold pocket watch and a tiny leather book. The book proved to be a missal, the Catholic vade mecum. It was difficult to open because the pages were caked together by a congealed maroon substance. The substance, I would soon learn, was dried blood.

At some point during this unauthorized reconnaissance, my mother entered the room, displeased that I had unearthed these household icons. But unlike my father, who would have knocked me clear across the room had he caught me prowling about the conjugal suite, my mother sat down and explained the provenance of these strange items. In olden days—actually, as recently as a decade earlier—people often died in their own beds; the oil, silver plate, and candles were stored in receptacles such as these to be used by the visiting priest when he came to administer the Last Rites. The oil was to be dripped on the forehead, as was the holy water; the silver plate was a "paten" used to catch the

Holy Eucharist should the priest drop it. The Eucharist, I already knew, was the body of Christ, or a reasonable facsimile thereof; for years I had looked forward to the day I would swallow the host for the first time, because the gifts children received when they made their First Holy Communion constituted the single biggest payday for fledgling soldiers of Christ in the entire liturgical calendar.

My mother now revealed that the gold watch and pocket-sized Bible had belonged to her brother Henry, who died in Alaska in 1949, a year before I was born. She was less than forthcoming with the details at the time, but when I prodded her over the coming weeks and months, she told me that her brother had run off to the state once known as Seward's Folly and landed a job as a longshoreman. She even had letters he had sent from Seward, Alaska. According to these missives, he was having a swell time of it up there in the frozen north, with no imminent plans to return to the East Coast. But then late one night, shortly after her marriage, she informed me, he was ambushed by faceless, nameless thugs and cut to ribbons in a dark alley. The body was shipped home along with Henry's personal effects, which included the gold watch and the blood-soaked missal, and was buried in a North Philadelphia cemetery. My mother did not explain what a longshoreman was, but it sounded fabulous.

Over the years, as my mother dolloped out snippets of information about her brother's tragically abbreviated life, I came to believe that my uncle Henry—clearly an urban maverick in the rambling, gambling, hell-for-leather Jack London tradition—was a lone wolf who had ditched Philadelphia, seeking a better life elsewhere, ultimately setting his sights on our remote, wide-open forty-ninth state. There he had many wondrous adventures. One night, or so I gathered from my mother's piecemeal account, he sprang to the defense of a black man who was being harassed by two other saloon patrons, the proverbial tough customers. But Henry, handy with his fists and always poised to defend the underdog, was not intimidated. The malignant racists were sent on their way, whereupon the badgered Negro fell to his knees and expressed his heartfelt gratitude to this Celtic Samaritan, a most unexpected champion in that benighted era. But later that night, upon exiting the saloon, Henry was pounced upon by this very same tandem of racist curs, stabbed in the liver, and left to bleed to death in a dark alley.

It isn't hard to see why Uncle Henry would immediately assume the role of my personal knight in shining armor. For years I carried his watch in my pocket and kept his blood-drenched missal secreted away in my chest of drawers. Given that I had already gobbled up juvenile versions of *Kidnapped* and *Treasure Island*, this rip-roaring saga was incredibly inspiring. From the time I first heard the word "elsewhere," I fashioned dreams of running away from home—to the Sahara, Tahiti, the Scottish Highlands. In my teens, I settled on Paris, then New York. But there was never any question of remaining in dull-as-dishwater Philadelphia. The ideal destination could be just about any port of call on the planet, so long as my father wasn't there. This would, of course, include Alaska.

My mother did not immediately tell me every relevant detail about Henry's early life, but over the years, the facts trickled out. Did he drink? Yes, but not to excess; unlike my father, he could handle his liquor. Was he a good student? No; people who grew up to be longshoremen rarely were. Did he get along with his father? Not really; in fact, they despised each other. While he was growing up, there had been numerous beatings, plenty of bad blood, the usual bevy of threats and execrations. As was so often the case in an ethnic group determined to populate the entire Eastern seaboard with children that at least one parent didn't really like, his mother may have been in his corner, but his father was not. Fusing this array of facts with my own adolescent conception of heroism, I fashioned an image of my uncle as a swashbuckling figure of gallantry and romance. If I couldn't have a living father I respected, the next-best thing was a dead uncle I adored.

At the time, there were only two other males in my extended family who were serious candidates for the retroactive homage I bestowed on Uncle Henry. The first was another dead relative, a man my mother referred to as Uncle Q, who had taught at West Point. West Point, to my ears at least, also sounded intoxicatingly mythical. Uncle Q, a considerably more tragic figure than Henry, was a confirmed bachelor gassed by the Germans in France during the First World War. He never recovered from this crime against humanity and eventually grew so weary of gasping for breath that he took his own life. I once compared photographs of the two men: Henry was a saucy lad cut from the *Captains Courageous* mold, Uncle Q a severe old Irish gent. Had Henry not existed, had he not insinuated himself into my existence with such fanfare, I perhaps would have adopted Uncle Q as my hero. But given the circumstances, and taking into account how much more picaresque a knife fight with subarctic scum seemed by comparison with a Hudson Valley suicide stemming from decades-old war wounds at the hands of the barbarous Huns, Uncle Henry beat Uncle Q hands down.

A somewhat less obvious candidate for full-bore adulation was my father's brother Johnny, still very much among the living. Strapping, not yet thirty, even better-looking than my handsome father, Johnny could lay claim to all kinds of handyman skills his older brother could not. He was also good around children. On the negative side, he had spent most of his adult life in the hoosegow. He would often materialize out of nowhere right around Christmas, laden with gifts purchased with the suspiciously large sum of money he had earned during his latest stint in the calaboose. This cash, we later learned, came from participating in medical experiments that would drastically shorten his life. No slouch, he was forever acquiring impressive new skills: One year it was carpentry, the next year, plumbing; the next year, the fruits of his diligence in electrician's school would shine forth. During his woodworking phase, when he found himself emulating the early stages in the career of his Lord and Savior, he produced a set of ornate, almost chic, wooden crucifixes he then dispensed as Christmas gifts. And if anything in the way of roofing or gutter repair needed to be done, Johnny was your man.

Uncle Johnny was the prototypical youngster who fell in with the wrong crowd at age fourteen or fifteen and henceforth was always in Dutch. In his case, the wrong crowd was the United States Navy, whose ranks he joined in 1944. Most of his offenses were petty: breaking into cigarette machines; walking off his bartending job at rush hour and leaving the watering hole completely unattended; routinely violating parole. Incapable of straightening up and flying right, he was always on the wrong side of the law.

On occasion, my father would take me or Ree along when he went to visit Johnny at nearby Holmesburg State Penitentiary, sometimes leaving us to cool our heels in the waiting room, sometimes leaving us outside in a nearby street unattended, with strict instructions to avoid talking to strangers. I was never sure whether he liked having company on his way to the Big House or thought it would cheer up his brother to know that his nieces and nephews were just a few hundred yards away and had not yet entered the recidivist mode. It was creepy waiting there inside the ominous fortress Uncle Johnny called home, but it was even creepier waiting outside. Here was yet another example of my father's idiosyncratic approach to family outings: Some kids went to see the lions in the zoo; we went to see Uncle Johnny in the slammer.

Other men in the family looked down on Johnny, not so much because he was a career jailbird, a second-story man, and a bail-jumper but because he drank wine (which was bad) and port (which was worse). This, to their way of thinking, epitomized Johnny: He was deliberately thumbing his nose at the official, culturally sanctioned beverages—beer and whiskey—that seemed to suit everyone else in the ethnic group just fine. Such behavior was an inexcusable deviation from Irish-American heterodoxy, which decreed that the imbibing of beer and spirits was acceptable in any social context, even if done to excess, but that the consumption of wine in any of its myriad manifestations identified one as a stinking lowlife, since wine was something Italians and Puerto Ricans drank.

Though she did not dislike him personally, my mother dreaded Johnny's Yuletide visits, which to her suggested a Dickensian irony on the part of the Keystone State penal authorities: Other families got Father Christmas; we got Uncle Johnny. Her apprehension about his visits was not predicated on his reputation as a hard case, as he was really quite a splendid fellow. Her concern was his influence on his malleable sibling, because when Johnny started quaffing the accursed, ethnically verboten fruit of the vine, he would invariably beguile my father into partaking of the abhorrent libation with him. My father succumbed, not because he enjoyed wine per se but because he wished to be chummy.

Unfortunately, wine made my father "rammy," causing him to become even more sullen, vindictive, explosive. Johnny, a convivial dipsomaniac, simply drank himself into a coma, then lurched off to bed. He would hang around for a few days, repeating this routine on a daily basis, promising that he would soon land a job, get back on his feet, and move into his own place. Then one day he would disappear. A few weeks later, we would get a report from Uncle Jerry or Uncle Charlie that he had again flouted the rules governing the commonwealth, landing him right back in the pokey. For the longest time, we honestly believed that Uncle Johnny could straighten out his life if he would only switch to a more salubrious beverage and evolve into a functional alcoholic like our dad. This was during the period when we still believed that alcohol itself was not the enemy, merely the dosage.

Always a pushover for entry-level iconoclasm, I admired Uncle Johnny because of his peripatetic ways, his refusal to take orders, and his insistence on drinking an ethnically prescribed refreshment that met with no one else's approval. Being a criminal did not sully his escutcheon in my book, given that the Count of Monte Cristo and the Man in the Iron Mask had also been wrongfully imprisoned after running afoul of the law, as had many of the Apostles and even Christ Himself. If anything, it made him seem more attractive, as hardened criminals were "tough customers" and I was not. Not until I found out that Uncle Johnny had a habit of going through women's pocketbooks foraging for cash, had a reputation as a light-fingered Louie, and was basically a small-time hood and nothing more, was I forced to purge him from my list of prospective role models, redirecting my idolatry back toward the martyred Uncle Henry.

As a child who was desperate to be taken seriously, I made sure that every new friend got to see that gold watch and that hemoglobin-encrusted missal, providing me with yet another opportunity to trot out the saga of Henry McNulty, Lone Wolf of the Kodiak. But I am not sure they cared, as many of them had their own gaudy skeletons in their family closets, and the story sounded a bit dodgy. When I entered college and began to consort with well-bred types whose family trees were devoid of murderers, drunks, and knife-wound victims, I would wait for an opportunity to recount the circumstances of Henry's demise. In the back of my mind I already knew that one advantage, and perhaps the only advantage, of growing up poor was having instant access to a rakish family tree, from which one could blithely exhume a few stiletto-filleted cadavers to bedazzle the gentry. Affluent suburban students I got to know in college could lay claim to embezzling uncles, predatory aunts who stripped to their foundation garments once they got a bit ginned up, and grandparents who had been the victims of bloody pogroms. But nobody I met ever had an uncle who got cut to ribbons in an Alaskan knife fight.

Somewhere along the line, Uncle Henry, man and myth, began to slip away. I never completely cut him adrift; he was always lurking there in the back of my mind as my personal Sergeant Preston of the Yukon. But as I grew older it became less and less politic to tell strangers that my uncle had finished second in a back-alley knife fight somewhere north of the forty-eighth parallel. This otherwise engaging anecdotal material was not the sort of thing you could use to impress girls. I also worried that my newfound friends, or their parents, might fear that the sins of the uncle would be visited upon the nephew, that the criminal urge might be congenital, that I, like my male forebears, might be the incarnation of the bad seed, with the mark of Cain engraved upon my very brow.

In retrospect, I realize that this casting about for role models was a crude attempt to assemble a personality with bits and pieces I picked up here and there from other people. It is difficult to grow up happy, much less sane, when there is no one in your social circle that you wish to resemble, when the men you most admire are murder victims, jailbirds, suicides, or a personable but generally unlucky religious leader whose mutilated corpse peers out at you from gruesome paintings mounted in every room in the house. To compensate for this, I manufactured my personality modularly. Men of the world, men-about-town like Uncle Jerry and Uncle Johnny and Uncle Henry and Uncle Charlie, transfixed me with their bravura style and bulging wallets and powerful scent of carcinogens, so I took careful mental notes whenever I found myself in their company, scavenging for bric-a-brac, annexing this or that chunk of their personalities, mixing and matching traits in an effort to simulate having an identity. Ultimately, this transformed me into a bit of a schizophrenic, so that by the time I grew up, I had not one personality but half a dozen. Still, in deciding which persona to adopt in this or that situation while going about my daily life, it's always been nice to have so many choices.

Despite the potent influence of these powerful, intriguing men, I bore no real resemblance to any of them and knew that I never would. It was true that they were larger than life, but that was only because the life I was leading was so small. They were tougher than me, coarser than me, better versed in the ways of the world than I could ever hope to be. They were spectacularly colorful; they drove big cars, smoked huge cigars, drank mammoth tumblers of whiskey, and used cryptic expressions like "*Schwärze,*" "conniption," "killjoy," "Death Row," and "Jewish lightning." They had access to far-flung regions of the English language to which minors were not invited, bandying about phrases like "He took the five-finger discount," "It knocked me for a loop," "He's still wet behind the ears," and "He got caught playing a tune on the cash register." They were tough in the clinches; they knew how to put bad actors down for the count; they despised men who took a powder, went into the tank, threw in the towel, or took French leave. They were "solid citizens," and solid citizens never used prissy, pantywaist words like "poppycock" or "balderdash"; they preferred earthy terms like "malarkey" and "cold-cocked" and "horseshit," and whatever else they may have done in their lives, they did not row crew. For this alone, they seemed worthy of knighthood.

They knew all about Skid Row. They could immediately ascertain who was a little light in the loafers, who was not playing with a full deck, who was a punch-drunk lollapalooza, and who was most likely to take a dive. They liked Gritty Carbuncle in the fifth at Aqueduct, though only to place, and were sure as shootin' that Sugar Ray Robinson would take out Kid Gavilan with just one punch, because Gavilan was a tin can, if not an outright palooka, who couldn't fight his way out of a paper bag and was, in any case, so skinny he had to come out twice just to make his own shadow. They rarely hung fire, preferring to risk the whole kit and caboodle on one shot at the brass ring. Though I mostly had no idea what they were talking about when they used these expressions, to me it was all hypnotically exotic, and before long I, too, was talking about cold-cocking punchy stumblebums and dispatching their sorry asses straight to Queer Street. After that, it went without saying, everything would be copacetic.

This program of modular personality assembly manifested itself most dramatically in 1959, when I fell under the spell of a barrel-chested war hero named Len Mohr. Len was the proprietor of a tumbledown clothing store about a mile from my home. Because his prices were so low and because the store was the kind of unprepossessing dump where the working class felt right at home, my family became regular patrons. Len took quite a shine to me, because I was bright and polite and asked tons of questions about the medals he had hanging on the wall.

At the ripe old age of thirty-two, when the Japanese launched their sneak attack on Pearl Harbor, Len had enlisted in the marines, landing a position as a drill instructor, teaching young men how to box. For the next couple of years, he organized boxing exhibitions as entertainment on troop ships, sometimes acting as referee. Then, despite his advanced years, he persuaded his commander to let him participate in the invasion of Iwo Jima. On the wall not far from the cash register hung a couple of medals he had won for his valorous actions. My dad, by contrast, had served as an infantryman who may have fired a few shots in anger on an island the Japanese had already abandoned, caught malaria, got shipped home, went AWOL, got into trouble with the MPs, and ended up doing three years' hard time in a Dixie military prison. His transgressions earned him a dishonorable discharge, a fact I unearthed while researching a school project. This was a career-wrecking badge of shame that would haunt him for the rest of his life. Len Mohr had his war, my father quite another.

One day when I was getting fitted for some back-to-school shoes, Len asked my mother if I could work for him. The arrangement he proposed was that I put in two hours every day after school and work from nine in the morning until seven at night on Saturday. The salary was $6 a week, hardly a king's ransom but not an out-and-out insult. I was all in favor of the idea, as was my mother, because it would give me a sense of purpose and provide me with a little bit of pocket money for the first time in my life. Asking an eight-year-old to work twenty hours a week probably wasn't even legal back then—though child labor laws were rarely enforced—but inasmuch as the job had the potential to save my life, I grabbed it.

By the standards of the retail sector, where merchants tended to be sallow, ectomorphic, and decrepit, Len cut a fine figure. He was roughly six feet tall, heavily muscled, with a stomach like granite. He sported a magnificent lion's mane, and nothing gave him more pleasure than to sweep his hair down over his forehead, shake it wildly, then whip it back into place, after which he would lovingly run a metal comb through that thicket of massed tendrils. He would do this several times a day, making quite a spectacle of himself in the process. He never cut his hair short, not even in the summertime, when the entire planet was baking. He was as intoxicated by his hair as any sixteen-year-old girl girding for conquest before her vanity table. His grooming tics evoked Samson, scourge of the Philistines, perhaps signifying a subconscious fear that his seemingly boundless retailing powers would vaporize were his locks ever shorn.

Even in photographs from his younger days, you could see that his hair was always amazingly copious and thick, an iconoclastic image, given the grooming mores of the era. After he left the service, Len never again got his hair cut like a marine; he always looked like Johnny Weissmuller in his Tarzan the Ape Man mode. This was most unusual, given that Len was a jarhead who had fought with valor in the living hell of Iwo Jima. Moreover, the era we were living through was a buttoned-down, straight-arrow entr'acte between the flashy forties and the swinging sixties, when white men sported close-cropped hair and lightly starched personalities to match. This juxtaposition of seditious hair and middle-of-the-road GOP values made an unusual combination. But from Len I learned the most valuable lesson of all: that if you had money, you could do whatever you damn well pleased.

Len's Clothing Store was a two-story stone structure drowning in faded yellow stucco, with crimson trim adorning the doors and windows. Defiantly ugly, it achieved the almost unimaginable distinction of being regarded as an eyesore by the neighbors even though it stood just a few yards from the rubbish-strewn railroad tracks, adjoined a dingy, poorly maintained social club, and sat no more than a stone's throw down the road from a heating oil company's fleabag headquarters. The building looked diseased, as if jaundice had devised a mechanism for expressing itself in the patois of commercial architecture. Len did not care about the store's outer appearance, nor how it looked on the inside, which wasn't all that much snazzier. I never got the impression that Len actually needed to earn any money, which was good, because the store never generated much. One torrid day in August of 1961, we took in a grand total of $2. This may have been some sort of retail record, even in the notoriously tightfisted Quaker City.

Len's principal source of income was the stock market. He had made a tidy fortune speculating on sizzling new issues in the late 1950s and would later make a killing during the Kennedy administration, cleaning up on a group of legendary stocks called the Nifty Fifty, plus a handful of brash new outfits like Ling Electronics and National Video. Though I did not learn this until much later, some of the massively hyped, self-levitating issues he favored, many of them the brainchildren of enterprising rogues, subsequently imploded, wiping out immense paper fortunes. In my thirties, when I worked for *Barron's* editor Alan Abelson, I found out that he had written disparagingly about these companies right around the time I was working for Len, warning readers that the whole thing was a house of cards, that investors should get out while the getting was good, before the sharpies fleeced them. But most of them did not.

Len, who read the *Wall Street Journal* from cover to cover every day, did not read *Barron's,* so I am not sure whether he headed for the exits before the bloodbath occurred or went down with the ship like everybody else. He certainly loved talking about his investments, affectionately circling their spasmodic gyrations in the newspaper stock tables and regaling me with the juicy details of their latest vertiginous exploits. To Len, the stock market was a Balzacian saga, with the same heroes and villains resurfacing again and again. None of this meant anything to me at the time; Wall Street was as foreign to me as the lute. Nobody I knew owned stocks. I did not even know what stocks were, only that they were associated with Republicans. Nor did I know what bonds were, only that they were no fun to talk about, even for Republicans, which is why

Len didn't own any. I had no idea what Republicans were or what they stood for; I only knew that whatever they stood for, my family stood for something else, though there seemed to be less money in it. I knew that Republicans liked Nixon, while we liked Kennedy, and that members of the political entity inexplicably nicknamed the Grand Old Party could detect electrifying qualities in Dwight D. Eisenhower's personality that were not apparent to the naked eye, and probably still aren't.

Len had grown up in North Philadelphia, a few blocks from Connie Mack Stadium—the ballyard named after Cornelius McGillicuddy, the ostentatiously patrician, maddeningly unpredictable owner and manager of the Philadelphia Athletics. Connie Mack, who always wore a three-piece suit and snappy headgear, had built a magnificent team in the 1910s, winning several World Series championships, but had then broken the city's heart by capriciously dismantling it. He had assembled an even more potent squad in the late twenties—purists believe the 1929–1931 A's were the best team to ever take the field—but enraged by his avaricious players and the state's refusal to alter its notorious blue laws, which banned all commerce on Sunday, including sporting events, he busted up that club as well. This broke the city's perennially broken heart for a second time, and this time it stayed that way. The A's were listless and appalling for the next twenty years, usually finishing last or next-to-last, and by the time they limped off to Kansas City in 1954, the Phillies had supplanted them for pride of place in the city's affections.

The upscale A's had always been the Republican team, while the inept Phillies embodied the sewer values of the Democratic Party, and by the time I was born, the city was turning solidly Democratic. The A's could boast of their glorious tradition, which they later revived in Oakland, after their disastrous sojourn in Kansas City; the Phillies, except for two brief, shining moments, have been disgracing themselves both on and off the field virtually without interruption since 1883. Nothing in American history is more astonishing than the ability of the Philadelphia Phillies to maintain an enthusiastic fan base, given that the club, by any objective, nonemotional, nondelusional analysis of the factual data, is the least successful franchise in the history of sports. This attests to the fact that there's no fool like an old fool, that youth is wasted on the young, and that a sucker is born every minute—except in the Quaker City, where the pace at which women give birth to chumps may move along at a slightly snappier clip. In my family, for instance.

Len was the youngest son of a man who was by then the oldest living firefighter in the City of Brotherly Love, as well as its last surviving tiller-man. Mohr père was at least ninety when I met him, a widower living alone in a typically joyless North Philadelphia row home and a bit hard of hearing. I did not know what a tillerman was at the time, only that he was the oldest one extant, and that after him there would be no others. Very few white people were still living in the neighborhood by this point, but this was his home, and he was not leaving it. Like my uncle Joe, he had an ornate spittoon sitting in the middle of his living room but not much else. He was not a charmer. I never heard Len talk about his mother. His older brother, on a dare, had dived off a cliff into a creek or pond and died on impact when his body splintered to pieces on the rocks below. He was still in his teens when this occurred; he had leaped off the cliff to impress a girl. Len frequently warned me that the best swimmers were the ones most likely to die in the water, as they were the ones who took the most chances. Given that I did not learn to swim until age thirty, this admonition was unnecessary. Besides, I was not the kind of person who would ever jump off a cliff, least of all to impress a girl.

Len had a high school education, no more. Working as a salesman for several years before launching his own operation, he had parlayed his fortune into a well-appointed house in Bala Cynwyd, Pennsylvania, a ritzy suburban hamlet poised just across City Line Avenue on the tony Main Line. Scions of tillermen who hailed from the streets of North Philadelphia were not supposed to end up on the Main Line or in any other tony locality, and Len was proud of his achievement. But his accomplishments were his and his alone; he felt that most of the people who ended up in slums deserved to be there. He identified with the class he had joined, not the class from which he had sprung. Anything that smacked of class warfare was anathema to him; men made their own breaks, period.

One day I got to see where he lived. The house was a graceful Colonial with a manicured lawn, a white picket fence, and an Airedale despotically frolicking behind it. Len would constantly expound on why Airedales were tougher than German shepherds or Dobermans; he had convinced himself that there was an ongoing argument regarding the relative fighting abilities of these breeds—indeed, that the dispute was the center of a national debate that had been raging since Grant took Vicksburg. Airedales, he grumbled, suffered from a deceptively cuddly image—those avuncular little goatees didn't help—and this explained why they had made no formal combat appearance in the Pacific theater. Yet, when the chips were down and an Airedale was locked in a battle royal with a Doberman or a German shepherd, it was invariably the Airedale—no longer so cuddly, no longer so cute—that would prevail. He never divulged the source of his data, but I eventually came to the conclusion that he ceaselessly wandered the streets of Bala Cynwyd keeping his eyes peeled for Dobermans and Alsatians that his pet Airedale could savage just so he could pad the statistics.

Len's wife, Barbara, whom he referred to as Babs, was a White Russian who was reputed to have served as a translator at the Nuremberg trials. Of his three children, the one he talked about most was a son named Bing, who hated school and had opened an auto-repair business at the age of sixteen. This would have been something of a disappointment to many fathers, as few would dream of prevailing in the rag trade just so they could bankroll their kid's career as a grease monkey. But Bing made his own rules, and Len respected them. Each of his two daughters was a nurse, each married to an osteopath. I never met either of them, as they never visited the store. They were allegorical creatures who inhabited some vaporous paramedical utopia and were seen only in photographs. They, too, resided in swish neighborhoods. Osteopaths at the time were viewed as witch doctors by society at large, but Len clearly reveled in having bookend sorcerers for sons-in-law, as it was in his nature to go against the grain. All in all, it was quite a family.

By the time I met Len, the Mohrs, to use one of his catchphrases, were "feeling no pain" financially. Len drove a gray-and-white Pontiac station wagon the size of Kentucky, played pool on a sleek table in the basement of his house, got to wear the kinds of fancy Ban-Lon sweaters he would never dream of selling to his roughneck clientele, and was the beneficiary of seemingly unlimited free time. He was never down in the dumps, rarely lost his temper, didn't hold grudges, was always chipper and upbeat. He was the first man I ever met who did not drink to excess—to the best of my knowledge, he did not drink at all—and the first potential role model who was neither pushing up the daisies nor pulling hard time.

As noted, Len's dilapidated clothing store was located in a humdrum, out-of-the-way neighborhood. There were no other retail establishments nearby, save a grocery and a convenience store, not much parking, and not a whole lot in the way of pedestrian traffic. It was as barmy a location for a clothier's as any I have ever seen; opening what he referred to as a haberdashery where he did was like opening a nightclub in a cemetery. It wasn't just a case of our being off the beaten track. We were marooned.

The store occupied the entire first floor of the two-story building. Upstairs was a space where Len stored—"concealed" is more like it—stock he had given up any hopes of selling. I always thought of this room as his personal shrine to Saint Jude, the patron saint of hopeless causes, which in this case involved vintage women's footwear. Len allowed me to go upstairs exactly once in the seven years I was on his payroll, and only then to see if pigeons were flying through a broken window and nesting up there. They were not. What I did find were hundreds upon hundreds of shoeboxes filled with fading, decaying, unsightly, ludicrously out-of-fashion alligator-skin wedgies. For whatever the reason, Len wanted me to see them, but only that once. Perhaps it was his way of discouraging hero worship on my part, since this hidden cavern of unsold shoes provided incontestable evidence that even the master of retail sometimes nodded. Shakespeare, Bard of Avon, had his *Pericles, Prince of Tyre;* Len Mohr had his alligator-skin wedgies.

Beneath the store was a dank, unfinished basement with a floor made of some harsh substance that seemed to antedate coal. The first room one ventured into was empty, but the second had a toilet mounted clumsily on a pile of concrete blocks. There was also a sink but no hot water. It was as black as night down there—the only illumination provided by a naked forty-watt bulb suspended from the ceiling—and it reeked of oil. It had the feel of a dungeon, a pit lacking only a pendulum. There were no rats on hand, though there should have been; perhaps they, too, had been put off by the scent of kerosene and pulled up stakes. I dreaded going down there—I kept expecting Charon or Nosferatu to turn up. Because of the condition of the lavatory, it would mortify me when female customers would ask to use it, as I did not deem it appropriate for women to relieve themselves in such unladylike surroundings. When they resurfaced, they would try to act as if they had not just visited a cesspool. Sometimes their clothes would be smudged with dirt. It was not at all refined. I could never understand why a man as prosperous as Len didn't bother to install a presentable bathroom in the building where he spent most of his waking hours. Apparently, he didn't want people getting into the habit of using it. Their first visit was usually their last.

Len sold cheap, serviceable clothing intended to be worn by working-class people who were going nowhere fast. The product mix included black naval officer's brogans, Wrangler jeans, Fruit of the Loom underwear, Converse sneakers, Hanes sweatshirts, and masses of off-brand merchandise. Our inventory consisted almost entirely of attire Len himself would not have been caught dead in, dapper ex-marine that he was. He stocked virtually no women's or girl's clothing, because he believed that females were fickle, that feminine styles quickly went out of fashion, and that when you tried to reap the distaff whirlwind, you always ended up stranded with a funeral pyre of out-of-favor goods you would never be able to unload. What's more, it was merchandise that would take up valuable retail space forever, because Len would never admit that he was wrong about anything, so he would never get rid of old stock, no matter how unlikely it was that he would ever sell it. Instead, he would stuff it beneath tables already groaning under the weight of men's slacks or sequester it upstairs in his retail equivalent of a mausoleum, his own personal potter's field for alligator-skin wedgies.

This was not because he was cheap; it was because he had inexhaustible faith in his abilities as a salesman. By virtue of being a crackerjack salesman, Len had amassed enough cash to get his own business off the ground. But to remain a crackerjack salesman, he needed to believe that there was nothing he could not sell, no matter how unfashionable, grotesque, or *dépassé,* given a favorable economic environment and a suitably impressionable customer. On the back wall hung a rack of men's outerwear: dozens of blue denim jackets that were popular with men of all ages, and an assortment of reasonably snappy windbreakers and rain slickers. But all the way over in the corner hung a foreboding collection of merchandise that even the most wretched, clownishly attired consumer would steer clear of. Much of it was plaid, but plaid in the wrong places. The top-of-the-line items in this fashion ghetto were a pair of dinky golf jackets that nobody in this defiantly working-class neighborhood would ever dream of buying. You couldn't even get anybody to look at these Medusas in gabardine: One glance and the customer might turn to Naugahyde. "Moving the merchandise" was a very popular expression back in that era, but this merchandise never, ever budged.

It is worth noting that in the late fifties and early sixties, irony had not yet arrived in America, and certainly not in Philadelphia, so no secondary market of snarky hipsters salivating over the prospect of sporting fusty old duds at their tongue-in-cheek social gatherings yet existed. This was the era of shiny, pointy-toed Cuban-heel shoes and space-age fabrics like Orlon; everyone wanted to look suave and cool, like Chubby Checker. It would never have occurred to anyone in that social milieu to deliberately dress like a fuckhead.

Len was an extremely generous man. True, he would never extend credit to his customers, because he believed that extending credit to the misbegotten merely encouraged them to become even more misbegotten. But he would give people things, as he had the common touch. He realized that one of the most important elements in dealing with the poor was to enter their physical space without acting as if you were going to contract leprosy. He would drive me home to the project at night and not worry about getting his station wagon nicked or his tires slashed. He would drop off turkeys for poor people the night before Thanksgiving, which required venturing into their crummy neighborhoods. And he would make surprise deliveries of clothes to the unemployed, usually merchandise that had been hanging around for a year or two but not the out-and-out slop that nobody wanted.

This I could not understand. Why, I badgered him, didn't he just off-load those wedgies? After all, beggars couldn't be choosers. But he would not be persuaded. He was like Lord Jim, eternally seeking to atone for that one irretrievable moment when his nerve had failed him. Or like Henry Hudson, convinced that if he could just have one more crack at it, he would find that elusive Northwest Passage. This was not about money. This was about exoneration.

Once, at Christmastime, I asked Len why he did not stuff our pathetic inventory in the back of his station wagon and give it away to the poor. He would not hear of it; he would never engage in such shabby largesse. He was far too much of a gentleman to fob off pitiful trash on some starving, one-eyed invalid and act like he was doing him a favor. Christmas was a time of rejoicing, he reminded me, and it was hard to believe that anyone would start jumping for joy after waking up on the twenty-fifth of December to find that Santa had left a pair of fifteen-year-old alligator-skin wedgies under the tree. Poverty was bad; anachronistic footwear only made things worse.

Len's Clothing Store was, in many respects, the proverbial enigma wrapped inside a mystery concealed within a conundrum. Consider the communications network. For whatever the reason, Len had no personal telephone in the store; instead, he had a pay phone rigged up behind the counter. But no one except him was allowed to use it, because no one—including me—was allowed anywhere near the cash register. Not once was I on hand when the man from the phone company came to empty the coin box; for all I know, he turned up just once every twenty-five years, because Len never spent any money on the phone. Instead, he would ring his wife according to a prearranged code shortly before closing the store, then hang up. Seconds later she would ring back. He would tell her that he was on his way home. She would say, "Good." That was the only time the phone ever got used. Even as a kid, I had suspicions that the phone company's business model was defective.

My father always believed that Len operated the store as a "front," that he was in fact a bookie. He may have said this because he hoped it would diminish my employer in my eyes. I did not know what a bookie was when I started working there, but by the time I was twelve or thirteen, I did. I was sure that Len was not a bookie, because the phone did not ring with the frequency needed to maintain a gambling operation, and because the only sports in which he expressed any interest were baseball and boxing and golf, but not college football and certainly not pro football or basketball, cornerstones of the wagering industry that Len despised. Also, he was not Italian. More to the point, when was the last time anyone heard of a German-American bookmaker?

At first, I was not sure whether Len viewed me as a protégé who might one day step into his shoes and lead his emporium to even loftier heights—perhaps by unloading those accursed wedgies—or whether he simply enjoyed my company. Eventually, I decided that it must be the latter, since he knew that I had my heart set on becoming a priest, not a merchant. Though adept at straightening stock, folding shirts, and lacing shoes, I was never more than an adequate salesman, as I lacked what was known in the trade as moxie, aka "the tinker's *cojones*." At the first sign of resistance from a customer, often in response to a garment he or she deemed culturally repellent, I would back down. Len would not. Len was a master at steering our clientele toward purchases they did not want to make—in some cases, purchases that every fiber in their being cried out against.

Not a churchgoer, and most assuredly not a Catholic, Len nevertheless encouraged me to improve my vending skills, insisting that this would make me a more effective plenipotentiary of the Lord later in life. His rationale was simple: Pushing the word of God was like pushing any other product; learning how to persuade priggish, recalcitrant customers to choose one type of footwear over another would stand me in good stead the day I had to persuade some filthy heathen to choose Christianity over cobra worship. Len did not understand that while deceit might be the cornerstone of the salesman's craft, it was not a marketing tool available to me, since lying was a mortal sin. He refused to view his sales spiels as deceitful; it was more a case of banging the drum slowly and gilding the lily fast. When teenagers would come in seeking the kind of fleetingly fashionable attire we never carried, he would devise mythical scenarios and resort to time-honored schtick to create the impression that the merchandise we did have in stock was preferred by all the glamorous athletes and movie stars of the era, that the customers should thank their lucky stars merely to be offered this once-in-a-lifetime opportunity to add such eye-popping treasures to their emaciated wardrobes.

"I had to order these shoes specially from Monte Carlo and get them sent up by cargo plane from the Panama Canal," he would cheerily declare. "Jack Paar wears these shoes; Sandy Koufax swears by them; Burt Lancaster wears this exact same brand. I actually lose a dollar on every pair I sell, but that's okay, because the volume overcomes the loss."

Sometimes when customers would divulge the extortionate price they had paid for a shirt or a pair of pants bought elsewhere, Len would ask if they had received a complimentary kiss with their purchase. His modus operandi when he did not have the products people wanted was to resort to his own special brand of ridicule, intimating that the only men who would wear such items were limp-wristed Neapolitans and jaded *Schwärze* of dubious moral character. By dint of his resplendent manliness, his massive chest, his amazing hair, his flashy sweaters, his cutting-edge Hush Puppies (later viewed with contempt by coy fashionistas but at that time universally deemed the apotheosis of casual chic), the Marine Corps regalia hanging on the walls, and the aura of liberation from all financial worry that he exuded, Len was usually able to convince even the most obstinate customer that he would be a fool not to snap up the goods that were being proffered so altruistically at such a massive discount to their true value.

It is probably not going too far to say that Len viewed his sales mission from an evangelical perspective; that he believed he had been put on this planet to preach the old-time religion of black lace-ups and thermal underwear and to persuade the ovine public to resist the meretricious, come-hither appeal of patterned acrylic jumpers and Italian loafers with toes shaped like a marlin's proboscis. He was here to protect working-class people from their own worst instincts, to shield the proletariat from fads, whimsy, flights of fancy, lapses of sanity. To accomplish this, he would sometimes resort to logic, sometimes to teasing, and, when all else failed, to outright abuse.

"What are you, meshugah?" he would ask a dumpy middle-aged

man vainly trying to shoehorn himself into a pair of jeans two sizes too small.

"What are you, meshugah?" he would ask an ugly, poorly groomed factory worker eyeballing the fancy dress shirts that, because they required cuff links, had been designated as demographically off-limits to the proletariat.

"What are you, meshugah?" he would demand of the bespectacled pipsqueak gazing covetously at the heavy flannel shirts in the middle of an August heat wave, shirts that were worn only by he-men. None of our customers was Jewish, but they all seemed to know what the term "meshugah" meant. If nothing else, Len had succeeded in bringing Yiddish to the monolingual goyish masses. Most of them were so much in awe of Len's personality, so solicitous of his approbation, so emotionally servile, that they would abandon their original intentions and purchase whatever he deemed appropriate for their personality, physique, skin tone, sexual orientation, economic class. They were not our customers; they were our marionettes.

Many of our customers *were*, in fact, meshugah. Orders of shoes came in sets of two dozen, arranged in sizes that corresponded to the theoretical distribution of shoe sizes throughout American society. Because the popular sizes quickly disappeared, frantic young men hell-bent on looking their best come Saturday night would try jamming their feet into shoes that were a full size too small, sometimes two sizes too small. This was the only time Len would retreat from the hard-sell mode, begging these young men to be reasonable, imploring them not to throw away their podiatric future for a brief roll in the feathers with some Manayunk-based harlot, steering them toward more realistic sizes in styles that fit them even if they did not please them. But sometimes the customers persisted; young men, in particular, would rather be able to dance on Saturday night than to walk on Sunday morning. And then we had lost their business forever.

Len had no way of knowing this, given how shabbily I dressed, but, like many of our customers, I too harbored clandestine dreams of fashion conquest. My fifth-grade class, boasting a multicultural panorama decades ahead of its time, included three bullies: a hulking Caucasoid named Eddy Sawyer, who pounded me straight into the pavement one afternoon; a stocky black youth named Joseph Lynch, who was more of a henchchild than a full-blown thug; and a rake-thin, good-looking boy of indeterminate ethnic provenance whose name I have long since forgotten but whose attire will live on in memory forever. The common wisdom was that this boy was Hawaiian, because he had jet-black hair and smoldering eyes and did not look like the Puerto Ricans or Chinese in the neighborhood. I think his name may have been Vincent. I also think he may have been Cambodian.

Unlike the other two bullies, who were dangerous only if provoked, Vincent was always looking for trouble. He was an unbelievably vicious youth, with a malevolent set to his teeth, and I am sure that he eventually came to a sorry end. Be that as it may, he was a snazzy dresser, what was known at the time as a Fancy Dan. Unlike the rest of us, who mostly wore interchangeably bland getups, this debonair child psychotic always sported a flashy jet-black suit. From the time I started working for Len at the princely sum of $6 a week, I had visions of buying a suit exactly like Vincent's. Throughout my childhood, I was convinced that if I could only raise enough money to acquire such a suit, my life would change overnight. To me, the suit—particularly the jacket—was invested with insuperable magical powers. Enveloped in its ebony magnificence, I would be able to impress girls, stir the envy of boys, cow the bourgeoisie, realign the constellations, impersonate an Apollonian Hawaiian.

Of course, in order to buy a jet-black suit, I would have to make the purchase at some other store. This was out of the question, because Len would have felt betrayed. Whenever I did report for work wearing a shirt or jacket I had not purchased from him—and he always sold me clothing at a 70 percent discount—Len would act stunned, as if Benedict Arnold had just sauntered into his establishment, with Maréchal Pétain, Ethel Rosenberg, and Judas Iscariot in train. What was the point of risking his life on that hellhole of Iwo Jima if his protégé was going to turn up in a shirt like *that*? "That outfit makes you look like a smacked ass," he would snicker, or "Why would anyone want to walk around looking like a smacked ass?" or "Have you noticed that there seem to be an awful lot of smacked asses among young people today?" In Len's circumscribed view of the sartorial cosmos, the world was divided into two distinct groups: people who bought their clothing from him and people who looked like smacked asses.

I never did get around to buying that suit, because every time I came within sight of my goal, something bad would happen and my tiny nest egg would disappear. One night, when I had saved up $32, putting me within striking distance of that mesmerizing outfit, I chipped a tooth playing football. The tooth got infected, neuralgia set in, and by Saturday night I was sporting an abscess the size of a golf ball. As we had no family dentist—after my mother was induced to get her teeth pulled out at age thirty-nine, she seemed to give the orthodontic community a wide berth—it was impossible to receive treatment until the following Tuesday. The tooth-industry butcher recommended by a sadistic neighbor sedated me with some sort of buy-one-get-three-free nerve gas, but it never took complete effect, and throughout the operation I could see a throbbing volcanic mass swelling up in front of my face, primed to explode. Through a haze of pain, I felt the backwoods oral surgeon yank the teeth out one by one and then lance the abscess. He did not cover his profession in glory that afternoon; I could have managed just as well with a string, a doorknob, and a knitting needle—or a pair of pliers. The procedure was expensive, and as we had no insurance, my piggy bank got cracked open immediately. That was the last time I thought about buying any jet-black suits.

"You don't want to be a clotheshorse anyway," my mother consoled me. She was right: I was not a clotheshorse, and I did not need that suit. But I wanted it; I wanted it more than I ever wanted anything except the English racing bike my uncle Charlie bought me. To this day, I believe that if I could have only gotten my hands on that jet-black suit, everything in my life would have been different. There would have been much more drama and general gaiety at the very least, and it would have occurred earlier and lasted longer. I might have been named interim chairman of the Commerce Department or recruited to fill a surprise vacancy at the Académie Française or nominated to serve in an advisory capacity—perhaps functioning as an éminence grise—in some postcolonial transitional government. Later in life, when I began dressing entirely in black, friends theorized that I did this in imitation of Johnny Cash or in homage to Samuel

Beckett or as a way of vicariously experiencing the visual splendor of the clerical vocation that had eluded me, or even because black clothes have a way of making a 210-pound man look thinner. But I think it was because of that Hawaiian kid. Better late than never.

One day after I had been working for Len for six months or so, a group of boys slightly older than me began to make a commotion at the front of the store.

"Show us Lieutenant Leto!" they demanded. "We want to see Lieutenant Leto!"

"The lieutenant is still sleeping," Len replied, trying to calm them down. I could tell from his impish demeanor that this was not the first time he had rebuffed such a request. "He's not coming out today. He needs his beauty sleep."

"Please show us Lieutenant Leto!" the boys insisted. "Please!"

"The lieutenant has gone AWOL," Len would tease them.

"Please show us Lieutenant Leto!"

This was a ritual that was repeated again and again throughout my seven-year stint in this far-flung corner of the retail sector. Boys would clamber for an appearance by Lieutenant Leto, and Len would act completely uninterested. He was not going to respond to pressure just because of the blandishments of a few rowdy teenagers. If they expected him to give in, they were going to have to show him that they really meant it. Only if they literally got down on bended knee and begged him would he drop his blasé attitude and accede to their requests for an appearance by Lieutenant Leto. As soon as he felt that the charade had gone on long enough, he would reach down under the counter and extract a filthy, decaying brown paper bag. This he would plunk down onto the counter. From within, he would now produce a human skull, which still had a few teeth dangling from the roof of the mouth.

"He must have been in a crap game that night," Len would say, chuckling as he brandished a wad of bloodstained Japanese bills lying at the bottom of the bag. "That was the last time he felt lucky."

He would then allow the boys to play with the skull, provided they did not rattle the teeth, several of which were coming loose. After the boys left, Len would return the skull to its final resting place beneath the cash register.

"He was the first man I killed," Len later explained when I asked for more details about the strange odyssey of Lieutenant Leto. "We came up behind the Japs and shot them, then I chopped off his head, dipped it in high-octane gas, and wrapped it in a canvas bag. It's called a marine's pillow."

What I remember most vividly from this incident, and from many subsequent appearances by Lieutenant Leto, was how natural it seemed at the time that Len should have a human skull wrapped in a brown paper bag stuffed away under the counter in his store. I was not horrified by Lieutenant Leto's residence in the store, nor did Len's behavior strike me as ghoulish; I had no frame of reference for this experience. V-J Day was a scant fifteen years in the past; the Japanese had waged a barbaric war against us; this being the case, the act of decapitating a stranger and bringing his skull home as a combination trophy and conversation piece seemed a perfectly acceptable course of action. To this day, when I hark back to Lieutenant Leto's splashy debut that afternoon, I do not feel the revulsion I should. This is because it is impossible to retrofit emotions: If I was not horrified then, it is difficult to be horrified now. But I also think it may have something to do with growing up in an environment where abnormal behavior was the norm.

My father was highly upset when informed of the whereabouts of the unfortunate Lieutenant Leto's noggin, and for a while there was talk about making me quit my job. But my parents needed the $6 I brought home every week, and in the end my father, who had served in the less overtly theatrical United States Army, simply wrote off this incident as macabre but predictable Marine Corps behavior.

"Those guys are so rah-rah," he would say.

Rah-rah, indeed. But I liked the rahness of Len's rah, and my father knew it. I liked everything about Len: his breathtaking mane of brown hair, his Ban-Lon sweaters, his scuffed Hush Puppies. Most of all, I liked his medals. Almost from the moment I began working in the clothing store, I was aware that he was taking on the role of a surrogate father. At several points, he offered to adopt me, an idea I sometimes encouraged, even though there was little likelihood that I would ever leave my mother and sisters behind. The truth was, a defection like that would have looked bad on my record; it would be like slipping away from the stagecoach station under cover of night, abandoning the wounded to a grisly fate at the hands of the Apaches.

While Len probably knew all along that adoption was not in the cards, he still acted very much in loco parentis. He taught me how to banter with strangers in the way that men do but boys don't. He taught me how to tell stories, piling up detail after detail, occasionally taking a brief parenthetical detour, always making listeners wait for the big payoff; though because I was Irish American, I already had a head start on this sort of thing. He taught me how to throw a curveball, how to dance, and how to box, never failing to remind me, "Lead with your left." Once he even cut my hair. This was during a period when I briefly disliked my hair more than I disliked my father.

My hair was perfectly straight and blond until the age of thirteen; it had the texture of braised straw. First it was blond, then dirty blond, then brown, but it was always entirely inanimate and never did anything but droop down over my eyebrows in a style evoking Teen Hitler, Austrian Cornball. Throughout this era, I dreamed of waking up with jet-black hair—to go with my jet-black suit—a raven-hued mane that I could slick back like Ricky Nelson or the hotshots on *Route 66*. I conducted various experiments to make my hair look better—pompadour, bangs, wispy sideburns—but nothing worked. Out of the blue, Len suggested a buzz cut, using a pair of electric shears he just happened to have lying around, as if he were holding them in reserve in case a battalion of hirsute paratroopers stopped by, desperate to get spruced up for the woodchopper's ball. Len assured me that a buzz cut would not only keep me cool but make me look cool. This theory, I soon learned, had no basis in fact; the buzz cut made me look like Jimmy Crack Corn incarnate.

During the dog days of summer, Len and I would spend the long afternoons tossing a tennis ball back and forth, listening to the radio, straightening stock, waiting for customers to straggle in. We also did quite a bit of wrestling, madly careening around the store, sending the clothing flying this way and that. On days when business was slow, which it often was, Len would give me boxing lessons. All afternoon we would slug it out, pummeling each other from one end of the store to the other, with Len ceaselessly preaching, "Lead with your left, jab with your right." Or maybe it was the other way around. Len insisted that even a man of the cloth might have to defend himself from time to time, but this flew in the face of everything I had ever been taught about Christ, whose pugilist skills, if they existed, were never mentioned in the scriptures.

Despite Len's best efforts, these boxing lessons came to naught, as I was puny and weak, and had already noticed that all the people who liked to fight were bigger than the people they liked to fight with. Len maintained that the bigger they came, the harder they fell, but this I did not find to be the case. To the contrary, what I observed as I grew up was that the bigger they came, the faster everyone else fell. While I was still marking time in East Falls, waiting to bulk up, I learned to align myself diplomatically, often tenuously, with boys who were bigger and meaner than me, boys who could use help with their homework. The mythology of urban survival asserts that boys from bad neighbor-hoods grow up to be tough, but in my experience, boys who grow up to be tough sooner or later get flattened by boys who grew up to be tougher or who have more tough boys in their entourage. The boys who survive growing up in rough neighborhoods are the ones who become cunning, who see trouble coming and either befriend its practitioners or get out of their way. Len could not fathom such timidity and tact, because he was a marine, and marines believed in slugging people.

Len was also determined to take my education in hand. He was a voracious reader, but, like many men who embark on a lifetime program of self-improvement, he rarely read anything worth reading. He was the only person I ever met who had a subscription to *U.S. News & World Report* and actually seemed to enjoy it. Even then, this was unheard of. Graphically stultifying, *U.S. News & World Report* was the consummate symbol of the Eisenhower era. It was dry. It was sober. It was about as interesting as a thumbtack. But every week Len read it devoutly from cover to cover. It spoke his language, and he its.

Stacks and stacks of motivational guides by droll pinheads like Dale

Carnegie and Norman Vincent Peale were piled high on the counter, right beside the cash register. Len would read them and reread them, convinced that each time he plunged back into their well-thumbed pages, he would unearth yet another pearl of wisdom that had previously escaped his gimlet eye. Often he would tell me to go back to the shoe department, sit myself down, and feast on the adventures of that irrepressible go-getter Henry Alger or that indomitable tycoon J. P. Getty. But even as a child, I found these books sappy and hackneyed and smug, so I read *Aquaman* instead.

"Can't means *won't!*" was the sort of Babbittian flummery these books purveyed. "Get there the first-est with the most-est" was another axiom. "There are no atheists in foxholes" was Len's favorite, though this flew in the face of everything Americans believed about all those Red Chinese soldiers advancing the cause of godless communism in Korea, and seemed doubly illogical because Len himself gave no evidence of believing in God. These exhortations and bromides were of varied provenance; some sounded like they had emanated directly from the lips of Benjamin Franklin or Madame Curie or Ethan Allen, the good old Green Mountain Boy himself; others sounded like something Yvonne De Carlo or Ethel Merman might have said.

Len also devoured weird, pseudoscientific books illustrated with elaborate cranial charts and cephalographs depicting the interests, passions, and capabilities one could "scientifically" detect in the brains of Johann Sebastian Bach, Napoleon Bonaparte, Robert E. Lee, Henry Ford. These diagrams, visual paeans to one-dimensional men, persuaded Len that captains of industry never read novels, that fiction was for women and wastrels, that successful men shunned any reading material other than books that would make them even more successful. The diagrams and graphs suggested that Bach was a shallow, narrow-band doofus whose only real talent lay in the field of music, an idiot savant who would have had a hard time cutting the mustard in any other line of work. But that was hardly a criticism; shallowness was fine as long as it was profound shallowness, focused shallowness, passionate shallowness. Len could never understand why I gave the thumbs-down to his reading suggestions, preferring the escapist fiction of Robert Louis

Stevenson, Lew Wallace, Percival Wren, Zane Grey, Jules Verne, H. G. Wells, and the rest of that crew. But then again, I suppose that anyone who got revved up reading *U.S. News & World Report* didn't need Edgar Allan Poe to supply any thrills.

Throughout my seven-year apprenticeship at the store, my father came in no more than a handful of times. Once, when he was out of work and we were close to starvation, he asked Len to lend him ten bucks. A few weeks later, he gave me two fives and told me to repay the loan. Len made no comment at the time, but a few days later he said that my father had rubbed him the wrong way because he had borrowed $20 and repaid only $10. I had no way of knowing if this was true but suspected that it was. Len never asked for the other ten bucks; it was the last time we discussed the subject. Their only other contact occurred when my father miraculously amassed enough cash to buy a 1935 Buick that Len's son Bing had raised from the dead. Bing was a master at restoring seemingly defunct junkers to a reasonably functional state, but he warned my father that if he pushed the Buick past the 45 mph mark, it would die on him. It was the first car we ever owned, so we were overjoyed when he forked over $35 for the roomy Capone-era conveyance and brought it home. He wrecked it in two days. He confiscated my wages to buy a new battery, but it was no use; the Buick was down for the count. Afterward, the cruddy old bomb sat at the bottom of our cul-de-sac for a few weeks. We tried playing in it, but the upholstery was prickly and retained the August heat, so it wasn't much fun. Eventually, this glaring symbol of my failure as an intermediary got towed away, though the afterglow of my complicity in this disaster lingered for years.

Even to a child, it was obvious that there was something unusual about the Len Mohr philosophy of commerce. For example, he was always ready to drop everything, lock up the store, and drive over to Connie Mack Stadium a few hours before a ball game. Len had once owned three parking lots a few hundred yards from the stadium; the lots had provided a steady stream of income back in the early fifties, when the A's were still in town and Robin Roberts and the Whiz Kids were fielding a string of uncharacteristically competitive Phillies squads. But those days were gone, as were the A's. Two of the lots Len had sold off; the third was on the block. So far, no takers.

It wasn't merely the fact that he liked to close up shop in the middle of the day that branded Len an iconoclast. It was his attitude toward the Phillies. True, the summers were equatorial, making it pointless to hang around waiting for customers to drag their carcasses in. True, down at the stadium, after wrapping things up on the parking lot, we could at least take in the last few innings of the game. But the Phillies, a Chaplinesque aggregation of bozos, invalids, and slobs, always lost. Two years after I began working for Len, the hometown heroes dropped twenty-three games in a row, a record that will never be broken, and if it is, only by the Phillies. One year earlier, manager Eddie Sawyer quit after the first game of the season, declaring, "I'm forty-nine years old and I want to live to be fifty." In light of these facts, Len's attitude confused me. I could understand why he would close the store in the middle of a boiling hot summer day. But why he would close up just so we could drive over and see the Phillies is beyond me. He hated the sons of bitches.

There was no use searching for explanations, though. That was the way he was; he played by his own rules. And over the course of my apprenticeship, I would come to realize that Len viewed shopkeeping almost exclusively from a recreational perspective. He ran his operation along the lines of a rural general store, where windbags and curmudgeons would gather on the front porch to fret about the weather or taxes or expound their dopey theories about the revival of the gold standard. It didn't matter to him whether they bought anything. The regulars knew, without being able to access the precise terminology, that Len thought of his store as an agora, a gathering place for schemers, social climbers, con artists, dreamers, ne'er-do-wells, tarts, and screwups. Len loved to hear about their latest adventures; he reveled in the human comedy. From his point of view, and probably theirs, his goofball clientele were a pack of naughty scamps who trooped in once a week to report on their latest scrapes, and to describe the latest pickles they had gotten themselves into, seeking his advice, his input, his commiseration, and, if possible, his approval. He had a special soft spot in his heart for crackpots.

The vagabond crew of regulars was a rich and variegated lot. There were the Ferrante brothers, a pair of humongous siblings who ran a fuel company fifty yards up the road. All day long, all week long, they would be out on the road, pumping heating oil into people's homes, tending to their business. Then the weekend came, and with it, a desire to relax, socialize, spread their cash around. Because they smelled to high heaven, they were allowed onto our premises only on Saturday night shortly before closing time, because even after such a brief visit, we'd still have to keep the windows open all day Sunday to allow the stench from their stink-bomb bodies and putrid clothes to dissipate, making it possible for commerce with the nonmephitic to resume on Monday. The younger of the two was a live wire with a bawdy juvenile sense of humor; he had a forty-eight-inch waist, fairly ample for that era, fairly ample for his height: about five-seven. His older, taller brother, a Brobdingnagian sourpuss, logged in with a sixty-two-inch waist, perhaps more. He bore a striking resemblance to Stalin's trusty old hatchet man Nikita Khrushchev, though in those days people thought that anyone fat and unpleasant-looking resembled Khrushchev. Because Len had a contact inside a firm that made industrial uniforms for porcine men—he referred to him as Omar the Tent Maker—the *fatso fratelli* would waddle in roughly once every four to five weeks to purchase new duds.

The younger brother was fond of me, perhaps because I laughed at his jokes, which were not especially funny but were delivered with foundation-rattling Sicilian gusto. He was the kind of man who would gleefully array a bunch of matchsticks on the counter, with three matches representing the missionaries and three representing the cannibals, and then ask me to figure out how to safely ferry all six of them across the river without ever leaving a single missionary on the shore with any two cannibals, who would, of course, immediately eat him. Fully aware that I was preparing for a career as a missionary, he probably thought this exercise might come in handy at some point down the road when I crossed paths with man-eating infidels. But the fatter, older brother never stopped scowling at me, as if my antiseptic eighty-five pounds were a calculated rebuke to his miasmic flab, when in fact I was skinny only because I never got enough to eat.

It was especially endearing that the younger brother could not remember the punch lines to his own jokes; a few weeks after he showed us how to ferry the missionaries and cannibals across the river without getting any of the missionaries eaten, he returned to the store and sheepishly begged us to explain the solution to him. The brothers constantly talked about bailing out of the oil business and getting into something more dignified, but this was clearly not in the cards, as people who could not remember the answers to their own riddles were lucky to be employed in the first place. Despite the fact that it was impossible for the Ferrantes to expunge the rank scent of oil from their clothing, hair, skin, and car upholstery, both of them were married. Len and I always wondered what their wives smelled like.

Another regular visitor was a man named Horrie, short for Horace, who lived with his mother a few yards up the street in a darling little row home. By the looks of things, nobody had ever explained to Horrie that underwear was reusable, so every Saturday afternoon he would sally forth and purchase six new pairs of jockey shorts, six athletic tee shirts later known as wife beaters but in those innocent times still referred to as dago dining jackets, and six pairs of black nylon socks. We never knew what he did with the underwear after he wore it—we sometimes speculated that a forest of soiled skivvies was slowly accumulating in his backyard—but Len was grateful for the business.

Horrie, who had no visible means of support, would spend hours and hours outside his mother's house painstakingly, almost amorously, polishing his radiant, midnight blue Cadillac. On Saturdays he would come in and talk to Len about the car, which was undeniably a thing of beauty. Oddly, for a man who lived and died for his automobile, he seemed to spend very little time behind the wheel; in fact, no one ever saw him driving it. One day when I inquired about this, Len explained that the magnificent but entirely stationary vehicle did not have an engine, at least not a working one, but that Horrie had vowed to buy one just as soon as he got a job. This event would occur at some unspecified point later in the millennium. Years after I left Len's employ, I heard that Horrie got into a fight with the dreaded highway patrol the very night he finally got the Caddy up and running, that the coppers beat him senseless, and that they then impounded the car. But I refused to believe this story, as it was too sad.

Yet another regular visitor was a man who would disappear for months at a time, shipping out to Greenland, where he was supposedly assembling a war chest large enough to move his family to Sarasota, Florida, the land of dreams. He worked as a night watchman, though what he was watching by night during those interminable Greenland winters was never disclosed. It may have been cod, perhaps thermonuclear weapons. This was in the early sixties, before the Citrus State had been overrun by developers. Every so often the man would come into the store and show Len brochures depicting parcels of land that could be scooped up dirt-cheap way down yonder in this tropical paradise. His family, left behind while he flitted off on his frosty expeditions, had no desire to leave Philadelphia, but each time he came back from a winter in the glacial north, he seemed even more determined to relocate to the Sun Belt. It was very unusual to meet Philadelphians who worked in Greenland in those days; Pennsylvanians have long been the least migratory of Americans, and people from Philadelphia never go anywhere, convinced that they have everything anyone could possibly want right there in the bounteous Delaware Valley. Now that I think back on it and reflect on the man's boundless optimism, awesome reservoirs of pep, and determination to get the hell out of town, it seems less and less likely that he was a native of the City of Brotherly Love.

At least once a week, Len received a social call from a thirtyish chap who lived a few blocks north of the store, where he nursed grandiose dreams of a political career. John was five-feet-eight, good-looking in that jowly, indeterminate way so many Irish Americans are, and blessed with the gift of gab. Philadelphia politics were dominated by tough, ethically suspect Irish Catholics, men who knew where the money was and how to steal it, and who knew that tough, ethically suspect Italians were warming up on the sidelines, waiting to steal whatever the Micks left behind. If you were going to steal, so their credo stipulated, you'd better steal fast. John, who was by no means a bruiser, dreamed of displacing these scoundrels or, if this proved impossible, swelling their ranks. Periodically, he would run for insignificant local offices to which he had no chance of being elected. After his most recent drubbing, he would hunker down with Len in our makeshift situation room, and the pair would conduct a point-by-point postmortem, diagnosing John's latest failure to win the plaudits of the hoi polloi. Mostly, he ran for the school board. He did not have a rigid, much less a well-thought-out, political philosophy; he was from the classic throw-the-bums-out segment of the electorate that honestly believed that the devil you didn't know was better than the devil you did, though not even they were sure why. Such a constituency, no matter how vocal, no matter how stroppy, was rarely numerous enough to ensure their champion's electoral victory.

Flabbergastingly vapid but quite full of himself, John would rattle on and on about his big plans while Len listened patiently with an amused expression on his face, every so often interjecting one of the many pearls of wisdom he had gleaned from Dale Carnegie: "Can't means won't," "Fortune favors the brave"—then occasionally tossing in "If a bricklayer can lay bricks, why can't a plumber lay plums?" for comic effect.

I am not sure if Len ever resorted to the expression "Big hat, no cattle" to describe his visitor, but he did use phrases like "You've got champagne taste with a beer pocketbook" and "You can't make a silk purse out of a sow's ear." I was jealous of the way Len used the English language like a gun rack from which he could select the weapon best suited to incapacitating the prey at hand. There we'd be, with John gasbagging about his latest cockamamie scheme to vault to the top of the political world and depose the scum who dwelled there, and Len would send him crashing back to earth with an "All talk, no action" or a "Crap or get off the pot" or a "Sure, you and how many marines?"

I did not get the feeling that John took any of this criticism personally; he loved to bask in Len's man-of-the-world aura, perhaps in the misguided hope that if he hung around this Solon-by-the-Schuylkill long enough, he might acquire Len's wit, his acumen, and perhaps even his barrel chest. John, who was astonishingly grandiloquent for a man who still lived with his mother, tended to speak as if I were not even there, as if a real fireball like him was too important to palaver with a callow youth, a wee nipper, a nobody. I never paid attention to anything he had to say, as he was bombastic and flatulent and had a weak chin and was obviously going nowhere fast. But I always kept my eyes on Len, who seemed to find John's improbable tales of derring-do and high electoral adventure inexhaustibly amusing. John was one of those unfortunate individuals who had trouble reading body language, who did not grasp that when Len uncrossed his arms, donned his reading glasses, and went back to scrutinizing that week's edition of *U.S. News & World Report,* it meant that the consultation was over. What could be more humiliating, then or now, than being told that one's Svengali would rather read *U.S. News &World Report* than talk to you?

One day when his paperweight protégé was vacating the premises, Len told me to go outside and take a gander at his car. From the top of the steps, the two-door sedan, a late-fifties Rambler, looked ordinary enough, but then, moseying around to port side, I realized that it had no door on the driver's side, that a gigantic strip of thick plastic had been attached to the space where the door should have been. One thing I must say on John's behalf, though: As he was pulling away from the curb, heading back to man the hustings of his mind, he briefly caught my eye, and not for a second did his expression betray even the slightest embarrassment that he was driving a car that was missing a door. For in the cosmos he inhabited, no matter what the external evidence might suggest, he was a man on the move, a cat on the make, a diamond in the rough, a pearl among swine, a young man to keep your eye on. He was in his own world, and probably still is.

Skintight slacks came into fashion in the early 1960s, and not a moment too soon for a woman Len referred to as Kaye Sera, who had the most pugnacious, territorially acquisitive backside I have ever encountered. Universally viewed as a tramp, Kaye had a husband no one ever saw, two children no one liked, and two buttocks no one ever stopped talking about. Never much of a shopper, she was forever hauling her tarty derriere into Len's establishment on Saturday afternoons, propping it up against a table laden with our competitively priced men's dress shirts, and engaging Len in mildly suggestive banter. Not a pretty woman, though by no means hideous, Kaye had by this point transformed her visage into a puffy clown face after decades of applying mounds of pancake makeup to its neutral surface.

Quite a different matter was her pampered, capacious rear end—a veritable force of nature, a genetic miracle, a neighborhood legend by virtue of its prodigious girth, Jello-O–like suppleness, gratifying ubiquity, and willingness to duke it out with all comers. Local opinion was divided on whether her skintight white slacks had been spray-painted directly onto her cheeks by person or persons unknown, or whether she gained posterioral purchase via an oversized, ingeniously crafted shoehorn and the adroit use of hard-to-obtain Sumatran unguents that helped ease her stupendous glutes into the flimsy trousers that always seemed nine sizes too small to handle the thankless assignment they had been handed by the pitiless gods of the netherworld. My personal theory was that she probably squatted down on the ground and started wiggling into her slacks early Wednesday morning; put in a long, hard day of squirming and wriggling both Thursday and Friday; and, through sheer willpower and ferocious dieting, finally managed to negotiate the airtight garment's passage over the summit of her buttocks by late Saturday afternoon, by which point she was sufficiently presentable to waddle out of her house for her gay weekend promenade. Though a compulsive giggler and a first-class nitwit, she meant no harm and in her own squalid little way exuded an ineffable floozie charm. She was best known in the neighborhood as the woman least like any of our mothers. This included the mothers who were drunken sluts.

Of all the picaresque characters to frequent Len's Clothing Store, there was none whose visits I welcomed more than Abe Hirshberg's. Abe was the last of the red-hot ethnic stereotypes, a salty-tongued refugee from the garment district who worked as a jobber, haunting the least charming districts in the city hawking odd lots of clothing known as closeouts to small-time merchants like Len. It was merchandise in styles that had not so much been discontinued or superseded as repudiated. This was in the days before discount chains like Wal-Mart wiped establishments like Len's off the face of the earth and put jobbers like Abe out to pasture for good.

Abe tooled around in a cruiser-class Lincoln Continental stocked to the gills with off-brand merchandise that ranged from the nonessential to the farcical: shirts that were already three years out of fashion, long-extinct fads like pedal pushers or Dr. Kildare jackets—briefly a hit among teenagers—and other well-traveled flotsam and jetsam of this general ilk. Abe hated opening the trunk of his car, because if he didn't sell a substantial portion of its contents by the time he left, he would need at least two people to sit on it and get it closed again. And that meant forking over a tip.

Abe was about sixty-five when I met him: short, bespectacled, wrinkled in places where no wrinkles should exist. Half the time he spoke in English, the rest of the time in Yiddish. In either vernacular, his conversation was a nonstop string of threats, execrations, epithets, exclamations, exaggerations, exhortations, oaths, and heartrending appeals for mercy. He swung wildly back and forth between Willy Loman, the Merchant of Venice, and the Iceman (that Cometh). He was fond of invoking the God of Israel and invariably likened his private-sector misfortunes to the destruction of the Temple. He thought of Len as a cross between Charles Atlas, George Reeves, Adolf Eichmann, and the emperor Titus. He was perpetually scribbling illegible notes in an elephantine notebook that had hundreds of bits of paper sticking out if it, writing down orders that had not yet been agreed upon, as if the very act of committing them to paper invested them with legal finality. The notebook contained so many orders, one would have thought Abe was a millionaire many times over, that in visiting us in East Falls, he was merely slumming it. This is the way he looked at it, too. From the first time I saw him, I understood that, in Abe's view, deigning to set foot in a two-bit dive like Len's Clothing Store was an act of supreme altruism—because he had places to go and people to meet. Interesting places. Important people. Not tightwad sons of bitches like Len Mohr, spawn of an accursed race, who would literally make that poor son of a bitch George Washington scream for mercy before he'd part with a goddamn dollar bill earned at his hole-in-the-wall dump and all-purpose shit hole, the prick Hun bastard.

"I have tickets to the theater. My wife is waiting for me at the front door," Abe would say. "Please: Nineteen dollars a dozen is my best offer."

Len would tell him to pack up his lurid castoffs and get lost.

"You are crucifying me!" Abe would tell Len tearfully when he refused to take the nightmarish merchandise off his hands. "You are literally drinking my blood."

At this juncture, Abe would protest that the Wanamakers and the Bloomingdales and the Lords and the Taylors and all of his other imaginary contacts in the haberdashery stratosphere never treated him like this, that the abuse he was enduring tonight—tantamount to lèse-majesté—was beyond the pale. When this failed to produce the desired effect, which it usually did, he would ostentatiously ferret out his fancy gold watch and gaze at it with an expression of mock terror, as if ten more minutes of pointless dickering with a cheapskate ballbuster like Len Mohr would compel him to cancel his long-anticipated nightcap with the Maharini of Annapur.

Nobody else talked to Len like this. Everybody else treated him with boundless respect and admiration, bordering on fear. Not Abe. Because of Len's tenacious refusal to part with his money and because of his Teutonic background, and because of, well, everything, Abe viewed him as Antiochus himself, scourge of the Israelites.

"Open my veins, go ahead!" he would shriek at the top of his voice. "Put my head under the wheel and run over it, you bastard."

The first time I saw Len and Abe in action, I was only nine years old. It was a Saturday night, just before closing time, and Len and I were turning out the lights. Suddenly, I heard the sound of something incredibly heavy being dragged up the front steps. Now the outer door creaked opened. Heavy breathing, more sounds of scraping and dragging. Then the inside door burst open and in lurched a short, perspiring old man, dragging what was easily the planet's oldest, largest, filthiest suitcase behind him. It looked like a going-away present he'd been handed by the prophet Elijah after his well-attended bar mitzvah in 874 B.C.

"Get out of here, and take that garbage with you!" Len would bark, making a halfhearted attempt to block his path. "We're closing."

"Five minutes is all I ask!" Abe would thunder, mopping his brow and feigning his twelfth coronary. "Five minutes—is this too much to ask?"

Len would then relent, and Abe would wearily undo the leather straps that bound the suitcase together. From within its fearsome recesses would cascade a tsunami of down-market merchandise. It suggested that Abe had made a Faustian bargain with a Mephistophelian middleman who agreed to provide unlimited access to clothing nobody wanted in exchange for his everlasting soul. *Pledge me your wife's soul and I'll throw in some manufacturer's seconds closeout hosiery.*

When I think of Len today, I picture him and Abe Hirschberg screaming epithets at each other as Abe scuttles down the staircase with his suitcase in tow. *Two-fifty a shirt is my last offer. They're pink; how am I going to sell pink shirts to Polacks? At my age, do you think I enjoy this? That's your problem. Do you think I need such melodrama? That's also your problem. Twenty-nine bucks a dozen, with three XLs, and you've got yourself a deal. Careful, Abe: Don't go flying ass-over-tin-cups. Twenty-nine bucks, that's the best I can do for you. Well, that's not good enough. For this I drove all the way here on my weekend? Apparently. For this I drove twenty-five miles out of my way? So it would appear. And don't let the door hit your ass on the way out. You goy son of a bitch. Same to you, Schweinhund. Make it four XLs and you've got yourself a deal. Fine, but at this price, I must be meshugah. Done, you prick. But I am only doing this because my wife is waiting at the front door with my sickly grandchildren. Did I tell you Esther has pleurisy? I thought it was leprosy.* In the end, after witnessing scores of these bravura performances, I realized that these two men were in love with each other, joined at the retail hip. In the best of all possible worlds, they would have been buried side by side in a cemetery that admitted only grand masters of feigned ethnic antagonism.

But then again, who needs the aggravation?

One afternoon, completely out of the blue, Len announced that he had invested in a company founded by a group of local businessmen that would provide financial backing for a promising young boxer. By the sound of it, most of the other men in the Cloverlay group were high rollers. I am not sure how or when Len and these captains of industry crossed paths or whether he merely purchased a few shares of stock that they issued, but I assume the whole thing had something to do with the boxing matches Len used to referee in clubs in North Philadelphia. The boxer in question was a hard-hitting brute who had taken the gold medal in the 1964 Olympics but was now slaving away in a local slaughterhouse. The backing company, by tossing a few clams his way, would enable him to quit his job and focus on his real objective, which at this early stage was to turn professional and wangle a rematch with the one fighter who had bested him in the Olympic tryouts a few years earlier. The man who prevailed in that three-round set-to went by the name of Buster Mathis. The man he outpointed was named Joe Frazier.

Because I was only a kid at the time, because I knew nothing about boxing, and because I had no way of knowing that Joe Frazier would one day become the heavyweight champion of the world, I didn't think much of this venture. When Len would talk about perhaps dropping by the North Philadelphia gym where Smokin' Joe worked out, I expressed no great interest in going. This may have been because Len used to ref fights in a gym nicknamed the Blood Pit, and this didn't sound like the sort of place a pasty-faced teenaged boy would feel comfortable.

For the next few years, Len would simply not give the Smokin' Joe Frazier saga a rest. Just as the Nifty Fifty had dominated our conversations a few years earlier, Len now had a bee in his bonnet about the fearsome young bull in the Cloverlay stable. Not every kid gets to work for a man who is one of the original backers of a future heavyweight champion of the world, and even as a teen, I should have realized that there was something special about this. But at the time I didn't care one way or the other. Like most young people of the era, I would soon become contemptuous of Frazier—unfairly, I realize in retrospect—and idolize Muhammad Ali, not only because of what the former Cassius Clay seemed to stand for but because young people are so easily bowled over by the kind of high-profile insolence Clay was famous for.

Slowly, just beneath the surface, tension began to develop between Len and me. Just as every son has to kill his father, I now had to kill my surrogate father. Though I respectfully stayed abreast of Frazier's progress as he disposed of a series of stumblebums, then an Argentinian slugger named Oscar Bonavena, then a gifted but undersized veteran named Eddie Machen, I did so with no great enthusiasm. Things were changing on other fronts as well; I was, in the words of my employer, "feeling my oats." I questioned the wisdom of escalating the war in Vietnam. I spoke my mind about Nixon and Eisenhower. I upbraided Len for using terms like "*Schwärze*" and "Jewish lightning." I stopped reading ostensibly enlightening articles he had circled in *U.S. News & World Report.* All of a sudden, I knew everything.

Len and I never reached the point where we openly feuded or ceased to enjoy each other's company. But things did change. From the beginning, Len could not understand why anyone in his right mind would want to be a priest. He was even less clear as to why anyone would devour novels by Faulkner and Fitzgerald when he could more profitably devote his time to biographies of Andrew Carnegie or books with diagrams depicting Alexander the Great's brain in its prime, before Aristotle's most celebrated student started hitting the hard stuff.

Len knew that I was not enthralled by retail. He could see that I was bored silly by all the Frazier hoopla, that like everybody else under the age of twenty-five, I was solidly in Ali's corner. He could sense that a wedge had developed between us. Earlier, things had been different. When I was about twelve and my father's drinking was getting completely out of hand, Len had proposed adopting me, or at least arranging for me to spend my final year before entering the seminary in his home. Because there was no real social congress between Len and my father, I have no idea how these negotiations would have proceeded. I only know that after we moved out of the project and across town when I was thirteen and I stopped working for Len every day after school, the adoption talk ceased. Now I saw him only once a week, taking a long bus ride from my new neighborhood back to the old one. He continued to pay me $6 a week, though now I was earning in a single day what I had previously been paid for twenty hours of work. But after a few years, I wearied of the long commute and grew tired of giving up my Saturdays. I had new friends now, and I wanted to spend more time with them. One day I was offered a job as a clerk in a pharmacy in my new neighborhood. I accepted it. Breaking the news to Len was the hardest thing I ever had to tell anyone in my life.

I visited the store a few times during my last two years in high school, dropping by to purchase clothes, which he always sold me at a ridiculous discount, and I stopped in a few times after I entered college. After that, our paths parted. Years passed. My mother said she'd heard through the grapevine that he eventually retired to Florida, but I had trouble believing this, because Len never took vacations, wasn't crazy about direct sunlight, and seemed to be the kind of man who was born to die in the retail saddle. He lived to be ninety-one, just like his father before him. But after that visit in 1971, I never saw him again.

I have often asked myself why I never went back to visit Len after I left college. Perhaps it is because of the ruthlessness of the young, the obsession with staking out one's own terrain, escaping from the patriarch's shadow. Moreover, I did not want to be reminded of the past, and East Falls held almost nothing but bad memories. Most likely, I did not want to see Len again until I had made my mark as a writer, an occupation he had always disparaged, and by the time that happened, he had left the stage. Ironically, I achieved professional and financial success at the same age as Len: in my late thirties. Success was the theme that dominated our relationship; it was the thread connecting all our conversations. In the World According to Len Mohr, it was better to fail at something you wanted to do than succeed at something you didn't; success on anyone's terms other than your own was failure. I had no quarrel with these axioms, which proved a steady source of inspiration during the long years I could not get anyone to publish my work because I wanted to write like this and they wanted me to write like that. But by the time I was successful, Len's store had been shuttered.

Throughout my relationship with Len, I understood exactly what I was getting out of it: six bucks a week and a daily trip through the looking glass. But what did he get out of it? I never knew. I could never pinpoint what Len saw in me, since my father had done such a superb job convincing his children of their inherent worthlessness. Perhaps he detected something in my personality—orneriness—that he liked because it mirrored the orneriness in him. Or perhaps this was not a trait he had detected but one he had spawned. The negative side of the relationship was that Len could never stop thinking of me as a child. This became apparent the last time I saw him, when I was twenty years old and brought along my latest girlfriend to meet him. The reception was cool; he was cordial but by no means effervescent. I may not have realized it earlier, but I realized it then: Len was devastated when our seven-year liaison came to an end. He did not go out and find another stock clerk to replace me. He did not bring any new protégés on board. He was no longer in the market for surrogate sons. And when I went to see him that final time, I could see that it was the boy that he missed, not the man I had become.

Assessing those years, a case can be made that Len's Clothing Store was not the ideal environment for a young boy. What with middle-aged vixens whose buttocks were exploding out of their trousers and foul-mouthed middlemen swearing like sailors and fat slobs who smelled like roughnecks from Kuwaiti oil fields stinking up the joint and decapitated skulls rolling around under the counter, perhaps I would have been better off if I'd signed up for a paper route or shined shoes or delivered circulars or stayed home. But until I met Len, my life was featureless and gloomy. The people who congregated around the store were all defective in some way; they were off-brands, marked-down merchandise, damaged goods, closeouts. But they made swell company, and they held out the promise of a better world, a world bristling with the unexpected. Most important, none of them were cruel. They provided a respite from the dark hegemony of my father. It was true that I wished away my childhood, working twenty hours a week; there was never any time for Little League baseball or Pop Warner football, no time for after-school activities, not much time for play. No matter. Without that job, without that sliver of self-respect my piddling wages provided, I would have gone down for the count. Len had hired me for the hell of it, not because he deliberately set out to save my life. He saved it anyway.

When I grew up and told friends about Len and Lieutenant Leto and our rogues' gallery of exotics, they often reacted as if these people were grotesques. They were the kinds of weirdos and losers and head cases we go out of our way to shield our middle-class children from; the closest either of my children has ever gotten to a bona fide screwball is me. Perhaps my friends are right; perhaps these people were grotesques; perhaps they were in many ways pathetic. But when I see them now, gamboling across the landscape, they seem like commedia dell'arte characters who brought sunshine to my youth. They were certainly a whole lot more fun to be around than the hedge-fund managers and politicians and

American Studies professors and editors of glossy magazines I would meet later. What's more, they all possessed an unusual brand of courage. Unlike most of the interchangeably successful people I have met in my professional life, the oddballs who frequented Len's Clothing Store had assembled their personalities from whole cloth. They were not generic; they had not been churned out on an assembly line; they were, to use one of Len's stock phrases, the real McCoy.

Especially Kaye Sera. Kaye was a plain-looking woman with a gigantic ass who'd been cast adrift in a blue-collar neighborhood in a blue-collar town in an asphyxiatingly conservative era, but she risked everything because she wanted to look like Sophia Loren. To some, this may seem like a trashy dream. But it takes a million times more guts to be a working-class femme fatale who flaunts her fat ass in a straitlaced community that frowns on this sort of thing than to be a soccer mom tooling around the suburbs in a socially sanctified vehicle with a bumper sticker proclaiming her unswerving allegiance to a dink presidential candidate who got creamed four years ago. Some people have attitudes. Some people have balls.

This brings me full-circle back to Uncle Henry. Years passed after I stopped worshipping him on a daily basis—decades, in fact. Then, in 1984, my youngest sister, Mary Ann, got married to a tall, strapping Irish American named Tom Farrell. Tom's father, a member of the Philadelphia Police Department's bunko squad, did not drink. Neither did Tom. Neither, as far as I could determine, did anyone else on his side of the family. At the wedding reception, the libational schism between the two families was reflected in the seating arrangements: The Queenans faced the Farrells across a strategic divide—drinkers on one side, teetotalers on the other—with the neutral bridal party holding court nervously and, for the most part, abstemiously at the middle table connecting the two wings.

That afternoon, I was seated next to my mother's younger sister, Cecilia. My aunt was an Irish-American beauty whose beloved husband died quite young; she never remarried, and there was always about her a sense of dreams gone awry, of the rose whose fragrance had been wasted on the desert air. My own theory was that she never found anyone to replace Bill Tierney, the love of her life, and accepted the fact that one love of your life was enough. I had always liked my aunt, and after everyone had a few belts, I asked her if she and my mother did not sometimes miss their brother Henry.

"No," she replied unhesitatingly.

"You didn't? I just thought . . . well, he was your brother. . . ."

"Why would we miss him? He was a bad actor," she added, by way of clarification.

"What does that mean?" I inquired.

And then it all came out. Uncle Henry had, indeed, fled Philadelphia for Alaska, but not to fulfill any burning ambition to start a new life. He'd fled because he owed money to the wrong people, and the wrong people wanted it back. Yes, he had found work in Alaska, but he hadn't died there; he perished in a knife fight somewhere in Washington State. And he hadn't died while defending a Negro; he'd apparently been killed after confronting one. He was bad news, and the world was better off without him.

One afternoon a few years later, when I was driving down to Atlantic City with my mother, then in her eighty-sixth year, I asked her to tell me the truth, the whole truth, and nothing but the truth about her brother. She did, at least to the extent that she could recall all the relevant data. Bit by bit she filled me in on the missing details about Henry's life, the ones she had suppressed for so many years. He had been a troublemaker. He had been a bum. He had been murdered, and there was nothing heroic or romantic about his demise. He had sired a child out of wedlock, then left his wife behind in the City of Brotherly Love. The woman never saw any of the insurance money after he died; my mother and her sisters pocketed it. Times were tough; funerals were expensive. The common-law wife got stiffed.

Many years after Henry's death, Aunt Cecilia discovered that she had the same last name as an executive at the factory where she worked. Buttonholing him one day, she learned that he had never known his father, who had died out in Alaska when he was still an infant. A family reunion was organized. Henry's widow, still living, did not attend. By the end of the family gathering, Henry's son had a somewhat clearer idea of who his father was and how he died. Shortly thereafter, my aunt lost her job. There were no more family reunions.

From the time her parents passed away in the mid-1940s, my mother had always known that Henry's number was up, because her mother was the only family member willing to "stay in his corner." My mother was not surprised when she learned that her brother was dead, having long ago resigned herself to the fact that sooner or later he would come to a bad end. Like her own husband, Henry had gone absent without leave.

"He was always in some kind of trouble," she explained as we headed toward Atlantic City, where she could work the slots and forget about her marriage. "He just wasn't going to play ball."

When all the facts were in and the exact sequence of events was set in stone, it was clear that Uncle Henry had not been the hero I had taken him for as a child. If anything, he was a hood, a ne'er-do-well at best. Still, I was amazed at how quickly his sisters had been able to jettison his memory. He was disposable. A lot of young men were back then. The Depression and the war had hardened these women. They had married well to good men who died too soon, or married badly to bad men who died too late, or married safe, uninteresting men and then led long, safe, uninteresting lives. From the start, these women understood that life was not going to be a bed of roses. You had to batten down the hatches, cover up the windows, and get on with it. Man overboard.

None of this changed my feelings about my dead uncle. The legend of Uncle Henry had served me well through the darkest of times. And so, for my purposes, whatever his failings, he will forever remain the dashing, romantic figure who came to the defense of a harried black man in an Anchorage bar and paid for it with his life. In my mind's eye, he is like the Empire State Building: No matter how many overwrought skyscrapers hammy plutocrats erect in Chicago and Malaysia and Canberra and Battery Park, the Empire State Building will always be the tallest building in the world. And Henry will always be the daring young man who ran off to Alaska to start a new life. Just because something isn't true doesn't mean you shouldn't believe in it.

Chapter 6. **The Parting of the Reed Sea**

Throughout grade school, I had few second thoughts about entering the seminary. Admittedly, I was under unrelenting pressure from nuns and priests and relatives to don the Roman collar; they were forever pulling me aside and asking, "Do you still think you have a vocation?" as if it were possible to respond, "No." Still, it would be dishonest and self-serving to say that I entered the Maryknoll Junior Seminary because of prodding from adults. I did it for the aforementioned reasons: a craving for prestige, an aversion to working at a nine-to-five job, and most important, an all-consuming desire to get out of my father's house forever.

When I was in eighth grade, I won a citywide diocesan contest for an essay in which I defended the Latin mass and cautioned the Church about the perils of tossing tradition overboard. The Church chose to ignore my warning. The Cassandra-like essay itself has long since disappeared; no one in my family would be sentimental enough to hang on to such an extraneous oddity. But they did keep the trophy, a nifty marble-and-gold affair with an engraved image of a disembodied hand grasping a stylus and pressing down on what appeared to be papyrus. That my father never hocked it to some shady pawnbroker is one of the great surprises of my life; what stayed his hand was probably fear that filching a quasi-iconic object awarded by the Church might constitute some variation on the sin of simony and result in his spending an additional thirty-five centuries burning in Hell. Catholics were superstitious about these things.

Classmates knew that I was laying the groundwork for early canonization, but they did not hold it against me. To the extent that it was possible, given my aggressively publicized dreams of being decapitated or crucified, I tried to fit in. Though I did not swear, abstained from shoplifting, and rarely got into fights, I did do many of the other things that school-age children did: trespassing on private property, ringing the doorbells of the superannuated to scare the living daylights out of them, egging windshields. But I never got into any real trouble, the kind of trouble that would permanently seal off escape from an economic class whose charms had long since worn off.

Others did. Behind Saint Benedict's church was a playground/parking lot where boys were allowed to play softball after school. Because the rear of the church, which faced the schoolyard, housed a set of ornate stained-glass windows, we were not allowed to swing away toward left field. Since most of us were right-handed, this was a great inconvenience but one we grudgingly accepted, as there was nowhere else in the neighborhood to play baseball. When the pitch came in, we would dutifully aim our bats toward right field or lay down harmless bunts that wormed their way up the third-base line. One of the boys in my class was an abysmal athlete, but he participated in our games anyway, as he reveled in the camaraderie. We liked him well enough during school hours but didn't welcome his presence on the playing field afterward, because we feared that he would one day take a full cut and blast a softball right through Saint Anthony's stained-glass testicles, bringing down the curtain on our games forever.

I did not rat out the hooligan when he took one uppercut too many, and this probably reassured my classmates that, at least in this instance, I was not yet working on the side of the angels. I was also present and accounted for when two altar boys locked a tipsy Father Aloysius inside the walk-in safe where the parish's chalices and monstrances and ciboriums—as previously noted, my favorite vessel—were stored, and again I held my tongue when he sobered up and started banging on the vault door, bawling his eyes out, wondering who could possibly derive pleasure from such a heartless prank. I was reasonably certain that God would ignore my complicity in these transgressions, as the alternative was to be shunned, spat upon, or pummeled senseless by my less devout peers. Throughout my childhood, during which I remained adamantly short and stringy, with a physique the texture of noodles, discretion always seemed to be the better part of valor.

I served as an altar boy straight through grade school, during which time I continued to interact with a series of uninspiring clerics. A German-American parish priest, one of those addled anti-Semites who seem to be unaware that Christ started out life as a Jew, had received a dispensation to use white wine, as opposed to red, when serving mass; apparently he suffered from some offbeat oenological allergy. Altar boys habitually quaffed a swig or two of the celebrant's wine before mass, and I was no exception, but I was shocked the first time I chugged a few ounces of his personal reserve; consulting the bottle, I found that what he was guzzling was some sort of Riesling or Chablis. *Oh, dear: Father Fancy-Pants!* The notion that Christ's Most Precious Blood could have a sweet taste to it had never occurred to me; it was probably the moment I began to suspect that the concept of transubstantiation might be grounded in metaphor.

The priest, who lived to be ninety-one, had a habit of giving rides to teenaged girls on their way home from high school, a practice that was frowned upon by everyone except the teenaged girls, who gleefully pocketed the twenty-five-cent bus fare they would otherwise have had to shell out. He used to say the nine o'clock mass on Sunday mornings, which was the service every student was required to attend, because otherwise the nuns would have had to monitor all the other masses, from six in the morning until noon, and count heads to make sure no one was playing hooky. He always jump-started his homilies by informing the adults in the room that he would have nothing to say to them, that he was only interested in talking to the young people, because this was their mass, not their parents'. After this contemptuous introduction, he would deliver his rambling, incoherent sermon in a weird, high-pitched voice, serving up a needlessly effusive mixture of high dudgeon and baby talk. He had gotten it into his head that this gibberish was a crowd favorite, as was the man who spouted it, though in fact we all hated his guts.

Throughout these years, as my respect for missionaries grew in inverse proportion to my contempt for diocesan priests, ruggedness continued to be one of the main selling points of the Maryknoll order. Missionaries were manly men. Missionaries were serious. Missionaries did not get locked inside safes, they did not talk like two-year-olds, and they most assuredly did not drink Chablis. They also did not have names like Aloysius. And soon I would be one of them.

This, at least, is what I hoped would happen, but then reality reared its ugly head. Much like Christopher Columbus wading ashore on San Salvador and immediately realizing that, whoever the natives of the island were, they were definitely not canny middlemen in the Indian spice trade, I experienced a similar sense of disillusionment when I arrived at the Maryknoll Junior Seminary, officially, the Venard Apostolic School, in Clark's Summit, Pennsylvania, on September 11, 1964. The Venard was a tidy cluster of stone buildings perched hopefully atop a hill looking down on the drowsy hamlet of Clark's Green, which itself towered over a petite, somniferous way station called Chinchilla, which was located about eight miles outside Scranton. Scranton was known up and down the East Coast, and perhaps even farther, as a first-class dump, only slightly more enticing than its twin city, Wilkes-Barre, which lay coiled in wait sixteen miles down the road, like the uglier of the Siamese twins. Wilkes-Barre was famous for exactly one thing: Mr. Peanut had been born there in 1916. Scranton could not even lay claim to that. Thus was I introduced to the meaning of the word "Podunk."

I am not sure how a boy of thirteen who, save for that one trip to upstate New York, had never been anywhere except Philadelphia and the Jersey shore could instantaneously discern how awful Scranton was, but I could. Clearly, nothing exciting had happened there in decades; it was like walking into an Edward Hopper painting, where you got the feeling that all the wild, fun-loving people had already blown town, leaving behind only the brooding buildings and desolate streets. The Mafia had been active in Scranton during the Prohibition Era, but even the Black Hand had long since pulled up stakes, taking their bootlegging brio with them. I was old enough to know that Philadelphia had a reputation for being parochial, conservative, working-class, short on hoopla, and I knew that this reputation was well deserved, as people in the Delaware Valley worked hard at being uninspiring. But Philadelphia was a real city, with subways and trolleys and crooked politicians and a downtown and buildings that rose higher than four stories and two rivers and a zoo and ghettoes and organized crime and millions of inhabitants and department stores with names like Strawbridge & Clothier and local lore and graft and a nickname. By comparison with sarcophagal Scranton, Philadelphia was Byzantium. And I wasn't even in Scranton. I was eight miles outside it.

Neither of my parents could accompany me to the seminary that first day, as my mother was recuperating from having her gallbladder removed, and my father had to work. So I trekked north to Scranton with my aunt Cassie on a banged-up old Trailways bus, then caught a local bus to Clark's Summit. My aunt was not especially devout, but she did like an outing. She was very impressed by the facility that greeted us in Clark's Summit, particularly the quaint monastic touches. As we entered the grounds we spied, just off to the right, a little pond ringed by pine trees; in the back of the main building stood a well-maintained baseball field and a functional basketball court. Off to the left were a barn and a nondescript building where some of the priests and all of the brothers lived. The main unit, which housed the dormitories, the classrooms, the refectory, and the administrative offices, was a conventional ecclesiastical structure, vaguely Mediterranean in style, with a bell tower at its apex. It was a nice spread the Maryknolls had, a haven from the world of Mammon, but I was already beginning to realize that the world of Mammon was in my blood, that rustic charm made me queasy.

Aunt Cassie stayed most of the afternoon. I'd never been anywhere near as close to her as I was to her husband, Jerry, who, like most nattily dressed men, was much more likely to spread his money around. But I made sure to kiss her goodbye when she left, because a fixture of family mythology was the time my father—her brother—refused to kiss her at the 30th Street train station the day he shipped out for the South Pacific in 1943. He'd given her the high hat, or so he later claimed, because he hadn't wanted to be embarrassed in front of his friends. Aunt Cassie never forgave him for that slight, and he himself never stopped ruing his caddishness that day, for if he had been killed in action, this icy adieu at 30th Street Station would have been her very last memory of him. It was odd that my father so often mentioned this incident, because he was not an especially affectionate person, nor was she.

After Aunt Cassie left, I began my new life. Many of my classmates were already suffering from homesickness; some were actually in tears. The priests told us that the surest antidote for homesickness was sports. The most persuasive of them was Morgan J. Vittengl, a stocky, striking-looking fellow who resembled the actor who would betray Clint Eastwood in *The Outlaw Josey Wales,* a film that had not yet been made. Vittengl, who taught European history with considerable style but little insight, promptly organized a game of five-on-five basketball on the courts that lay slumbering in the shadow of the bell tower. I had never met anyone named Morgan prior to this, and certainly not a man of the cloth; every priest I'd come across up until then was named Patrick or Michael or Vincent or Joseph (gaudy Hibernian names like Brendan and Sean came later, when the Irish had enough money to move to the suburbs and send their kids to private schools and could afford to be more blatantly ethnic). To this day Morgan J. Vittengl strikes me as a jaw-droppingly suave handle—more like a nom de guerre—a name that might easily have belonged to a swashbuckling adjutant gallivanting through the swamps of Ole Virginny with Jeb Stuart himself.

It was priests against babes in the woods that afternoon—again, Morgan's suggestion. I did not know how to play basketball at the time, having spent my entire childhood working in retail, and had never gotten any pointers from my father, whose attitude toward the sport was one of unalloyed revulsion. Father Vittengl was an ursine, territorial type, and he and his fellow servants of the Lord pounded the stuffing out of us. They boxed us out with their massive buttocks, smacked and tripped us as we dashed downcourt, smashed our pansy jump shots back into our faces, and fouled us at will. I was not sure at the time if any of these missionaries had ever had their fingernails torn out by the godless Red Chinese, or had their eyes kept pried wide open with bamboo splints for ninety-six hours straight by bloodthirsty Mau Maus, or had their guts spilled onto the sands of Corregidor by bayonet-toting minions of the Empire of the Sun rehearsing for the Bataan Death March. But there was clearly something about fresh-faced young boys with full sets of appendages that stuck in their manly craws, because they were certainly in a cantankerous mood that day. They must have beaten us pale, slack-jawed neophytes about 87–13. That really improved things on the homesickness front.

The next day school began, and we all settled into a rigid daily routine: early-morning mass, classes, lunch, more classes, several hours of manual labor, a few hours of sport, dinner, study hall, evening chapel, bedtime. On Sunday afternoons, we were allowed to vacate the premises for four hours; most of us wandered into Clark's Green or Chinchilla to purchase records or books. Books had to be submitted for review to the rector or one of his assistants, who examined them carefully, eyes peeled for Satan's wily input. If nothing offensive was found within, the freshly purchased reading material was stamped APPROVED BY THE RECTOR. Books that were not approved were confiscated and destroyed. Anything pertaining to war or diplomacy or nuclear devastation was acceptable; anything mentioning lingerie was not. My collection included a few trashy westerns with names like *Barranca!* and *Forced March to Loon Creek,* popular classics like *The Rise and Fall of the Third Reich,* and the madcap right-wing screed *None Dare Call It Treason,* which my uncle Jerry had given me. This legendary volume—the lunatic's bedside companion in the early 1960s—pilloried gullible Americans for ignoring the threat posed by the heathen Russkies, the atheistic Red Chinese, the Christ-hating Cubans, and the Democratic Party. I read the book to be nice to my uncle, who may have been a member of the Reds-under-the-beds John Birch Society at the time, but *Forced March to Loon Creek* was a lot more fun.

By the time I entered the seminary, my family had escaped from the housing project. Because both my parents were now working—at least for a while—we felt that we were moving up in the world as a family unit. But occasionally I would be reminded that the trajectory of our ascent was not uniformly vertical; on two separate occasions I was taken aside after dinner and told by the bursar that the checks my parents had sent me had bounced. Apprising me of this in hush-hush, conspiratorial tones, he conveyed the impression that Mom and Dad had just purloined the emerald-encrusted scepter from the tomb of Sargon II. The checks were for $5 apiece. My parents would never send cash through the mail, because they viewed all postal workers as confederates of Ali Baba. By sending a check, they were perhaps also expressing a desperate hope that by the time I cashed it, there might be enough money in the bank to cover it. More often than not, there wasn't. This left me out of pocket for the next ten days or so, until another check arrived. Obviously, we were not yet out of the woods.

After the euphoria of flight from my father's necropolis wore off, I began to examine the situation in which I now found myself. It would be going too far to describe my emotional state as one of homesickness, as I certainly did not pine for my home per se. But I did miss my city and my neighborhood, as I was now stranded in the boonies. Previously, I had defined myself as Catholic, white, male, working class, Irish American. Nobody I knew back home harped on the fact that we were Irish Americans, because everyone in my social circle was Irish American, or acted like it. Self-conceptualization was never a problem: We told great stories, we had an odd, unsetting sense of humor, we were fiercely devoted to our mothers without actually enjoying their company, we wished our fathers were dead, we spent most of our lives being depressed, we drank ourselves to early graves, we were Irish. And there were a lot of us. We were not the fish; we were the water. But now, left to my own devices in the wilds of northeastern Pennsylvania, I realized that what I really was, was an urbanite.

Most of my classmates in the seminary were not. From the outset, it was possible to detect a deep cultural schism that bifurcated the school. There were ninety-three students in all, about equally divided between big-city kids and rubes, many of whom came from farcical places like Mingo Junction, Ohio, and Fair Haven, Michigan. The big-city kids liked to smoke, listen to rock 'n' roll, smuggle in banned books, play sports, and manufacture any excuse to get off campus. The rubes liked to help Brother Eric slaughter cows. Few of my classmates seemed particularly interested in religion; they were never devout in the way Saint John Bosco, or the saint I had mistaken him for, was.

To this day, I have no idea what most of us were doing there. Some were innocent bystanders press-ganged into the priesthood by overly devout parents. This was definitely true of the handful of shanghaied Hispanics enrolled in the school. While many of the rubes were clearly lost souls looking for high adventure, country bumpkins duped into thinking they could find it a few miles outside Scranton, Pennsylvania, a substantial portion of the student body consisted of those sorts of tough, mean, ambitious Irish and Italian youngsters who have always swelled the clergy's ranks without conveying any discernible aura of saintliness or compassion for one's fellow man. A handful—the ones who immediately signed up for roles in the school production of *Twelve Angry Men*—were either gay or veering in that general direction. And a fair number of the students were exactly like me, scrawny adolescents with fathers who didn't like them. We were the ones who viewed the Church primarily as an escape hatch from reality.

Years later, I would read a novel called *The Dark* by the very capable Irish writer John McGahern. The hero is a young boy who enters the seminary to get away from the depredations of his sadistic, dysfunctional father, only to find that the Church is not much of an upgrade. As McGahern makes clear, this standard-issue CV is a cliché among the Irish. You become a priest, or you become a cop, or you become a criminal. But you do it to escape from a drunk, not because you genuinely seek to lay smooth the path of the Lord. Willa Cather once said that there are only a handful of story lines in all of human existence, yet everyone acts as if his or hers is unique. Only later in life do we learn that many others have trod an identical path, that our lives are largely generic.

Shortly after I arrived in Clark's Summit, the Phillies began the most startling collapse in the history of baseball. Considered no more than a so-so team coming out of spring training, the Phils enjoyed a Cinderella season, taking over first place on July 16 and remaining atop the standings until the final week in September. The Quaker City, whose largely working-class population was still reeling from John F. Kennedy's assassination the previous November, literally quaked with joy. Most of the city, anyway: Down in North Philly, in the slums that ringed Connie Mack Stadium, people were not having a Cinderella season. One sweltering June evening, riots erupted.

Because of the riots, because of the city's dismal self-image, because of JFK, the Phillies' magical season assumed a symbolic heft far beyond the events that transpired on the playing field. But as was so often the case in this luckless metropolis, the fairy tale would not have a happy ending; the team's miraculous performance from the beginning of April until late in September was merely a prelude to disaster. Two weeks before reaching their first World Series since 1950 and only the third Fall Classic in their macabre eighty-one-year history, the hometown heroes boasted a seemingly insurmountable six-and-a-half-game lead over their closest rivals, the St. Louis Cardinals, with just twelve games to play. Then, unbelievably, they managed to lose ten straight games and the pennant. The horrific streak ended on the next-to-last day of the season, when they beat the Cincinnati Reds, as they did the following day. But it was all for naught: The Cardinals, after dropping the first two games in New York, set down the puny Mets 11–5 on Sunday and won the pennant by a single game. The Cardinals went on to win the World Series, besting the Yankees in a seven-game slugfest few remember, because to sports fans the words "Nineteen sixty-four" are synonymous not with the Cardinals' unlikely come-from-behind triumph but with the Phillies' epochal meltdown.

Throughout their collapse, my mother would send me two-day-old newspaper clippings chronicling the team's latest misadventures. Even though I already knew what had transpired in these games, I devoured every word, perhaps hoping that if I pored over them long enough, Chico Ruiz would not steal home in a 1–0 Reds victory and manager Gene Mauch would reconsider his decision to start his ace pitchers Jim Bunning and Chris Short on two days' rest, thereby wrecking their arms. Watching the Phils blow the pennant was the worst thing that would ever happen to me in my life as a sports fan; nothing ever took the disappointment away. It was a title the Phils hadn't expected, and didn't really deserve, but as it was right there within our grasp, the city felt that its guts had been ripped out when victory was torn away from us. As the well-traveled backup catcher Gus Triandos whispered tearfully moments after the season ended, "Some guys want to guzzle the champagne. I only wanted a sip."

No sipping this time out. The Phillies were not going to the Fall Classic; matinee idol Johnny Callison, the club's cannon-armed right fielder, was not going to be the Most Valuable Player; and I was now beginning to harbor vague suspicions that God might not be looking out for my best interests. The champagne would remain on ice for another sixteen years until the Phils finally did win the first championship in their long, stomach-turning history. But not even that could erase the heartbreak of 1964, an anguish I could share with no one at the time because, inexplicably, given that we found ourselves in the Keystone State, I was the only native of Philadelphia. Throughout the Phillies' meltdown, fully aware that I had spent much of the past summer waving cars onto Len's parking lot right down the street from Connie Mack Stadium, my new classmates never stopped reminding me what a massive tank job was taking place 125 miles to the south. This was not very Christian of them. Of course, in the grand scheme of things, I should have realized even then that none of this truly mattered. But if none of it mattered, why did I feel so bad?

All the normal rites of passage occurred in the seminary. I began to smoke the demon weed. I took up the guitar and, like many guitarists, quickly became as proficient on the instrument as I was ever likely to get. I added a full six inches to my height. I learned to play basketball, partly because my father hated it but mostly because it took my mind off baseball. Overnight, my hair went from being completely straight to being an unruly mess, and while this doubtless has a perfectly logical genetic explanation, I prefer to think that overhearing one too many anecdotes about massacres in the Belgian Congo may have been responsible for this sudden follicular eruption. From that point on, I made sure that my hair was always cut short, because Maryknolls equated wavy hair with unkempt hair, and unkempt hair connoted contempt for authority, a deplorable need for attention, and perhaps even a seditious temperament.

Now fourteen, I started to think about girls in a way I had not before, certainly not the way I had thought about them when I first set up that makeshift bedroom tabernacle so many years earlier. Girl-watching could be done only from afar, as the seminary was virtually monochromatic, genderwise. The only women with whom we had any regular

contact were the cabal of French-Canadian nuns who did all the cooking and mending and washing for the priests but spoke no English. They
belonged to an obscure order that did its recruiting in the most forlorn
corners of rural Canada, and they served the same function as those
tiny birds that hitch a ride on the snouts of rhinos, removing vexatious
lice in exchange for protection from predators.

In recognition of their astounding self-abnegation—performing menial
tasks for clergymen with whom they could not even communicate—the
nuns were presumably assured a place in the Kingdom of Heaven. They
were forever smiling, and a bit on the chirpy side, but what I remember
most about them was that, even by the doleful standards of pulchritude one
tends to associate with women who have taken the veil, they were pretty
hard to look at.

I cannot say for sure how well they fared in the cognate realms of
laundry and dry cleaning, nor what their seamstress skills may have
amounted to; but turned loose in the kitchen, they were hell on wheels.
The meals they served up were so hair-raising—charred potatoes, cal-
cified string beans, hamburgers redolent of death—that they made me
pine for my mother's seventh-rate but not explicitly life-threatening
cooking. The only thing they got right was baking bread, which was so
crusty and sweet that some of us would sneak down and filch a few slices
when they were not looking, even though we risked severe reprisals if
we were caught. These slices tasted delicious when the bread was hot
and fresh and right out of the oven but had no taste at all the next day
when distributed for meals, by which time the individual loaves were
solid enough to pinch-hit with. The nuns, so it would appear, had been
planted in our midst to toughen up our intestines and prepare us for
toiling in foreign climes, where we could expect even less agreeable
food. Their approach to cuisine was overtly recriminatory; they were
not so much bunglers as *saboteuses*. They swept into a room full of meat,
fruits, and vegetables and made sure that no one came out happy. The
rustic Canucks of marriageable age they'd left behind could not have
been sorry to see them go.

The only other females we ever saw were girls from a nearby reform
school. Even from a distance, they looked less errant than pestiliential,

not like naughty girls who needed to be grounded but like molls who needed to be executed. No more than a handful of my classmates at the Venard grew up to be priests, but I am sure some of the girls from the reform school grew up to be criminals. In its stated objective, neither institution was terribly successful.

I became much more intrepid during this period, sneaking off campus during recreation period one afternoon and wending my way down the hill to a W. T. Grant's department store in amorphous Chinchilla, where I bought a copy of the Beatles' 45 "Eight Days a Week." This earned me the gratitude, if not the respect, of the handful of upperclassmen who did not view the Beatles as a threat to Christian values. The junior and senior classes, mostly effete, anglophobe traditionalists, took the position that folk music (Peter, Paul and Mary, Odetta, Pete Seeger, the Kingston Trio, the New Christy Minstrels) was a force for social good, while rock 'n' roll was a depraved art form that celebrated carnal lust. Underclassmen made no attempt to challenge this view, conceding that folk music boasted infinitely more intellectual content than rock 'n' roll. But folk music's merits notwithstanding, we preferred the harsher, less moral, less cerebral genre epitomized by the Beatles, the Kinks, and the Rolling Stones, not only because it was a socially acceptable way of thumbing our noses at our elders but because it did not involve the banjo.

I learned the art of diplomacy in the seminary. I was compassionate toward a boy who was afraid to let anyone in the locker room see what he believed to be a grievously undersized penis—a gallant gesture on my part, considering how mercilessly he ridiculed my sad, arcless jump shot when we were out on the basketball court. I was less compassionate toward a boy who refused to bathe. But in neither case did my compassion extend to actually intervening when the upperclassmen lowered their sights on the two unfortunates. In the first instance, they ripped the towel away from the young man's hips, causing him to erupt in tears, though in the long run the assault was probably good for him, as it immediately became clear that his penis was no more undersized than most. The upperclassmen's ministrations were less well received by the boy who refused to bathe, a Rust Belt stalwart who literally stank to high heaven. Though many felt that he was only getting what he had coming to him, this did not make his howls of protest any less searing when a gang of seminarians overpowered him, stripped him naked, forced him into an industrial-sized sink, and scrubbed him down with a bath brush. This was painful and humiliating; they enjoyed it and he didn't. He felt betrayed that none of us had defended him, and even though he smelled like rancid cheese, he was right to feel that way. We were supposed to be Soldiers of Christ, and Christ would not have abandoned even the smelliest adherent in his hour of need.

The priests didn't always behave so well, either. The first weekend of every month was brightened by Visitation Sunday, when parents and relatives were free to enter campus at one in the afternoon and stay until five. They were also allowed to take us off the grounds to a restaurant or a department store if they liked, but because it was usually my mother who came to visit, and because my mother did not drive, and because we didn't have a car anyway, the two of us generally spent the afternoon wandering around the seminary. I recall no details about her visits, other than that she made them, which my father did not. He never visited the seminary the entire time I was there, a warm-up for never visiting the university I would attend four years later, not even on the day I became the first person on his side of the family to graduate from college.

Visitors could bring in as much food as they liked; the cargo was then carried by students to their assigned table in the refectory. Here, six of us broke bread together three times a day. Seating arrangements changed each month, but I used my influence with a couple of upperclassmen to get myself assigned to the same table as the Italians, because they had the best food. Though I had been raised to mistrust, if not actually abhor, Italians, there was no denying that the cuisine favored by this reputedly shifty ethnic group had ours beaten hands down. So I stopped hating them at an early age, deciding to hate Episcopalians instead. One boy stands out in memory: Every month his parents brought him huge aluminum trays overflowing with lasagna, prosciutto, capicola, foot-long salamis. I did not especially care for the boy, who hailed from New York; we did not have much in common. But I sure liked his mom's cooking. Meanwhile, my mother would turn up with her statutory, store-bought pineapple cheesecake. Until I went away to the seminary, I honestly believed that the pineapple cheesecake was the most sublime of mankind's wondrous inventions and also assumed that it was the most universally revered. Now I learned otherwise.

After our visitors left, we were allowed to polish off as much of our bountiful harvest as we liked, with the proviso that at the end of the meal, the cornucopia of delights would be commandeered, mixed in with the booty amassed from all the other tables, and redistributed to the entire student body throughout the coming week. My lifelong aversion to socialism probably dates from this moment. The lasagna, the sausages, the prosciutto, the brownies et al. rarely reappeared on the seminarians' tables; more often than not, they surfaced the next night on the table at the front of the refectory, where the priests sat. The salamis, the brownies, the capicola sat up there on the head table, taunting us, teasing us, serving as cruel, tantalizing symbols of our impotence before our masters. This was exactly the way I imagined things happened in Outer Mongolia and Cuba and Albania and the Ukraine: The commissars promised the masses that the fruits of their labors would be pooled together and redistributed so that everyone got their fair share, but instead things always ended up with the Central Planning Commission stealing all the pastries.

Realizing that we were being royally screwed, some of the seminarians told their parents to bring less food. Not the Italians. Every Visitation Sunday, I would sit there with my olive-skinned *amici* after our parents had left, and we would force-feed ourselves everything in sight. Down our adolescent throats we would jam hot sausages, fettuccine drowning in seven cheeses, potato gnocchi, spinach ravioli, fresh cannolis, and even Mom's pineapple cheesecake, consuming these delights in no particular order. Like detainees in Stalag 17, we were not going to let our treasures fall into the hands of the enemy; we'd rather puke up our guts for three days running. Admittedly, walnut-laden brownies and overcooked Genoa salami served with a heaping portion of greasy pineapple cheesecake—all washed down with a vatload of RC Cola—made a disgusting combination. But if self-induced nausea was the only way we could keep our rightful property out of the mouths of the clergy, then nausea it would be.

One youth from the Buckeye State was even more daring than the rest of us; he used to hide his foot-long salamis in his closet—inside his shoes—doling out a slice at a time to bunkmates, both to keep us happy and to keep us quiet. Someone must have ratted him out, though, for one spring evening, our hall monitor came sweeping through the dorm room on a surprise inspection. This was unfortunate timing, because at that moment we were all clustered around a contraband transistor radio listening for reports from the second Sonny Liston–Muhammad Ali fight, which was taking place in Lewiston, Maine. As soon as the priest flicked on the lights, we shut off the radio and plunged beneath our covers. The priest found the stash—I always suspected that the Lord of the Sty had informed on the Boy with the Golden Salami, though this may have been more because of the obvious olfactory link between the two than because of any clear-cut evidence of betrayal—and by the time we turned the radio back on, the one-minute-forty-two-second fight was over. We were not at all happy about this. Shortly after that, the boy who never bathed got held down for his brutal scrubbing.

Almost no one who passed through the Maryknoll Junior Seminary between 1964 and 1966 became a priest; the institution was padlocked in 1967 and sold to the Baptists a few years later. This is not surprising. The decline of the Catholic Church in America had begun in the early 1960s, when the nation was torn apart by political, racial, generational, and cultural conflict. The Church was being challenged on all fronts—it was reactionary, it was insensitive, it was too dependent on hoary ritual and archaic mumbo jumbo, it was not sufficiently consumer oriented—and in an attempt to short-circuit these criticisms, a bevy of mutton-headed attempts at modernization was put into place. One was deep-sixing the Latin Mass; another was deemphasizing the organ in favor of the guitar; a third was the introduction of a sinister camaraderie among parishioners, manifested in compulsory handshakes and prefabricated words of mandatory cheer. In the essay I had written the previous year, the prize-winning composition whose admonitions the Vatican had inexplicably chosen to ignore, I had singled out the repudiation of the Latin Vulgate as an innovation that would destroy the Church in America; had I written the same essay just a few years later, I would have thrown in a few choice words about the threat posed to Catholics everywhere by the introduction of folk masses. In my opinion, no institution could long survive a rupture from its ancestral cultural moorings; by encouraging feeble young clerics to array themselves against the forces of Lucifer armed only with the instruments of cabaret, the Church was attempting to achieve with the hootenanny what it could no longer achieve through faith. In these assumptions, I was proven woefully prescient.

Despite the *seismic events* that were *rocking* the Church to *its very foundations* in that *tumultuous era*—yes, this is the way people used to talk in the 1960s, especially on television—more than a few of us might have persevered and become priests if only the men who ran the seminary had tried to meet us halfway. They did not. In fairness to them, they could not. Their lives had been too hard and, in some cases, too long, and it clearly irked them that ours had not. They were missionaries, not nursemaids. Their courage and travails notwithstanding, the men who ran the seminary made poor guiding lights for boys of our age, particularly in that era. If learning to be like them was what was required to edify the heathen, then the heathen was probably going to remain unedified.

The Maryknolls did not fail me, however; I failed them. From the day I started my new life in Clark's Summit, I knew I would soon be ending it. The seminary was, for all intents and purposes, military school for soldiers of Christ. Life in small-town America struck me as electrifyingly dopey, and by this juncture I was starting to realize that I had probably never had a vocation in the first place. One problem was my deteriorating relationship with God. A sine qua non for success in the spiritual realm was faith: In order to be a good priest, you had to believe in God. But my faith in God had never extended much further than lack of faith in my father. God was an affable abstraction; my father was not. To me, God was a talisman, a rabbit's foot, a good-luck charm useful in combating evil spirits. But He was never immanent or real in the sense that I could feel His radiance enveloping me. I had less trouble believing in the devil, who kept bouncing around from Berlin to Peking to Moscow. Even in college, where rehearsed contempt for organized religion was de rigueur, I could never bring myself to dislike God in the way that atheists did, pillorying Him with a virulence so out of proportion to His alleged failings that the denunciations themselves seemed to confirm His existence. I never hated God; I simply never felt His presence. All those years I had been serving mass in my bedroom and acting out scenes from *The Lives of the Saints,* I had told myself that rock-solid proof of God's existence would one day manifest itself to me, though perhaps not in Philadelphia. This never happened. It was exactly like rooting for the Eagles: No matter how much I wanted to believe that they would one day win the Super Bowl, I never really felt that they had it in them.

Things might have turned out differently had the faculty included a few priests who combined intelligence and piety with a bit of pizzazz. It did not. Father Casey, the rector presiding over the seminary, was a case in point. He was the classic, no-nonsense tough guy, short on warmth and humor, with the physical appearance of a leg-breaker Dutch Schultz might have sent over to collect from an obstinate bookie after Gallant Knave finished a surprising third in the Preakness. Still only in his thirties, but creating the impression that he'd been around the block a few times, Father Casey made no effort to conceal the disdain he felt for us. His face perpetually wore a malignant smile; he resembled Jack Palance in *Shane,* or perhaps a calculating spider awaiting a meal he planned to enjoy immensely. When we gathered together in the assembly room late every Saturday afternoon for his weekly review, he would spend about fifteen minutes updating us on how useless we were, as if it had somehow slipped our minds. The whole time he was talking, he would fiddle around with the sleeves of his cassock and play with the bridge of his Clark Kent eyeglasses, as if he was getting ready to slug somebody. We were all afraid of him, not because we feared physical violence, which was never threatened, much less meted out, but because there was something about his blast-furnace scorn that made us feel that we would never be men. Those of us who had contemptuous, condescending fathers now realized that we had jumped out of the frying pan into the fire. There was nothing soft or sentimental about Father Casey; personality-wise, he bore as much resemblance to the ingratiating, compassionate Lamb of God as Erwin Rommel. Putting a man like that in charge of boys struck me as hopelessly counterproductive, especially when you were trying to attract those boys to a profession where staffing problems was becoming an increasingly serious issue. Cracking a smile just to lighten the mood every now and then wouldn't have hurt; for Christ's sake, we were only kids. All of this suggested that, however strong its hiring record over the previous 19½ centuries, the Church was now in a bit of a slump.

The only priest I both liked and admired was Father Ratermann, a crotchety varmint who taught Latin and Greek and moderated the speech club and the debating society. Of indeterminate age, Father Ratermann was a tall, rail-thin curmudgeon who had a slight hitch in his step, seemed to be speaking out of the side of his mouth even when he wasn't, and squinted. He had served seven years as a missionary in Guatemala, and looked like he had missed a few meals out there, as if all those tortillas and maize had not agreed with him. He looked like the brainy fellow in the IRA movie who, though he does not actually kill the informer, makes the phone call to the provos pinpointing his whereabouts. He was gently abrasive, caustic, fun to be around. A few other priests didn't mind us; he actually seemed to like us. He encouraged me to read Martial and Juvenal, not just Caesar's *Gallic War*; he was the first person in my life to describe me as a cynic, an observation I may have incorrectly interpreted as praise. Very few of the students could understand his sly sense of humor, certainly none of the plowboys. Unlike most of his colleagues, he was cerebral, intellectually adventurous, and did not give the impression of being especially deferential toward his superiors. He looked about as much like a reaper of wheat or a harvester of papayas as Kublai Khan. With an intellect and a sense of humor like his, he should have been a Jesuit; what he was doing in the Maryknolls was beyond me. It was thus a bittersweet irony that the only Maryknoll who ever inspired me in any way is the one that inspired me to leave the Maryknolls.

From the purely pedagogical standpoint, amazingly enough, the seminary turned out to be much less stultifying than I had expected. Though Father Ratermann was the only four-star standout, Father Vittengl was certainly a solid professional, and most of our teachers were competent at the very least and, in some instances, enlightening. The only exception was Father Trettel, the retiring little priest who taught theology. All along, as I had been preparing to enter the seminary, I was aware that missionary orders did not place much emphasis on scholarship. So I was not surprised that the priest assigned to teach us the subtlest, most arcane elements of Church doctrine was a bit of a chucklehead. A country bumpkin, he had been shipped off to the junior seminary in all likelihood because he could never learn the Swahili word for Sanhedrin and was thus incapable of explaining the concept of transubstantiation to closed-minded Third World cannibals. Those in the know theorized that Father Trettel had been assigned to the freshman class with the express purpose of instilling humility in us. But at the same time, his inept pedagogical technique, his earthy malapropisms, and his hysterically amusing attempts to navigate from the beginning of a sentence to the end provided a strange brand of backhanded encouragement to the entire student body. His very existence seemed to be the Maryknolls' way of saying: "If this guy could get himself ordained, anyone can. You boys are in like Flynn."

Father Trettel was a thoroughly nice man, a gentle soul without an ounce of malice in him, but because he was not especially bright, he could make neither heads nor tails of the scriptures and had no more idea than a budgerigar why Pontius Pilate was so supine in the face of the ostensibly powerless Pharisees or why Origen of Alexandria castrated himself. Because of this, he frequently found himself mired in doctrinal quagmires from which he could not extricate himself. He would start off by trying to explain the concept of eternity—when, for instance, did it start?—only to lose his train of thought. Or he would forget the narrow, technical definition of "simony," the cryptic transgression against the law of God that had provided me with so many hours of entertainment as a child and remains to this day the sin I would most enjoy committing if time and circumstances permitted. He was also weak on such subjects as how Jesus managed to surgically reattach the severed ear of the high priest's servant on the Mount of Olives on Holy Thursday without impressing His captors and could not readily recall either the advice the Witch of Endor offered to Saul or whether he had taken it.

One afternoon, Father Trettel informed us that Moses had not led the Israelites across the Red Sea, eight miles wide and a thousand feet deep at its narrowest point, but rather across the Reed Sea, a series of nearby marshes. This was back in 1965, when the Church was making a frantic—albeit belated—attempt to reconcile the scriptures with science, to tone down any discussion of burning bushes or self-levitating divinities or descending tongues of flame, to deemphasize the necromantic overtones to Christ's raising of Lazarus, to stop concealing the literal truth of these events beneath the all-encompassing cloak of metaphor. By advancing the clever but somewhat loopy Reed Sea explanation for the flight of the Israelites—a theory he had not devised himself but had read somewhere—Father Trettel was attempting to demythologize one of the least plausible events in biblical history. In effect, he was laying the blame for three thousand years of nonstop confusion at the feet of shoddy translators, who, in another context, might have confused the Danube with the Dunube or the Mississippi with the Mippississi.

I shall never forget the look of surrender on Father Trettel's face when one of the more persnickety students raised his hand and pointed out that the name Red Sea could not possibly be confused with Reed Sea, because the Bible had been written in Greek or Aramaic or Hebrew or Yiddish or Coptic, meaning that the Red-Reed mix-up would have had no opportunity to come into play. Anyway, if Moses and the Israelites could so easily cross the Reed Sea marshes on foot, what would have prevented Pharaoh's army from doing exactly the same? Father Trettel made a halfhearted attempt to convince us that this admittedly perplexing wordplay might parallel an identical case of mistaken aquatic identity in these other languages, but he was at a loss to explain away the fatal submersion of the entire Egyptian army in what appeared to be an innocuous swamp. Vanquished, he merely gazed off into the distance, the way Ronald Reagan so often did toward the very end of his presidency, and smiled.

"Well, it all gets very confusing back there in history," he said.

Father Trettel had another ceremonial function, also designed to teach us the virtue of humility. Catholics are not allowed to receive the Holy Eucharist while in a state of mortal sin; one of the most serious offenses a soldier of Christ can commit, it can lead to excommunication, an eternity in Hell, death, or blindness. Because all ninety-three of us were soldiers of Christ, it was impossible for us to attend mass in the morning and not receive Holy Communion, because that would indicate that we were guilty of having committed some mortal sin we had not yet owned up to. Realistically, the only mortal sins seminarians were capable of committing on a day-in, day-out basis were "impure thoughts" and "impure deeds," as there was nothing worth stealing and very little worth coveting on campus grounds. "Impure thoughts" and "impure deeds" were Church-sanctioned euphemisms for "fantasizing about girls, usually scantily clad," and "masturbation." If you did not receive Holy Communion each and every morning, it could mean but one thing: You had been physically desecrating the temple of the Lord (or at least one section of the temple) in bed under cover of darkness the night before. True, it was theoretically possible to be guilty of the sins of sloth or envy, or to have plotted the rector's death, but no one would have believed anyone who tried using such far-fetched, recondite excuses to explain why he had forgone receiving the body and blood of Christ.

Complicating matters was the fact that confession was held every evening immediately after dinner and every morning immediately before mass. This meant there was never any reason not to receive Communion. Evening confessions were held in the chapel, morning confessions in a tiny office directly adjoining it. Evening sessions were lightly attended: Any seminarian who had already made up his mind to masturbate later that night would be wasting his time going to confession a few hours earlier, as he would have to come right back for another breast-baring the following morning. On the other hand, no one wanted to be seen lining up outside the office for confession every single morning, because then everyone could see that the penitent was an unreconstructed sex maniac. None of us honestly believed that God would condemn us to an eternity in Hell for sloth or envy or even gluttony, but we were concerned that masturbation might do the trick, because masturbation involved the penis, and the penis was the Scourge of Christ.

Until my arrival in the seminary, I had never had any objections to the sacrament of confession, because in the churches I attended as a child, Father Confessor was always seated behind a grate, concealed inside a dark booth, making it impossible for him to identify the transgressor. Though it was mortifying to admit to impure deeds the first time I went to confession, this shame quickly passed, as I soon realized that priests had heard it all before and nothing shocked them. Like most boys, I tried to disguise my voice and sound like an Okinawan stevedore when I catalogued my sins; I also got into the habit of shaving a few digits off the weekly carnal tally, confessing to ten impure thoughts and three impure deeds since my last confession a week earlier, when the actual grand total was more like one hundred and fifty. Confessors rarely upbraided us for these rote sins of the flesh; they seemed to accept that it was all part of growing up. They merely advised us to avoid "proximate occasions of sin"—any place girls might turn up—and to try to think about the Blessed Mother swaddling the Baby Jesus whenever we caught a glimpse of a girl's underwear or spied a photo of Marilyn Monroe busting out of her nightie. I tried to implement these cerebrally prophylactic gambits many times, but they never worked.

It was a shock to all of us when we arrived at the seminary and discovered that confessions would not be held in private booths, the way they were back home, but in a brightly lit room, with Father Confessor ensconced in an armchair with his head turned slightly away from us, his hand cupping his eyes, like a child counting to ten before declaring, "Ready or not, here I come!" Worse yet, Father Confessor was none other than Father Trettel. This meant that anytime a seminarian had been plundering the temple of the Lord the previous evening, he had to join the queue outside that make-do confessional with all the other perverts and wait for a chance to confess his sins to a teacher whose class he would be attending later that day. It would have been so much nicer if our confessor were the bursar or the dean of admissions or one of the other priests we rarely saw, but this was not seminary policy. We all lived in terror that the normally soft-spoken Father Trettel might suddenly whirl around and confront us when we admitted to our insatiable carnal appetites, crying out, "You committed *how many* impure deeds *how many times* since six o'clock last evening? What, are you going for the school record?"—and that he might say it loud enough that everyone standing outside could hear. I have always believed that Father Trettel's designation as our confessor was a deliberate ploy to reduce the number of smart-ass comments he got in class. A fourteen-year-old boy is far less likely to ridicule a simpleton when the simpleton is in possession of the fact that the boy manhandled himself eight separate times the previous evening, four times while fantasizing about Marilyn Monroe, four times while fantasizing about reform-school girls. And even the number eight might be a lowball figure.

Father Trettel was the only priest at the seminary who could accurately be described as slow on the draw. But, like many other clerical orders, the Maryknolls had an ancillary wing consisting of brothers. Brothers, by reputation, were hardworking holy men who had never been formally ordained as Christ's terrestrial ambassadors. Because of this, they were prohibited from performing such lofty clerical functions as celebrating mass, or hearing confessions, which necessitated making snap moral judgments. My father, who was much given to the gratuitously contrary defense of untenable positions, maintained that brothers were every bit the intellectual equals of priests but were so humble and self-abnegating, so convinced of their own unworthiness in the eyes of God, that they had forgone the prestige that attended members of the priestly class. None of us believed this. Brothers in our eyes were the liturgical equivalents of dentists; they didn't have the chops to crack the starting lineup. They were like the youngest sons in Mafia families who were handed no-show desk jobs at the Department of Public Works while their older brothers got to go out and actually kill people.

The brothers at the seminary were doled out the emphatically menial tasks of slaying cows, raising vegetables, plowing snow, repairing plumbing. They weren't particularly sociable, especially not to seminarians who thought they were superior to them, because in the world according to us, smarter meant better. The only seminarians whose company the brothers enjoyed were the plowboys from God's Country: bovine, standoffish lads who reveled in the aroma of manure and the fragrance of pigs' gonads. These were the boys many of us suspected would one day become brothers themselves, as soon as it had become obvious to their superiors that they lacked the skills needed to preach, teach, counsel, heal, or heap contumely upon unreconstructed Bolivian sodomites.

I did not divulge my flagging enthusiasm for the priesthood to anyone at school, and I certainly never mentioned it to my father when I went home for Thanksgiving and Christmas vacations. After eight years of ostentatious rehearsal for seminary life, a vocation was not something I could easily relinquish overnight. This situation called for finesse; it had to be handled with kid gloves. I would gut it out in the hinterland as long as possible, and with any luck I might survive until it was time to attend college. But there was no realistic possibility of my ever joining the clergy. This may have had less to do with loss of faith in God than loss of faith in northeastern Pennsylvania, where the laughs were few and far between. Unlike real-life high school, where students could amuse themselves by wrapping their parents' cars around telephone poles or falling to untimely deaths from ice-covered bridges while engaging in alcohol-fueled horseplay, nothing exciting ever happened at the seminary, in part because there were no slutty girls to blunt our judgment and goad us on to disaster. The year before, two sophomores had feigned rubella or scarlet fever so they could be sent to the infirmary, where they were caught in flagrante delicto and promptly expelled. Phone calls were made; parents were summoned; the boys vanished into the gloaming. The news of their concupiscent hijinks had come as a surprise to everyone concerned; the boys were very well liked and sorely missed. That was about as far as the conversation went.

It is impossible for the uninitiated to imagine how gingerly the subject of the love that dare not speak its name was treated back then; even though we all knew that a couple of priests who had a habit of smacking our bottoms were a bit forward, no one ever mentioned being molested, because no one ever was. The only time the subject ever came up was when the anecdote about the two frisky sophomores was revived, always with the observation that they had been apprehended in flagrante delicto. I never found out what in flagrante delicto meant in that case, whether the pair were merely jacking each other off or cuddling or smooching it up or perhaps engaging in something immeasurably less hygienic; I did not know at the time what to do with a girl, much less with a boy. Nobody ever got caught in flagrante delicto during my solitary year in the seminary, which was a great loss, as an excommunication-level offense like two boys giving each other clandestine blow jobs surely would have spiced things up considerably.

"Bored witless" was an apt description of my psychological condition that winter; I would literally do anything to escape the seminary grounds. I joined the speech team, even though I did not feel comfortable speaking in public, because I had nothing to say. I also joined the debate team, visiting high schools all over the Greater Scranton–Hazelton–Wilkes-Barre metropolitan area, facing off against a legion of pockmarked, bespectacled adolescent boys and pouty coeds shoehorned into taut sweaters, arguing with rehearsed vehemence that nuclear deterrence would not work because the Soviets were untrustworthy swine. Or, when it was time to switch sides and defend the nuclear-deterrence proposition, swearing on a stack of Bibles that it would work like a charm, for even the Russians occasionally behaved sensibly.

I was much more effective when arguing in the negative than when defending the affirmative, because the team on offense was allowed to be mean and dishonest, which played to my strengths, whereas the team on defense was expected to be honorable and scrupulously fair. My partner on the debate team was an intense, thoughtful, gifted speaker, and I was a decent debater myself, if a bit on the duplicitous side. But the other members of the team were a nervous boy who played the Henry Fonda role in the school production of *Twelve Angry Men* and a dithering sort who already seemed sixty-five years old. It did not help that the aspiring thespian stuttered when he got riled up, nor that he rapped on the table, schoolmarm style, in a censorious gesture later popularized by the testy, condescending British prime minister Margaret Thatcher. Whenever we went out on a debate, our team would finish second or third, dragged down by the unimpressive scores of our outgunned colleagues. I didn't care; I was only doing it to meet pouty girls in taut sweaters.

To maximize the amount of time devoted to off-campus escapades, I also took a job as timekeeper for the varsity basketball team, even though I had no more than a passing familiarity with the rules of the sport. Nervous, clueless, panicky, I made a mockery of everything that timekeepers have traditionally held dear to their hearts. I would stop the clock or press down on the buzzer, indicating a substitution or time-out, with no reason for doing so, as if I had succumbed to a surprise attack of Saint Vitus' dance. I had no idea what I was doing up there with my thumb planted squarely on that machine, and while it is true that my training on the device had been woefully inadequate—"Here, kid; keep time for us!"—that is no excuse for my failure to improve my skills. The officials hated me, as did the coaches, the players, and most of the spectators. Although we were a microscopic school and were not officially included in any league, we usually held our own against similarly tiny institutions, but when we played against squads from bigger schools, they fish-gutted us. We also played an exhibition against a boys' reformatory, where we not only got ripped to shreds by the future repeat offenders but—due to the obvious travel restrictions—had to play on their home court. My, did those strapping laddies ever enjoy the annual visit from the lithe and lanky seminarians.

No matter how deplorable my timekeeping skills, I continued to serve in that quasi-chronometric capacity, because nobody else wanted the job, and, as it reduced my campus confinement by roughly ten hours a week, I would never have abdicated that post without a fight. It did not matter to me how depressing the cataleptic backwaters we visited proved to be; the ugliest small city was infinitely preferable to the comeliest hamlet. One night, a bunch of us drove all the way up to Binghamton, New York, battling a driving rain that Noah himself would have found a bit excessive. It was a sixty-mile jaunt, and the whole time we were motoring along, we could see almost nothing in front of us. Just outside Binghamton, we hit a dog hard enough to kill it. We dragged the bloody carcass off to the side of the road, scattering innards all over the interstate, then resumed our trek to the abbatoir masquerading as a gymnasium, filled to the rafters with dyspeptic townies who had come out to support their team. Because the out-of-bounds area along the sidelines was only about two feet deep, we were forced to stand cheek-by-jowl with this neolithic crew throughout the game. I doubt if they were Catholics; for all I know, they may have been Empire State

Druids. We lost by forty points, the spectators despised us, and on top of everything, we had to drive back to the seminary at midnight in an even worse storm, keeping our eyes peeled for yet another frothing cur that might tempt fate by trampolining into the grillwork. I didn't care; it was still better than staying at the seminary. At least we got to see girls. Girls with the charm of Gorgons, but girls all the same.

Insensitive but by no means oblivious to the general mood of the academy, Father Casey and his staff realized that we all found life in Clark's Summit a bit on the sclerotic side. They chose an unconventional method for defusing the tension. One day the school held a raffle whose top prize was permission to go into Scranton for the day. The prize did not include bus fare or free transportation to Scranton; it consisted solely of *permission* to go there. It was like raffling off weekend passes to the Strait of Magellan. One of my friends won the prize and included me in a group of eight boys who made the pilgrimage into the brooding, pointless municipality. When we got there, there was nothing to do but freeze. We spent the whole day wandering around the exanimate downtown, drifting from one scuzzy store to the next, buying records we did not want and books we did not intend to read. If we had been ordinary high school boys instead of seminarians, we might have bribed a wino to buy us a bottle of cheap rotgut or hooked up with some ripe local colleens, if only for a bit of repartee and a glimpse of stocking. But we were seminarians, lofty-minded virgins prepping for sainthood, so the notion of indulging in that sort of saucy caper never even occurred to us.

Somewhere along the line, our doomed octet got separated. At the end of the afternoon, a couple of us missed the last bus to Clark's Summit, so we had to walk the eight miles back to campus, staggering along the side of the road for what seemed like days as night engulfed us and our stamina fled. We felt like idiots. We were sure we were going to die out there, unmourned and unloved, breathing our last on the shoulder of an inconsequential road that provided a direct link between Scranton and nowhere. As luck would have it, we did not die. We returned to the seminary too late for dinner and, in punishment for violating curfew, were forbidden to leave the grounds for the next month. Nobody bothered asking how our day in Scranton had worked out; they had a pretty good idea that it was not like an evening in Venice.

Because my existence up until then had been structured around a career in the Church, it was going to be difficult to extract myself from this situation and start a new life. I shared the news about my loss of faith with no one, not even my sisters, so no one suspected that I was preparing to leave the seminary as soon as a suitable pretext presented itself. When this might occur, I was in no position to say. In the end, I decided that I would simply allow events to take their course and let the chips fall where they may.

Events did take their course. One night shortly after Christmas, a bunch of my underclassman chums were fooling around in the auditorium, flailing away at the guitars, pounding on the drums. For reasons I have never understood, I seized a microphone and launched into an impersonation of Mick Jagger, who had not yet become internationally famous but was already displaying a somewhat camp disposition. The impression extended no further than puffing out my lips in simian fashion, and pointing at an imaginary audience in that limp-wristed manner Jagger so often would, as if he were Charles II proffering his hand to a cheeky commoner. It was a terrible impersonation but a great hit with my friends, who persuaded me to enter a talent contest that would be held at the seminary the following month. I had never before stepped onto a stage and had no desire to; nor at the time was I especially fond of the Rolling Stones. Peer pressure alone must have induced me to toss my hat into the ring.

Our makeshift band "practiced" every night for a month, miming the Stones' crackling rendition of Chuck Berry's "Around and Around." I suppose it was a nice way to pass the time, at least for them. The big night finally arrived. All the seminarians, all the priests, and all the brothers were in attendance that evening, not sure what to expect. The sisters stayed home, cooking inedible meals and praying in a bucolic, sixteenth-century French so impenetrable that not even Le Bon Dieu could have made heads or tails of it. I do not recall who preceded or followed us; I do have some hazy recollection of a couple of students warbling corn-pone folk songs with little passion or conviction and of a couple of boys delivering sententious speeches from time-honored plays. Even by the standards of a junior seminary that was training young men to be tillers of soil and planters of yams, the talent show was pretty thin on talent. At last it was my hooty ensemble's turn to perform. Nervous, anxious for this ordeal to be over, I meandered out on stage sporting a filthy sweatshirt and a silly wig and brandishing a pair of cheap maracas. A helpful assistant cued up "Around and Around" on a turntable backstage, and I launched into my impression as the four boys in my "band," all of whom had now turned distressingly meek, pretended to play their instruments. Twenty seconds into the song, the record skipped. We stopped, waited for the record to start again, then took another crack at it. The record skipped a second time, then a third, and finally we gave up. We could not have been on the stage more than ninety seconds—two minutes, tops.

We may have coaxed forth a few laughs that night, or at least a few smirks. I believe there may even have been a smattering of applause as we wrapped up our performance. There was no applause from Father Casey, however; he took in the performance with the rapture of a Savonarola. Our eyes briefly met as I descended from the stage, and I could see that he was not one bit amused by my tomfoolery. My impersonating the posturing, ridiculous Mick Jagger must have struck him as a poke in the eye, as conduct unbecoming a member in good standing of the Church Militant. Maryknoll missionaries were supposed to be tillers of soil and pullers of teeth and bringers of light and fishers of men. They were not supposed to be clowns. I am not sure Casey even knew who Mick Jagger was, but the damage had been done. From that night until the very end of the school year, Father Casey never said a word to me. But from that moment on, I knew I was a marked man. And so my career as a seminarian began to slouch its way toward its ignominious conclusion. I now knew that I would never be a priest; Casey knew that I would never be a priest; we only needed to put the finishing touches on my official exit from the Maryknoll community.

Here, I took a surprisingly hands-on role in orchestrating my future. Already known as a capable writer—no great accomplishment in this congress of poltroons—I was invited to guest-edit the student newspaper. It was a Maryknoll tradition to let freshmen put out the final issue of the paper, and this year my number had come up. Sharing this honor was a bright, sober chap, who four years later would resurface as my roommate in college. Not much of a student but every inch a patriot, Bill Beazley would join the Air Force Reserve Officer Training Corps at a time when making such a choice was by no means a popular one, going on to serve in Vietnam. He was a straight arrow in the seminary, he was a straight arrow in college, and for all I know, he may be a straight arrow today. I, on the other hand, was not.

Bill and I had no idea how to put out a newspaper. We knew that newspapers relied on news, but there was no news in the seminary. The paper was only four pages long, so we crammed it full of sports stories and articles entitled "Passion Reading Set for Holy Week" and "Farewell to Brother Eugene." Shortly before we shipped it to the printer, a "bazaar" was held at the seminary. There were games and music and refreshments and a Name That Hamster contest in which students paid a nickel for a chance to confer both a first and a last name on a lively white rodent. This was the Maryknoll idea of fun. At the end of the festivities, the first name was drawn from a jar; it proved to be Omahard. I never found out which of our classmates had scrawled this, much less what it meant. It sounded pastoral. The second name withdrawn from the jar was "Casey." Everyone thought this was terrifically entertaining, because whatever handle students may have suggested as a first name on their raffle tickets, they had all written "Casey" on the second, making some sort of derisive nomenclature inevitable. Bill and I must have found this impish ploy outrageously amusing, not to mention newsworthy, because we chose the hamster-naming event as the lead story in our edition of the newspaper, with a photo of the feisty rodent peering out from beneath the headline OMAHARD CASEY RIDES AGAIN!

Via intermediaries, Bill and I soon learned that neither our overall story sense nor our headline-writing skills had found favor with the powers that be. The headline was suppressed, and replaced with the less incendiary FRESHMEN ARE HOSTS AT SUCCESSFUL BAZAAR. No one said anything specifically menacing to me, but I knew I had committed a fatal faux pas. A month later, each and every student was invited in to

chat with Father Casey and review his progress toward the goal of ordination. Bill was in and out of the rector's office quickly; he returned
the next year, though by the time his seminary years were over, he, too,
had ceased to believe that he had a vocation. My conversation was even
briefer. I entered the office and sat down as Father Casey stared at me
with the sort of disdain that, even by his standards, seemed just a smidgen frosty. We chatted a few minutes, and then he said, "You weren't
thinking of coming back here next year, were you, Queenan?"

"No, Father, I wasn't."

"Good luck, then."

And so my career as a seminarian came to an end.

Now it only remained to break the news to my family. This proved much
less difficult than I had expected. Returning home for summer vacation, I went back to work for Len, played baseball, started a rock band,
bided my time. Not until the third week in August did I work up the
nerve to tell my mother that I had no plans to return to the seminary.
She relayed this decision to my father. I suppressed the information that
I had not actually been invited back to Clark's Summit for my sophomore year, though I think my mother may have received some paperwork to that effect. Certainly, the uncharacteristic silence from my old
recruiter friend and erstwhile career counselor, who had nurtured my
dreams throughout grade school, was something of a giveaway. To all
intents and purposes, without officially being expelled from the seminary, I had been cut from the team.

I expected this news to be greeted with the same shock as Edward
VIII's announcement that he was abdicating the British throne, but it
was not. If my mother was at all upset to learn that my vocation had gone
up in smoke, it was mainly because we would now have to go through all
the rigmarole of getting me enrolled in diocesan high school, and it was
already late in the summer. By this time she had gone back to work and
had a completely new agenda. The dreams of her children did not loom
large, if they loomed at all, as, for the first time in years, she had other
fish to fry. My father, to my amazement, was indifferent to the news; the
disclosure that his son would never have the opportunity to transform

bread and wine into the body and blood of Christ didn't faze him in the least. It took me a long time to understand why, as I was still a child, and children know nothing. Then one day it came to me. The last thing my father wanted was a son in a position to upstage him, a son invested with the moral authority to chastise him, to rain down fire and brimstone from an unassailable perch atop the moral high ground. The last thing he wanted was a child who had succeeded in doing something he might have enjoyed doing himself; after all, becoming a Trappist monk had been his burning ambition as a youth. The renunciation of the only dream I'd ever had enthralled him; he could not have been more pleased. He had always known that I would fail, he had warned me since birth that I would never amount to a pimple on an elephant's rear end, and to him my failure was neither a surprise nor a disappointment. Failure, in his estimation, was nothing to be ashamed of. It was our oldest family tradition.

Chapter 7. **Twilight of the Apothecaries**

The men who served as shining beacons to me as a child had strong personalities. They also had remarkable hair. Self-made clothier Len Mohr, haberdasher to the proletariat, sported a lustrous lion's mane that retained much of its original chestnut hue well into his fifties. My uncle Jerry cultivated a crop of spiky hair that stuck straight up in the air, as if the carcass of an unfortunate porcupine had been glued to his skull. Finally, there was my uncle Charlie, the guitar-strumming ward heeler whose job it was to make sure that on Election Day the people's voice was heard loud and clear, but only if the people were Democrats. Even at an advanced age, he would continue to fuss about with a pint-sized pompadour, applying wax to its surface in the vain hope of infusing it with something approaching Gibraltarian stolidity. In his mind, it was never too late to be stylish, even if his thinning hair served no other purpose than to cue fond memories of earlier, more hirsute days. In their own little way, all the manly men whose manliness I strove to emulate as a child were smitten by their hair. Perhaps they believed that as long as a man had his hair, he was not yet in the process of dying. Or perhaps they honestly thought they had "the look."

These otherwise dissimilar individuals sported hairstyles best described as "quirky." Yet the most memorable hairdo of them all belonged to Glenn Dreibelbis, who employed me in his apothecary during my last two years in high school. Viewed from the front, Glenn appeared to be totally hairless, a self-depilating sort who had made a preemptive decision to throw in the towel and divest himself of all but the most minimal cranial finery at an early age, since he was already going bald anyway. His head was virtually devoid of any protective or ornamental camouflage, save for a thin gray sliver of vestigial fur lurking all the way in the back, where the head joined the shoulders.

This ambiguous coif evoked none other than Friar Tuck, who adamantly refused to cut off that anemic, redundant halo of hair that snaked its way around the lower portion of his skull, as if a geriatric caterpillar were slumbering there.

It was not clear how long ago Glenn had shorn what must have been but skimpy locks in the first place. A few times I asked to see pictures of him when he was younger to ascertain whether he had once been a strapping youth with a full head of hair, but these photographs never materialized. Well into his fifties when he hired me as a stockroom clerk, delivery boy, cashier, and general factotum, he always wore a brief, tight white pharmacist's jacket rippling over his formidable paunch and was forever chain-smoking mentholated cigarettes, contemptible items he gave no sign of enjoying. His gait suggested that of an oversized gnome, advancing with weird little prancing steps, like a timid dancing bear not yet sure he had clinched the job with Barnum & Bailey. He wore battered Hush Puppies and covered his head with one of those unfortunate mashie hats that would be popularized by Alan Alda and Woody Allen in the 1970s, when self-emasculation came into vogue. Glenn was ahead of his time, but in the wrong way. Or perhaps it would be fairer to say that he was simultaneously both ahead of *and* behind the times. The composite image—beer gut, surgical jacket, chrome dome, Kool filters, Tilley hat—was not an attractive package; he was as unprepossessing a man as I have ever known.

Glenn (né William, but he never used his first name) was born in the coal-mining hinterland of central Pennsylvania around the time the Great War broke out. Anthracite was not in his future. He must have quickly made it clear to his Swiss-American family that he had no intention of pursuing the almost compulsory regional profession, for he cleared out in a hurry. Never in the time I knew him did he ever mention coal, not even as a serviceable fuel. Instead, he trundled off to the big city to become a pharmacist, then, after getting his degree, wended his way to New York, where he pitched camp in Greenwich Village. The Village was to be the alpha and omega, the triumph and tragedy, of his existence. While sowing whatever wild oats were in his power to sow, he lived smack-dab in the epicenter of Depression-era Bohemia. This was, it should be noted, a time when Dylan Thomas and his merry retinue were still very much on the scene, as were innumerable other poets, musicians, and subversives, though, judging from the historical record, not an enormous number of countercultural pharmacists. These were Glenn's days of heaven.

Then overnight everything changed. He met a woman from out of town, fell in love, got married, and was somehow induced to relocate to Philadelphia, where he opened a demure apothecary in a quiet, mildly prosperous community called West Oak Lane. There, he spent the rest of his life wishing he were somewhere else. Philadelphia in the 1950s was not a dream destination; it was intergalactically renowned for its lack of nightlife and was not all that much more bubbly by day. Philadelphia was a town, so the saying went, that pulled up its sidewalks at dusk. In fact, to this very day, most American cities pull up their sidewalks at dusk, but due to its proximity to voluptuous, fun-loving New York, Philadelphia has always been singled out as a drowsy municipality where nothing exciting ever happened, in sharp contrast to raucous Minneapolis, bacchanalian Cleveland, and sybaritic Des Moines. Whenever Glenn spoke of those golden days in New York, he made his forced evacuation to Philadelphia sound like Napoleon's retreat from Moscow, perhaps even his exile on bleak, rat-infested Saint Helena. The rest of his life was anticlimactic; till his dying breath, he would rue the day he left New York. It did not help that bit by bit, week by week, the charming neighborhood where he ran his business was becoming less charming; by the time my family showed up with our foolproof ability to make a bad situation worse, its decline was in full swing. Glenn was a sweet, generous, fascinating man, but by the time I hired on, life had broken him.

From the moment we moved to West Oak Lane, a quaint, leafy district whose vaguely Episcopalian name hinted at an elegance it aspired to without ever fully achieving, I was enthralled by the pixielike one-story apothecary at the corner of Chelten Avenue and Limekiln Pike. Prior to this, the word "apothecary" had not been part of my lexicon. In the housing project, when we needed prescriptions filled, we shopped at a dive called Major's Drugs, an unkempt, all-purpose emporium that, in addition to such staples as bedpans and trusses, sold cupcakes, ice cream, cigars, newspapers, magazines, and condoms to a somewhat mangy clientele. Whatever else it may have been, it was not an apothecary.

Glenn took the palliative arts seriously, referring to his sugarplum establishment as an apothecary, rather than a drugstore, because the term "apothecary" bespoke refinement and tradition, while "drugstore" bespoke retail narcotics. He had the same attitude toward the word "pharmacy," which to his ears sounded coarse and industrial. The paned windows of his colonial-style shop were adorned with brass scales and goosenecked vases filled with colored water; beside them sat framed illustrations depicting famous moments in medical history. Striking images of Galen and Hippocrates peered out at passersby, conferring an anomalous classical panache on a neighborhood with few other direct links to the Peloponnese.

Unlike most drugstores of the time, Glenn did not stock magazines, newspapers, or beverages, nor did he sell greeting cards. That, in his view, would have been tacky. He did stock candy and cigarettes; in fact, he changed his own brand every week or so, never quite finding a taste that suited him, inevitably reverting to Kool Filters, a brand at the time associated with jazz musicians, many of whom would go to an early grave. He was never without a cigarette in his mouth or on his person; he was incapable of starting a conversation without first lighting up what he referred to as "cancer sticks," but it was obvious from the pained expression on his face that the Kool Filters gave him no pleasure. This was in 1966, two years after the publication of the landmark Surgeon General's Report that decisively linked cigarette smoking to lung cancer. I admired the massive cultural dissonance and absence of logic in Glenn's approach to life. He was employed in a distinguished wing of the medical profession, he earned his daily bread by helping others recuperate from various diseases, he knew that smoking was no good for him, yet he puffed away like a blast furnace. Any pharmacist worth his salt must have been aware by this late date that such a deplorable vice was at odds with the emerging ethos of the health-care establishment and thus constituted some form of emotional spittle directed at the panjandrums of the healing class. But Glenn did not care. He was beyond caring.

Glenn didn't like to go anywhere near the cash register; he hired students as helpers in large part because he hated dirtying his hands with what he referred to as "filthy lucre." I worked for Glenn every Monday, Wednesday, and Friday for two hours after school; every Tuesday and Thursday from seven till nine; and every other Saturday from one until five. I was paid $1 an hour. Throughout that stint, he could never bring himself to hand me the $13.10 ($14 minus 90 cents in taxes) I was owed; my wages were always waiting for me late Saturday afternoon in the top drawer of a filing cabinet in the back room. Not once did I see Glenn physically dole out the cash; he always acted as if stealthy water sprites had deposited it there while his back was turned. Around him, one always sensed that the mere act of exchanging specie or even talking about money would have encrusted our liaison with slime, dragging our otherwise highbrow relationship straight down into the gutter.

Glenn insisted that the shop be spectacularly clean at all times; one of my jobs was to dust off the shelves and merchandise every three days, a task I did not enjoy one bit. I also had to wash the three picture windows, which, because they were each divided into twelve frames, necessitated my carefully rearranging the scales and illustrations and vases so I could climb into the window casement. In the front window sat a clock, accompanied by a photograph of whatever happened to be the major piece of news that day. A deliveryman from the news bureau popped in every afternoon with a fresh black-and-white glossy to slip into place. It usually involved somebody like Fidel Castro or Martin Luther King or Sandy Koufax. The news was mostly bad, except when someone who had once met Sitting Bull turned a hundred. The window cleaning was a cumbersome operation; one day I knocked over the most ornate of the vessels containing the colored water, dispatching it to an untimely death on the tiled floor below. It was the only time I saw Glenn angry; the fluted glass receptacle was an heirloom of some sort, one of a kind; it was a symbol of all the good times gone bad. He never replaced it.

Glenn felt that background music added a soothing ambience to an apothecary, but the music he chose was repellent: a string of excruciating instrumentals derived from golden hits of the thirties, forties, and fifties. They were shopworn tunes, so familiar that even though they featured no vocals, the listener could hear the lyrics in the canyons of his mind, reminding him, in case he had forgotten, that there was, indeed, a summer place, beyond the blue horizon, where one could stand on a corner, watching all the girls go by—several of whom bore a stunning resemblance to the girl that married dear old Dad—before returning to either Sorrento or Capistrano, whichever was more convenient. I was never allowed to switch channels, certainly not to Top 40 stations, because Glenn believed that pop music was crass and hopelessly out of synch with the rhythms of medication. Once, without his knowing it, I switched on the November 19, 1966, Notre Dame–Michigan State classic that would decide the national championship and listened with bated breath to the barely audible broadcast all afternoon. This epic showdown, one of those Games of the Century that usually end up being duds, was the most breathlessly anticipated sporting event of the year, if not the decade, but Glenn would not give me authorization to listen to it, deeming sports idiotic. There were, at that time, no more than four people in Philadelphia who shared this opinion. The game ended in a tie.

Glenn's attitude toward the radio was completely utilitarian: Ambient music was one of the costs of doing business, but nobody said he had to like it. Most people of that era accepted it as gospel truth that without a song, the day would never end, but Glenn did not agree. For him, music existed purely as a mood-setting device; he believed that if Galen and Hippocrates were still among the living, they would be operating upscale apothecaries where saccharine renditions of "I'm Gonna Wash That Man Right Outta My Hair" would perpetually chug along in the background. Muzak and commerce went hand in hand, but that was about the extent of it. He was the first person I ever met who not only had no taste in music but to whom music was not even important. Today all sorts of people feel that way.

I have no idea what Glenn's personal life was like; he never spoke about his wife and rarely mentioned his daughter. As had been the case with Len's wife and two daughters, my new employer's family never once visited the store the whole time I worked there. On the professional level, Glenn was a drug-industry ronin, a masterless samurai. As he explained it, pharmacists had once been radiant stars in the medical constellation, luminous planets giving off only slightly less light than physicians. Back in the first half of the century, when hanging out a pharmacist's shingle was considered a lofty achievement, it was not unheard of for druggists to ring a physician immediately after receiving a prescription and question the dosage or even suggest an alternate medication. There was a reassuring collegiality between doctors and druggists; they were joining forces to ensure that the patient got the best possible treatment. The role of the pharmacist then was not unlike that of the House of Representatives: to advise and consent. But by the time I started working for Glenn, pharmacists were beating a fast retreat before the onslaught of the drug companies.

By 1966, working as a pharmacist entailed little more than counting out an infinite series of antidepressant pills purchased by women who hated their husbands and weren't all that fond of their kids. Twenty Valiums. Thirty Valiums. Forty Valiums. With the audacious scumminess that is their calling card, drug companies had seized control of the health-care industry, seducing crass, easily manipulated doctors into becoming robotic shills who were only too happy to prescribe the same high-markup medications over and over again. The position of pharmacist was fast becoming menial and ancillary, the druggist serving as little more than a gatekeeper between listless physicians and a catatonic public, a mere cog in the Great Mandala of sedation. I could tell from the increasingly brief telephone chats Glenn had with the new breed of avaricious, condescending young physicians that they had no interest in his input. They were the ones who made the diagnosis; they were the ones who wrote the prescription; his job was to fill it. No further jawboning was necessary. Got it, Pops?

The only time Glenn displayed even the slightest interest in his now-eclipsed profession was when some Precambrian crone dragged her carcass into the shop, brandishing a tube containing the very last driblets of some Hoover-era balm useful in relief of rectal measles or psoriasis of the trachea, a prescription originally written in 1937. Then Glenn would spring into action: He would haul out his capacious mortar and equally daunting pestle, exhume a bevy of antediluvian jars and bottles garlanded with cobwebs, and spend the next fifteen minutes whipping up some quasi-medieval ointment, salve, potion, lotion, paste, elixir, or cream. In a poignant, Proustian moment, Glenn's face would now turn rosy red, illuminated by a jubilant smile, as he returned to the golden days of pharmaceutical derring-do he had known in his youth.

By the time I came on board, Glenn was rapidly seceding from a profession that no longer honored its members. Like an aging desperado who has hung up his guns, only occasionally emerging from retirement in the direst emergency, he would sit in the back room of his tiny but well-appointed establishment and occupy himself with just about anything that did not involve the career for which he had been trained. He would ensconce himself in his swivel chair and chain-smoke cigarettes as he indulged his assorted hobbies. One was reading about the bygone splendors of Olde New York; often I would hear him chuckling merrily at the exploits of Diamond Jim Brady, Dutch Schultz, Fiorello La Guardia, or Legs Diamond, swashbuckling fixtures of Gotham mythology whose adventures were chronicled in a pile of mildewed biographies that were never terribly far from his reach. But often, he merely dozed.

Initially, Glenn hired me to man the front counter. But after I'd been ringing up sales and waiting on customers for a while, he designated me his official aide-de-camp. He would lay out the prescriptions, place the relevant tubes or canisters atop them, and wait for me to come in after school to count out fifteen thousand sedatives. Meanwhile, he'd snuggle into his swivel chair in the back and read about the dexterous thugs who ran Tammany Hall or the astounding legerdemain of that irrepressible robber baron Jay Gould. He was also partial to the adventures of one Toots Shor, a still-breathing restaurateur, raconteur, bon vivant, and all-round high-stepper who operated a famous restaurant on Fifty-first Street, just off Fifth Avenue, that was home for many years to New York's most fabled ballplayers, lounge lizards, politicians, scribes, and gangsters.

Allowing a sixteen-year-old boy, not yet in possession of a high school diploma and boasting no formal training in the pharmaceutical arts, to fill prescriptions was in brazen violation of every Food and Drug Administration stricture on the books. Had I been a maniac, an anarchist, or even a garden-variety knave, I could have easily dispensed the wrong medicine or jacked up the dosage so high it would have sent half of our dysfunctional clientele to the loony bin. Looking back on it, I recognize that I, too, was in brazen violation of FDA policy regarding who could and could not dole out powerful antidepressants, and might conceivably have done a stint in the slammer for my transgressions. But at the time it all seemed like innocent fun, the urban equivalent of cow tipping or impregnating minors down at the old fishing hole.

America teems with bogus eccentrics, most of them wealthy poseurs whose rehearsed eccentricity evaporates the first time anyone mentions the yield curve. They falcon or collect vintage addressing machines or take up the viola da gamba in a shabby attempt to camouflage the pallid hues of their personalities. Glenn, on the other hand, was the genuine article, a twenty-four-karat oddball who navigated perilously between the shoreline of lucidity and the shoals of lunacy. Needless to say, he occasionally ran aground. But unlike those who were not playing with a full deck because they had been born "odd" or had suffered some emotionally paralytic trauma somewhere along the line, Glenn had deliberately removed the high cards from the deck, substituting jokers. Unlike so many people of that era, who were famous for taking brief, well-publicized, transparently hedonic sabbaticals from society before going back to work for Morgan Stanley, Glenn had really and truly "dropped out."

One of the strangest contours of Glenn's personality was his obsession with fire. He would sit in his creaky old chair, gleefully listening to reports of serious conflagrations on a police-band radio concealed in the storage room, on top of a refrigerator. Meanwhile, I would be out front medicating another three dozen zombies masquerading as housewives into a state of rapturous catatonia. The illegally obtained radio—John Q. Public wasn't supposed to be listening in on all this stuff—suggested a talking breadbox. It sat right next to a Himalaya of banned medications, beloved painkillers of a bygone era. Glenn kept them tucked away for emergencies or on the off chance that opium-laced cough medicines might one day come back into vogue. It was Hophead Heaven back there; had any of the local losers known of its existence, they would have blown the back door off its hinges and made off with enough mood-altering potions to keep them squirrelly till Amelia Earhart made her long-overdue return.

While Glenn and I were conversing about one thing or another, the sound of dispatchers yakking to firemen was constantly cackling away in the back room. Even when he was standing at the front counter, gas-bagging with customers about their rheumatism, chancres, or impending death from melanoma, Glenn would only half listen to what they were saying, his left ear always cocked for scintillating news from the pyrotechnic airwaves. It was the same procedure during his conversations with me; there I'd be, gamely feigning interest in the awful truth about Lucky Luciano's shadowy dealings with mobbed-up dermatologists or Commodore Vanderbilt's cornering the steamboat market back in 1862, and he'd suddenly jerk forward, put his fingers to his lips, then mince back to his lair with that signature gait of his, like Rumpelstiltskin trying to sneak up on the miller's daughter, or, if she was not available, Rapunzel herself. Now, he could listen more intently to the news emanating from his contraband appliance.

"I'm telling you, if that baby goes to five alarms, I'm closing this joint!" he would exclaim. And, by God, he would close it, just the way Len used to padlock his clothing store and scoot over to the ballpark on slow afternoons. No matter what time of day it was, as long as there was a fire burning out of control somewhere within a ten-mile radius, Glenn would send me on my way, lock up, and giddyup over to the scene of the blaze in his glitz-free baby blue Volkswagen Beetle.

For official consumption, Glenn was doing this as a member of the Second Alarmers, a cadre of concerned citizens who, out of an ingrained sense of civic duty, would gallop off to major conflagrations and distribute coffee and doughnuts to firemen. They even had their own divine little Second Alarmers truck, the very height of hobbyist preciousness. But the truth of the matter was, Glenn was a textbook example of the wholesome pyromaniac, a scamp who was enthralled by fire, not only because of its immense destructive power, nor because of the heroism of the men who battled it, but because of the sheer drama generated by the incendiary event itself.

A couple of times he asked if I would like to tag along and watch a building or two burn to the ground. No, I would not; fire never held any allure for me, and it was hard to see how my watching someone's possessions go up in smoke could be much fun. Besides, I could still remember that little girl who'd burned to death back in the housing project. Anyway, I was always the type who would rather play football with friends than witness the economic ruination of strangers.

Glenn was a serious student of the lore of combustion. At the drop of a hat, he would launch into an impassioned spiel about notable conflagrations he had witnessed, the most memorable of which was a granary fire in the 1950s that sent thirty-five people to the hospital. Other people liked to reminisce about neighborhoods that were now slums. Glenn liked to reminisce about neighborhoods that were now cinders. Manhattan fascinated him because of the glittering skyscrapers that would tower over the city until history had run its course. The only things in Philadelphia that interested him were buildings that had already burned to the ground.

Sadly for my employer, as for any devout firebug, Philadelphia, with few tall buildings, had trouble generating enough full-blown fires to keep him occupied. Stymied, he began casting about for another hobby. It wasn't going to be stamp collecting. Whittling never came under serious consideration. He definitely wasn't going to become a bird-watcher. Mercifully, neither the harmonica nor the hammered dulcimer ever entered the picture. Then one day, straggling in from school, I detected a fragrant aroma emanating from the back room. It smelled . . . well . . . piquant. Lo and behold, as I discovered when I made my way to the rear, Glenn had reinvented himself as a chef.

I could not imagine what had set this off, though one theory is that Glenn qua apothecarist delighted in the physical act of mixing substances together, in the same way that painters enjoy the visceral act of painting. Once the opportunity to use his hands on a daily basis was usurped by drug companies, he needed a substitute. Not really a gourmet, and having given no prior indication of any special interest in the preparation, presentation, or consumption of food, Glenn overnight decided to shed his identity as a pharmacist and henceforth tread the path of the epicure.

The fruits of Glenn's initial foray into the realm of the culinary was a modest beef stew he cooked on a Bunsen burner he kept in the back room. At least I thought it was a beef stew; subsequently, he would inform me that the concoction I'd been invited to tuck into was a *boeuf bourguignon* he had whipped up by consulting one of that era's trendy cookbooks, something along the lines of *Cuisine of the Dordogne for an Overweight Planet*. Glenn enlisted me and my friend Richie Giardinelli, who also worked in the apothecary, as guinea pigs in this exciting new enterprise. He would always have a meal waiting for us when we came in after school and would perch himself on the far side of the table like a voyeuristic gargoyle, chin resting on his hands, watching with shimmering glee as we devoured a repast he hoped would elicit the highest encomium imaginable. Alas, Richie's mother was a fantastic cook, hardly a rarity among Italian Americans, so he found the whole undertaking a bit goofy. I was in a completely different situation. My mother was arguably the worst cook in the history of Western cuisine, so I was all in favor of Glenn's setting off in this bold new direction, as the vittles were quite tasty.

Like most real-life chefs, Glenn had no interest in eating what he prepared; his pleasure came from giving pleasure to others. Cautious by nature, the hedgehog rather than the fox, he kicked off his second career with mildly adventurous dishes such as coq au vin, chicken with forty cloves of garlic, and linguine in vodka sauce, but quickly progressed to much more exotic fare along the lines of bouillabaisse and Welsh rarebit. As soon as I opened Glenn's front door after school, I could smell the bouquet of whatever he was working on wafting in from the storage room he had now transformed into a gremlin's keep. I had my favorites—Welsh rarebit was not one of them—and was grateful for his generosity and industry.

My sole beef with these impromptu meals was the diminutive portions he served; the birdlike offerings were perhaps West Oak Lane forerunners of nouvelle cuisine. I would have gleefully welcomed heartier portions while dining chez Dreibelbis, because I was furiously trying to bulk up so I could fend off bullies, including my father. At the time I worked for Glenn, I weighed only around 145 pounds, soaking wet.

The pivotal event in this era was my mother's decision to go back to work after a sixteen-year absence from the ranks of the employed.

This was a heroic act that enabled us to rent a house in a decent neighborhood, escape from public housing forever, and bid farewell to white trash, hooligans, guttersnipe, and scum. But it was also an emotionally transformational experience for her, because it meant that she would no longer be financially dependent on her husband. Her initial duties at Germantown Hospital were relatively menial, but when the Medicare program was introduced in 1965, she was put in charge of the collections desk. She remained in this position until her retirement twenty years later, after which she would endlessly reminisce about her time at the hospital, not so much because she was excited by her duties or her interactions with colleagues but because she enjoyed work in the abstract sense. For just as a house with a porch and a garden and a puppy gives a family a sense of dignity no apartment unit can confer, having a job gave my mother back her life.

Because she had white-collar skills that my father did not possess, she was soon earning more than he—before long, considerably more. This, for the first time ever, gave her the upper hand in the relationship. She immediately capitalized on her good fortune by devising a schedule whereby he would work nights and she would work days. This way, she would be asleep by the time he got home, and he would be asleep when she left in the morning. The arrangement meant that they only had to see each other on weekends, if either of them so desired, and sent a pretty clear message to her husband that she despised him. Their marriage, long a travesty, had now descended into the realm of farce.

In all likelihood, my mother had handed him an ultimatum: Either he would agree to a schedule that would get him out of the house during most waking hours so the rest of us could breathe, or she would throw him out. Of course, the four of us were hoping that her job would pay enough so she could turf him out into the street forever, but this did not come to pass. Constrained by the teachings of the Church, by the social mores of their class, and perhaps even by the delusional notion that a bad father was better than no father at all, she could never quite persuade herself to bring down the curtain on their pointless liaison forever. More important, neither of them ever made enough individually to support a decent standard of living; only by pooling their salaries were they able to lift us above the poverty line. My father grudgingly accepted this arrangement, because he had no other choice.

In the two years I worked at the apothecary, my father's downward trajectory continued, as if he was unaware that the bottom he was seeking had already been hit. His drinking and depression intensified; his fury at the world reached a maniacal level. Now he was a human powder keg. His rage mystified us, given our improved financial condition. But as was always true in his sector of a congenitally spiteful ethnic group, he viewed a wife's good fortune as a husband's disgrace. With his spasmodic employment history—fired, quit, fired, quit—he could no longer find work as a truck driver or even a deliveryman. The best job he could wangle at this late date was as a security guard at nearby La Salle College. This was a position that literally required no skills other than the ability to remain upright for eight hours a night. He did not like his job and had good reason not to. Even in those days, when the occupation was relatively new, security guards were figures of mirth. No one took them seriously; they did not get to carry guns; they were derided as "rent-a-cops."

This epithet enraged them. Cops in Philadelphia were feared but respected, particularly Frank Rizzo's leather-clad, jackbooted highway patrolmen. Security guards, by comparison, were thought of as impostors, cartoon cops. They dressed like policemen in the same way that stubby-legged little girls dressed up like ballerinas, but realistically they were in the same class as apprentice clowns who were permitted to wear rubber noses and oversized shoes but weren't allowed to be funny. My father spent the rest of his life taking jobs as a security guard or a night watchman at various academic institutions, apartment houses, and hospitals, and at all of them he made less money than my mother. In theory, the influx of extra cash should have cheered him, as a huge financial weight had been lifted from his shoulders. But because men who earned less than their wives were viewed with contempt—particularly in bluecollar neighborhoods—and because money cannot buy happiness, her good fortune simply reinforced his own perception that he was a failure. Unlike Glenn, who was not so much a failure as a has-been, a onetime success whose services society no longer required, my father did not have the financial resources to indulge any personal whimsy to allay his disappointment in the way his life had turned out. He would not be going out on any gleeful forays with the Second Alarmers. No *boeuf bourguignon* lay in his future.

Throughout these years, everyone in my family devised stratagems to avoid seeing him. Whenever they were on the premises simultaneously, my mother would barricade herself in her bedroom with that old standby, a stack of newspapers containing all sorts of bad news it was not in her best interest to read. Ree worked at a dry cleaner's and spent every free weekend with my uncle Jerry and aunt Cassie out in the suburbs. Eileen developed her remarkable singing voice, made a lot of friends, excelled at school, and otherwise kept a low profile while plotting her escape to New York City. Her plan, the details of which she loved to recapitulate to the rest of us, was to graduate from high school at noon, grab a snack, jump on the one-forty-five train to Gotham, and never come back. I think she may have kept the latest timetables hidden away in her bedroom just to make sure she didn't miss the train.

Keeping out of his way was not easy, as my father never stopped treating Eileen as his personal nemesis, the one child too many who had broken the back of the family financially, the one responsible for our losing the house on Russell Street. To him, she was less a daughter than a writ of execution. Mary Ann, our little sister, was usually left to her own devices; her sunny disposition may have enabled her to survive those years reasonably intact, even though she spent more time in my father's company than the rest of us. Ree, Eileen, and I always felt that Mary Ann had gotten off easier than her siblings, that she did not suffer routine physical abuse the way the rest of us did. We were also jealous of her, because she was cherubic and peppy, and because we believed that she was far and away our father's favorite. But this was an honor with few perks; it was like death by firing squad rather than death by hanging.

My personal diversionary strategy throughout these years was diabolically cunning: I made sure that when my father was home, I was not. I worked, studied at the library, played basketball, played football, played baseball, played pinochle, played guitar in a rock 'n' roll band called the Phase Shift Network. I was recruited into the band by a close friend I had taught to play guitar, with mixed results. He then switched to the bass, a wise decision, as bass players were always in demand. Jaw-droppingly suave for that era, let alone that neighborhood, Joe Alteari was the first person I ever knew that dared to appear in public clad in paisley and somehow managed to pull it off. This may have been because he was Italian, and Italians felt at home in regions of the fashion world where less exotic ethnic groups feared to tread. The newest member of the band, he was also the one who was most sensitive about its image. From the moment he joined up and got the lay of the land, he was deter-mined to stage a palace coup and purge the current rhythm guitarist from the ensemble, thus freeing up a space for me.

This closet conspiracy was fueled neither by malice nor by caprice. The guitarist, whose horizontally manicured bangs reflected the chill-ing influence of Prince Valiant, played a lime green Gretsch guitar, the sort of gaudy, high-priced instrument favored by foot-stompin', finger-pickin' hillbillies. Such an instrument, whatever its merits on technical grounds, was woefully out of place in a cutting-edge band like the Phase Shift Network, whose repertory ranged from Jimi Hendrix to Cream to the Doors but specifically excluded any material targeting the wangdoo-dle set. Given these circumstances, Roger Heiser simply would not do.

Roger had another serious drawback: He was a member of the Order of DeMolay, named after the last Grand Master of the Knights Templar, who was accused of witchcraft by the French clergy and burned at the stake in 1314 after undergoing unspeakable tortures. One of the most serious charges leveled against Jacques DeMolay and his *confreres* was that they asserted their fealty to Satan by puckering up and smooching the anuses of heathen house cats. Though no one in the band ever made much of an effort to ascertain Roger's feelings about the clandestine foibles of the Knights Templar, it did not help that this otherwise likable florist's son, Childe Templar or not, was not much of a guitarist. This unlikely combination of continental flamboyance, medieval depravity, nocturnal cat worship, possession of a hopelessly unfashionable musical instrument, and a tendency to highjack acid-rock numbers like "Eight Miles High" with his Foggy Mountain Breakdown strumming proved fatal, and the unfortunate youth was chucked out of the band. The ensemble's reasoning was that, knowing what we did about the Knights Templar, an oddball like Roger simply could not be trusted when the lights went down. But in all honesty, I think it was the lime green guitar that did him in.

Rob Weiss, the singer in our band, soon became my best friend. Rob's parents, the first Jews of my acquaintance, took an immediate liking to me and opened their doors on weekends whenever my father was on the warpath. The Weisses lived in a middling neighborhood teeming with Eastern Europeans, including a number of vindictive Ukrainians hell-bent on wresting control of Kiev back from the Soviets. The Ukrainians were fun to be around, if ever so slightly insane. The Weisses' neighborhood was better than ours, but not for long; it, too, would soon disintegrate into a slum, the way all North Philadelphia neighborhoods eventually turned into slums.

Judaism was terra incognita for me. My parents were not virulent racists or anti-Semites, though black people and Jews eavesdropping on some of their conversations might have had a hard time believing it. They mostly treated people as they found them. But they had a strange way of talking about other ethnic groups, using a tidy collection of euphemisms they shared with everyone else in the white working class. My mother liked Negroes who were "educated" and Jews who were not "pushy." It was odd to upbraid other people for being insufficiently "educated" or excessively "pushy" when you were married to a man who pissed into the sink and passed out facedown into the carpet, but that was the way she spoke.

When Irish Americans wanted to establish their bona fides in regard to blacks or Jews, they would say things like "I was standing on the corner in the rain, and this very nice Jewish girl came up and gave me her umbrella" or "A very nice colored man gave me his seat on the bus." These anecdotes were transmitted with a sense of befuddlement at the gallantry of the ethnic benefactors in question, leavened by a ham-fisted self-congratulation at being progressive enough to give credit where credit was due. Not all Jews were cheap, was the subtext of these testimonials, not all Negroes were ignorant and dangerous. Many were, but not all. The nicest thing you could say about Negroes in this environment was that they were "refined," unlike the cannibals who lived right next door to them.

There was nothing especially mean-spirited about this way of talking; white people acted as if affectionate condescension was magnanimous, perhaps even gutsy. What I learned growing up was that blacks and Latins were to be feared, Jews distrusted, Italians avoided, and Poles ridiculed—but always on a case-by-case basis. Wasps we had no frame of reference for. All we knew about them was that given half a chance, they would row crew.

The Weisses were unlike any family I had known up until then because both parents had white-collar jobs—Mary as an inventory clerk, Joe as a credit manager, first at a famous downtown department store called Lit Brothers, then at Temple University Hospital. They were also the only family I ever met that was headed by a Joseph and a Mary, which seemed like both a cultural and a statistical deviation from the norm. What the Weisses were doing with the most Christian names in all of creation was beyond me, though it would have seemed even stranger had either of them been born in Nazareth or Bethlehem in upstate Pennsylvania. Fond of books, fond of music, fond of life, the Weisses would take day trips and sometimes overnighters to New York City every couple of months to see topflight Broadway plays. Trophies they bagged included both Zero Mostel and Topol in *Fiddler on the Roof* and Lauren Bacall in *Applause*. They usually stayed at the Essex House, with its dazzling view of Central Park.

Even though producers of that era still staged tryouts in Philadelphia and Boston before opening in New York, the Weisses liked to see the shows in the big city, recognizing that a day in Philadelphia was merely a day in Philadelphia, while a day in New York was not. They gave the appearance of walking on air when they returned home Saturday evening or Sunday afternoon, because, in fact, they were. To me, these excursions to Gotham were the height of sophistication, the sort of thing no adult in my family, my neighborhood, or my ethnic group would ever dream of doing. The people I grew up around were perfectly happy to dismiss New York City as dangerous, overpriced, iniquitous, and extraneous. They were misinformed and aimed to keep it that way. Rob's parents felt otherwise.

By the time I was a senior in high school, the Phase Shift Network had been renamed Stained Glass, and the Weisses knew all about my family situation. I was always welcome in their home. I taught Rob how to play guitar and spent many Saturday nights sleeping on his bedroom floor, avoiding my rampaging father. Rob and I played a lot of music together, but his passion for performing dwarfed mine. No more than a passable bassist, a so-so guitarist at best, a singer whose gifts never extended very far beyond the realm of adequacy, I was a musician whose career was one long rehearsal for being an ex-musician. No matter what band I played in, the band was never in demand. I understood that the end was near when we rechristened our psychedelic wedding combo Baby's Death. Now we were even less in demand. I may have played music as long as I did only because I liked being around the Weisses.

My family's everyday existence improved significantly after we escaped from the project. When we moved into a real house in a real neighborhood, as opposed to the converted garrison where we had been interned for four years, we found ourselves in a proper community with cute little grocery stores and pizzerias and Chinese laundries and even an oyster house. Best of all was the Number 6 trolley line right down the street, which would ferry us to the subway stop a mile or so away, where we could grab a train downtown, where the bright lights awaited us. No longer did we feel inferior, shipwrecked. For a while there was even hope that the removal of the welfare stigma might enable my father to quell his demons and pull himself together. But this hope proved illusory.

Before we moved to West Oak Lane, my father still adhered to a few rules that, he believed, insulated him from the charge of being an alcoholic. One, he did not drink in the morning. Two, he did not drink on the Sabbath. Three, he did not bring distilled spirits into the house, and if he did, he hid them. Four, he did not sit on the front steps and get loaded with the riffraff. Five, he did not get so drunk that the police had to be called in. Six, he did not mix beer with whiskey in "depth charges" or boilermakers. Seven, he did not drink on the job. This was his credo. Now everything changed. He drank all the time, he drank anywhere, he drank anything, he drank with anybody. He had gone someplace from which he was not coming back. Just as he had done when both his parents breathed their last in the spring of 1944, he had gone absent without leave. But this time, he was going AWOL for good.

One event that helped push him over the edge occurred in Dallas, Texas, on November 22, 1963. Like most Irish Americans, my father took John F. Kennedy's death personally. Because he was the son of penniless immigrants and grew up in an era when the Irish were despised, JFK's murder seemed to epitomize everything that was wrong with America; the Gracchan tribune of the workingman had been slain, and once again the Catholics had gotten the short end of the stick. But unlike most other Irish Americans, who were reasonably happy with the way things had turned out for our ethnic group in recent decades, my father never got over JFK's assassination.

While Kennedy was alive, my father, like 7.5 million other Americans, purchased a comedy record called *The First Family*. The LP featured an assortment of little-known comics and bargain-basement thespians acting out ostensibly humorous vignettes featuring the president, his brother Bobby, his wife, Jackie, and such notorious political figures as Nikita Khrushchev, Chairman Mao Tse-tung, and Fidel Castro. The man playing JFK was a Massachusetts stand-up comic and musician by the name of Vaughn Meader, whose voice and inflection bore a remarkable resemblance to the president's. Of course, this could be said of just about any male between the ages of sixteen and eighty-five who was a native of Boston.

The First Family was the fastest-selling record in American history, and only the fourth to sell a million copies. Forty years later, I flew out to Monterey, California, to interview the man who had dreamed up the *First Family* concept. From him I learned that the album had been recorded in front of a live audience the night JFK went on television and warned the Soviet Union that if they did not pull their nuclear missiles out of Cuba, the United States was prepared to go to war. The sequestered audience, entirely oblivious to Kennedy's speech, was laughing quite enthusiastically at the First Family's foibles. They were probably the only people in the United States of America who were laughing enthusiastically that evening.

As is so often the case with pop cultural supernovas, *The First Family* was not an especially funny record, and it has not stood the test of time. What sounded witty then sounded hokey later. But there is no denying that the lighthearted material was tremendously appealing to everyone in my family back in 1963, not just because of the contrived romance of Camelot that swirled around the Kennedy White House but because it made my father laugh, and anything that made him laugh made him less likely to hit us.

Shortly after Kennedy's death, the abrasive comic Lenny Bruce gave a performance at a well-known nightclub in New York City. Bruce had a habit of wandering onstage and fussing about with newspaper clippings before officially launching into his act. On this occasion, he kept his fans waiting nervously for several minutes before approaching the microphone, staring at the audience, and rasping, "Boy, is Vaughn Meader fucked."

Fucked and then some was what life henceforth held in store for the luckless Bay State artiste. Nobody who loved JFK—their numbers, of course, did not include the many, many southerners who received the news of Kennedy's assassination with visible equanimity—wanted to see or hear Vaughn Meader after November 22, 1963, because seeing him only reminded them of Kennedy's death. My father was perhaps the lone exception to this view. Whenever he went on one of his benders, he would wobble into the dining room and load his badly scratched copy of *The First Family* onto our cheap, tinny portable record player. Then he would jack up the volume full-force, blasting the shopworn routines through the entire house. Sometimes he would do this at three in the morning, even though he knew that his children had school the next day and that his wife had a responsible job. Pillows wrapped around our heads, always fearful that he would set the house on fire, we could hear him downstairs, weeping and knocking over furniture, lamenting the lost splendor of Camelot. Sometimes he would give hell to Chairman Mao; other times he would mock, chastise, and even mimic Castro. I suppose, looking back on things, that this behavior may have been poignant or sad, or at least signified the presence of deeper emotions. But at the time it merely seemed terrifying.

When I came home from work on Saturday nights after trekking halfway across Philadelphia on the K bus, my father would force me and my sisters to watch *The Jackie Gleason Show*. Gleason was a beloved Irish comic whose success conferred a vicarious sense of achievement on unsuccessful Irish Americans. In this, he was heir to the mantle once worn by Jimmy Cagney, a tough little Mick if there ever was one, who was to the Irish what Frank Sinatra was to the Italians: the proud ethnic who refused to change his name or his attitude merely to get ahead. Gleason, who seemed less plangently Irish than Cagney but Irish all the same, had starred in a popular show called *The Honeymooners* in the early days of television and had performed admirably as a pool shark in the 1961 film *The Hustler*. Cagney's mother, it just so happened, was part Norwegian. But never mind.

Now, a decade after *The Honeymooners* had ceased taping, Gleason hosted a popular variety show that originated in Miami Beach. The show featured an assortment of comic skits, some of them funny, some less so. Each and every broadcast ended with Gleason in the role of an irascible bartender conducting an exasperating conversation with a barfly named Crazy Guggenheim. Crazy Guggenheim was a daffy, incoherent drunk, a fountain of malapropisms and homespun idiocy. My father adored this character; the closing segment in the taproom was the high point of his week. The sequence always wound up with Frank Fontaine, the man who played Crazy Guggenheim, turning on the just-add-water charm that is the stock-in-trade of the Irish and warbling some mawkish ditty like "Let Me Call You Sweetheart" or "I Love You Truly." Fontaine's comic material was pitiful, and his singing was worse: phony, sentimental, needy. I loathed both him and his alter ego; I hated the way he repackaged a vice that had ravaged a million families into something innocuous, laughable, sweet: a cute ethnic tic, like the funny little Frenchman with his beret, his Gauloise, and his baguette. Gleason's addled associate was widely viewed as a lush, a rummy, or a tippler who'd had a snootful, when what he was, in fact, was a drunk. This is the term I have long preferred when describing an alcoholic, because its harsh, primordial texture captures the essence of the beast. "Drunk" is a coarse, besodden word that deprives the waterlogged quadruped of even the tiniest pretension to dignity. It makes a drunk sound like what he is.

One of the tried-and-true stratagems of the accomplished alcoholic is the defective-memory gambit: If I was so drunk that I cannot remember doing something, then, *quod erat demonstrandum*, I didn't do it. One night when I was sixteen, I came home to find that the blue velour wing chair that dominated our living room was absent from its usual place of honor. A snap reconnaissance revealed that it was lying on its side in the backyard, where my father had heaved it in a fit of rage the night before. This was after tossing a handful of beer bottles through the window, showering glass on my mother and my sister Ree, while they were hanging laundry. Now the chair looked not so much ejected as dead. The most upsetting thing about this incident was that the blue velour wing chair was a cherished family possession, the nearest we ever came to an heirloom. Though it was tatty and stained and rickety, the velour was so elegant by comparison with the chintzy fabrics we were accustomed to that the chair had come to assume in our minds the jaded majesty of a Louis XV fauteuil. I gathered it up and returned it to its rightful position in the living room, and my mother made sure that the windowpane was replaced. None of us ever mentioned the incident, nor did we attempt to pinpoint what insult or slight had precipitated such an explosion. This would only have rekindled my father's ire, ensuring that even more chairs would go flying.

Events like this reinforced the sense that we were living in an asylum. Sleep was fitful, because we were always waiting for the lunatic-in-chief to fall asleep with a lit cigarette and incinerate the entire family. Yes, there are instances where inmates in such a facility might actually prefer death to life. But nobody wants to die in a fire. My sisters and I had not always viewed our father as a menace, as our implacable enemy. It had taken years to get to that stage. But by the time I was in my early teens, that juncture had arrived because his continued existence threatened ours. Our attitude was simple: We wanted him dead or we wanted him gone. The only positive thing he could do for us now was to walk in front of a truck or slit his own throat. Or, as insurance against a Rasputin-like escape from the clutches of the Grim Reaper, both.

Glenn knew none of this, as my mother always encouraged us to keep the truth about our home life "under our hats." Unlike Len, whom my father envied and disliked, Glenn never infiltrated his consciousness. He was too prim and respectable to pose any kind of threat. He was pudgy and soft and drove a baby blue Volkswagen, which was neither a manly vehicle nor a virile hue. Anyway, he was a pharmacist, the bush-league version of a physician. Though our house sat no more than a hundred yards from the apothecary, I am not sure the two ever met. If they did, I cannot imagine what they had to say to each other. The only thing I ever told Glenn about my father was that it wasn't worth getting to know him.

One day Glenn asked if I would like to spend a Sunday in New York. I had never been to New York; the closest I'd ever gotten was Trenton. Glenn picked me up at three in the morning and we headed north, adhering to some meandering itinerary that carried us toward Perth Amboy. At this point the vehicle abruptly veered east. A stickler for detail, and no stranger to romance, Glenn wanted me to see Manhattan for the first time while standing on the deck of the Staten Island Ferry. It was important to him that I be immediately, and quite hopelessly, smitten by New York. With the trusty old Staten Island Ferry gambit, he was pulling out all the stops.

Such high-pressure sales tactics weren't really necessary; from the moment I laid eyes on the Manhattan skyline, I understood that New York was a question that had only one answer. Still, just to be on the safe side, Glenn piled it on thick. He started out by treating me to breakfast in Little Italy. Then we motored all the way up Park Avenue and down the Great White Way. We drove east on Fifty-seventh Street and west on Forty-second. We visited Harlem, Wall Street, Rockefeller Center, Central Park, the Brooklyn Bridge, Lincoln Center, and Greenwich Village. He took me to Chinatown for lunch, just to show me what a proper Chinatown—as opposed to Philadelphia's junior-varsity version— looked like, and then wrapped up the festivities with a banquet in Sheepshead Bay. A rube off the streets of Philly didn't have a chance in the face of such an onslaught; the deck was rigged, and the fix was in.

Watching a young man fall in love with a city that he himself had foolishly jilted was a bittersweet triumph for Glenn; it was as if he were converting me to a religion he had unwisely abjured. Still, it was obvious that my enthusiasm, my sense of wonder, and my refusal to take any-thing for granted elated him. He'd taught me a lot about New York over the two years I'd been working for him, and I had learned my lessons well. I understood that Chinatown and Central Park and Saint Patrick's Cathedral and Harlem were mythic. I needed no one to explain to me the symbolism of Wall Street or Madison Avenue or Times Square. I knew all about the sonnets and bonnets at the Fifth Avenue Easter Parade. The day I saw New York was the day I saw the future. And even though my affection for the city would never extend to its sports franchises—to start cheering for the pathetic Mets or the accursed Yankees would be a betrayal of my roots—I had already decided that one day I would come to live in the Empire State, and that once I did, I would probably be stay-ing. Countless times over the years, I have reminded myself that New York is not my home; that despite the passage of years, I am only pass-ing through. But the idea of leaving it remains beyond contemplation. When I fantasize about other lives I might be leading, I have no trouble visualizing that first day in Paris. What I cannot visualize is that last day in New York.

Adults hate to arrive at the point in their lives when young people start offering them advice. They hate it even more when the advice is worth taking. As crime mounted and our trusty old clientele either returned to dust or absconded to antiseptic Jersey suburbs, I urged Glenn to sell his business right away, while it was still possible to fetch a decent price. By now, my family was getting ready to move again, spurred on by gang violence that had become rampant in the neighborhood. But Glenn refused, adhering to the dictum that things could not get better until they got worse. Things did not get better. One night, a hood came in, put a gun to Glenn's head, forced him onto the floor, and emptied the cash register. Glenn was not harmed, but he was terrified, and that was the end of his apothecary days. Shortly thereafter, he sold the store and took a job at a suburban hospital filling prescriptions. There he no longer cooked Welsh rarebit and no longer served up bouillabaisse. His days as a free-wheeling entrepreneur were over.

After I moved away from West Oak Lane, I stopped by to visit Glenn a few times; but once I entered college, after he had padlocked his operation, I never saw him again. The hospital where he worked was not easy to reach by public transportation, and I did not drive, and I was busy with my studies, and I had a girlfriend, and so on and so forth. I did learn from my mother that things continued to go badly for him over those last few years. But things were not going badly for me. So Glenn dropped out of my life.

Losing contact with the two men who had meant so much to me growing up has always been a source of regret. But I was reluctant to renew contact with them until I had made something of myself, and by the time that happened, they were gone. I am not even sure they would have been happy with the results; if they were seeking a clone or a reflection, I could not accommodate them. The whole time I was living in the shadow of these men, I knew that I would not grow up to be anything like them. I had no intention of being a marine, a boxer, or a retailer, and I certainly had no desire to be a pharmacist. Glenn was bald and tubby and wore a silly hat and drove a misshapen baby blue Volkswagen that I, the prototypical teen, was mortified to be seen in. At a time when people were still driving flashy Thunderbirds and Mustangs, Glenn had already surrendered to lackluster functionality. It was hard to square this with his passion for the improvident Jay Gould, the freewheeling Diamond Jim Brady, and all the other rakish heroes of the Gilded Age. Still, by observing him, being inspired by him, taking a bit of this and throwing away a lot of that, I managed to cobble together a personality that would stand me in good stead for the rest of my life.

When a child grows up to be the person he dreamed of becoming, it is easy to forget that his dreams did not always seem attainable. Without Len and Glenn, I would have been sucked into the void. This is not so much because of the wisdom they imparted, nor even because they kept reminding me that there was light at the end of the tunnel. It was because they taught me that the light at the end of the tunnel was meaningless unless you were willing to go into the tunnel. These otherwise very different men taught me that there were two kinds of people: the ones who thought the world was a dangerous place, and the ones who did not. My father feared the world; it was an adversary to hide from.

Len and Glenn went out to meet it head-on and encouraged me to do the same. They taught me not to throw my life away, because I was not going to get another one.

Neither of these men has ever left my thoughts. They are a link with a now vanished urban, working-class world that was neither hopelessly dangerous nor ludicrously synthetic like the twee districts that ring Center City Philadelphia today, rechristened with smarmy names like Northern Liberties. Len and Glenn were unpredictable and difficult to get a read on and in some ways strange, but they were authentic and original and irreplaceable. And now they are gone.

One afternoon toward the end of our relationship, I strolled into the apothecary, smelled something funny, and discovered that Glenn was expanding his horizons yet again and morphing into a *Braumeister*. Earlier that day, he had excavated his long-dormant home-brewing paraphernalia and concocted a potent beverage he identified as mead. Mead, sophisticates will aver, is a yeasty libation that reached the height of its popularity in the thirteenth century, right around the time Gandolf of Frith slew Wamba the Stoat Fetcher. That Glenn was going off in this unanticipated feudal direction seemed par for the course; he was always a man out of time. From that point on, he kept a creditable supply of home-brewed mead on hand, never failing to hand me a flagon when I reported for work after school, thereby ensuring that I would be ever so slightly blitzed as I was counting out a few hundred Valiums for our reliably inanimate clientele. Once again, the very act of delegating official pill-counting authority to a high school student with no formal training in the pharmaceutical arts, a youngster who was well and truly ripped after imbibing such a powerful, neomedieval brew, was in blatant contravention of long-standing FDA policies regarding sobriety in the workplace, especially at the secondary-school level. Glenn did not blink an eye. He was the most persistently, defiantly, authentically unhinged person I ever met.

In the end, what I valued most in these two men, apart from their decency, was their wholesome eccentricity. Unlike my father, whose antisocial approach to life always culminated in mayhem, Len and Glenn demonstrated how it was possible to thrive in this society even though one had in some sense seceded from it. When I see Glenn in my mind's eye, he is not the defeated chain-smoker lying facedown on the floor with a gun pressed against his temple amid the ruins of his apothecary, but the mad scientist brewing a fresh vat of mead for the bibulous pleasure of his teenaged assistant. When I think of him, I see him in Sheepshead Bay, gobbling up his oysters, or in McSorley's Old Ale House, quaffing a beer. I see him in Greenwich Village, standing on the spot where Dylan Thomas busted a gut, or on 125th Street in Harlem, or on the footsteps of the Cathedral of Saint John the Divine, the half-finished temple that will still be under construction the morning of Armageddon. Finally, I see him in old Times Square, telling all the boys on Forty-second Street that he will soon be rejoining them, and this time for good. His beady Swiss-American eyes are sparkling now; he is once again the boy from coal country who came to the big city in search of adventure. In a nation of fakers and poseurs and bogus mavericks and phonies, Glenn was the real thing. His was an apothecary like no other apothecary the Keystone State had ever seen, and for twenty-four months I was lucky enough to work in it. Those who speak ill of pharmacists in my presence do so at their peril.

Chapter 8. *C'est magnifique, mais ce n'est pas la guerre*

At the time I was attending it, Cardinal Dougherty was the largest Catholic high school in the world. To me, this is a fascinating résumé entry, like once having worked as a mason on the Great Wall of China; but even though I have gone through life clamorously making my quaint, statistically improbable educational pedigree known to strangers, always expecting them to be impressed, they never are. Perhaps it is because they do not believe me, suspecting, not without some justification, that Catholics have a tendency to fudge the numbers.

When I graduated, in 1968, shortly before the school began an inexorable decline that would reduce its size by 85 percent, Cardinal Dougherty boasted an enrollment of sixty-five hundred. This was five times the size of the college I would attend. Years later, when I would encounter alumni from the same graduating class, they would act as if we were comrades in arms, battle-scarred veterans of Belleau Wood or Antietam. In fact, having matriculated simultaneously at a school the size of Cardinal Dougherty gave us roughly as much in common as two tourists who had once been in the same train station in Stuttgart. I never felt like I was in high school; I felt like I was in a half-dozen high schools.

Students were assigned to one of three sections—Academic, Business, and General—based on their perceived cerebral skills. Once a student had been dispatched to the section deemed most suited to his gifts, he could never transfer out. This meant that by age thirteen, at least one incontrovertible, life-altering decision had been made for each student as a result of a calibration process of questionable merit. There were the anointed ones, there were the runners-up, and there were the castoffs. Those in the top Academic section were viewed as college material; those in the Business section would make fine bureaucrats; those in the General section would go to Vietnam to fight a war they were not going to win. Without the deferment from the draft that was awarded to college students, boys had a good chance of ending up dead in Southeast Asia. Many of them knew this, but there was little they could do about it. The rest of us had other options.

The students assigned to the Business section were a mystery, like the ancient Phoenicians or the lost masters of the oud. They inhabited a netherworld, marooned between those who were indisputably bright and those who were not. Their predicament evoked the specter of Limbo, that murky, poorly signposted halfway house between Heaven and Hell populated by those unfortunate enough to die unbaptized. Unlike Purgatory—which Catholics saw as a minimum-security detention facility of the mind, a rehab center where sinners underwent a middling level of chastisement for an indeterminate period before finally being allowed to enter the Kingdom of Heaven—Limbo was an extraterrestrial waiting room where infants, well-meaning heathens, and freelance holy men like Mahatma Gandhi sat around until the Four Horsemen of the Apocalypse finally cantered in. Only at the End of Days would the Good Book be opened and everyone who had ever drawn breath would learn what his eternal reward was to be. But it was clearly understood that Gandhi and Aristotle and Plato and all those unchristened infants could be kicking around Limbo for a long, long time, as their cases fell between stools, and the Last Judgment was hardly nigh.

A nun once told me that the actress Jennifer Jones, despite a generally immoral life pockmarked by numerous affairs and brazen appearances in a handful of steamy movies, would probably be dispatched to Limbo when she died, in recognition of her fine work in the 1943 film *The Song of Bernadette*. Implicit was the belief that God would turn a blind eye to Jones's torrid onscreen affair with William Holden in *Love Is a Many-Splendored Thing*, ignoring that provocative, canary-hued swimsuit she pranced around in, fetching lass that she was, because *The Song of Bernadette* was one of the very few films ever made about southwestern French Catholic teenaged schizophrenics that was not teeming with factual inaccuracies and glaring doctrinal errors. Limbo was a place for people who hadn't really done anything wrong, blameless folk who were not so much in the wrong place at the wrong time as not in the right place at the right time. It was the same with the Business section: These students were neither inside nor outside life's rich feast. They were marking time in the vestibule, cooling their heels.

Escaping from the Business section once you were in it was tantamount to escaping from Alcatraz. Many tried; few succeeded. The same was true of the lower Academic section. My junior year, I met a young man who, having fared poorly in grade school, was remanded to the bowels of the Academic section B-6. Belatedly, it became clear that Leo was much too bright to be cast out into the pedagogical darkness; he even tried to get himself promoted to a higher grade, where he belonged. But the éminences grises who ran Dougherty feared that this would set a bad precedent, as, in their view (the ultimate statement of Catholic orthodoxy), all precedents were bad. And so, they refused.

One day, an insurgency of the type one rarely encounters outside motion pictures erupted when a grassroots campaign was mounted to get Leo elected president of the senior class. This terrified the administration, as Leo was considered a free spirit, and free spirits were dangerous. Leo won the contest in a walk, amassing votes from all three sections, effortlessly defeating the assorted goody-two-shoes and hale-fellows-well-met slated for greatness by the administration, all of them from the top Academic section. Their numbers included the usual assortment of brownnosing stalwarts and yes-men, as well as a sensitive type who wrote the kinds of precociously wise short stories about soldiers dying young that made one wish a pipe bomb would explode in his locker.

Leo subsequently fared poorly in one of his classes, an event almost certainly orchestrated by the administration, and because of this he was stripped of his post. On the yearbook page devoted to the officers of the class of '68, there are photographs of the vice president, the secretary, and the treasurer. Leo is nowhere to be found. It was as if Joe Stalin himself had popped by and assisted the yearbook editors in airbrushing him out of history. After graduation, Leo made his way to Georgetown University, where, I believe, he was preparing for a career as a lawyer. But one afternoon, having misplaced the key to his mother's home on a return trip to Philadelphia, he tried to climb in through the second-story window, fell to the ground, and died. His life, however brief, would have made a great movie, but had it been less brief, it would have made a great life. His strange, unnecessary death haunted me. Nobody ever said that life was fair, one is constantly reminded, usually by people least in a position to know. Fortunate sons are particularly fond of mouthing such clattertrap. Leo was not a fortunate son.

It was not all that common for a student in B-2 like me to strike up a friendship with someone in B-6; in a system that thrived on social and intellectual segregation, this was like a Hottentot consorting with an Eskimo. I do not remember how or when we first crossed paths—Leo lived in a better neighborhood than I did—but it was probably on the bus. Befriending anyone outside one's class or neighborhood was rare; the social system fostered loyalty to a tight enclave of the similarly gifted, the similarly inclined, and the similarly financed, and in any case lifelong friendships with denizens of one's own neighborhood—to the exclusion of everybody else—was a Philadelphia tradition. I never felt part of Cardinal Dougherty, which was miles away, and catered to a better class of people than my family. To me, Cardinal Dougherty was neither iconic nor memorable; it was a building where I went to high school. As a result of its size and social structure, there were literally thousands of classmates I never met while enrolled there, including a man who grew up to be the Hanging Judge, a folk legend famous for presiding over on-the-spot trials of rowdy carousers at Eagles football games. Many alumni continued to treat Dougherty as the centerpiece of their emotional lives decades after matriculating; for some, those high school days were the happiest they would ever know. But I didn't set foot again in the building for forty years. And that visit would have no sequel.

Cardinal Dougherty consisted of a single large building with flanking wings. It was a modern, antiseptic structure—by no means vast, by no means hideous—though its facilities were almost actionably meager. During gym class, hundreds of us would sit in the stands and watch other classes play basketball, as there were not enough courts to go around. We were supposed to be doing our homework, but mostly we liked to watch the boys smack each other around and take dozens of ill-advised jumpers, all the while hoping that someone would suffer a career-ending injury or get pummeled into a coma. The next day, these same boys would sit in the stands and watch us play, wishing us exactly the same.

Directly north of the school stood a gigantic field—wide as the steppes and equally devoid of landscapers—upon which someone in authority could easily have given the order to erect dozens of basketball courts to accommodate the ludicrously underserved student population. But no one ever did. We were told that the archdiocese had long-term plans for this property, though we never learned what these plans were. We never went outside during gym class, not once in four years; the running track and the football field were off-limits to anyone but the varsity athletes. Decades later, the field still lay empty. A popular theory bandied about at the time hypothesized that the Catholic Church was patiently waiting a full half-century to make a killing in a real estate boom, which, in the end, never quite materialized. Knowing the way the Church operated, there was a good chance it would hang on to that tract of land forever. Having survived the property-devaluing hijinks of the Vandals, the Jutes, the Visigoths, and the Huns, not to mention the depredations of the Vikings and the Moors, the Catholic Church definitely knew how to ride out an adverse economic cycle.

In the 1960s, no one was required to pay tuition to attend a diocesan high school; it was simply thought of as public school for Catholics. Students did not have to be Catholics to enroll at Cardinal Dougherty; they merely had to attend religion classes, like the rest of us, and pretend to be interested, like the rest of us. Receiving no funding from the state, the schools were maintained through the auspices of the Church itself, which viewed public schools as the spawning grounds of Satan: hotbeds of atheism, ignorance, and depravity. This was not far from the truth, as Philadelphia's public schools had already plunged into a maelstrom of mayhem from which they would never resurface. Even though our classes were much larger than those in public school, the quality of education was demonstrably better, as was the overall atmosphere, if only because bringing meat cleavers and sawed-off shotguns to class was frowned upon by the archdiocese.

At Cardinal Dougherty, troublesome students were given a warning or two, perhaps suspended once or twice, and then shipped off *in aeternum* to one of the unappetizing public institutions, which served as unofficial landfill for parochial refuse. Because public high schools were so dangerous, with student bodies that were overwhelmingly black and poor, the mere threat of expelling a student from a Catholic institution, where the student bodies were overwhelmingly white, was usually sufficient to whip troublemakers into shape. Teachers only needed to say, "You'll end up at Daniel Boone," to strike terror into the most recalcitrant Irish-, Italian-, or Polish-American heart.

Though the girls outnumbered the boys at Cardinal Dougherty, the school was not, technically speaking, coeducational; rather, it was co-institutional, with girls on one side of the building and boys on the other. The student cafeterias were separated by a ten-foot-high wall, though sometimes, for no good reason, a panel door connecting the two halves of the gigantic refectory was left open, allowing the boys to sneak a peek at the girls and vice versa. The sexes were not allowed to socialize during school hours; male students caught gazing at the girls through that aperture were sometimes arraigned on charges of "mental rape" by puckish though dysfunctional priests and sent to detention. The system bred not so much misogyny as mystification; if the girls were close enough to look at, why were we forbidden to look at them?

This policy of straitjacketed gender segregation was unbelievably daft, the brainchild of overqualified eunuchs and flagellants manqué. Everything imaginable was done to prevent us from meeting Catholic girls; as a result, many of us ended up consorting with Jewesses, a development that seemed to fly in the face of everything the Church had been trying to accomplish since Caiaphas pusillanimously remanded Christ to the custody of Pontius Pilate. Others found favor with culturally adventurous Methodists or Episcopalians; I got my first blow job from a fallen-away Lutheran and remember it to this day as markedly less than satisfactory.

Even dismissal was conducted in segregated shifts. The girls got out at 2:45, the boys at 3:00, the girls at 3:15, the boys at 3:30. Students were forbidden to loiter around the premises after dismissal, making it even more difficult to meet members of the opposite sex. The girls who did stick around, the ones who salivated at the thought of riding home on the boys' buses, were generally viewed as cheap sluts. This was not always a criticism. Female students wore long green gabardine sheaths that made them look like bean stalks. Many looked like chubby bean stalks. The girls who liked to hang around until the boys got dismissed looked like bean stalks of easy virtue. Even when they wore their skirts thigh-high or the most provocative kneesocks since Salome was in pigtails, they remained about as sexually alluring as turnips. There was nothing fetching about them. They simply looked desperate.

With one notable exception, nothing important ever happened to me at Cardinal Dougherty. I developed no lifelong friendships, fell in love with no girls, joined no clubs, succumbed to the influence of no mentors. The school was located several miles from my home in a snooty neighborhood, and most of the students looked down on anyone living in a racially mixed community. As a result, I never felt at home there. I had close friends, true, classmates I genuinely liked, but these friendships did not endure very far into adult life. Because of this, my memory of those years is hazy, with few vivid images standing out. Cardinal Dougherty was staffed by a team of dedicated, generally competent diocesan priests, supplemented by a small group of lay teachers, all of them male. The school, as one would expect of an institution operated by a sect that had once threatened to incinerate Galileo, was stronger in the arts than the sciences, with the physics department in particular standing out as a ratiocinative Death Valley.

Due to the demands of work, I did not try out for any sports teams, though the only one I would have had a shot at in a school that large was cross-country. For purely philosophical reasons, I did not work on the school newspaper. Like all high school newspapers, ours was staffed by preening twits who wrote in a style best described as Lycée Hemingway: "We were on the street. There were three of us. There were three of them. We were white. They were not." I had already decided that I wanted to be a writer when I grew up, but I did not want to write like Ernest Hemingway, if only because everyone else did. I did not want to write some of the time the way he wrote all of the time, and I did not want to write most of the time the way the windbags on the newspaper wrote all of the time. Moreover, I could not see the point in publishing anything until I had something to say. I did not have anything to say until I was thirty-five and even then, not much.

Nothing served up in my high school literature classes played any role in my becoming a writer. I never strolled into a classroom and fell under the spell of a charismatic teacher, the way I had when I studied Latin with Father Ratermann in the seminary. I would not encounter another inspirational teacher until college, but by that point my career path was clear, so inspiration was no longer required. Whatever encouragement I did receive as an adolescent came from my father, a high school dropout who had somehow intuited that literature was a balm and a beacon, not a dead amphibian to be carved up in a laboratory. Writing, he understood, had cathartic power; putting words on paper enabled the otherwise impotent to exert a measure of control over their environment, to transform reality in all its cheerlessness into something more to their liking. Being a self-loathing drunk did not automatically disqualify him as a mentor; as I would later learn, most writers were self-loathing drunks. It came with the territory.

After he was dead, when I was casting about for material I could use to spit-shine his memory, I would recall the moment when the notion of making a living as a writer first entered my head. It was when I was ten years old and he gave me my first writing job, as his official stenographer, a position I continued to hold straight through high school. My father, as previously noted, was the sort of person who regularly threw fits. Social injustice, endemic political corruption, the rise of rock 'n' roll, and the depravity of Negroes were the themes most likely to set him off. But unlike other hard-drinking men, he would not let it rest there. Instead, his apoplexy nudged him toward the epistolary mode. Sometimes when he had worked himself into a fit of sufficiently high dudgeon, he would announce his intention to write an angry letter to the editor of the local newspaper. There were three Delaware Valley newspapers at the time, but the one that most incensed him was the *Evening Bulletin,* which he ceaselessly denounced as the mouthpiece of the plutocracy, the pawn of the feckless GOP.

Because his handwriting was atrocious, because he was physically lazy, because he was usually too juiced up to focus his eyes, and because I was in no position to refuse him, he insisted that I transcribe his denunciations precisely as he dictated them and then mail them to the targets of his displeasure. Whenever he plunged into one of these dyspeptic moods, he truly seemed to have taken leave of his senses, just like the rest of those prolix lunatics who never fail to end their letters to the editor without announcing that they are canceling their subscriptions for good, as if this would imperil the financial well-being of the publication. The difference was his prose. Most people who fire off angry letters to the editor write the way they speak: like billygoats. My father, by contrast, had a touch of the poet; his turn of phrase and choice of words were things of beauty. He had read Charles Dickens, Jack London, F. Scott Fitzgerald, Theodore Dreiser, Sinclair Lewis, the Brontës. He could recite portions of "The Charge of the Light Brigade," "The Song of Hiawatha," "The Wreck of the Hesperus," "Paul Revere's Ride," and a sizable chunk of Mark Antony's funeral oration from *Julius Caesar*. He was surprisingly fond of Cato the Elder, otherwise lightly regarded in the Quaker City. In short, he knew whereof he spoke. Or, rather, he knew whereof they spoke and imitated their way of speaking.

His jeremiads were, accordingly, laced with poignant imagery, edifying turns of phrase, and a lofty, tongue-in-cheek style he may have appropriated from Mark Twain, filled with pithy phrases like "More in sorrow than in anger, I take my pen in hand" and "Come not between the dragon and his wrath." At this late date, I can no longer recall what the letters were about, nor the specific outrages that triggered his ire, but they usually included a handful of fulminations against the house vampire Herbert Hoover, whose heartless economic policies had driven the workingman, yea, verily into the shadow of the Valley of Death. There was an anachronistic quality to these attacks, as Hoover, be he villain, stooge, or nincompoop, had been out of office for around thirty years. But a feud was a feud, and a bloodsucking leech was a bloodsucking leech.

Unlike my father, my high school literature teachers did not know whereof they spoke, nor whereof anybody else spoke. They spoke anyway. The syllabi they arrayed against us like Imperial Rome's merciless legions at Masada were unilaterally punitive, consisting of narcoleptic stories by Nathaniel Hawthorne, dreary sludge by Thomas Hardy, lunkheaded prose by John Steinbeck, and a cornucopia of hooey by that stable of braying jackasses whom high school literature professors have always revered. They were quite taken by *The Glass Menagerie*. Quite taken indeed.

Just to put everyone in an even more homicidal mood, teachers would occasionally throw in a few morsels from Chaucer, a perennial hit with high school boys. Never truly sold on the notion that great literature could appeal to us on its own merits—an assumption that was probably true—they forced us to parse and diagram sentences, ferret out cryptic metaphors, and use every last ounce of our sleuthing capacities to pin down the messianic imagery in *Moby-Dick*, though we were never sure whether Captain Ahab, Ishmael, or the whale himself was the Christ figure. Even when they introduced us to undeniably great writers like Joseph Conrad and Henry James, they insisted on our reading their most demanding novels, the ones we were far too young to appreciate, nineteenth-century masterpieces that, however brilliant, would automatically tax any teenager's patience, if only because of the archaic language. Our teachers did not care. The quality of mercy was a concept that could gain no purchase in their stalagmitic hearts.

I spent my last two years at Cardinal Dougherty hiding in the back of the class, concealed behind a sowlike creature named Arthur Prendergast. It was Prendergast's girth that enabled me to read the complete works of Ian Fleming, Arthur Conan Doyle, and Ray Bradbury without getting caught by my instructors. Arthur fell into that class of mildly jolly individuals who seem to have been born old and never been young, though it is closer to the truth to say that that they were born fat and had never been thin. Concealed behind this affable razorback, I was able to do a tremendous amount of casual reading, and for this I was eternally grateful. Meanwhile, all the boys up front were being systematically driven out of their minds by clerics delivering listless harangues about the pulverized dreams of the doomed tobogganer Ethan Frome or the moral inflexibility of that honey-tongued Dixie barrister Atticus Finch. My classmates had done nothing to deserve this. They were, to borrow one of my father's favorite citations, more sinned against than sinning. They were truly the Holy Innocents.

I had one or two memorable teachers in high school; most of the others were dullards or flunkies. My history professor in junior year was a flashy blade in his early thirties who wore ritzy clothes, was rumored to be the son of a wealthy man, and, much like my third-grade teacher, Miss Needham, was suspected of having taken a poorly paid teaching job primarily as a stunt to infuriate his well-heeled father. Nothing else, we felt, could explain his presence among teen mortals; a teacher's salary in a Catholic school wouldn't keep him in worsted slacks, much less double-breasted trench coats. This was in the year 1967, when American fashion standards were coming apart at the seams. Mr. Rotchford was an obdurate holdout, the last Beau Brummel, a fiercely stylish chap determined to ride out our long national fashion nightmare.

It was almost impossible then, and is surely impossible now, for a young man teaching high school in an American city not to come across as a dweeb, a suck-up, or a schlub, but this was not the case with Angelo T. Rotchford. Unlike his colleagues, he did not wear serviceable penny loafers and regimentally striped ties, but Milanese slip-ons and teal cravats. Eschewing corduroy jackets with ghastly velveteen patches on the elbows—the uniform of so many pedagogues of the era—he opted for sleek cashmere blazers. He most certainly did not wear what my twelve-year-old son would later derisively refer to as "teacher pants." His peers shopped at the House of Sears & Roebuck; his charge card read "House of Burberry." By comparison with the rest of the staff—half of them fatsos in fraying cassocks, half of them string beans in weather-beaten cords—he was Süleyman the Magnificent.

Mr. Rotchford was a very capable teacher with a sharp sense of humor, and we all admired him. This was almost unheard of among students at that time, because teachers were generally viewed as jailers or snitches. If I do not recall anything in particular he had to say, I have no trouble recalling his affectionately irreverent attitude toward the subject matter, and of course, his fabulous duds. His colleagues were far less memorable, in either the sartorial or the pedagogical department. My physics teacher in senior year was a diminutive, mirthless loner who derived enormous pleasure from watching boys paddle each other. An accommodating sort, he supplied the paddle. Some of the boys found this funny, but I did not. The beady-eyed, poorly shaven hobbit was transparently depraved, but not very tall, and even at that tender age I understood that height trumped authority. By this time, I was six feet tall, and sixteen years of life with an ogre was more than enough preparation for two semesters with a reptile.

Dismayed by this weird mélange of voyeurism and bargain-basement deviancy, a group of us approached a priest we admired and asked him to have a word with our professor, but nothing came of it. Shortly before school ended, the pouty gnome threatened to flunk half the class, thereby preventing us from entering college, thereby exposing us to the prospect of being called up and sent to Vietnam. Cooler heads prevailed, and our F's were upgraded to D's and C's. It was revelatory that the powers that be would step in to address the grading issue but did not seem terribly concerned about the wayward dwarf's unnerving predilections in the disciplinary realm.

A few teachers tried hard but fell short of the mark. Father Calpin, our chemistry professor in junior year, was a meek and pious soul with a heart of gold, who would obligingly step out of the room for a few minutes during exams, thereby enabling the less gifted students to copy the answers off the more gifted ones, and thereby get into college. But as soon as we found out—through channels—that he suffered from a heart condition, we moved heaven and earth to polish him off by Thanksgiving: grasshoppers in the desk drawer, bowling balls rolling around the stadium seating, frisky rodents cavorting in the closet, and, of course, that trusty old favorite, explosions in the lab. The fact is, we found out that he had a heart condition from a priest we liked who specifically requested that we go easy on him. To this day, I cannot imagine what he was thinking of. Father Calpin himself took no offense at our attempts to send him to an early grave, dismissing our stunts as harmless adolescent hijinks. A living saint, he eventually won us over. By Christmas we had stopped trying to kill him, and by Easter we weren't even making all that much of an effort to induce a stroke. But right up to the end of the year, we kept on stuffing those grasshoppers in the desk drawer just to watch him go flying out of his chair.

Our religion instructor during sophomore year was one of those dif-
fident, cerebral sorts who were often found in Catholic colleges but rarely
in high schools. His assignment to Dougherty seemed to constitute
some form of ostracism by the diocese, or perhaps a test of his mettle,
though once he'd been around us a few weeks, he may have interpreted
it more as a reprisal. He had come to the right place to get his mettle
tested, because no one in our class was interested in anything he had to
say. Not one of us cared about Vatican II, an event of stupendous importance that was much in the news those days. None of us cared about the
freshly unearthed Dead Sea scrolls, which were all the rage. And it goes
without question that none of us made any effort to behave.

Frustrated, he took to grabbing students by the collar and giving
them three sharp smacks across the face. He referred to these as "three
smashes," which sounded more like "thwee smathes," as he was afflicted
by a pronounced lisp. He was a magnificently homely man, with a face
like a Komodo dragon. He also had a tendency to bite down on his
tongue when he hit a student; as the victim's face was practically adjoining his at the time, it was hard for the miscreant to avoid giggling, since
it always appeared that the priest was choking on a wiener the size of
Denmark. Smirking, chuckling, or any other form of physiognomic
insubordination could lead us into uncharted waters: four smashes, five
smashes, sometimes as many as six. Prickly, but no idiot, he did not try
smacking any of the larger, tougher boys.

He was not a vicious man, merely outgunned. At the outset, he was
fond of me; aware that I had only recently left the seminary, he assumed
that I was fully conversant with the latest developments in the Curia.
But I was not at all fond of him, as he was an unsightly goof, and once or
twice I deliberately put him in situations where he had no choice but to
retaliate. Getting him to smash me in the face apprised my peers that I
was no longer a pious seminarian but just another run-of-the-mill punk
like them. There was nothing especially unwholesome about these measures; in fact, there was something nostalgic about his lighthearted retribution. I thought he was silly; I did not think him cruel.

The absence of pedagogical mentors was a source of no concern during my high school years, as I was getting all the motivation I needed

from my two employers. But if I did not have an inspiring teacher, I did have an inspiring subject: French. I was smitten by the French language from the first time I heard it uttered and have remained infatuated ever since. This unlikely romance had begun to flower five years earlier, when I stayed up late one Saturday night to watch the classic black-and-white film *Beau Geste* with my father. *Beau Geste* was a hell-for-leather saga about three English brothers (Ray Milland, Robert Preston, and the fantastically miscast Gary Cooper) who run off to join the French Foreign Legion after a precious jewel disappears from their aunt's home during an impromptu séance. The story kicks off in the rolling English countryside, but most of the action takes place in the swirling sands of the Sahara. There, at Fort Zinderneuf, a desolate military outpost in French West Africa, two of the three boys fall prey to the sadistic martinet Sergeant Markoff, played with demonic glee by Brian Donlevy, who was nominated for the Oscar as Best Supporting Actor for his performance. Ultimately, reviving a tradition from the games of their youth, two of the boys give the third what they refer to as a "Viking's funeral": a huge floating bonfire, with a dog buried at the corpse's feet. The dog in this case was Sergeant Markoff, by this point very much dead. The film was based on Percival Wren's immortal novel of the same name, one of the most popular works of fiction ever published. It sold millions of copies, was translated into countless languages, and was made into four feature-length films, not counting a dire parody called *The Last Remake of Beau Geste*. Sadly, Wren and his work are now completely forgotten. This is unfortunate, since *Beau Geste* had everything a young boy could possibly ask for in either a book or a film: honor, romance, intrigue, swordplay, surprise attacks by bloodthirsty Tuaregs, heroic deaths, fatal confrontations with corrupt authority figures, and first-rate funerals. Not to mention hell-for-leather.

Forty years after seeing the film, I sought out Wren's final resting place, in a village a few miles down the road from my wife's birthplace in the Cotswolds, and deposited a wreath of flowers on his disintegrating, poorly maintained grave. I felt that I owed it to him, for, from the moment I first saw the film inspired by his novel, I had dreamed of living in France, even though none of the action takes place there and even though none of the actors was French, most assuredly not Gary Cooper. Years later I discovered that the French Foreign Legion at the time of *Beau Geste* consisted almost exclusively of lowlife thugs who had taken it on the lam, one step ahead of the coppers, and not dashing English public-school boys on the prowl for a ripping good time. By that point, it did not matter. The spell had been cast.

The spell was certainly not cast by any members of Cardinal Dougherty's modern-languages department. My first French teacher was a wraithlike Polish American well into his thirties. He was bespectacled, pint-sized, studious, and a bachelor. He was not French Foreign Legion material. Mr. Stan was a perfectly nice fellow who once told me that I resembled Julius Caesar, which seemed like a compliment until I found out that Caesar was a fat, bald, epileptic bisexual. I liked Mr. Stan well enough until the day he began tormenting a Venezuelan boy who showed up in the middle of the year. Spanish was Carlos's native tongue, but he was incapable of learning French: This enraged Mr. Stan, who insisted that, as the languages were cousins, Carlos had a head start on the rest of us and should be able to speak *sans accent.*

It made no difference to him that the new arrival was simultaneously struggling to learn English; that it was difficult for native Spanish speakers to master Italian and French because the very similarities of the languages confused the issue; and that, on top of everything else, Carlos was not especially bright. Carlos's ineptitude was not a crime in our eyes, but it was to Mr. Stan, who treated him with a disdain and cruelty woefully out of proportion to his failings. Still, in the end, we were no better than our teacher, profiting from his badgering of the cowed Caraquenian because it diverted attention away from our own linguistic deficiencies.

My French teacher during my junior and senior years was a pompous buffoon, a fiftyish cleric who referred to himself in the third person and whose familiarity with Gallic civilization was limited to owning a couple of Maurice Chevalier records and being in firm possession of the fact that Quasimodo was a Paris-based hunchback. He would sit in the front of the class with a papier-mâché model of the cathedral of Notre Dame poised on his desk and proceed to butcher nursery-school words like *la chaise* and *le stylo*, all the while sporting a self-satisfied grin suggesting that he had just edged out Jean-Paul Sartre, Henri de Montherlant, and Simone de Beauvoir for the Prix Goncourt. He knew as much about French as the rest of us knew about bathosphere maintenance.

This did not matter. As I had never before met anyone who had been to Paris, the very sound of words like *baguette* and *gendarme* seemed insanely exotic to my ears, evoking lofty dreams of refinement, elegance, and escape, even when massacred by a halfwit cleric. True, I had grown up around working-class people who spoke Italian, but in my social set Italian was derided as the grubby patois of duplicitous lily-livers who were constantly siding with the Germans in world wars and then thinking better of it. This stereotype prevailed even though all the Italians we knew, including my uncle Sam Mazzarella, had grown up on the banks of the Schuylkill, and quite a few of them had fought valiantly in the Second World War on the American side. But at the time, the Italian tongue had none of the sex appeal it would later acquire; Italian—or, heaven forbid, Spanish or Yiddish—did not evoke the Louvre or the Eiffel Tower or Claude Monet or Napoleon's electrifying triumph at Austerlitz. It was a peasant lingo spoken by greaseballs from South Philly who sold cheese in disconcertingly large quantities to timorous merchants who had no obvious need for daily dairy deliveries of such magnitude. French, by contrast, conjured up fanciful images of Charlemagne, Charles Martel, the Three Musketeers, the Man in the Iron Mask, the French Foreign Legion, and the old crowd pleaser herself, Joan of Arc.

From this point on, I thought of the French language as my exit visa out of the working class. On one side of the door lay poverty, prejudice, ignorance, gloom. On the other side lay affluence, sophistication, luxury, and perhaps even happiness. In my mind, success and happiness were inexorably intertwined with high culture. Growing up to be rich meant nothing to me, because the newly rich were renowned for their vulgarity, and if you were still vulgar, you were still poor. Anyway, I grew up being taught that the rich proceeded directly to Hell after they died and stayed there for the rest of eternity, and nothing I have learned since then has given me any reason to think otherwise.

Until I stumbled upon the splendors of the French language, religion had been the dominant element in my life. Now the Book of Revelations and the Holy Bible were supplanted by *Madame Bovary* and *Père Goriot*. This transformation was something I tried to keep under my hat. Len would have felt betrayed by such prissiness; Uncle Jerry would have been horrified; Glenn would have been baffled as to why a thrill-seeking young boy would start obsessing about Paris, France, when he could simply buy himself a train ticket and mosey eighty-five miles up the track to New York, New York. This was yet another instance where I simply held my tongue, deeming discretion the better part of valor.

Although my seduction by French civilization was genuine, spontaneous, and irreversible, quickly evolving into a passion that would last a lifetime, the original motivation for my francophilia was somewhat less than pure. From the outset, I viewed speaking French as a skill I could easily master and then throw back into my father's face. In retrospect, it is amazing how circumscribed my world was by my attempts to belittle my father in retaliation for his belittling me. But this was war, and the wedge between us widened every day: Every book I read, every movie I watched, every idea I assimilated furnished yet another tool to aid me in my flight from my father's economic class, a class I sought not only to exit but to disown. The ironic part was that my father, endowed with a sophistication and a curiosity about the world that were not commonly associated with the proletariat, had in some way prepared all of us to secede from the class he had been born into.

Because he was not a dunce, because he valued books and film and music, he had, without realizing it, armed his children with the skills they would need to escape from a class in which he himself was trapped for life. It was a class from which, had the opportunity ever arisen, he would have joyously taken flight as well. But because he could not escape—hamstrung by the dishonorable discharge, the shabby work record, the addiction to alcohol—he resented anyone who could. Though he did not really want us to grow up to be like him, warning us to avoid the mistakes he had made—dropping out of school, going AWOL, emptying every whiskey bottle in the Delaware Valley in the hopes of eventually finding the one whose contents would bring him happiness—he begrudged us every step we took away from him.

Nothing sickened him more than the thought that his children might get the life that he wanted. He was a true child of his tribe: If you were in, he was out; if you were up, he was down.

When I began studying French history, no one impressed me more than Joan of Arc. I had quite a crush on the Maid of Orléans throughout high school; she seemed to be the apotheosis of teen chutzpah. By a strange coincidence, at the same time that I was daydreaming about Saint Michael, Saint Catherine, and Saint Margaret—Joan of Arc's unexpected confidants—wondering if there was any possibility whatsoever that one of them might put in a late-twentieth-century appearance, however brief, in my neighborhood, my father actually did begin hearing voices. Shortly after John Kennedy was assassinated, a tragedy that seemed to affect our family even more than it affected JFK's, my father got into the habit of staying up all night, first talking to himself, then weeping, then conversing with a series of incorporeal interlocutors whose ranks ranged from Saint Peter to the recently deceased Pope John XXIII to Jesus Christ Himself. Hidden away upstairs, self-mummified in our sheets, we could hear snippets of these conversations, which always reached the critical moment when my father would come right out and ask the Son of God precisely how he fit into His divine plan and what specific duties he was expected to fulfill between now and the hour of his death.

A pioneer in the field of extraterrestrial badinage, my father had convinced himself that even though he was but a lowly security guard and an alcoholic, the Lamb of God should be expected to have his personal file right there at his fingertips and be more than ready to drop everything and supply him with a few pointers on how he might upgrade his performance as a Christian. The notion that Christ had nothing better to do with his time than to mentor delusional alkies was the height of arrogance, illustrating that come-as-you-are chumminess that has now become a staple of American religion. Christ the Savior never answered any of my father's questions, preferring to maintain the distance for which He is famous. This did not prevent paterfamilias from keeping up a one-sided dialogue with the Messiah throughout my high school years and well into college.

It should have come as no surprise to any of us that he was engaging in these fruitless colloquies with the Son of God, because nobody else in the house was going to speak to him unless coerced. If we were very quiet and he was not especially drunk, he would stay out of our rooms and leave us alone. To help things along, we would make sure to go to the bathroom before bedtime, ensuring that our bladders were empty, and take special care to not allow the bedsprings to rustle beneath us. But if he detected even the slightest sounds of movement in our rooms, he would stumble to the foot of the stairs and ask one of us—usually me—to come down and talk to him. This was not in the way of an invitation; it was a command performance. The subject of our witching-hour confabs was usually subversive Negroes or the war in Vietnam, conversations that always ended in arguments, as my father viewed all of us as being in league with Martin Luther King Jr., Stokely Carmichael, Fidel Castro, Bob Dylan. We feuded without end during those late-night summit conferences, though the arguments never came to blows, because I always backed off when I saw him get that unmistakable look in his eye that presaged violence. Night after night, he would sit there, smiling, perhaps recounting an amusing story about something that had happened at work—like the man who took umbrage when told that he could not make love to his wife in a semiprivate room at the University of Pennsylvania Hospital because it contravened hospital rules—and then I would go off to get myself a glass of water or use the bathroom or tie my shoe, and when I turned back to face him, I would find Hyde in the seat so recently occupied by Jekyll. Then the gloves would come off and the high-octane goading would start: "I see that your old friend H. Rap Brown is back in town . . . ," "I see that your pal Martin Luther King is stirring up trouble in Georgia . . . ," "I see those instigators are trying to bust up a block out in Folcroft." To the extent that it was possible, I would try to avoid taking the bait, having considerably less interest in Martin Luther King's career than my father thought. Then, when he started to turn vicious, I would mentally catalogue all the misfortunes he had suffered, taking due note of the bullet wound he had once absorbed, and remind myself that I was still giving away fifty pounds. At which point, I would decide not to push it. Not yet, anyway. All in good time.

When he was extremely drunk, and extremely upset at what Martin Luther King had done to his old neighborhood, both of which made him desperate for company, he would barrel into our rooms and kiss us in a nauseating simulation of paternal affection. This was even worse than listening to him. Yet, no matter how bad things got, I honestly believed that time was on our side, that sooner or later we would all escape from this Quaker City concentration camp. I spent most of my childhood dreaming about adulthood; there was no mileage in being a kid. No longer being young had been my driving ambition since I was nine; the only thing I wanted out of my childhood was an end to it.

To the extent that it was possible, I avoided my father. We all did. We took jobs or joined clubs or feigned illnesses or manufactured excuses for sleepovers. This worked for a while. Then one night when I was sixteen years old, he asked if I was still giving my $13.10 in earnings to my mother every week. It was suppertime; the whole family was seated at the dining room table, eating food we did not especially care for. He was drunk when he asked the question, spoiling for a fight.

"When I was your age, my mother didn't have to ask me for my pay when I came home from work," he noted, launching into one of his favorite spiels, once again conjuring up the reliably unverifiable mythology of the Great Depression. I do not remember the exact words I used in response to this latest tirade, but it was something to the effect that I needed the money to pay the $15 fees for the college applications I was filling out. This was not what he wanted to hear.

"You don't have to worry about that," he snapped. "Haven't we always taken care of you?"

I thought about that for a second, then threw caution to the wind. "Actually, you've never taken care of me," I replied, emboldened by a temerity that had not existed five seconds earlier. "So I'm taking care of it myself."

Life changed in the next fifteen seconds, both his and mine. Livid, not quite believing his ears, he half leaped, half lurched out of his chair and circled around the table. I jumped out of my chair and bolted into the living room. He followed me, closing in, ready to charge. I could see that he planned to punch me. I had other plans. I punched him. I'd punched people before, so it wasn't terra incognita. I cocked my right fist, aimed, took a short, healthy swing, smacked his forehead, swatted him away. *Use your jab, use your jab,* as Len used to say. It wasn't a hard punch, certainly not a haymaker, but it was solid enough for him to know he'd been hit. Then and there, the topography of our lives shifted. From the moment he came barreling into the living room, he was a different person in my eyes. What I saw was no longer a dangerous man armed with his fists and a belt. What I saw before me was a paunchy, middle-aged drunk who couldn't take me in a fair fight. What I saw was a bully getting a taste of his own medicine.

My mother and sisters intervened; no more punches were thrown. Fleeing the house to stay overnight with a friend, I understood that the Rubicon had finally been crossed. I still feared my father; in a way, I now feared him more than ever. But I no longer feared him enough to let him hit me again. The next day, via reliable neighborhood intermediaries, my mother let it be known that it was safe to come home. She must have given the old man yet another of her toothless ultimatums: Lay off the kids or you and I are going to call it quits. I am not sure that he dreaded being separated from his family, but he did dread losing his wife's income. Without her paycheck, he'd be out on the street, down on Skid Row. I avoided contact with him for the next few days: I was out with my band, I was out at my job, I was out playing basketball, I was out. Stewed to the gills when the incident occurred, he retreated into the reassuring amnesia that alcoholism confers on its acolytes and pretended that the whole thing had never happened. Not once for the rest of our lives did we ever talk about the events of that evening. He never again asked if I had volunteered to give my paycheck to my mother. Nor did he ever try hitting me again. He understood that those days were now over; that if he used a belt, I'd use a tire iron. One thing was clear to both of us: If he wanted a punching bag, he'd have to look elsewhere.

For obvious reasons, this made him dangerous. From that day onward, I never went to bed without jamming a chair up against the door and making sure that a butcher knife was lodged safely in the cowboy boots that sat beside my nightstand. I was sure he was only biding his time, waiting for revenge. I was biding my time as well, waiting to be accepted into college so I could clear out of there forever. I never slept well in my father's house again. And I never turned my back on him.

I was a short-timer now; the finish line was in sight. Once high school was over, once I went away to college, the life I had been looking forward to for so many years could begin. It would be my life, and neither Dr. Jekyll nor Mr. Hyde was going to be part of it. As one of my instructors might have put it, in his maladroit, mangled French, *plus c'est la même chose, plus ça change.*

Chapter 9. **Second Fiddle**

One Saturday morning when I was long past my childhood, my wife phoned from her car and asked me to switch on the radio and identify the piece being performed on the classical music station. I was in a rush that morning, so I tuned in quickly, listened to a few measures, and told her that it sounded like Dvořák's Cello Concerto. Then I hung up. A few minutes later, motoring along in my own car, I switched on the radio just as the piece was reaching its conclusion. I then phoned my wife and said that it was Schumann's Cello Concerto she'd been listening to, not Dvořák's, and I was sure of it. A few minutes later, when the performance finished, the announcer came on the air and said that listeners had just been treated to a stirring rendition of Robert Schumann's Cello Concerto in A minor.

I knew the composition was Schumann's because there are only a handful of cello concertos in the active canon, and only the famous ones ever get played. These are by Camille Saint-Saëns, who began giving public violin recitals at the age of two; Johannes Brahms, who as a young man used to thump the ivories in a Hamburg bordello, permanently souring his attitude toward women; Edward Elgar, who was ignored at the beginning of his career and ridiculed at the end; the aforementioned Dvořák; and Haydn. There are also formidable cello concertos by Benjamin Britten, Richard Strauss, and a handful of others, but they are almost never heard on the radio and would never be confused with Schumann's.

While it is true that Schumann may fleetingly sound like a few of his contemporaries, none of them wrote famous cello concertos, so when my wife asked me to identify the piece, I knew that it could not be by Beethoven, Liszt, Berlioz, Schubert, or Mendelssohn. Identifying Schumann as the composer was child's play for anyone familiar with classical music. More impressive was when I identified Jacqueline du Pré as the soloist. But here I was simply making an educated guess: There are only a few recordings of Schumann's Cello Concerto in existence, and because of her gifts, plus the aura of tragedy that surrounded her— she died at age forty-two of multiple sclerosis—du Pré's recording is one of the most frequently aired on the radio. So all in all it seemed like a reasonable hunch.

Anyone who loved classical music could pull off a stunt like this; a close friend, from a more prosperous background than I, can name the key a piece is written in, which I cannot. People like this, people who regard classical music as something akin to oxygen or sunlight, are harder and harder to find in a nation that seems forever poised to revert to its backwoods roots. This is especially true the farther one shimmies down the economic ladder: It goes without saying that people who grow up in humble row homes are unlikely to listen to "serious" music and even less likely to perform it. Susan Orsini was an exception.

I met Susan Orsini the day I graduated from high school. The encounter would change my life, making it both different and better, not just during the time we were together but forever. Our meeting was the result of happenstance; there were 1,435 students in the graduating class at Cardinal Dougherty, and the only municipal facility large enough to accommodate such a dense throng was Convention Hall, a cavernous auditorium that sat at the edge of the University of Pennsylvania campus. Convention Hall was the home of the Philadelphia 76ers, who had won the NBA championship the year before, fielding what was then considered to be the single greatest team in the history of the league. Game five was the first basketball game I ever attended, and by far the most memorable, though pro basketball was so poorly thought of in Philadelphia at the time that my friend Tom Smith and I simply walked up and bought tickets a few minutes before tip-off. There were five future Hall of Fame players on the floor that evening: Wilt Chamberlain, Rick Barry, Hal Greer, Nate Thurmond, and Billy Cunningham, not to mention the redoubtable Chet "The Jet" Walker. Never again would I attend a game showcasing such a dazzling array of talent.

I met Susan because my name began with a "Q" and hers with an

"O," and at graduation we were lined up backstage in parallel lines (girls in one row, boys in the other) right next to each other. After four years of never being allowed anywhere near the girls on the other side of the school, we were now instructed to parade out onto the stage in tandem as if we were all the best of friends. This was perhaps because the Catholic Church abhorred sex but revered symmetry. Though not beautiful in the narrow, technical sense of the word, Susan was one of those girls whose vivaciousness made her seem beautiful: If she could not be the prettiest girl in the room, she would act as if she was. She had a lithe figure, an imperious smile, piercing, somewhat conspiratorial eyes, and lustrous brown hair. As soon as she opened her mouth, I knew that she had more going for her than any other girl I had ever met.

We talked about this and that backstage, and at some point I volunteered the information that I was a musician of sorts. So was she. I played guitar; she played violin in the high school orchestra. I knew that Convention Hall was the only venue the Beatles had not sold out during their 1964 American tour. She did not; popular music was not her forte. She was headed off to Washington in the fall to study music at Catholic University. I was heading directly across town to study literature at Saint Joseph's College. We hit it off.

Up until that backstage encounter at Convention Hall, I had never met anyone who played the violin. In the neighborhoods I grew up in, some toothless old drunk might occasionally hammer out a polka on the accordion, at least until the neighbors threatened to call the cops and have him stuffed into the meat wagon, or some wine-soaked *paesano* might warble a few tremulous bars from *Rigoletto,* but that was about as cosmopolitan as things ever got. If people played anything, it was the drums. Violins were not part of the equation, nor were French horns, oboes, bassoons, harps, piccolos, harmoniums, or celestes. When I met Susan, I knew that I was entering an exciting new world that had previously been inaccessible to me. Anyone could read good books and watch good movies, the way I had been doing for years. But dating a violin player was like joining a club where they wouldn't let you in unless you were refined and well-spoken and promised to never play the sound track from *Under the Yum-Yum Tree* at three o'clock in the morning. It was a never-never land, a foreign country I had previously visited only in my dreams. I made sure I got her phone number.

By a strange coincidence, Susan knew one of my closest friends, Mike Craig. Mike was the boy who had looked on in African-American disbelief when Monsignor Collis visited the seventh-grade class at Saint Benedict's and told everyone to be extra nice to the Queenans because we were the first white people to move into the neighborhood in years. Mike was hosting a graduation party that night, with my band, the Phase Shift Network, or Stained Glass, or whatever we were calling ourselves at the time, providing entertainment of a sort. Three songs into our set, during our routine evisceration of Cream's "Tales of Brave Ulysses," I looked up and saw Susan standing directly in front of the bandstand. She was wearing red culottes with a white top, and by this point I was quite taken with her, particularly in this fetching strawberry-shortcake incarnation. We started dating the next day and soon were seeing each other two or three times a week. One Saturday night, we went all the way downtown to eat at a famous restaurant and then hailed a cab to a fancy movie theater and took in the just-released *2001: A Space Odyssey*. She told me that the opening theme had been written by Richard Strauss, "The Blue Danube" by Johann Strauss, and the ambient music by an Eastern European composer named György Ligeti. I erroneously assumed that the two Strausses were related and did not learn until much later that one of them had briefly been on the führer's payroll, though after the war he insisted that he had never really cared for the Nazis and only accepted their paychecks in the service of his career. The other Strauss had no fascist skeletons in his closet. Susan and I dressed to the nines for the outing, as going downtown to see a first-run movie was special.

Susan came from a better economic class than I did. Though the Orsinis lived in a tiny row home, it was in a nicer neighborhood than ours. Her father had a steady job; her mother was quite witty and sophisticated; and the very fact that one of their three children played the violin indicated that they had aspirations far beyond those of my own family and a bit of spare cash to help make those dreams come true. A golden child, Susan liked to be entertained, so I was going through my money fast. But she was worth it.

Susan tagged along to a few of my band's rehearsals, but she was never terribly fond of rock music, especially not the brand we played: Bar Mitzvah Acid Folk. A student of the classics and an intense performer, she made little effort to disguise her contempt for our bilious musicianship. Most people found us vaguely amusing, but she did not. As the summer progressed she began teaching me the rudiments of serious music. She loaded me up with LPs by Bach, Liszt, Chopin, Brahms. She told me to go home and listen to them carefully, and then the next time we went out, she would quiz me about each composition, asking if I had noticed how a theme was introduced in the first movement, then disappeared, then resurfaced in a slightly different form in the final movement. She took me to two free concerts by the Philadelphia Orchestra at the Robin Hood Dell, their summer home in Fairmount Park. I do not remember the names of the soloists or the pieces performed, as my thoughts were focused elsewhere.

Susan also lent me several fusty music-appreciation books that I found dry and indifferently written. But when she gave me a book chronicling the lives of the great composers, I was bowled over. Prior to meeting her, I had always associated classical music with nose-in-the-air stuffed shirts and had no idea that Mozart died a pauper, that Schubert never owned a piano, or that Stravinsky used to pass along commissions to Erik Satie, who worked cheap. Now that we'd gotten the class-warfare thing out of the way, the musicians seemed as real to me as John, Paul, George, Ringo, and Elvis.

I came late to a love of music. From the time I was small until the moment I heard the Beatles' "Love Me Do" in November 1963, I had regarded music in primarily disciplinary terms, as just another form of punishment my father could inflict on his family because he was stronger than us. While it is true that, at least by the standards of the workingman, he had relatively good taste in music—he was fond of Frank Sinatra, Ella Fitzgerald, Count Basie, etc.—he simultaneously had very bad taste in music, as he was quite taken by such hokey trifles as "Volare" and "That's Amore." My father's generation never forgave society for sending them off to rescue civilization from Hitler and Mussolini and then repaying them with Bill Haley and His Comets. Enraged that the music they loved was now considered passé, they retaliated with kitsch. I did not stop hating music until I could stake out some terrain of my own, and even though I would soften over the years and revise my earlier opinions about Sinatra, Dean Martin, Tony Bennett, and a few others, there are certain artists and certain songs I can never hear without cringing. To me, the names Bing Crosby, Perry Como, Jerry Vale, and Julius LaRosa are like Pol Pot, Ivan the Terrible, Jack the Ripper, and Zog.

Though young people at the time made no effort to conceal their feelings on this matter, adults could not get it through their heads how much we despised their music. One day, the nation's most esteemed Champagne Music maker, Lawrence Welk, fired a singer named Natalie Nevins from his popular Saturday night television program, a show my father had forced us to watch since it first began airing in 1955, provided we had a television at the time. Nevins was a belligerently perky chantoozey whose greatest crime, so the rumor mill had it, was attempting to upstage the mule-faced bandleader with the Wiener-schnitzelian accent. But others said he dumped her because she was late for a plane.

A high-ranking priest at Cardinal Dougherty had the last name Nevins, and word got out that Natalie was his sister. One day, a rumor began to spread that a schoolwide letter-writing campaign was being organized in the hope that Welk would change his mind about canning Miss Nevins after receiving sixty-five hundred irate missives from Philadelphia high school students vowing to boycott the program forever if this very fine, though perhaps overbearingly bouncy, singer was forced to walk the plank. Some of the students who would be asked to write these letters were already donning preposterous sixties camouflage— wide-wale corduroy bell-bottoms, paisley dress shirts, granny glasses— and slipping off every weekend to a Center City dive called the Trauma, where they got to inhale overpriced reefer and ogle scantily clad tartlets while bands with puzzling names like the Village Fugs hacked their way through such catchy tunes as "River of Shit" and "Slum Goddess of the Lower East Side."

At the first concert I attended at the Trauma, a gang of bikers had a bit of a dust-up with a quartet of goonish record-company representatives after the men in suits refused to stop heckling Jesse Colin Young & the Youngbloods, who had recently deserted Mercury Records for RCA. The Youngbloods' limp signature tune exhorted the youth of America to (1) smile on their brothers; (2) get together; and (3) love one another, if at all possible, right now. The band was so strapped for material that they had to play their two big hit songs—the other was "Grizzly Bear"—twice in each set. The Youngbloods and the motorcycle gang were not a natural fit, but the bikers, to their credit, apprised the four well-turned-out goons that their antisocial behavior was ruining things for the other patrons. When the goons did not take the hint, they beat them on and about the head, smote them hip and thigh, and threw them down the stairs.

Teenagers witnessing this episode with a mixture of apprehension and self-congratulation—"No two ways about it, Tom; we're men!"—were not likely to sign any petitions begging Lawrence Welk or anyone else to reconsider a seemingly impetuous personnel decision. Especially those, like me, who had been press-ganged into watching his show in the first place. I never found out how many letters Dougherty students ended up writing to the bandleader, if any, but Natalie Nevins did not keep her job.

By the time I met Susan Orsini, music had become the center of my universe. My bandmates in tow, I would rush out every weekend to hear the likes of Jimi Hendrix, Cream, the Doors, Jefferson Airplane, the Kinks, Big Brother & the Holding Company, the Mothers of Invention, Procul Harum, Sly & the Family Stone, Quicksilver Messenger Service, Steppenwolf, the original Fleetwood Mac, the Grateful Dead, and, whenever possible, the Rolling Stones. For reasons he never made clear, my father did not object to any of these bands, but he refused to let us play any songs by the Beatles within the confines of his house. Shortly after the lovable Liverpudlians made landfall in America, a Catholic newspaper published an article branding them minions of Lucifer, scions of Baal, and wolves in sheep's clothing—the malefic trifecta—whose sole purpose in life was to corrupt the youth of America and lead them down the road to rack and ruin. After reading this, my father never relaxed his animosity toward a pop combo that, by comparison with many other ensembles of the time, seemed cheerful, upbeat, innocuous, and actually kind of cute.

When the Beatles appeared on *The Ed Sullivan Show* on three consecutive Sundays in February 1964, my father refused to let us watch them. He also refused to let us go out and watch them elsewhere. He forced us to stay indoors, staring at the clock, fully aware of what we were missing, while the sands of time ran out. It was as if he were inviting us, nay, encouraging us, to slip rat poison into his lager. The most disorienting thing about his cruelty was that it had no detectable pattern or theme, as he didn't object to our watching the Rolling Stones on a Saturday night variety show called *The Hollywood Palace,* nor did he raise a fuss when we reserved the console to watch Jim Morrison & the Doors the night they appeared on *The Ed Sullivan Show* four years later. None of this made any sense, because the Stones and the Doors really were minions of Lucifer and made little effort to disguise it.

Once Susan entered my life, pop music began to diminish in importance. This was partially because everything anyone needed to know about pop music he knew by the time he was fifteen, whereas classical music could keep a person occupied for a lifetime. Pedagogically speaking, Susan did not believe in starting at the bottom and working your way up. She refused to begin my education with *Night on Bald Mountain* or *Pictures at an Exhibition;* she did not buy into the theory that those who dipped their toes into the water with *The Four Seasons* would ultimately acquire a taste for Bach's *Magnificat.* To her, it made more sense to start on the mountaintops (Beethoven, Mozart, Schubert, Wagner), then work your way down through the lower peaks (Ravel, Prokofiev, Bizet) until you finally reached the cities of the plains, where Aaron Copland and Nikolai Rimsky-Korsakov would be waiting for you. If you felt comfortable down on the flat, dry mesas, where *Billy the Kid* was always galumphing along in the background, that was fine. But you shouldn't start down there.

Susan was a fountain of informed opinions, and soon I had annexed all of them. She told me that that Dmitri Shostakovich could have been the greatest composer of the twentieth century were it not for the psychotic meddling of Josef Stalin, who kept threatening to kill him if he didn't start writing more music that celebrated the inevitable, though somewhat delayed, triumph of the industrial proletariat over the bootlicking forces of capitalism. She told me that the reason no one ever accused Brahms of writing half-baked incidental music—even those who disliked Brahms—was that he destroyed everything he did not want published, which Mozart did not. She told me that Gabriel Fauré was the greatest composer American audiences knew nothing about, with Leoš Janáček a close second.

Because I was thoroughly unschooled at the time—a tabula rasa, as she put it—this approach worked to perfection; I quickly, if not immediately, grasped why Haydn was superior to Borodin, why Delius was not in the same league as Berlioz, why Schubert was a colossus and Albéniz was not. Because of Susan's inflexibly patrician tastes, which I quickly acquired, it took me years to work my way backward and learn to appreciate the less obvious charms of the second- and third-tier composers, to understand that even if Jacques Ibert was not as brilliant as Giuseppe Verdi, Jacques Ibert was nevertheless brilliant.

Susan adored the titans, but she also made a place on the shelf for curiosities. Shortly after she began tutoring me, we went downtown on a record-buying expedition, during which she monitored my purchases with a martinet's rigor. She informed me that I must, must, must pick up Glenn Gould's 1955 recording of *The Goldberg Variations*, Vladimir Horowitz's haunting interpretation of Liszt's *Années de Pèlerinage*, and Rudolf Serkin's elegant rendering of Beethoven's *Moonlight, Pathétique,* and *Appassionata* sonatas. Also on the compulsory buying list were Beethoven's Third, Fifth, and Seventh symphonies as performed by Wilhelm Furtwängler and the Vienna Philharmonic, Bruno Walter's bracing set of Brahms's four symphonies, and Igor Stravinsky's *Petruschka* as played by the Boston Symphony Orchestra with the very capable Pierre Monteux at the helm. But she also pressured me into buying lesser-known works like Paul Hindemith's *Symphonic Metamorphoses of Themes by Carl Maria von Weber.* This is a beautiful, thoroughly accessible little number that—like Vaughan Williams's *Sinfonia Antarctica* and Josef Suk's Serenade for Strings—should be in the standard repertory but isn't, because for some reason music lovers who ought to know better have never taken a shine to it. The recording I bought was by the Philadelphia Orchestra under the baton of its longtime conductor Eugene Ormandy.

Susan had strong opinions about conductors and shared the reigning view among those in the know that the Hungarian-born Ormandy was a lightweight, a dud, a high-class hack at best. Advocates of this theory dismissed the bald, chubby Ormandy as a recycled fiddle player who had been lucky enough to inherit one of the world's greatest orchestras from the legendary Leopold Stokowski, but that his basic function was to serve as a diligent curator until a better conductor could be found. Soon, I began to express similarly strong opinions about conductors, voicing the view that Ormandy was a lightweight, a hack, a reconditioned Magyar fiddler who functioned purely in a curatorial capacity until a better conductor could be found. It was exhilarating to reach a point in my life where I could cavalierly toss around such opinions, casually slandering one of the world's most famous conductors and looking down my nose at some of its most revered composers. This brand of aspirational haughtiness—condescension from below—made me feel like a member of the elite, a North Philly cognoscente, if you will. This was what I had always imagined life would be like once I got called up to the majors.

I spent much of that memorable summer trashing Ormandy within earshot of anyone who would listen. It did not concern me, or deter me, that none of my friends had any idea what I was talking about, as they knew as little about classical music as I had known just a few weeks earlier. Throughout those months, I honed my material carefully, sharpening my rhetorical weapons for the moment that would inevitably arrive when I started college and would cross swords with someone foolish enough to try defending Eugene Ormandy. Armed with Susan's blast-furnace contempt—which I borrowed from her without actually asking, much the same way Patroclus filched that suit of armor from Achilles—and emboldened by my rapidly expanding knowledge of the classical idiom, I felt that I would soon be ready to sally forth and emasculate the philistine. Woe betide the benighted clod who dared venture into my wheelhouse.

A few weeks after I met Susan, a second unexpected development occurred. My mother came home and announced that we were moving to the 5200 block of North Second Street in a neighborhood called Olney. This was literally right around the corner from the Orsinis, who lived on the 5200 block of American Street. What's more, for the first time since our exile from Russell Street, we were actually going to buy a house, not rent one. Even better, at least from the ethnic-ambience perspective, the neighborhood was filled with Germans and Italians instead of the usual down-market Irish, Poles, and blacks we were used to. Olney, in fact, was a Reich-leaning enclave where the FBI had busted up pro-Nazi bunds during the Second World War, and it still evinced a low-key "Axis in exile" flavor. But that didn't matter to us; we were willing to let bygones be bygones. Naturally, we were excited at the news that we would be moving, as West Oak Lane was rapidly turning into a slum, with teenage gangs shooting up rivals all over the place, on one occasion right down the street from our house. Alas, we had no way of knowing that Olney's best days were behind it.

Buying a house in a neighborhood that was heading south fast continued our venerable family tradition of urban leapfrogging. We would escape from a rapidly decaying neighborhood, skip past one that was decaying at a slightly more temperate pace, and then pitch our tent in a neighborhood poised on the very precipice of decay. But we did not know that at the time. For now, the bad times lay in the future; when I was seventeen, it was a very good year. Moving to Second Street was the most exciting thing that had ever happened to me, not only because I was smitten by Susan but because I was smitten by what Susan represented.

After we got off welfare and moved from the housing project to West Oak Lane, we were sure that the excision of this enormous social stigma would improve my father's disposition. But his disposition did not improve, partly because he hated his job as a security guard, partly because he realized that his children rarely saw a speeding truck without wishing he was under it, partly because our new neighborhood quickly fell apart. We had similarly high expectations when we moved to Olney, but they, too, were soon dashed; not long after we moved in, the old people who had maintained their homes so well for so many years began to die or move out, and what my parents referred to as "a rough crowd" moved in. We were now hemmed in by voluptuously unappealing Eastern Europeans—Iron Curtain white trash—who held all-night pool parties in their postage-stamp backyards, inviting my father over leer at hard-core pornography on their colossal basement TVs even though they knew that he was a religious man and despised them. Our new neighbors were industrious palookas from far-flung communist climes who had come to America seeking a better life, but for them a better life meant a closetful of Dallas Cowboys tee shirts, cheap porn, and the opportunity to use the word "nigger" twenty-four hours a day in an incantatory style, as if repeating it often enough would make the subways safer.

In short, moving to Olney did not work out the way I had hoped it would. A summer with a fairy-tale beginning gradually turned somber as my relationship with Susan took an unanticipated turn. As the day of her departure for college approached, Susan grew distant, no longer interested in traveling downtown to see arty movies, no longer interested in teaching me the difference between a fugue and a chaconne. Pygmalion, it would seem, had wearied of Galatea. Shattered, puzzled, I barraged her with phone calls—fruitlessly, as she was never in—and walked down American Street every twelve minutes to see if she would ever resurface. Because we seemed to have hit it off so well, I was baffled by this glacial onslaught. I did not see her for one solid month. Then, a few days before she left for Washington, she called and suggested that we get together for a chat. I was excited and relieved, but not for long. Over coffee she told me that she had big plans for her life, and none of them included me.

"I'm going to Catholic University to major in music, and after that I'm going to get a job in a small orchestra," she explained. "I'm going to work hard, I'm going to meet a conductor at a small regional orchestra, and I'm going to marry him. I'm not coming back to Philadelphia after I graduate. There's no point in our continuing this."

Because I was already crafting dreams of being a writer when I grew up, I resented Susan's acting as if she was the only one who had big plans for the future. But there was no denying that her grand strategy was better thought out than mine and that, even if I was going places, I wasn't going there as fast as she was. She was taking off for the nation's capital; I was staying behind in Philadelphia. She was headed for a prestigious Catholic university that attracted students from all over the country; I was headed for a Catholic college attended mostly by commuters. She had specific goals mapped out, with a clear idea of how to achieve them; I was still in the murky, jailbreak phase of my existence. Susan did not want me to write to her, and she did not want me to come down and see her in Washington, D.C. We'd had a nice summer fling, but the fling was over.

Though I did not see her my entire freshman year and was crushed that she did not phone over the holidays, I quickly met another girl who did return my calls. She, too, took over my life. Marguerite, who had grown up poor and fatherless in the slums of North Philadelphia and was now living in the housing project we had fled five years earlier, was one of nature's miracles. She had been born with nothing, but viewed this as a fact, not a verdict. Like Susan, she seized the role of mentor, teaching me everything she knew about jazz and poetry. She took me to an art museum for the first time in my life; she gave me my first book of poetry; she bought me a ticket to my first foreign film, *The Organizer*, starring Marcello Mastroianni. From Marguerite I learned about Yusef Lateef, Charlie Mingus, Ornette Coleman, Pharoah Sanders, not to mention Ingmar Bergman, Federico Fellini, Jean-Luc Godard, and Giorgio de Chirico. From her I learned that it was possible to visit the main branch of the Public Library in Logan Square and borrow recordings of Duke Ellington trading solos with John Coltrane, and to listen to them on turntables in a special room reserved for music lovers. From her I learned that the Philadelphia Art Museum, a sandbox for the rich, had an ancillary function as a sanctuary for the poor. Marguerite, a product of the slums, knew that if you were standing in front of a Brancusi and the light hit it just right, you could briefly forget that you were poor. She never took beauty for granted, because beauty was a finite resource, especially in Philadelphia. To those who had grown up around beautiful things, a museum was the cultural equivalent of a billiard room; to those who had not, a museum was Valhalla.

I was fiercely proud of the cultural armament I was strapping on these days, and particularly proud of my francophilia. But I always hid the French books when I came home, because I was aware of their powers to enrage. Like most alcoholics—indeed, like most ex-alcoholics— my father could never abide not being the center of attention. None of us was ever allowed to read a novel or listen to music in peace; if you were up in your bedroom, minding your own business, humming along to a pop song that had made your life worth living for the past three weeks, he would wait until the dramatic crescendo arrived, then force open the door and tell you to lift the needle off the record so he could remind you how much he disliked Martin Luther King and everything he stood for, even after Martin Luther King was gone. When he saw one of us curled up on the sofa with a book we were obviously enjoying, he would tell us to put it away and come out to the kitchen for a stiff drink. In issuing this command, he would invariably repeat his favorite cautionary tale, an urban myth that had absolutely no basis in fact. "You don't want to be like that kid at Penn who read so many books he ended up blowing his brains out," he would warn us. "All work and no play makes Jack a dull boy."

I was not a dull boy, and my sisters were anything but dull girls. He knew this, yet the fact brought him no joy. He was not so much jealous of who we were as who we might become. He saw the ship leaving the harbor, and if he couldn't be on it, he'd just as soon it went down with all hands. It never crossed his mind that our good fortune could be his to share; he could not imagine his children returning later in life to act as his benefactor or seek his counsel the way children had been doing since time immemorial. He was convinced that he was beyond forgiveness, incapable of understanding that while forgiveness cannot always be earned, it can always be granted. But he wasn't going to hold his breath waiting for that to happen. He had seen the future. And it didn't include him.

Chapter 10. **Management Potential**

In the 1960s, irate students would often stage violent protests, seizing control of university buildings and refusing to be dislodged until their grievances were addressed. These grievances were compiled in a list of "non-negotiable demands," which usually called for an immediate end to the war in Vietnam, the elimination of racism and poverty, and the emancipation of women. Occasionally, someone would drop in something about migrant workers. Until these non-negotiable demands were met, or at least negotiated, students would remain holed up inside the administration buildings, to the consternation of the faculty, the police, and most of the alumni. The students did not care; they would not be moved. For these were the Days of Rage.

At the college I attended from 1968 to 1972, exactly one insurgency of this nature occurred. Whether the war in Vietnam, endemic racism, or institutional poverty ultimately made it onto our list I cannot say, but I do recall our ultimatum that the administration reassess its draconian policy regarding library hours and keep the building open until midnight—or risk the consequences. The administration took our other demands under advisement, but quickly moved to extend library hours by hiring additional personnel. Our victory complete, we returned to our dorms and the uprising came to an end. This was the sixties. This was Saint Joseph's College. And these were our Days of Rage.

Saint Joseph's College, founded in 1851, had long had a reputation as an above-average liberal arts institution that also boasted an impressive physics department. It was located at the western edge of Philadelphia, straddling City Line Avenue, which was actually Route 1. This was the busy thoroughfare that separated the tough-as-nails City of Brotherly Love from the affluent Main Line. One side of the campus was in Wynnwood (which some called Overbrook), a formerly upscale community that was steadily taking on a more hardscrabble edge. The other side was in Lower Merion Township, where names like "Latch's Lane" abounded, as Lower Merion was nothing if not prim and traditional. Saint Joseph's catered to Irish-Catholic alumni of local Catholic high schools, with a fair number of Italians thrown in for ethnic balance. The majority of the students were commuters, though this would change, as over time the composition of the student body became less urban. The school prided itself on producing the kinds of solid citizens that kept places like Philadelphia running smoothly, as well as quite a few people who went into the insurance business. It also produced a handful of high-powered entrepreneurs, the occasional captain of industry, and assorted clergymen. One of its most famous alumni from that era went on to become secretary of the navy under Ronald Reagan. This was not perhaps the career goal Saint Joseph's always managed to foster, but it was the kind of goal it aspired to.

My decision to attend Saint Joseph's was predicated on a number of factors that had nothing to do with one another. One, I was pretty sure I could get in. Two, I suspected that I could get financial aid, as both the federal government, under Lyndon Baines Johnson, and the state of Pennsylvania were spreading a fair amount of cash around in those days. Otherwise there would have been no chance of my going to college. Even though everybody I knew was trying to drive LBJ from office, we didn't mind taking his money.

Factor number three was the family tradition of attending the school: My cousin Jimmy, who sold me a life insurance policy before my voice had changed, graduated in 1960, and my cousin Joey, the roly-poly sourpuss with the blabbermouth mother and the father who professed to be the smartest mail carrier in Quaker City history, got his diploma four years later. Neither of these relationships would have inspired me to follow in my cousins' footsteps, but because Jimmy and Joey's parents were constantly rattling on and on about the school, it may have made me feel a more intimate emotional connection.

There was never any possibility of my attending Penn or Haverford— too ritzy—much less applying to any university out of state. That was the sort of thing people like Susan Orsini did, people who had quantifiable talents and big dreams. My dream was to make a living by ridiculing people, and it didn't seem to matter all that much where I got my degree, as one couldn't actually major in satire or invective. Temple University—Saint Joseph's for Jews—never came under serious consideration, nor did Philadelphia Textile (too industrial), Penn State (too rah-rah), or Villanova (too effete). People with my background despised the tony and all its works, and Villanova, which suffered from the delusion that it was Notre Dame (just as Notre Dame suffered from the delusion that it was Harvard), radiated toniness. It basically came down to this: If you were attending a school where you could effortlessly get yourself mugged within three blocks of the campus, then your alma mater could not possibly be regarded as tony. Things simply didn't work that way.

The only other strong contender was LaSalle College, which had once employed my father as a security guard. LaSalle was a perfectly respectable institution, and I could have gotten a fine education there, but as it was only a couple of miles from my house, and as half my graduating class at Cardinal Dougherty planned to enroll there, it was never on my short list. I wanted to get away from it all, and going to school way over on the west side of Philadelphia would make me feel that I was venturing out into the wide world and setting off on some big adventure, even though Saint Joseph's was only two long bus rides from my home.

Another major factor in my decision to attend Saint Joseph's was the abiding allure of the Society of Jesus. The Jesuits had a reputation for intellectual acuity, deviousness, and a tendency to ignore everyone else and play amongst themselves. I liked that. Even though I had struck out as a Maryknoll, I had long believed that, had the Jesuits operated a junior seminary when I was thirteen years old, I would have almost assuredly continued down the path toward ordination and become a priest. I am not sure why I clung to this belief so obstinately, given that I did not believe in God and had been obsessed with females since age fourteen. But I did.

The final reason I chose Saint Joseph's over all the other local schools was that throughout the 1960s, it fielded a superb basketball team. Despite the college's puny size—around 1,250 students—its Hawks regularly competed for the national championship. In retrospect, I now accept that this was probably the single most important factor in my decision to go to Hawk Hill. It may have been the only one.

The spring before I began my studies, I was taken on a campus tour by a member of an organization called the Crimson Key. Part booster, part catechist, my tour guide was attired in a maroon jacket, gray trousers, a white shirt, a maroon tie, and a pair of spit-shined black lace-ups. He assured me that I would be happy at Saint Joseph's, though I am not sure how he could have possibly known this, since he had only just met me and I was not wearing a tie that afternoon. I for my part was not so certain I would be happy there, as one of my top criteria in selecting an institution of higher learning was finding a school where I would not have to wear socks. The sockless look seemed to me to be the very height of sophistication, but if the Crimson Key wardrobe was any indication, no one at Saint Joseph's went in much for that sort of thing.

Turning a corner toward the end of my visit, we stumbled upon a throng of slovenly attired students gathered around a pudgy young man in a fringed buckskin jacket who was emptying a plastic bag filled with goldfish and stuffing them down his throat. The students, many of them sandaled and sockless, were egging him on, and he seemed to be having a ripping good time himself. The tour guide, miffed that these scuzzy lowlifes had gone and spoiled everything just as he was getting ready to close the deal, bitterly referred to them as "slimeballs," and tried to pull me away. But I insisted on staying, purporting to be mesmerized by the vivid socio-anthropological elements implicit in this baroque tableau. I was later told that the boy clad in buckskin was attempting to set the world record for goldfish consumption, but I refused to believe this, as he seemed more of a clown than a competitor, and at no point did he appear to be the kind of person who could start out as a myth and then become a legend. Still, the presence of these slobs, deadbeats, and wastrels allayed my fears that the student body at Saint Joseph's consisted only of go-getters and straight-shooters, and played a large part in my decision to spend the next four years of my life there.

Until 1968, Saint Joseph's was populated by serious, sober, sensibly attired young men who needed eighteen credits of theology and eighteen credits of philosophy in order to graduate. After 1968, the weirdos in the buckskin jackets gradually began to infiltrate the student body. Very few of these students were authentic hippies; people from West Philadelphia and the immediate suburbs of Delaware County rarely had the chops to pass themselves off as authentic bohemians; they always looked as if they were merely out trick-or-treating. Most of them, I suspect, were ringers: lacrosse players masquerading as hashish aficionados and devotees of Kahlil Gibran in order to impress girls. If this was their objective, they had come to the wrong place; Saint Joseph's did not admit women until my senior year. These ersatz flower children were never numerous enough to challenge the reigning ethos of the school, but there were enough of them to make the nerds and jocks that had previously dominated campus life feel nervous, fearing that a cultural Armageddon was nigh.

The residence hall I lived in during my freshman year was filled with jocks and nerds. Some of them were majoring in food marketing, an abstruse field that was a Saint Joseph's specialty. The food marketing majors had their very own food marketing library, though no one ever knew what they did in there. Other residents of Simpson Hall would go on to do graduate work in advertising at Ohio State. It was as if they had strolled right out of a scene in *The Graduate* and were curious to know if anyone would like to discuss the investment potential of polyurethane, while downing a martini or two and nibbling on some canapés. They despised me and my roommates, dismissing us as unkempt, hirsute hippies who had no respect for authority and refused to join fraternities. I was neither unkempt nor especially hirsute, and I generally did have respect for authority, provided the authority figures were sufficiently numerous and scary-looking. It helped if they had tattoos. But the upperclassmen were right on the money about the fraternities. I gave them a wide berth for the same reason I stayed away from the Boy Scouts: I never joined anything, I didn't like the way they dressed, and frankly I found the whole thing just a bit homoerotic.

The upperclassmen had a special animus toward my roommate Steve. Steve was a courtly, soft-spoken Italian American who was reportedly in the process of flunking out of every major Jesuit college on the eastern seaboard. By the time I came onboard Steve already had Boston College, Holy Cross, and Fordham under his belt, and as soon as he'd taken his scalp on Hawk Hill, he could head south to Loyola of Baltimore and Georgetown to complete the mission. (Saint Peter's in Hoboken and the University of Scranton were optional.) The first part-time catatonic I ever broke bread with, though a very engaging one, he would spend days upon end gazing up at the ceiling, smoking one Marlboro after another and listening to Beethoven piano sonatas, which did very little to improve his mood. Then, every three weeks or so, he would suddenly jump up and do something, like read a newspaper or start an argument, or ask if anyone wanted extra anchovies on their pizza. It was hard to draw a bead on him.

One weekend, Steve invited me down to his home in Vineland, New Jersey. Over dinner, his father told me, in a crestfallen tone of voice, that he had once entertained hopes that Steve would be the first Italian-American president of the United States.

"Don't you need a college degree to get elected president?" I inquired, unable to resist such an inviting setup line and overjoyed to be in the presence of a patriarch who didn't seem likely to take offense at such impertinence, much less slug me. But Steve's father did not find that remark one bit amusing, and I was not invited back.

The big problem at Simpson Hall was this: The upperclassmen didn't like our attitude. For generations, it had been a Simpson Hall tradition for upperclassmen to bring their meals into the dorm on lunch trays borrowed from the nearby cafeteria, then pile them up at the foot of the stairs, where freshmen were expected to make a nice, neat stack and return them at the end of the day. My third roommate, Bill, who had been my classmate and coeditor at the Venard four years earlier, was already in the ROTC, and was preparing for a career in the military, so he had no objection to this otherwise demeaning chore. But while I did not mind accepting ceremonial abuse from full-grown men, I drew the line at accepting it from boys. If the upperclassmen wanted those trays returned to the cafeteria, they could do it themselves.

My roommate Fred went one step further. An irreverent hippie, Fred had grown up in Yardley, Pennsylvania, a village just across the river from Trenton, New Jersey, which had no great tradition of irreverence. A history major intent on becoming a lawyer, he was the kind of jocular, impudent individual whose applications Saint Joseph's had gone out of its way to discourage since its inception. One Sunday night, returning from a visit home, I found Fred standing by the bay window in our bedroom, sailing a mass of soiled lunch trays out into the void and down onto the lawn that separated Simpson Hall from a public school in the back. Though large and unwieldy, the trays glided along at a lovely pace if launched with sufficient verve and grace. Week after week, Fred and I would meet up on Sunday evening, down a quart or two of the toxic collegiate beverage Ripple, and toss a hundred or more of those trays into the backyard, all the while listening to the Velvet Underground and discussing Schopenhauer's debt to Kierkegaard. Presumably, the upperclassmen then collected the trays in the morning and sheepishly returned them to the cafeteria. They would have dearly loved to haul us before the authorities and bring us up on charges of aerodynamic hooliganism, but Fred and I were never apprehended in flagrante delicto, and emphatically protested our innocence when any suggestion was made that we would engage in such a perverse strain of vandalism.

One evening a snowstorm blew through campus after we had turned in for the night, and the following morning when we got out of bed the lawn was covered with a hundred or more V-shaped lunch trays that had wilted and curled in on themselves. With that, the powers that be decided they had had enough. They replaced the oversized trays with plastic carriers less than half their size; these didn't glide smoothly and were no fun to play with. The administration also ruled that henceforth no one could remove lunch trays from the cafeteria. Fred now channeled his rebellious streak into the less reprehensible, less destructive pastime of Frisbee, and the upperclassmen had to eat in the cafeteria like everybody else. Now they really hated us.

At Saint Joseph's College I began to bury the past and invent a new persona. Nobody there cared what economic class I came from, or that my father was a functional derelict, and because so many of us went around in shabby clothing with disintegrating shoes and no socks, we all looked like paupers anyway. Once I realized that America was a country where white people could pass themselves off as whomever they liked, provided they still had some teeth, I began to mothball the anecdotes about Alaskan knife fights, bullets in the cerebellum, lengthy stints in the Big House, and all the other colorful lore of the petty criminal class into which I had been born.

Obviously there were times when my background came in handy. For example, when preparing a family history for my Introduction to Western Civilization course, the banner year my father went through thirteen different jobs was a morsel of information I could use to great advantage. Other students could produce documents linking them to people who had lived many centuries in the past; one classmate could even lay claim to an ancestor who had fought with William the Conqueror. This cut no ice with our teacher. To Dr. Schmandt, being related to William the Conqueror was an accident of history, like being Bram Stoker's third cousin, but nothing more. A student's provenance from such a dazzling forebear did not make his research paper any better, unless the student could show how this rarefied bloodline had exerted some demonstrable effect on his current economic situation or psychological frame of mind. Anyway, no one in Philadelphia would ever be impressed just because you said you were descended from a Norman. By contrast, being the son of a man who had gone through thirteen jobs in a single year was almost magical; it was the stuff of socioeconomic legend; it tied the indoor record for domestic calamity, inability to toe the line, and refusal to kowtow; it was as exotic as having a mother who had once trained polar bears.

But I no longer wanted to be exotic, or perhaps I now wanted to be exotic only in the same way everyone else was exotic. Little by little, I started to do things that people from my background did not normally do. I studied Eastern philosophy. I read the complete works of Maxim Gorky, without being told to. I made friends with a boy who was slated to appear in a Cap & Bells production of *Julius Caesar* with the entire cast dressed up in *Star Trek* costumes. Or maybe it was *Macbeth*. I definitely began to put some distance between me and the proletariat when I joined the Zarathustra Philosophical Society, chaired by a boy from

Atlantic City who once blasted a softball right through a classroom window, then defended himself by asserting that the window did not exist. The Jesuits on the disciplinary committee had no problem with this line of reasoning, it being the Age of Aquarius and what-not, provided the student agreed to pay for the window.

I took a Greek theater course with a bearded scholar named Dr. McDonough, who was said to have used powerful computers to prove that *The Iliad* and *The Odyssey* had been written by the same man. McDonough's ingenious approach while he was up at Columbia University was to compare meter, sentence structure, and the frequency with which certain words and images appeared to prove that the twin pillars of Western literature had been written by one and only one author. According to his data, the man's name was Homer. He was good fun when you got him off topic and he started talking about his colleagues in the classics department; but he was an abysmal teacher, as he was far more interested in dead Greeks than in live Philadelphians, so I quickly stopped attending his classes. One January evening, my good friend Chris Taylor and I discovered that we were studying for the same final exam in the same Greek course, even though we had never crossed paths in McDonough's classroom. This was quite an achievement, given that there were only about eight of us in the class and Chris and I were roommates.

We were also roommates when we took John Mullen's eighteenth-century literature course. That was one class I never cut. A stocky, caustic, debonair war vet and Saint Joseph alumnus who had grown up in that mysterious district of South Philadelphia where Irish-Catholic Republicans not only lived but apparently flourished, Mullen was an expert in Augustan literature. He knew everything there was to know about Jonathan Swift, Alexander Pope, John Dryden, Samuel Johnson, and all the other acid-tongued misanthropes that thrived in the early 1700s. None of them tolerated fools gladly, and he didn't have much time for fools himself. In that era many of our teachers were making an effort to take us seriously when we voiced our daft opinions or advanced our inane theories, as the young were then fleetingly viewed as repositories of wisdom. But Mr. Mullen could never conceal his amusement when a student opened his mouth to say anything, because students never had anything to say. That's what professors were for.

Eighteenth-century literature was going out of style in the late sixties, but then again so were Chaucer and Western civilization, and Mr. Mullen didn't care much one way or another whether students enjoyed the material contained in the syllabus. I certainly did, but then again, I still read Chaucer. One afternoon, Mr. Mullen's three o'clock seminar coincided with a momentous gathering at the Alumni Field House, the barn at the edge of campus where the basketball team practiced. Devastating rumors had begun circulating that Paul McCartney was dead, and to stave off a rash of suicides and fire bombings and nervous breakdowns, a symposium of sorts was convened, gathering together a glittering array of the Delaware Valley's most admired pop cultural luminaries and avatars of taste. These experts vowed to deconstruct the discordant images of an unshod McCartney shuffling through the crosswalk on the cover of *Abbey Road*, as well as the hidden messages contained in the lyrics of "I Am the Walrus," not to mention the ambiguous photographs included in the artwork accompanying *Magical Mystery Tour*. This way, we could ascertain once and for all whether Paul McCartney was still among the living and make plans for the remainder of our lives accordingly.

The afternoon of the summit conference, Mr. Mullen turned up for class as usual, said a few words about our upcoming assignments, and then announced: "In light of the epochal developments taking place over in the field house today, I wouldn't dream of detaining you to discuss *Gulliver's Travels*." He then dismissed us. Everyone was shocked.

"I guess beneath that tough exterior, he's a nice guy after all," one of my classmates said.

"No, he isn't," I replied. From that moment on, I wanted to be exactly like John P. Mullen: Suave. Debonair. Aloof. Condescending.

Around this time, I also fell under the spell of a French teacher named Tom Donahue. He, too, was a graduate of Saint Joseph's; he, too, had grown up on the streets of Philadelphia. He introduced me to Eugene Ionesco and Jean Genet, lent me enigmatic plays by Fernando Arrabal and Robert Pinget, and counseled me to dump Kurt Vonnegut and Joseph Heller and take a crack at Honoré de Balzac and Gustave Flaubert. One day he organized a field trip to New York City, where a bunch of us dined at a restaurant whose décor consisted entirely of materials pertaining to Napoleon Bonaparte. These objects included paintings, photographs, ashtrays, souvenir mugs, matchboxes, and even a Corsican-themed puzzle mounted on the walls. There may even have been a shawl or two.

We also visited the Museum of Modern Art, where I got to see *Les Demoiselles d'Avignon* and *Le Douanier* Rousseau's crackpot paintings for the first time. Later that evening we went to the Barbizon Plaza Theatre and saw Madeleine Renaud in Samuel Beckett's *Oh les Beaux Jours*. Renaud, one of France's most brilliant actresses, was married to Jean-Louis Barrault, the French Laurence Olivier, best known for his role as the doomed mime in *Les Enfants du Paradis*. When the curtain came up, Renaud was buried up to her waist in sand; by the end of the play only her neck protruded. About ten minutes into the proceedings, a crotchety old cuss seated not far from us drew himself up, began brandishing his cane in an ominous manner, and started bellowing, *"Merde! Merde!"* or words to that effect. Later that evening, as we were walking down Sixth Avenue to the train station, I asked Tom if the man with the cane was a plant, if Beckett had written a part for an irate spectator. Tom didn't think so, though Genet had done this sort of thing in *Les Paravents*, his four-and-a-half-hour play about the Algerian War. Any way you looked at it, I'd come a long way from the East Falls Housing Project.

At the end of my freshman year, Richard Nixon, never one to lie down on the job when an opportunity to torment my family presented itself, closed down the federal program that had been bankrolling my education. Because I had a 3.9 grade-point average, my mother and I ultimately were successful in persuading the financial aid office to award me an academic scholarship. But housing, meals, and books I would have to pay for by myself. Having already gone a bit overboard in the book-buying department, I would now need to move back home for at least part of the summer and put a few bucks together. The downside of this was that I had to see my father. The upside was that I got to see my mother and my sisters, at least until Ree and Eileen caught that train to New York. This was the one good thing about going home. The only good thing, in fact.

For the next four years, I worked at summer jobs, raising just enough cash to pay for off-campus housing during the school year, as well as concert tickets, alcohol, and the kinds of invigorating but only marginally nutritious food that college students have always favored. I did not spend any money on drugs, as drugs always seemed to be widely available, funneled to all and sundry by elusive benefactors named Vega, Mellow, or Shelby. Moreover, because of my blue-collar background, I always preferred alcohol to hallucinogens anyway.

At my previous jobs I had been employed by fascinating, self-made men from whom I would draw inspiration that would last a lifetime. Now I would be exposed to a different type of man. Legend has it that while campaigning in the West Virginia primary in 1960, John F. Kennedy visited a coal mine. Outside the cavern stood a line of miners, waiting to shake the candidate's hand. As Kennedy emerged from the bowels of the yellow-dog Democratic earth, he was approached by a man who asked point-blank, "Did you ever have a job?" Kennedy thought about it for a second, then replied, "No. Not really." To which the miner said, "You didn't miss much."

The working-class men I met on my summer jobs shared this opinion. Some, no more than a handful, were the sorts of archetypal lunch-pail heroes who have always made America great and, had they lived elsewhere, would have made those countries great as well. But a lot of them were slobs. In the summer of 1969, I worked sixteen hours a day for one solid month, first on the night shift at a bubble-gum factory a mile from my home, then all day long at a gas station right around the corner. The men who worked at the factory, mostly pulling down a few bucks more than the minimum wage, were a relatively cheerful, engaging group of fellows. The men in the gas station, also bringing home slightly more than a pittance, were miserable pricks. The gas station attendants and car mechanics were all white; the workforce at the bubble-gum factory was racially mixed. The ethnically heterogeneous group learned how to get along; the men in the homogeneous group were always at each other's throats. What conclusions social scientists might draw from this data I cannot say; ethnic diversity might not even be relevant. But I think it was.

At the time, I was little concerned about such matters. I didn't take these jobs because I thought they would be interesting or because I thought I would learn anything that would be useful to me later in life. I already knew that poorly paid jobs merely led to other poorly paid jobs, and I had long since ceased believing in the secret wisdom of the proletariat. I took these jobs because I was desperate to raise cash to rent a room off campus so that I could read Tolstoy and listen to Fauré in peace. As paying for a place of my own necessitated a formidable war chest, I spent a couple of summers working myself into the ground.

I took the night job at the bubble-gum factory because of an accident during the day at the gas station. I'd started working at the filling station in June, intending to quit in August and attend the Woodstock Festival in upstate New York. But those plans went up in smoke after I stepped on a plank in the back of the garage and impaled my foot on a nail. Unable to walk, I was laid up for three weeks, by which time the festival was over.

In those prelitigious ages, there was no question of applying for unemployment benefits or suing anyone; working-class people didn't do that sort of thing. Nobody'd told me to step on that nail, nor was the unidentified party who had left that plank lying there willing to fess up and admit that he bore some responsibility for the mishap. The consensus was that I should have been more attentive while I was clambering around in the darkness looking for an inner tube, so I should simply grin and bear it, being as I was, in the patois of the filling station community, a dumb fuck. My friends motored off to Yasgur's farm without me and were promptly pulled over by Garden State troopers on the zany charge of "failing to make a good account of themselves on the New Jersey Turnpike." This specious, though undeniably creative, allegation was later dropped, but not before an inconvenient return trip to a court in northern New Jersey.

Both my coworkers and my father took malicious delight in my podiatric misfortune, the incident confirming their worst fears about the American educational system. Why in the name of Christ, they wanted to know, were we sending kids to hoity-toity universities if they were only going to end up shredding their feet on rusty nails? What good was reading Tacitus and Lucretius and Giraudoux if you were only going to end up hobbling around on crutches, they'd like to know, though they never actually cited Tacitus or Lucretius, much less the effete French playwright Jean Giraudoux, instead using the more general term "all those big shots."

This was back at a time when, if working-class people said or did anything malignant, untoward, or moronic, sociologists would argue that they had been "conditioned" to act this way, that their racial epithets or repellent behavior toward women were not prima facie evidence of stupidity or defective moral character or a generally feral lifestyle but the result of a top-secret disinformation program involving the surreptitious psychocranial implantation of dangerous or offensive ideas by the federal government or that shadowy social-engineering leviathan known as the Establishment. My pump-jockey cohorts behaved the way they did because they had been conditioned to act that way by the Hidden Persuaders; they did not dislike me personally; they did not think I was a commie or a fag; they did not wish me ill. They simply felt uncomfortable around anyone from their own class who was getting a higher education, understanding as they did that higher education was a repudiation of all that they were and all that they stood for.

What they stood for was nothing; people who are simply trying to survive are too busy feeding their families to symbolize anything. Decades later, when the emotional buffer of success allowed me to reflect on the pathologies of the working class, I no longer held a grudge against this coterie of ill-tempered drudges. They acted the way they did only because they were jealous of anyone who had a chance to avoid cleaning windshields for the rest of his life. Saddled with the workingman's ingrained contempt for the educated, they sought to buoy themselves with the reassuring belief that even though people like themselves could not tell William Shakespeare from Willian Penn, they made up for it by possessing inexhaustible reserves of common sense. Sure, college boys could tell you the importance of the Treaty of Utrecht or the causes of the Second Punic War. Some of them, the really clever ones, might even be able to untangle the relationship between Hasdrubal, Hamilcar, and Hannibal. But could they repair a carburetor or repoint a spark plug? My stepping on a rusty nail confirmed their worst prejudices; they found it side-splittingly amusing that someone so book-smart could simultaneously be so life-stupid. Today, I no longer hate them for snickering the way they did, though I hated them at the time. In retrospect, I realize that they simply could not help themselves. They were seeking solace from their miserable lives by telling themselves that a college education was not the be-all and end-all of existence, that they hadn't missed out on anything. They were like the bald man who consoles himself with the thought that at least he'll never end up like Absalom. They meant no harm by it. And, like I said, they were idiots.

The men who worked at the bubble-gum factory were cut from a different cloth and made much better company. It helped that they were not all white men, which the gas station attendants were; they didn't use the words "nigger," "shine," "rughead," and "coon" every ten seconds throughout their eight-hour shift the way the gas station boys did—with the occasional "spic" or "wetback" thrown in for ethnic balance. They also didn't keep eyeing you suspiciously, the way the grease monkeys did, suspecting that your failure to make regular use of such terminology meant that you were a nigger lover. This was an era when white people still used these terms within earshot of the reviled ethnic groups in question, whereas today they only use them in the privacy of their homes.

I landed the job in the bubble-gum factory because management was always looking for student help in the summer. I have no idea why college students were in such demand; we came cheap, but so did the retreads that punched the clock fifty-two weeks a year. One summer I worked the day shift on the packing line, stuffing freshly wrapped packages of gum into boxes, but the other three summers I signed up for the graveyard shift as a maintenance man, mostly mopping floors and disposing of trash. I was never terribly fond of bubble gum before I worked in the factory, and after seeing the size of the brassy, irascible rats that used to patrol the warehouse, I was even less of a fan afterward. But it gave me pleasure to tell people that I was now working the graveyard shift, because expressions like "working the graveyard shift" made me feel like a man.

The Fleer Corporation, best known for its Dubble Bubble gum, was a second-echelon operation that lacked the dazzling bravura of the industry giant, Topps. Whereas the Topps empire was sustained by young boys whose passion for trading baseball cards back and forth did not abate with the passage of time, Fleer's built its marketing strategy around the irresistible allure of cheesy prizes. The gum itself was revolting, so disgusting that even the rats were not all that taken by it, much preferring the staff's peanut-butter-and-jelly sandwiches, the rodent epicure's delight. The actual physical work at the factory—swabbing the decks, tossing out trash, scrubbing machinery—was mindless drudgery, not unlike pumping gas, and the time could pass slowly, especially if you showed up for your shift under the influence. What made working there tolerable, and even memorable, was that several of the full-time employees were, to use a popular term of that era, characters.

Night-shift bubble-gum factory employees did not arrive at such a career impasse by happenstance; the men assigned to the dawn patrol were all in some way defeated by life. But they seemed to understand that they had conspired in their own demise, either by failing to study hard in school or by hitting the sauce too often and too enthusiastically over the years. They regularly offered up comical tips for avoiding a similar fate, even though they knew there was no chance that I would follow in their footsteps, since the whole point of being a college boy was to put yourself in a situation where you could make a much better class of mistake with your life.

"There's no future in cleaning shithouses," one feisty white man well into his forties used to caution me as he pirouetted with his mop around the men's room. "No matter who tries to tell you otherwise, don't believe them. There is absolutely no future in cleaning shithouses."

"And Larry is the man who's in the best position to know," a somewhat younger black man named Melvin would chime in. "Larry has degrees in shithouse science from some of the finest institutions in America. He's forgotten more about cleaning shithouses than most people will ever know. And look where it's gotten him."

"It didn't get me any further than the shithouse!" Larry would proclaim. "So put that in your pipe and smoke it."

Larry and Melvin had regular assignments, carrying out the same basic chores every night. Larry cleaned the bathrooms, the cafeteria, and the offices; Melvin washed down the floors throughout the factory. The monotony of it all didn't seem to bother them one bit. The summer workers, students like me, often helped out with mopping the floors, but mostly took the jobs the older men didn't like or found too physically demanding to perform. One of these was loading up the trash receptacles out back with busted wooden pallets—skids, as they were called—that had previously been used to carry boxloads of the deadly provender that was Fleer's stock-in-trade. The trash receptacles, generally referred to as gondolas, sat at the edge of the loading dock in the rear of the factory. Once a gondola was filled to overflowing, a truck owned and operated by uncollegial Neapolitans pulled up, loaded it onto a flatbed, and hauled it off. Then an identical gondola was installed in its place. Tossing generic trash into these gaping maws was no big deal, but the skids were heavy, unwieldy, and jagged-edged, with nails sticking out, and if gripped without gloves or flung around in a careless fashion, they could easily shred one's fingers. That's why I always wore gloves.

The late sixties and early seventies were an era when Caucasian college boys working in factories during their summer vacations were in awe of older black men, viewing them as repositories of untramelled wisdom their own fathers did not possess. The older a black man was, and the less gainfully employed, the more likely he was to be a geyser of sagacity. Those of us who were working class ourselves were less receptive to these men's charms, as we had previously come into contact with elderly black men who had not proven to be astoundingly wise. But the middle-class boys from the ritzier neighborhoods were invariably smitten by these tough, well-traveled, inner-city solons, fawning like schoolgirls in their ebony presence.

The wise old black men, for their part, capitalized on this fulsome homage by getting the white boys to do the crummy jobs that they themselves abhorred. One such individual was a tall, heavyset man who presided over the garbage-disposal unit with a severity, detachment, and solemnity that suggested Pluto manning the reviewing stand in Hades. He walked with a limp, smoked like a chimney, and had a silky, sultry singing voice. A stickler for detail and a bit of a perfectionist in a job that required no perfection, he would instruct us to heave the trash into the gondola, chuck in the busted skids, then climb inside the tip and jump up and down on the accumulated refuse to compress it. Meanwhile, he would stand back and belt out the first few bars of "One Enchanted Evening" or "Lush Life," the most frequently performed numbers in his impressive, albeit limited, repertory. Occasionally, he would punctuate his regal, velvety Johnny Hartman impersonation with a procedural tip derived from his many years of experience in the waste-management sector such as, "More to the left" or "Watch out for that rat down by your foot." Once we'd hauled ourselves out of the gondola, he would press a button to activate a huge iron compacting device that would squeeze the trash far back into the recesses of the unit. Then we would start the process all over again, repeating it several times until no more trash remained.

I was never sure what this large, affable if somewhat distant man was seeking to accomplish through this convoluted exercise. The people who ran the factory did not care how tightly compacted the trash was, because a fixed number of gondolas were hauled in and out each week, and whether they were filled or not made no difference to anyone, least of all the Cosa Nostra. It was not as if this loading-dock Zorba was going to advance his career by getting us to climb into the gondola and jump up and down on the trash, since no one in management could possibly have any idea what was going on out there at three o'clock in the morning. The managers all worked the day shift; the closest thing to a person in a position of real authority on the night shift was the foreman, a tubby old man with the mournful eyes of an unpopular beagle, who rarely left his office and never spoke. In the end I decided that this Gautama of Gondolas, this Ramses of Refuse, had resigned himself to the fact that the closest he was ever going to get to legal redress for the myriad injustices that had been visited upon him by a racist society was the sight of two skinny white boys jumping up and down on a mountain of rotting bubble gum while trapped inside a trash compactor with a bunch of mean rats. Monday through Friday, thirteen weeks straight.

One night, one of the other students decided that it would be great fun to activate the trash compactor while I was still inside the gondola. There I was, bouncing up and down, trying hard not to look ridiculous, when suddenly I heard that horrible, overly familiar churning sound and turned to see the huge wall of metal surging toward me. It was the most terrifying moment of my life. The boy, whom I had not cared for previously and cared for even less now, immediately realized that the prank was unlikely to be received in the spirit in which it was intended. Judiciously, he turned off the device. Alas, the time for judiciousness had passed. I vaulted out of the gondola, screaming bloody murder, chased him, snared him, dragged him to the ground, straddled him, and began pounding him in the face. I hit him harder than I had ever hit anyone; I hit him until he cried. I did not lead with my left, as Len Mohr always advised; I simply buried my fists in his pudgy little face. After that evening, I did not punch anyone for thirty years; a combination of exhilaration at being in a position to beat someone senseless while occupying the unassailable moral high ground, coupled with horror at the capacity for violence that dwelled just below the surface of my personality, discouraged me from taking another swing at a human being until I finally stumbled on a second person who deserved it. What the boy had done was unforgivable—to this day I have nightmares about that trash compactor—but what I had done was cruel. He never came back to work. I never went back into the gondola.

Most of the cleanup jobs at the bubble-gum factory involved mopping, which I disliked intensely. But one night a week there was a way to get out of this onerous assignment. High above the factory floor sat a large metal funnel through which sugar seeped down to the machines below. The state health code mandated that the funnel be cleaned every week. None of the older men wanted to climb up into the rafters, because they were out of shape and afraid of heights. I wasn't. Once a week, I would haul myself up and pretend to be scrubbing down the cylinder's lining while I was actually reading an easily concealed paperback copy of *The Sun Also Rises* or *The Great Gatsby*. Since our supervisor was too fat to shinny up and see how the work was progressing, I could lounge up there for hours devouring the great classics of Western literature, occasionally banging on a wall to make it sound like I was actually working. I read *The Scarlet Letter, The Magnificent Ambersons,* and Guy de Maupassant's *Boule de Suif* while pretending to be cleaning that funnel. Maupassant had once written a short story in which a woman, asked to display her jewels, introduced her two children. My parents had not read it.

Experiences such as these are charming in retrospect, superb material for someone who plans to pursue a writing career. But I did not think of them as material while they were happening; at that point, they were the story of my life. Anecdotes about ripping good times in the bubble-gum factory are amusing only if the narrator is no longer stranded in the bubble-gum factory. The full-time employees were. To me, they were like recurring characters in *Great Expectations;* every summer when I came back to work, I couldn't wait to find out what had befallen them since the last rousing installment of *Adventures in the Confectionary Trade.* But there wasn't much in it for them; they had no expectations, great or small. They knew that one day we college boys would graduate and get real jobs and they would never see us again. It was nice to think that these decent, generous men had something of value to teach us about life. But it wasn't so valuable that any of us would ever be coming back for additional instruction.

Most of the men were amused by the college boys; if they resented us, it was not apparent to the naked eye. Louie was the lone exception. Louie was a short, squat Jewish man who always sat by himself in the cafeteria, eating a Delicious apple or a Bosc pear which he peeled in almost ceremonial fashion with a small, ugly-looking penknife. His face wore an expression of permanent apoplexy. He was probably in his late fifties, but he acted as if he had somehow managed to get on the wrong side of Nebuchadnezzar during the Babylonian captivity and had been suffering nonstop misery ever since. There was no way to get on his good side, because he didn't have one. Anything you said to him was interpreted as an insult; any comment, no matter how harmless, triggered a Krakatoan eruption. The college crew quickly learned that it was best to avoid him. But Melvin loved to give Louie a hard time, teasing him about his wife and his religion and what he did with the bedazzling sums of cash he was hauling down in the bubble-gum factory.

As soon as Melvin hit a nerve, Louie would eject himself from his seat and hurtle toward him, threatening to slit his throat with his puny penknife. At this point we would all jump up and beg him to quiet down, to let cooler heads prevail. Meanwhile, Melvin would laugh convulsively, having once again gotten his victim's easily gettable goat. The explosions were not playacting on Louie's part; even though Melvin could have broken him in half, knife or no knife, Louie was forever primed for action.

This intramural melodrama went on night after night after night. To be honest, it made lunchtime worth looking forward to, because no matter how innocuous Melvin's comments were, Louie always went after him with his ridiculous little knife—every single night. Melvin only had to say, "Hey, Louie, I was wondering . . . ," and Louie was off to the races. Louie truly hated Melvin, but because the rest of us laughed merrily at this nightly charade, he hated us, too. We justified our lack of compassion by telling ourselves that Louie's contempt toward black people, while clearly exacerbated by his relationship with Melvin, had certainly not begun there. The feud never ended; neither of them ever gave an inch.

Though I liked Melvin, I sympathized with his victim, wondering why his tormentor found it impossible to lighten up every so often, perhaps even give Louie the occasional night off. On the other hand, there was no earthly reason Louie had to take the bait every time, no reason why he had to go from zero to sixty in three seconds flat as soon as Melvin started needling him. I never in my life met a man locked in a more inflexible state of rage than Louie. And I never met a man with more ability to get under a man's skin than Melvin. I worked at a lot of jobs where one employee might sometimes give another a hard time, but it was usually done in a good-natured way. There was nothing good-natured about this.

One morning when I was late wrapping up my shift, I saw Louie gamboling out of the factory all dolled up in a business suit, white dress shirt, subdued tie, and black shoes, clutching a battered attaché case. I asked him where he was going, and he told me to mind my own goddamn business, nosy cocksucking parker that I was. That night, I asked one of the older men if Louie had finally had it up to here with Melvin's abuse and was looking for a new job. No, he explained; Louie had once worked as a salesman on Jeweler's Row downtown but had lost his livelihood a few years earlier. This may have been because even by the standards of ill-tempered jewelry salesmen, he was a bit too much of a pill. Ashamed to let his neighbors know how he now earned his daily bread, Louie went to work at 10:30 every evening clad in full white-collar regalia. He never returned home the next morning without first showering and shaving, removing any lingering vestiges of the fine white powder that permeated the factory, powder so pervasive it was impossible to keep off our clothes. How he thought this fooled his neighbors was a mystery; who wore a suit to the graveyard shift? Now I really wished Melvin would give it a rest.

To Louie, working in a bubble-gum factory, even as a janitor, was a step down. My father didn't see it that way, because a factory employee could always fight his way up the ladder of success, while a rent-a-cop like him was trapped for life in a dead-end job. One summer, because of staffing shortages, I worked the day shift at the factory. I did not enjoy the nine-to-five grind, because the shop floor was crawling with supervisors, which meant I had to work harder and there was no possibility of disappearing into a gigantic stainless-steel funnel and reading *The Idiot* all night. Looking on the bright side, working the day shift meant that I could spend the evenings drinking with my friends. Looking on the dark side, if I came to work hungover, it was that much more likely that I would get my hand jammed inside one of the machines and perhaps lose a finger. So there were trade-offs.

One afternoon during the summer between my junior and senior years, a boy who had graduated from Cardinal Dougherty the same year as I and had become an assistant manager in the bubble-gum factory, tapped me on the shoulder and asked if he could have a word. I was wearing a ridiculous white pajama-type uniform with a tatty mesh hairnet; I looked like the Michelin man after a stint on Devil's Island. He was dressed in white slacks, a white shirt, and a blue tie, the ensemble crowned by a snappy piece of headgear that was a cross between a pilot's cap and a kepi, as if the French Foreign Legion had inexplicably launched an airborne bubble-gum delivery unit. Usually when the managers took one of us college boys aside, it was to ask us to do them a favor and go into the bathroom and tell the regular workers to finish their joints and return to their workstations. Union rules prohibited managers from going inside the rank-and-file's bathrooms; they had lavatories of their own. I hated being given this task, because I lacked the moral authority to tell men ten to twenty years my senior to stop doing drugs, and because I feared that one day one of them might put my head through the wall to reinforce this point.

But rousting addled members of the goldbricking class was not what the manager wanted to see me about.

"We've noticed the way you handle yourself around the other employees," he explained, "and we think you've got real management potential. We were wondering if you might be interested in entering our management-trainee program."

I was always good at keeping a straight face, so I didn't snigger as the dour, intense, earnest young man delineated the package I was being offered. Though he had no way of knowing it, I was not staying up till four in the morning listening to Penderecki's *Threnody for the Victims of Hiroshima* just so I could land a job as a night manager in a bubble-gum factory. I politely told him that I would consider his proposal but pointed out that if I entered the management-trainee program, I would have to put off my plans to finish college and would then lose my draft deferment and would almost certainly get sent to Vietnam, where I might die. The young man himself must have wangled some kind of medical exemption from the draft, as bubble-gum manufacture was not an industry vital to the nation's defense. I was not going to college to get out of being drafted; I was going to college to get out of the working class. But I had no desire to go to Vietnam, nor did anyone else I knew. It was 1971, it was a war we all hated, and it was already lost.

My fellow alum went on to tell me that Fleer's would be willing to defray a good portion of the costs of my college studies, as it had his, provided the courses related in some way to the production, purveyance, or packaging of bubble gum. I thought this was quite hilarious and told everyone I knew about the offer. I omitted no detail—his grave demeanor, his obvious sincerity, the part about having "real" management potential, as opposed to the ersatz kind of management potential that was so common those days. My friends were amused. My sisters guffawed. My coworkers chuckled. My father was livid.

Not everyone living in the United States today can understand the symbolism of the terms "blue collar" and "white collar," but in that era a man who wore a white collar was going places and a man who wore a blue collar or a green collar or a brown collar or a gray collar wasn't. My father understood what it meant to be in management, even at some fifth-rate bubble-gum factory. Because he had clawed his way up to the periphery of the white-collar world when he worked as an expeditor at the appliance company, but had then been purged and cast back down into the proletarian darkness, he knew precisely what the difference between blue- and white-collar jobs was. To thumb my nose at an opportunity for a good salary and a pension and a future and a chance to wear a tie on the job was the height of arrogance and stupidity. This was not so much because he would have wanted the job himself—he hated wearing ties and taking orders from little shavers in kepis. It was because I acted like the whole thing was a joke.

"If that's all they taught you at college, you'll never amount to a pimple on an elephant's rear end!" he would exclaim, trotting out his most durable execration. He'd been using the same lexicon of denigration since I was five; there was no reason to break in any new material now.

My work schedule during the summer was crafted to make sure I was never in the house during his drinking hours. Because my shift started at eleven and my father did not come home from work until midnight, I could get through most of the week without seeing him. When I dragged myself in at seven in the morning, he would be in bed; I would sleep till noon and then go out with friends and play cards or have a few beers before going to work. True, occasional face-to-face meetings were unavoidable, on his days off, weekends, sick days, or nights when he returned early from work and wanted to talk. Until I graduated from high school, I had generally drunk beer when I was out with my friends, but once I entered college, I started to hit the hard stuff. This was mostly because of him. In order for me to stomach his presence, I had to be a couple drinks ahead of him before he walked through the front door. Throughout my senior year in high school and my four years in college, I always kept a bottle of cheap bourbon stuffed inside a boot in my bedroom closet, right next to my Bowie knife. An hour or so before I heard his footsteps on the porch, I would start swigging the whiskey, hoping that by the time he got home, I would be wasted enough to ignore him. The only way I could stand to be in the same room as a drunk was to be drunker. I rarely drank whiskey when my father was not around; I never developed a taste for it. I resorted to alcohol because it gave me the false courage I needed to stand up to him night after night after night. Undoubtedly, he and his father had developed a similar relationship back during the Great Depression, when talk was cheap but liquor wasn't.

It did not occur to me at the time that if I kept drinking like this, I might end up like my father. Everyone I knew drank heavily all the time without worrying about the consequences further down the road. If a man was a drunk, we believed, it was because he had flabby moral character, not because alcohol itself was dangerous, much less destructive or evil. Since I could handle my liquor, which several of my friends could not, there was no possibility of my ending up an alkie.

There were certain topics it was best to avoid in our house. You could not say a bad word against Police Chief (then Mayor) Frank Rizzo, by this point notorious for raiding the headquarters of the Black Panthers and parading them in front of newspaper cameras stark naked. It was a bad idea to talk about religion, politics, immigrants, or professional sports. It was also inadvisable to talk about college life, because words like "campus" and "syllabus" and "curriculum" evoked the specter of the gentry. I never let him see my grades in college—I graduated seventh in my class, first among liberal arts majors—because I knew it would trigger yet another discussion about how far Christ managed to get without a college degree. It was impolitic to joke about Christ in his presence; he would get rammy if he heard the word "geez" and did not take kindly to smart-aleck comments that Christ, when he did finally wrap up his terrestrial life that Friday afternoon on Golgotha, hadn't actually gotten all that far careerwise. It was equally unwise to remind him that, despite Christ's lack of a sheepskin, He had started out in life with a few obvious advantages: He was a fine public speaker; His earthly father, Joseph the carpenter, had taught Him a trade; He was divine. Sarcasm sometimes worked on my father, but not after the third drink, and not if the conversation involved the Lamb of God or anyone in His rough-and-tumble entourage. All in all, this was not a hospitable atmosphere for a first-generation college student.

"Why do you always keep a chair pressed up against your door?" he once asked.

"Because I'm afraid of ghosts," I replied.

"There's no such thing as ghosts," he said, "and even if there were, a wooden chair isn't going to keep a ghost out of your room."

"It's worked so far."

Purporting to be looking for a clean pair of socks or a subway token or a passage to India, my father had gotten into the habit of rifling through my things when I was out, eyes peeled for drugs. He was convinced that when I dragged myself in late at night, sporting dark sunglasses but no tee shirt and reeking of vodka, I had been out on the town doing LSD or heroin. Quite to the contrary, I'd been out on the town doing vodka. The Purple Jesus—vodka cut with grape juice—was my old standby; the religious symbolism was probably not accidental, though the concoction itself was revolting. While he never encouraged me to drink to excess, he always encouraged me to drink, if only to keep him company. On the more serious issue of narcotics, he, like most hard-drinking men of his generation, was convinced that drugs posed a threat to the republic. It was true: Drugs did pose a threat to the republic; the social carnage of the seventies would leave no doubt about that. But none of this had anything to do with me. If I posed a threat to the republic, it wasn't because I was shooting heroin. It was because I was drinking liquor, in any and all forms.

One day he confronted me with a vial of suspicious-looking tablets that he found in the top door of my chifforobe. He was certain they were contraband.

"I've got a friend down at police headquarters," he warned me, "and if he tests these pills and finds out that they're drugs, I'm not going to protect you."

"They are drugs," I told him. "They're painkillers for when you have a toothache. Try one."

In all likelihood, he never asked his friend down at police headquarters to test the Darvon compound I'd brought home from the apothecary, because his friend down at police headquarters did not exist. In any event, his fears were unwarranted. He never realized that no matter how much I wanted to belong to a loftier economic class, working-class values were so ingrained in my psyche that I would never dream of using drugs like acid or cocaine or heroin. Peer pressure alone precluded this: Working class boys, meaning virtually everyone I knew, drank liquor, which proved that they were men, while middle-class boys smoked reefer, which proved that they were beatniks or hippies or pussies or liked jazz. Within a few years, all this would change as the working class discovered not only the delights of daily drug abuse but the pleasure to be derived from mixing drugs with alcohol, especially when operating heavy machinery. But my attitude toward mood-altering substances never changed; I never developed a taste for drugs in any form. I had hand-stitched my personality by watching a procession of hard-drinking men drinking hard. None of them smoked joints. None of them would have dreamed of putting something in his mouth that had just been in another man's mouth. They had high standards of oral hygiene, but they also had a clear code of conduct. Men didn't swallow other men's saliva.

One summer day, my father and I drove to Wildwood, New Jersey, to experiment with a popular new ritual called a bonding experience. This was my mother's suggestion, and, as was often the case with her ideas, it was a bad one. We stayed at a nondescript boardinghouse my parents had been visiting for the past few years. We took some rides at the amusement park on the boardwalk, had a nice Italian meal, threw down a few drinks, and then went back to our lodgings. The sitting room in the boardinghouse was dominated by an upright piano, and my father, now feeling his oats, asked if I could bang out a couple of tunes for him and the other guests. What he had in mind was something along the lines of "Sweet Rosie O'Grady" or "Let Me Call You Sweetheart." I told him that I didn't know how to read music, didn't know any standards, and played the guitar, not the piano. This precipitated a lengthy, thermonuclear discussion of my failings as a human being and a son, because a son who loved his father—and, by extension, all of humanity—would have learned to play the piano, as opposed to the "banjo," as the piano gave ordinary people like him and the other people in the boardinghouse pleasure in a way the goddamned "banjo" did not.

"I don't play the banjo," I corrected him as the other guests and the landlady looked on in mounting dismay. "I play the guitar."

"Well, what's the difference between the banjo and the guitar?" he sneered. "Tell me, what's the difference between the banjo and the guitar?"

"Just drop it . . ."

"No, I want to know, college boy. What's the difference between the banjo and the guitar? Come on, tell me . . ."

The landlady eventually asked us to vacate the parlor, so we continued the conversation in our bedroom down the hall. It wasn't much of a conversation; I kept telling him to go to bed and sleep it off, and he kept asking me why I had never learned to play the piano, to the benefit of the faceless millions, and precisely what constituted the difference between the banjo and the guitar. I went outside and slept in the car that night, and the next morning the landlady told him that his patronage was no longer desired. We cut the bonding weekend short and drove back to Philadelphia.

"I'm sorry, buddy," he said as we motored through the wilds of south Jersey, "but no matter how hard I try, the two of us just seem to rub each other the wrong way."

It was true; we did. So we drove back home. I grabbed some clothes and went out and got drunk with my friends; he stayed home and got drunk all by himself. When he was younger and less maudlin, there were men who would drink with him, but those days were long gone, as were the men. Even men who drank too much and too often didn't want to do it with him. This was the last time we ever scheduled a meeting of the minds.

The piano episode underscored the fact that music, a social glue for many, never failed to divide my family. Toward the end of my stay at home, my father developed the habit of getting plastered and then putting the sound track to *Jesus Christ Superstar* on the record player. As was his wont, he tended to do this in the middle of the night. I have no idea where the LP came from; I think one of my sisters may have purchased it in a momentary lapse of sanity. *Jesus Christ Superstar* was brand-new at the time, and while uncompromisingly stupid, it was not completely unbearable in the way the scores to *Cats* or *Starlight Express* would be later.

My father, forty-two years old at the time the show first saw the light of day, clearly fell outside the demographic parameters Andrew Lloyd Webber was targeting. Yet, for whatever the reason, he adored that sound track and was particularly enamored of the bouncy, irreverent number in which Herod mocks the self-styled King of the Jews. Night after night, hour after hour, we would hear the man who had brought us into the world thrashing around in the dining room, juiced to the gills, listening to the same insipid song over and over again, constantly lifting the needle to repeat the exercise. We were never quite sure whether he was doing this because he pitied Christ or because he was starting to come around to Herod's point of view: that Jesus was an instigator and a bit of a goof. Blind drunk when he did this, he would often lose his grip on the needle when he lowered it onto the LP, scratching the record and causing it to skip and repeat. The CD player may have been invented to protect families like ours from such tribulation. This sort of behavior went on for years. Only much later in life did I begin to suspect that my revulsion for Webber's music, while genuine and spontaneous, may have had less to do with the composer than with my father. I am sure I would have grown up to hate Andrew Lloyd Webber anyway, as would be true of anyone who loved Schumann's Cello Concerto. But I might not have hated him as much.

Of course, had I not met Susan Orsini that fateful June afternoon in 1968, I might have grown up worshipping Andrew Lloyd Webber, like so many of my blockhead peers. Tellingly, the iron curtain Susan seemed to bring down on our relationship just before we both started college was not all that solid; I took her out several times during the subsequent summers, our friendship springing back to life once she realized that I no longer had my heart set on her and she no longer had to worry about breaking it. But our moment had passed, and neither of us made any serious attempt to recapture it. I did not see her much my junior year, perhaps once or twice, then one day my sister Mary Ann came home from school and announced that she had been killed in a car accident in Delaware while driving back to Washington. When I saw her parents at the wake a few nights later, I did not linger, as I felt that my very presence reminded them of the golden child who was no more. I never saw the family again after her funeral; I stopped walking down American Street forever. The Orsinis remained in that house as the neighborhood disintegrated, but a few years later my family moved away. And that was the end of that.

Susan was the first of my friends to die. When I knelt beside her casket at the funeral home the night of her viewing and stared down at her corpse, I could find no sign of the brassy girl who taught me that Debussy wrote his Études with the specific intention of driving his students to distraction, that Scriabin honestly believed he had unearthed a "magic chord." The morticians had flubbed their assignment; this was not the Susan I had known, not the Susan her parents had known, not the Susan any of us had known. Susan would never settle for something as glum and obvious as this wake. Susan had joie de vivre; when she was anywhere in the vicinity, the fireworks went off. The wax figurine lying in the casket was an impostor.

That night when I returned home, my father studied the mass card I brought back from the wake and asked how old Susan had been.

"Twenty-one," I said.

"Twenty-one," he repeated, bombed out of his skull, as usual. "Only twenty-one years old. So much talent, so much to live for. Why couldn't God take me instead of her?"

"Good question," I replied.

Immediately after Susan's burial, I went downtown to the Academy of Music and heard the Philadelphia Orchestra perform Brahms's Fourth Symphony. The orchestra was under the baton of the very old, very uncharismatic Eugene Ormandy, but that day, as if in her honor, Ormandy rose to the occasion. It was the first Friday afternoon concert I ever attended, but there would be hundreds and hundreds more, in Philadelphia, in New York, in Boston, in Chicago, in St. Louis, in London, in Paris. I would never go to a Friday afternoon concert without thinking of the day Susan was buried, though not in a spirit of reminiscence but of homage. Susan Orsini was the first girl to break my heart, but I would happily have had it broken a thousand times just to hear her talk once more about the solo viola passages from *Harold in Italy*.

A famous writer known for her incisive prose who then became a director of sappy movies once told me that when she left a newspaper job she dearly loved, she assumed that she would see many of her colleagues afterward but never did. This convinced her that people fell into broad general groups that were interchangeable, that if you moved from New York to Los Angeles or Berlin, you could effortlessly re-create your circle of friends back home by finding virtually identical replacements elsewhere. This is one of the casualties of growing up with money to burn: The well-heeled *are* largely interchangeable. There are a fixed number of roles to play, with a fixed number of themes, and everyone is handed his or her script at birth and then gets on with it, oblivious to the fact that they are merely types. There is the go-getter. The maverick. The hotshot. The recluse. The black sheep. The neurotic. The bohemian. The jerk-off. They are all in some ways different from one another but they are all fundamentally the same. They are unique in the same way that snowflakes are unique; no two are exactly alike, but they certainly seem identical to the naked eye.

Susan Orsini was interchangeable with no one. Suburban children trained in the classics are a dime a dozen. A violinist who grows up in a row home in Philadelphia is like Halley's Comet. In a world of subdued colors, Susan Orsini was a supernova. She was the only classically trained musician I ever met who was raised in modest circumstances in a working-class community, who did not attend a fancy prep school, who did not grow up in an environment of ease and comfort. The musicians who grow up to play in the great orchestras of America may be gifted as all get-out, but it is hard to tell one from the other. The musician who died in a car crash on a cold winter night in Delaware was one of a kind.

Meeting Susan would lead directly to the watershed moment in my life. As I learned more and more about the classics, I began to acquire arty LPs by the fistful. They were mostly meat-and-potatoes stuff—Chopin's complete piano works by the Brazilian wonder Guiomar Novaes, Schubert's Impromptus by Alfred Brendel. But there were also a few oddities thrown in—Webern's transcriptions of Bach, Messiaen's weird bird music, even a collection of sixteenth-century Spanish organ pieces—purchased for no other reason than to edify the vulgar. I adored these LPs and listened to them constantly; they were far and away my most precious possessions. The records were stored in a cardboard carton that sat at the foot of my bed. It was a collection of which I was enormously proud.

My belligerently proprietary attitude toward my record collection brought about the dénouement of my long, unsatisfactory relationship with my father. By the time I turned twenty, I had developed my own skills at sticking the knife in and breaking the human heart, having learned at the feet of the master. I knew that my deliberate scattering of dog-eared copies of Eugene Ionesco's La cantatrice chauve and Jean Anouilh's Becket, ou L'honneur de Dieu around the living room was simply a way of taunting him. These cultural talismans symbolized the dreams that lay within my reach but outside his: Bach would get me into graduate school; Courbet would facilitate my ascension into the middle class; Balzac would make me rich. Art, music, and literature, which had started out as diversions, had now evolved into artillery. My father's arsenal consisted of alcohol, brutality, and contempt; I fought back with Apollinaire, Brahms, and condescension. It was still unequal combat, as I was not yet capable of destroying him; but there was no doubt that the battle had been joined and the war would be pitiless.

One day when I came home, I found a half-dozen of my cherished LPs strewn all over my bedroom floor. Collecting them, I noticed that they were badly scratched, some beyond salvaging, some covered with beer stains. I gathered from my sister that my father had been listening to Chopin and Scarlatti while I was at work, with the usual results. The charitable view was that he was making an effort to extend the olive branch by putting *Movie Themes Go Mambo!* on the back burner and taking a crack at Mozart's Requiem. But all I saw was carnage. So I got out a piece of paper and wrote him a note:

> I DON'T MIND ANYONE LISTENING TO MY RECORDS. BUT IF
> YOU'RE GOING TO LISTEN TO THEM, TRY NOT TO SCRATCH
> THEM. AND PUT THEM AWAY WHEN YOU'RE DONE.

I was perfectly aware that leaving that sign on top of the record box was insanely provocative, that I was waving a red flag in a bull's face. I didn't care; I was spoiling for a fight. A few days passed, then one night I took the bus to Havertown to visit Uncle Jerry, whose wife had died a year earlier at the age of forty-nine. A heart attack had killed Aunt Cassie, though all the pills she was taking for various maladies may have helped. Uncle Jerry was having a rough time of it, but I was more than welcome to stop by, as he had always enjoyed my company. We were sitting in his living room, having a few drinks, when the phone rang.

It was my father. He was delirious.

"Did you leave that sign on those records?" he demanded. I could practically smell the liquor seeping through the earpiece.

"Well, they're my records—"

"Yeah, well, if that's the way you feel about it, pal, don't bother coming home tomorrow! I don't want you in my house anymore! I don't want to see your fucking face again! I don't need a son like you!"

Then he slammed down the phone.

I returned to the living room and had another beer. My uncle asked what all the fuss was about, and I told him. By this point, our relationship had changed. I wasn't a child anymore, and I wasn't a Republican. The hero of my youth, the man in the gray flannel suit and the natty fedora who used to take me out on his sales calls, had hardened as he grew older, becoming bitter and confrontational. I am not sure if this was the result of losing Aunt Cassie at such a young age; I knew by now that he was "a ladies' man" and had probably been a ladies' man straight through his marriage. In the end, I think the world turned gray because he had lost a sparring partner he had come to admire and realized too late that she was a born scrapper who could not be replaced.

That night, words were exchanged. Somehow, we segued from my father's drinking to Uncle Jerry's favorite topic: the iniquities of the Democratic Party. On and on he ranted about George Wallace and Stokely Carmichael and H. Rap Brown and *None Dare Call It Treason* and the John Birch Society and Tail-Gunner Joe and Barry Goldwater and that son of a bitch JFK and the tragically misunderstood Richard Nixon. In his eyes, everyone under the age of thirty was in secret contact with Chairman Mao and Ho Chi Minh; we were only waiting for nightfall so we could sneak up on the adults, slit their throats, and topple the republic. He didn't understand that long hair and disheveled attire and Eldridge Cleaver posters and Che Guevara tee shirts were virtually devoid of political content; that very little of it had anything to do with revolution or civil rights; that it was mostly about fashion. Even when I was sitting directly in front of my uncle, downing bottle after bottle of Carling Black Label beer, he must have thought I was doing it only to humor him, that I couldn't wait till he had gone to bed so I could get out my kit and shoot some horse or pop a few tabs of acid. He saw young people as the enemy of everything he valued—and I was young. Before my very eyes, my childhood idol had transformed himself into a cynical, middle-aged man who no longer believed in the American dream. Those face-offs on that hacienda-style chessboard seemed awfully far away now.

Shortly before he went to bed that night, Uncle Jerry stopped off in the living room for one final comment. "Your father may have his faults, but we all have faults. You have faults, too."

"I know that."

"Sometimes when I come down in the morning, you've put a half-bottle of beer back in the icebox," he continued. "If you don't put the cap back on, the beer goes flat and I have to throw it out. And sometimes you leave the mustard out on the drain board. So don't be too hasty in judging your father. We all make mistakes."

This said, he went off to bed.

Like many Americans of German ancestry, Uncle Jerry was tight with a buck. Incontestable evidence of this was supplied that night when I went upstairs and opened the medicine cabinet. There, arrayed before me, sat bottle upon bottle of sedatives and painkillers, the mélange of sleeping pills and assorted barbiturates that my aunt had amassed and had possibly mixed together in the fatal cocktail that inadvertently killed her. Though she had been dead for almost two years, Uncle Jerry had never thrown them out. Perhaps they constituted some idiosyncratic pharmaceutical memorial to his fallen spouse, or perhaps he was just cheap. The pills sat there, beckoning to me or anybody else in a suggestible frame of mind. I was tired now, worn out by a lifetime of discord and hatred. I was tired of all the conversations about Richard Nixon, Ho Chi Minh, Martin Luther King, Christ Our Savior. I may not have made a conscious decision to cash in my chips; I cannot even recall swallowing the pills. But I did swallow them, and I must have swallowed quite a few. Then I went to bed. I was going to drift off now. Things had not worked out the way one might have hoped. It was time to try something different.

The next morning, the phone began ringing. It rang for a long time. It was around ten, Uncle Jerry had already left for work, it must have gone on ringing forever. I finally answered it. It was my father. At least that's what I gathered, in my woozy condition. He was calling to apologize. I said that was nice. The receiver tumbled from my hand. He kept on talking, but I couldn't hear him. I was worn out. I needed to go back to sleep.

A few minutes later, the front door to the house came flying off its hinges. My father had called my uncle, my uncle had called the fire department, the firemen rushed me to the hospital, the nurses inserted a catheter in my penis and pumped my stomach. That hurt. Other than the catheter, I remember very little that happened that day. It was as if I was not even there, as if I no longer wished to be part of any equation that included me. Like my father when he had run away from the war, I'd gone absent without leave.

Chapter 11. **Walkabout**

The unscheduled theatrics of late August proved to be a stroke of tactical genius, bringing an elegant new structure to my relationship with my father. Henceforth, he was excised from my existence. From the time the firemen kicked in my uncle's door and carted me off to the hospital until the waning days of his life a quarter of a century later, we had almost nothing to do with each other. I had come to my senses. The spell had been broken.

Why I would risk ending my life rather than walking out of his is impossible to explain; nor do I fully understand why I spent so many years seeking the approval of a man I did not respect, much less love. It was perhaps because he was more than a bad father; he was a bad habit. Until I downed those pills, the idea of living the rest of my life without fashioning a workable relationship with my father would never have occurred to me. It would constitute some form of ethnic betrayal; Irish Catholics didn't do things like that: They might hate their fathers, but they did not turn their backs on them. Fathers were problems sons had to solve before one of them died. This, of course, was madness, the very thing people came to the United States to escape. But the logic that prevailed inside our house was the logic that holds sway in a bad dream: Until the sleeper is roused from his slumber, everything that transpires inside the dream makes perfect sense. My father was a nightmare from which his family needed to awake.

His were sorcerer's powers; stymied by life, he tricked his children into believing that they would never amount to anything either, that their sole function was to placate their household Svengali. We were citizens of a country that had only six inhabitants, a penal colony where everyone had his last name. Somewhere I had read that no matter how much Charles Dickens's father mistreated his family, Dickens never stopped loving him, in no small part because he was enchanted by his father's ne'er-do-well charm. For a time, I had similar feelings about my father, or at least that was the way I talked about him around my friends. My admiration for his sharp intellect and fine sense of humor and clever turn of phrase, and my envy of his abundant charisma and personal magnetism overshadowed my dread of his company. Those days were now past. Our relationship was a jigsaw puzzle I had been trying to assemble for twenty years with no hope of success, because too many of the vital pieces were missing or had never arrived with the original packaging.

From that time on, I operated as an independent contractor. I'd spent my entire life hoping to have a father like my friends' fathers— somebody you could look up to, somebody you could emulate, some- body you didn't have to arm yourself against with a Bowie knife. Now I realized that these options were not, and never had been, available. Acceptance of this fact was liberating: Neither his opinion nor anyone else's ever mattered to me again after that; I did not care if people dis- liked my work or my attitude or my values. I had squandered my youth trying to please someone who could not be pleased; now I would please myself.

It was euphoric to enter a world from which this lifelong nemesis had been purged. I would wake up every morning overjoyed to know that even if things turned out badly, at least he wouldn't be around to make them worse. From then on, I would spend a few minutes of every day in a state of private exultation, basking in the aura of his absence. He understood how I felt; the significance of my histrionic gesture that August night was impossible to misconstrue. When the squaws swooped down onto the Seventh Cavalry after the Battle of the Little Big Horn and began mutilating the troopers' corpses, they took special care to stick long knitting needles through George Arm- strong Custer's ears. They did this because they believed that nothing the Sioux and Cheyenne had ever said to him had gotten through. Now he could hear.

My father reacted to nearly losing his only son the way he reacted to all disasters: by retreating into the convenient obliviousness of the alkie and refusing to discuss it. Clearly, he was taken aback by what had occurred; with an infant sister already written up on his rap sheet, prematurely shipping a son to the morgue would probably have put the kibosh on any hopes of entering the Kingdom of Heaven. We never had another knock-down, drag-out fight after that, because to him my botched suicide attempt was proof of emotional delicacy, suggesting that the infrastructure of sanity in my personality was so fragile that an ill-chosen word might push me over the edge. From now on, he would have to walk on eggshells in the way only he could.

I spent two weeks in the hospital recuperating from the first twenty years of my life, then passed the remainder of the summer at friends' houses or in New York with my two older sisters. I cannot recall my first visit home afterward or when I next saw my father. He did not visit me in the hospital, not out of malice or indifference but because the professionals thought it would be a bad idea for us to see each other. A few weeks later, I moved into inexpensive lodgings my mother found in the classifieds, a functional little room on the third story of a stately home that sat two blocks down the street from Saint Joseph's College, directly opposite the cardinal's residence. There were two other tenants in the house: a hairstylist who looked like David Lee Roth ten years before even Roth dared to and a scrawny Chinese math major who drank like a fish, smoked like a chimney, spent twelve hours a day playing cards and the other twelve waiting on tables in a Chinese restaurant. It was as if he were competing for a coveted ethnic-stereotype award and wanted to make sure he locked it up early. He graduated summa cum laude, a remarkable achievement for someone who never went to class and never, ever went to bed.

My senior year in college was unexpectedly sublime. Because I had the highest grade-point average among liberal arts majors, I was eligible for an independent-study program called the College Scholar. It meant that instead of attending classes like everyone else, I could follow a directed-readings program and spend all my time exploring the world's foremost literary masterpieces. The whole thing was very sixties; who needed classes and teachers and peers and term papers when you could stay in bed, get loaded, and read *The One Hundred and Twenty Days of Sodom*? Freed from the normal constraints of the otherwise rigorous Jesuit curriculum, I devoured the works of Molière, Corneille, and Racine, as well as the collected plays of the career criminal Jean Genet and the right-wing Catholic poet Paul Claudel, whom I compared in an original though ultimately pointless honors thesis whose unsurprising conclusion was that Genet and Claudel had almost nothing in common, except that a lot of French people found them contemptible and annoying. I also read every play by Shakespeare's major contemporaries—John Ford, John Webster, Cyril Tourneur, Ben Jonson—arriving at the similarly unsurprising conclusion that, compared to the thirty-seven plays churned out by the Bard of Avon, their work didn't add up to much. It also didn't add up to much compared to the works of Molière, Racine, and Corneille or, for that matter, Claudel and Genet.

When I was not busy studying, I would attend any affordable concert in the tristate area, whether rock, jazz, or classical, only drawing the line at country-and-western—culturally irrelevant to a young urbanite—and folk, which made my skin crawl, as it had ever since I was first exposed to Pete Seeger and Phil Ochs and others of their pop Stalinist ilk back in the seminary. At these concerts, like everyone else in my age group, I would consume an intimidating quantity of alcohol, even if Mahler's Eighth was on the program. I also started dating a vivacious, ruddy-cheeked, raven-haired girl from the suburbs whose father had taken early retirement from the post office so he could sit home and read the Great Books. Every weekend when I turned up at her house, I would find him lounging in a recliner, working his way through Plato's *Republic* or *The Decameron,* a stein of beer poised on the adjoining table.

"That Boccaccio was sure a character," he would cheerfully greet me with as I strolled into his house. "By the way, there's plenty of Pabst Blue Ribbon in the fridge."

As soon as I had a cold lager in my hand, he would begin grilling me about the vital lie or the causes of the Peloponnesian War or whether Brutus was a hero or a snake to betray his good friend Julius Caesar, who may have been his bastard son via his mistress Servilia. Because he was a working-class man who had little formal education, it was sometimes difficult for him to grasp exactly what Plato or Suetonius or Gibbon was driving at in a certain passage, or to place Ernest Hemingway's no-frills style in historical context vis-à-vis Theodore Dreiser and Émile Zola. Still, there was something heroic about this menopausal self-actualization project, this armchair quest for the autodidact's Holy Grail. Out there somewhere, just beyond the horizon, lay a world of unimaginable splendor and sophistication, and though it might sometimes seem out of reach, if you kept on reading, studying, striving, you could one day arrive there. I admired him for his undertaking and continued to date his delightful daughter long after I knew the relationship was going nowhere, because I enjoyed his company at least as much as I enjoyed hers. In another life, he might have been my father. And a very good one he would have been.

One other memory stands out from my final year in college: the four-hour course I took every Tuesday afternoon at the Barnes Foundation, the secretive, pugnaciously antisocial art museum whose grounds abutted the campus of Saint Joseph's College on the Lower Merion side of City Line Avenue. For decades, the museum had refused to open its doors to the public, limiting its audience to authentic cognoscenti, whose ranks, it had decided, did not include art critics, museum directors, curators, art historians, or, for that matter, most cognoscenti. It was like one of those spooky South Philadelphia social clubs, which, by the very act of barring its doors to non-Italians, immediately deepened the atmosphere of intrigue and menace when in fact all anyone was doing inside was smoking *Toscanis* and hiding from their wives. In the case of the Barnes Foundation, its ardently publicized passion for obscurity and seclusion and its high-decibel entreaties to be left alone made people wonder exactly what was going on behind its locked doors. What was going on was simple: A bunch of crackpots, plus the half-dozen people in the art world they did not despise, were hiding indoors with $6 billion worth of modern art, gloating over the fact that only a few hundred museumgoers a year ever got to see their breathtaking collection of Soutines, and even then only because the foundation had a gun cocked to its head. Lots of museums are haughty, but the Barnes was downright mean.

Only recently had a lawsuit brought by the state of Pennsylvania compelled the furtive, spiteful institution to open its doors and let ordinary people see its fabulous collection. The Barnes, founded by a man who had made a fortune in the eyewash racket but was now long dead, had compromised with the authorities by deigning to allow a microscopic number of guests to visit the museum a few times a week, but only after securing hard-to-obtain reservations. The institution also announced that it would offer a ponderous art-appreciation course to select members of the community, whose numbers would include ten students from Saint Joseph's. Aspiring aesthetes were admitted only after a personal interview with Albert Barnes's mentor, coconspirator, and, some said, mistress, the lovely but very strange Violette de Mazia.

De Mazia, like Barnes, was quite the eccentric. Every Tuesday, once we had all been padlocked inside the museum for the entire afternoon—no one was allowed to leave early, not even if nuclear war erupted—she would waft into the main gallery clad in a billowing gown color-coded with the paintings to be discussed that day. She would then perch her sparrowlike body on a tall stool, stare at us from behind her dark sunglasses, and lecture in a high-pitched voice for four hours straight, vainly attempting to convince the ninety members of the class that there were no bulls or matadors or picadors or symbols of Spain's decline or its Catholic past in the Picasso painting hanging on the wall directly behind her, because paintings consisted only of color, light, geometric structures, shading, and amorphous, ineffable entities called "broad human values," which the rest of us referred to as "B.H.V.'s." The bulls and matadors were optical illusions.

Sometimes the anorexic Gaul would hang the paintings upside down to prove that a great work of art was equally riveting no matter which way you looked at it, but none of us had any idea what she was talking about, most certainly not the middle-aged Teuton with the black eye patch, who was widely suspected of being a Nazi spy—a latter-day Rip Van Winkle of fascist bent who had somehow managed to sleep through all the fireworks back in the forties and was now trying to make up for lost time by infiltrating one of the most esoteric corners of the art world.

De Mazia, a bantamweight, if that, would sit in exactly the same spot where Bertrand Russell once ensconced himself while he was giving a series of lectures that ultimately became *The History of Western Philosophy*. When Russell complained that the nudes were making it hard for his students to concentrate, Barnes more or less replied, "My dear fellow, what nudes?" It was that kind of operation.

Ms. de Mazia was an amazingly fine-looking woman for one so emaciated and advanced in years (she was already in her seventies but born in France, which gave her an unfair advantage over all the other women in the room), and Barnes's collection of Matisses, Gauguins, Renoirs, and Soutines was second to none, so I thoroughly enjoyed that course, even though, as soon as she started talking about broad human values and hanging the Picassos at cockeyed angles, I could see that she was as mad as a hatter.

Back home in Olney, which I rarely visited after Susan's death, things were much the same. In the long run, the near-tragedy of the previous summer had not noticeably improved my father's disposition. He continued to drink with homicidal zeal; he continued to conduct his nocturnal colloquies with invisible specters; he continued to sink into the abyss he had been sinking into since 1958. None of it was of any consequence to me; I would never live in his house again, and whatever happened to him from that point onward was his business. When people used the word "father" in my presence, it was like hearing a once-familiar term from a foreign language whose vocabulary I had now forgotten.

He may have felt the same way about the word "son"; whatever his views on the suicide attempt, our estrangement was complete. The rupture was cemented when I phoned home in May of my senior year to announce that an organization called the Alliance Française had awarded me a $2,000 scholarship to spend a year in France. My French teacher Tom Donahue had suggested that I apply for the scholarship at the end of my senior year, a suggestion I viewed as ludicrous because, even though I could read the language reasonably well, my spoken French was almost actionably bad. He assured me that this did not matter, because the Alliance Française promoted French culture, not French grammar, and as I had already read the complete works of Molière and Racine, something no one else under the age of twenty-one in the Greater Delaware Valley could purport to have done, I would have the inside track on the competition. He also said that he could arrange for me to be the final applicant interviewed by the Alliance board, loping in at dusk, by which point the judges would be so weary of perky Swarthmore francophiles smitten by the nuances of the future anterior tense that they would literally fall down on their knees and beg me to take the money.

This is exactly what came to pass: I entered the room and, when asked why I wanted to spend a year in France, immediately ran through the whole F. Scott Fitzgerald, Ernest Hemingway, James Joyce sleeping-on-the-floor-at-Shakespeare & Company-when-we-were-very-young-and-very-happy routine, then casually observed that every great non-French writer I could think of—Dante, Erasmus, Edith Wharton, George Orwell, James Baldwin—had lived in Paris, though none of them had died there. I had cribbed this material from Henry Miller, fully aware that, like many of Miller's assertions, it was not true: Oscar Wilde died in Paris, as did Samuel Beckett. Be that as it may, my spiel manifested an edifying, if jejune, savoir faire; my determination to become a writer was unquestionable; and at least I did not pretend to hold any special place in my heart for the vanished splendors of the future anterior tense, much less the preterit. They gave me the two thousand smackers.

In immigrant lore, when the eldest son becomes the first member of the family to graduate from college, and when he tops it off by winning a scholarship to spend a year in Paris, the parents react jubilantly. Even if no one else in the family has ever been to Paris or has any real expectation of ever getting there, the idea of spending a year in France is imbued with transparent symbolism; it is not some indecipherable cuneiform. But there was no rejoicing on North Second Street when my parents heard my news; they were charter members of an ethnic group that lacked the capacity to enjoy anyone else's good fortune. They knew that a year in France meant a lot to me, that it was far and away the most important event in my life. But it meant nothing to them. Their lack of enthusiasm did not derive from fear that I would get above my station and expose myself to the uninterrupted series of brutal disappointments that life held in store. Nor was their blasé response an expression of the equally popular Irish-Catholic belief that human existence was a zero-sum operation—that one man's success by definition was offset by another man's failure. It was simply a case of my news being irrelevant to them. They were working-class people; they had been beaten down by life. My good fortune was not about to raise their salaries, heal their illnesses, repair their appliances, fix their marriage. Joy was an emotion to which they had long ago lost access.

The year in France was much as I'd expected it to be: a dream come true. From the moment I stepped off the plane, exchanging the City of Brotherly Love for the City of Light, I felt that I had crossed into another dimension. Night after night in the peanut gallery at the Comédie Française. Twice-a-week concerts at the Théâtre des Champs-Élysées, where Stravinsky's *Rite of Spring* caused a riot in 1913. Lots of friends, loads of alcohol, tons of merriment. Hundreds of books, hundreds of movies, scores of plays, even a few tentative stabs at writing fiction. But mostly culture, sex, and liquor.

Certain memories stand out more clearly than others: A sixth arrondissement boardinghouse filled with Spaniards, Venezuelans, Japanese, Czechs, and Yugoslavs who were desperately trying to master a language they were obviously no match for. Meeting Jean-Louis Barrault, whose wife, Madeleine Renaud, I had seen at the Barbizon Plaza Theatre in New York two years earlier. Looking up to see snow falling on the Eiffel Tower on Christmas Eve. A strapping Finnish girl rowing me around in a dinghy on the Grande Jatte; a petulant Dutch woman explaining to me why Richard Brautigan beat Dostoyevsky hands down; a chic French-Canadian nurse introducing me to the most vital rite of passage of all: sex with someone who knew what she was doing.

There was also a brief fling with a moody Long Island girl who recruited me as her escort on a trip to Tangiers to buy Goulami beads. Along the way, we visited Pamplona, the Prado, and the Alhambra, none of which I ever saw again. More noteworthy still were my nightly subterranean encounters with a Japanese pastry chef studying at Le Cordon Bleu who kept me alive all winter by stuffing my face with the latest delicacy he happened to be concocting. Every night, I would careen into the boardinghouse at three in the morning from some Left Bank bistro and find him downstairs in the communal kitchen doing his homework. His homework was pastry. He would sit there and watch me ingest an entire cake or pie or *clafoutis* or flan, or a plateful of petits fours or *jésuites*, never expecting compensation or even thanks, only asking if tonight's treat was up to my usual standards. Sometimes I would bring along an undernourished friend. My unlikely benefactor from Kyoto didn't mind in the least. Seventy-five percent of my diet that year consisted of pastry: Now I knew what Marie Antoinette was talking about.

Finally, and perhaps most memorably, there was a chance encounter with a displaced francophobic Australian surfer that would result in a friendship that lasted forever, no matter how great the distance between us. I would never have met Mick had I not first crossed paths with his brash, fetching French girlfriend in a Montparnasse supermarket while she was engaged in what I believed at the time to be shoplifting, though she may have merely been straightening her poncho.

"Oh, you're American," she said, fiddling covetously with a rather plump rib-eye steak. "My boyfriend's Australian, but he can't stand French people. Why don't you come over on Thursday night for dinner?"

That friendship lasted a lifetime, too; she was a cook to be reckoned with. In the end, I didn't spend all that much time studying language and literature at the Sorbonne, which was what I was supposed to be doing, but there was certainly plenty of time for wine, women, and song. The entire year in Paris, for the first time in my life, I felt supernaturally happy, at least until the United States government, finally conceding that the war in Vietnam was lost, sued for peace, causing the dollar to crash overnight, and my money ran out, all thanks to that son of a bitch Richard Nixon, who had been the bane of my family's existence since 1958. When I was a little kid on Russell Street, I could never understand why my father hated Nixon so much. Now I knew.

One June evening at the end of that year, my French teacher, who had engineered my trip to Paris in the first place, turned up out of the blue. Diplomatically, over a smashing dinner he paid for, Nixon's disastrous foreign policy having left me threadbare, I confessed that while I had indeed signed up at the Sorbonne to take a few courses the previous September—primarily to get a student I.D., which allowed me to eat meals in university restaurants for thirty cents apiece—I'd spent most of the past ten months carousing.

"That's what we expected you to do," he said nonchalantly, never breaking stride as he worked on his couscous. "How's the ratatouille?"

After I returned to the United States, Paris refused to leave my thoughts. Philadelphia made sure of that. The City of Light resembles no other city on the face of the earth, as is widely known. But it is particularly dissimilar to the City of Brotherly Love, which is long on angst but short on charm. Paris was more than a moveable feast; it was a feast I never had to share with anyone else. The year I spent on the Rue Mayet was the touchstone I could come back to again and again; it was the year I nixed the official family credo and decided that life was to be seized by the throat, not merely endured; that it was a gift, not a chore.

My father could not understand how any of this had come about: My all-expenses-paid trip abroad had to be the work of fairies, gremlins, demiurges, succubi. In the emotionally cauterized mind of the Depression-era Irish American, good fortune is never earned, cannot last, and is probably the work of the devil. While I was away, there were occasional letters from my mother and my three sisters, but not one from my father, who was the only one in the family who actually liked writing letters. When I spent a king's ransom to phone home at Christmas from the post office, which, since I had no phone, was the only place I could make a transatlantic call, he was at work. I had forgotten that he always worked holidays, in part because he got paid double time but mostly because nobody wanted him around on Christmas, Easter, Thanksgiving, or even Flag Day. I spent eleven months not hearing his voice, nor he mine.

While I was in Europe, his drinking problems continued, but the number of family members on hand to terrorize had dwindled to a paltry two: my mother and my youngest sister, Mary Ann, still in high school. Ree and Eileen were long gone, sharing an apartment in New York City, both attending college. My mother continued to live with him and tolerate his abuse, though none of us had any idea why. The official explanation was that neither could manage financially on their own, though more likely she stayed with him because that was what Catholic women of her generation were expected to do. To leave him would be to admit defeat both as a Catholic and as a female. She did call the police several times when he got plastered, turned violent, chased her and my sister out the door, and locked himself in, and on more than one occasion she forced him to spend the night at his sister Rosemary's house, a few blocks away. Of course, it had been years since my parents shared a bed, so this was a marriage in name only. But she never formally threw him out of the house while there were still children living in it. There would always be a reconciliation, a halfhearted apology, a promise to lay off the sauce and "get help." But help, never sought, never arrived, and shortly thereafter the same destructive cycle would resume.

I returned to Philadelphia after my year in Paris, renting an apartment in a quaint suburban town ten miles north of my parents' home. As soon as I was set up in my new living quarters, I began preparing for a career as a novelist. I made a list of the 250 greatest books ever written, and over a two-year period I polished off all of them—*Ulysses, Buddenbrooks, The Brothers Karamazov, Moby-Dick*—convinced that if I read enough great prose, some of it might rub off on me. Things did not work out the way I had hoped; my fiction was dreadful. But I did not know this at the time, nor did I care.

During this period, I supported myself with a number of offbeat, and sometimes crummy, jobs. For six months, I worked on the assembly line at one of the most admired corporations in the history of addressing machines. I did this under the tutelage of a porky, nearsighted man who despised me. Assembling addressing machines was a lark for college boys like me, but he was no college boy, and this was no lark. I did not go out of my way to display contempt for the semiskilled milieu in which I found myself, but my attempts to disguise my true feelings were unsuccessful, as he clearly wished I was dead, along with all the other college boys who went slumming in factories for a few months before taking management jobs with IBM.

I also worked for a south Jersey term-paper factory, cranking out hundreds of inappropriately thoughtful essays, filled with facts I had pulled out of thin air, supported by footnotes I sometimes marshaled from sources that did not exist. What happened when those papers got turned in to professors by the legion of pinheads who patronized the term-paper factory is beyond me; few of our customers could spell Macbeth, much less explain what caused his relationship with Banquo to unravel. The job didn't pay much, but the hours were good.

For about a year, I worked at a gigantic supermarket warehouse as a "casual" laborer, doing all the tasks the older men did not have to do because they belonged to a powerful union and could do as they pleased. The job paid more than twice my salary at the addressing-machine factory. The older men on the loading dock were mostly high school dropouts, like my father, who would have cut off his right arm for a job like this. They responded to the good fortune society had showered on them by reporting for work bombed out of their skulls, refueling at break time on shots and beers purchased at a buck a pop from a fellow employee who operated an informal saloon out of the back of his station wagon. Some of the younger men also smoked reefer, though not in front of the old-timers, who viewed drugs as un-American and out of step with the ethos of the proletariat. As a rule, the younger men drank for the first four hours of their shift and got high the second four, while the older men drank only at lunchtime. Once everyone was suitably hammered, they would spend the rest of the night deploring their miserable lot in life, cursing management for forcing them to do what little work they did do, as if sulking was going to make the time pass any more quickly.

The old-timers manifested a curious strain of patriotism: Their cars were festooned with American-flag decals and coarse, jingoistic slogans; they approved of everything the Nixon administration was doing in Southeast Asia; and they bellyached ceaselessly about the threat posed to Americans by the communists among us. Yet they themselves were bereft of the virtues that had made America great: the belief in an honest day's work for an honest day's pay, a determination to improve one's skills and get ahead in life, a cheerful, upbeat attitude about the future. Mostly, they were grumpy mopes. Mostly, they were bums.

Casual laborers had to wait all day for a phone call informing them that their services were required that evening. No one got called back unless he had loaded one thousand boxes onto a truck the night before, a feat that was impossible to achieve without working through lunch breaks. One night, slaving away in the middle of the night, desperate to reach my quota, I found myself surrounded by four older men. They were the kind of men who munched on Red Man chewing tobacco not because they enjoyed it but because newspaper photos of murderous Dixie Klansmen invariably depicted them with a pouch of Red Man tobacco protruding from their shirt pockets, and the local canaille valued its iconic power. They were not especially scary, but they made up for this by being numerous.

"We don't work through lunch breaks," they informed me with that terse malevolence cowardly men can effortlessly muster when accompanied by several other terse, malevolent men. "Don't let us catch you working through your lunch break again."

I never did work through my lunch break again. I simply worked harder, because I wanted to raise enough money to move to New York or go back to France. I never worked anyplace where I more thoroughly disliked my coworkers or more resented the way some people took the American dream for granted. I liked them even less than the rats that came bounding out of the fifty-pound bags of dog food, because at least the rats had a solid work ethic.

During this period, I would occasionally see my father "socially." He would invite me out to lunch, regale me with a few vintage tales, then reach into his wallet and offer to cover the $12 check. Discovering, to his amazement, that his cupboard was bare, he would stick me with the bill and then shamelessly borrow a fresh twenty smackers. He was nothing if not bold. He would always order two Manhattans as soon as we arrived, then two more, as if he feared that the restaurant might run out of liquor or suddenly get padlocked following a surprise raid by the Feds. He would toss back a minimum of four stiff drinks, with a couple of beer chasers, each time we convened, after which he would drive home, well and truly ripped. This did not faze me. In my mind, he had already entered the lovable-rogue stage of his life: He continued to be dishonest and unreliable, but at least he did it all in a cheerful, almost scamplike, way. One day I asked him why he was drinking at eleven o'clock in the morning, as he had long adhered to the rule that a man who abstained from demon alcohol before noon ipso facto could never be accused of having a drinking problem.

"It's afternoon in Bangkok," he replied.

By this point, I had begun using my father as a punch line. I would regularly cite pithy phrases he used, such as "Work is the curse of the drinking man" or "When Queenan drinks, everybody drinks; when Queenan pays, everybody pays." Or I would adopt one of his time-honored gambits and bang on the hood of a car whose driver was madly klaxoning and sneer: "Your horn works, buddy. Why don't you check your lights?" All this was a ploy to turn my father into someone less villainous: a rapscallion, if you will, a jackanapes, a will-o'-the-wisp, but certainly not a churl. For years, I had viewed him as a monster. Now I viewed him as a clown.

We didn't argue anymore; on the rare occasions when we saw each other, we mostly reminisced about how wonderful things were back in what he referred to as "the good old days." The good old days were set in an era antedating the birth of his children; he never recounted cute little stories about things we did as toddlers, preferring to dwell on the exploits of Glenn Davis and Doc Blanchard in the epic 1946 Notre Dame game at Yankee Stadium. Like the Notre Dame–Michigan State Game of the Century twenty years later, that one ended in a tie, in this case with neither side actually putting any points on the scoreboard. Because children remember little that happened before the age of five, they must rely on their parents to confirm that they actually said or did amusing things as tykes. Every so often, it would have been nice to hear him talk about the times when his children brought him some small measure of happiness, the golden years before all his dreams got smashed by Eisenhower and Nixon and the 1958 recession. But he never talked about our childhoods. He talked about Notre Dame.

We had a few memorable outings in the last three years I lived in Philadelphia. One day he phoned and asked if I would help him pick up a mattress he'd purchased for ten bucks from a student who was graduating from the University of Pennsylvania. This was right around the time Nixon resigned from office, hauling his fluorescently duplicitous hide back to the Golden State, where he would no longer be in a position to inflict economic ruin on my family. When we convened at the frat house, I noticed that he had brought along a roll of flimsy string rather than a length of sturdy rope. I offered to run to the hardware store to buy a clothesline, but he said not to worry, the string would do just fine, provided we made sure it was attached tightly to the front and rear fenders. We tied the mattress onto the roof and scooted out onto the Schuylkill Expressway. It was windy that day, and we hadn't done much of a job securing the mattress, so as soon as the car hit cruising speed, the new acquisition came flying off the top. It landed directly in front of the car behind us, nearly causing an accident. The driver swerved and started honking his horn, mad as hell. In the rearview mirror, my father spotted a traffic cop about four cars back, so we took the next exit and high-tailed it out of there. It was a very fine adventure indeed, culminating in my father's trademark admonition "Don't take any wooden nickels."

He could be chummy enough when encountered on neutral ground, but behind closed doors the alcohol overpowered him. As he got older, he started calling in sick to work, often due to lack of sleep. He regularly stayed up all night listening to his barmy record collection, careening around downstairs, engaging in his soused Socratic dialogues with some unidentified, unseen co-monologist who may have been God, though it was not unheard of for Saint Jude, patron saint of lost causes, to put in an occasional appearance. My mother, as always, lived in fear that he would one day burn down the house with her inside it, just as he had supposedly burned down the house with his little sister inside it as a boy.

One day, against all odds, after thirty long years of marriage, none of them terribly pleasant, my mother announced that she had finally had enough. The straw that broke the connubial camel's back was my father's electrifyingly stupid decision to quit his job as a security guard at the University of Pennsylvania Hospital just six months before he would have been eligible for a modest pension. It was the kind of insanely self-destructive gesture at which he excelled; since the prospect of nursing a nice little pension may have been the only reason my mother hung on as long as she did, there was no further reason to stay. She knew that she should have heaved him overboard years earlier, when there was still time to salvage something out of our childhood. Unwisely, she had waited until all the children were out of the house before severing her ties with a man she had never loved. We had long believed that money lay at the core of this decision—the specter of the Great Depression hovered over our household, with each of these scarred children of the 1930s deciding they would rather live in despair than in poverty—but perhaps not. Perhaps she never truly appreciated how utterly he dominated our existence, how completely he blotted out the sun. Perhaps she needed to have all the buffers between her and her husband removed before she could finally realize what a horror he was. It had been a mistake to marry him; it had been a mistake to have four children with him; it had been a mistake to stay with him for thirty years. Better luck next lifetime.

She was happy to be rid of him, and happy to be rid of the house itself, a dingy affair that none of us ever liked and that we'd grown to like even less as the neighborhood deteriorated. My mother, who throughout the worst times had always clung to an improbable aloofness, trundled off to live in a sun-drenched little apartment in a much better neighborhood, leaving behind her useless husband and our abominable next-door neighbors, the smut-loving detritus from beyond the Carpathians. I do not even recall how I learned of this decision, only that I applauded it.

After the house was sold, my father vaporized. For a while, so the grapevine reported, he was staying with his surviving sister, Rosemary, a pudgy neurotic who lived a few blocks away in a three-bedroom house whose Venetian blinds had not been opened since Prohibition. Then, later on, we heard that he'd moved in with my uncle Jerry, whom I had not seen since the night I requisitioned the contents of his wife's medicine cabinet. Sometimes my father found a cheap room to rent somewhere; sometimes he would pitch camp in a men's shelter; sometimes he dropped from sight completely. The Bedouin phase that was to characterize the last two decades of his life had begun.

My mother kept vaguely abreast of his movements during this period, as he occasionally checked in by phone. She never changed her number, nor did she move to a new address without telling him. But she made it clear that she did not want him coming around. She never divorced him; she never sought a legal separation; but emboldened by the moral flaccidity that swept through society in the 1970s, she did finally work up the nerve to pull the plug on their marriage. Without this national shift in morals and mores, she would never have had the courage to leave him. But by the late 1970s, everybody was leaving everybody.

I had cleared out of Philadelphia forever by the time my parents threw in the towel. I returned to France in 1976, tracked down an English-woman I had met and fallen in love with two years earlier, persuaded her to move to New York, then induced her to marry me. While Francesca worked her fingers to the bone writing continuing-education scripts for films produced by the American Institute of Certified Public Accountants, some of them directed by a man who had previously directed episodes of the Gothic soap opera *Dark Shadows,* I started making my way in the world. I wrote four novels and more than a hundred short stories. My fledgling attempts were not successful; no one was interested in the novels, and the stories were purchased almost exclusively by literary magazines that paid in copies or by skin magazines that would juxtapose a story about the Mafia coming after God for gambling debts with photographs of women endowed with implausibly mammoth breasts. These setbacks I viewed as no more than delays: I understood that editors were reluctant to publish anything by an unknown, no matter how good, until the newcomer had obtained the imprimatur of a major magazine, newspaper, or eccentric millionaire. Editors did not march until someone gave them their marching orders.

It took me ten years to secure a foothold in the business; success eluded me until I gave up writing fiction, switched to journalism, and received the official laying-on of hands from *The New Republic* and *The Wall Street Journal.* After all those years in the wilderness—once receiving nine rejections in a single day—I was cordially invited into the house of mirth. This was almost certainly because the zeitgeist changed, and the fifty-year-olds who had been rejecting my work because I did not write like James Thurber and Peter De Vries—masters of wryness—were replaced by thirty-five-year-olds with little appetite for the wry.

The roadblocks along the way were of no consequence because Francesca and I were happy to be in New York and enjoyed each other's company. For me, the thrill of living with someone who gave not the slightest indication of latent insanity more than compensated for the fistfuls of rejection letters I received every day.

For quite a few years, the family had little contact with my father. His vanishing act suited us just fine; we would have been perfectly happy to never hear from him again or to read one day in the papers that he was dead. We did not feel sorry for him; we did not feel that he was entitled to our compassion, our sympathy, our cash. He was gone—and good riddance. Francesca, compassionate by nature, would sometimes encourage me to contact him, but I sloughed off these suggestions. Keeping my father at bay was almost a medical precaution; with his ingratiating Irish smile and beguiling demeanor, he could make you forget why you did not want him around in the first place. First he got into your house, and then he got into your heart. This was why I was always willing to send him money I did not expect him to repay but did not want him coming anywhere near me. During one five-year stretch, I saw him only once. He phoned us from the Port Authority around dinnertime, asking if he could stay the night. He was on the way back from a retreat at a monastery an hour north of Manhattan, but a heartless bellboy had filched his wallet while he was showering in a seedy hotel, and as luck would have it, he did not have enough cash to cover the return trip to Philadelphia. *The Case of the Purloined Portefeuille* was an old standby; I first heard him use it three decades earlier when describing an incident that had supposedly transpired at the North Philadelphia train station. This was at least the fourth time I'd heard him recount the story, each time embellishing it a bit, sometimes claiming that he had caught a glimpse of the thief's face, another time reporting that the thief was accompanied by a swarthy confederate to whom he passed the swag. We took him in for the evening, fed him, gave him some cash, then sent him on his way in the morning. He did not ask if he could stay a few days longer until he got on his feet, and not even my indulgent wife bothered to suggest that he do so.

The evening of that unexpected visit, father and son went out for a drink. After the usual preliminaries about the worthless Phillies, he said that he would have really appreciated it—indeed, would have interpreted it as a sign of respect—if I had consulted him before asking for my wife's hand in marriage. In slipping effortlessly into the role of the elder statesman, the wise, knowing patriarch to whom a measure of filial deference was due, he had somehow mistaken himself for the marquis of Tavistock or the fifth laird of Culloden. But then again, he had always been susceptible to periodic bouts of brain fever, during which he attempted to rearrogate to himself that vast array of paternal rights he had long since abdicated.

The years came, the years went. He was living here, he was living there. Did he work? Was he well? I had no idea. I was getting on with my life. His long absences transformed him into a harmless mythological creature; when the rest of us would gather at holidays, we could trot out our very finest material: *Remember the night he fell on the floor and broke his glasses, remember the night he fell off the fishing boat, remember the night he ripped the* NO PARKING *sign out of the sidewalk and hid it in the basement, remember the night he threw the beer bottles through the window?* We talked about him as if he were already dead; such wishful thinking was rooted in the hope that he would kick the bucket before reaching the age when he might expect one of us to take him in, because even though none of us was ever going to open our doors to him, one of us would have to draw the short straw and tell him that.

To our universal amazement, he picked himself up off the canvas and made an epic comeback. He got his drinking under control, found himself a cozy little apartment, landed a job as a doorman at a swanky apartment building across the street from the art museum. Now he was pulling down a decent salary, solid benefits, the works. Then something even more remarkable occurred: Around the time my daughter was born, in 1983, my parents reunited. This came as a shock to the rest of us, as it certainly seemed at the time they'd split up that the rupture was final.

It was not. Prepared to give the old reprobate another shot, forever hoping that the goodness abiding deep within him would one day burst forth in full flower, we thought this was very uplifting, almost sweet.

Throughout this interlude, we were beguiled into thinking that our parents' tragic saga might have a fairy-tale ending after all. "They look so cute together!" one of my sisters declared. They did, indeed. The prodigal had returned from his sojourn in the fleshpots of Gaza, and there would be much rejoicing over he who had been lost and was now found. A weak and sinning man had been saved by the love of a good woman, and thanks to my mother's prayers, the intercession of the Holy Angels and perhaps a bit of sub-rosa backstage intervention from the Lamb of God Himself, we might all live happily ever after.

Of this delusion we were promptly disabused. A few months after their rapprochement, my mother tossed him out onto the street, this time for good. In her recapitulation of events, my father, as soon as he had found a place to hang his hat, was back to his old tricks: stealing money from her pocketbook, tippling on the side, playing the music he wanted to hear at the volume he wanted to hear it, dictating what they would eat and when they would eat it, where they would go and how long they would stay. He was already skating on thin ice when he nixed the idea of visiting the casinos in Atlantic City two to three times a week, as this was the only place my mother ever truly felt wanted. Then one day he went a step too far: He left the gas jets on in the kitchen, with no flame burning, before shambling off for his morning constitutional. This suggested that he was oblivious to reality—losing his marbles—or had his eyes on her insurance money. Either way, he was more trouble than he was worth. Sayonara.

Before the final breakup, I visited my parents with my newborn daughter at Easter time. My father was now just this side of sixty, no longer young, but not yet old. We gathered at my mother's apartment and had a gay old time. Mom, in the bubbly phase of her manic-depressive cycle, was in high spirits, and my father was his usual loquacious self; he could always turn on the charm. Somewhere along the line he asked if he could speak to me privately. I assumed he was going to hit me up for a loan. This did not bother me. I had lots of money by this juncture, and his demands were invariably paltry. We stepped into the bedroom, and suddenly his expression turned serious. It reminded me of the times he would take off his glasses and put on his sanctimonious letter-writing face. It was the face of rehearsed, choreographed gravitas. It was the face of the world-class Celtic ham.

"Joey, I know I treated you and your sisters badly when you were kids," he began. "One of the things I've learned through Alcoholics Anonymous is that you have to admit that you've hurt people and let them know how sorry you are. I know that I did some bad things back then, and I apologize. Son, I'm sorry for anything I may have done to harm you."

Then he stuck out his hand.

I did not have it in me to forgive him, as absolution was not my line of trade, but I shook his hand anyway, if only because this creepy vignette made me uncomfortable and I wanted it to be over. Clemency was not included in my limited roster of emotions, but because he seemed to be making an effort to turn his life around, I did not express my true feelings at the time. Still, the whole thing rankled. I didn't like the way my father phrased his apology; it sounded like he was working from a script. I knew, of course, that the self-abnegation–by–numbers routine was a stunt suggested to people like my father by Alcoholics Anonymous. You had done many bad things and now realized that you were powerless before the fearsome suzerainty of demon alcohol, but you were man enough to fess up to your mistakes. You said a few words, you stuck out your hand—meekly, if you were any good at this sort of thing—your apology was accepted, and then everything was even-steven. It was, I believe, Step Number Five in AA's Golden Road to self-redemption. Or maybe Number Seven. The gauchest element in this procedure was that the drinker's victims were recruited—"commandeered" is a better word—into the ceremony, assigned the unfulfilling role of cogs in the miscreant's wheel of redemption. Accepting the proffered apology was de rigueur, for without it, the penitent substance abuser might relapse, if only out of disappointment at being denied absolution.

Nothing my father had done in all the years I'd known him infuriated me more than this fleabag apology. By this time, of course, America had entered a dismal era when alcoholics demanded ceremonial exculpation for their wrongdoing because they professed to be powerless before their addiction. They were like Austrians trying to explain away Hitler: Forget all that Anschluss unpleasantness; we were victims, too. Where alcoholics had long been viewed as selfish people with flabby wills, they now professed to be saddled with a misfiring gene that made it impossible to resist the allure of the bottle, or afflicted by rogue enzymes that did not break down the amino acids in their eighth martini properly. Alcoholism was no longer a sign of weak moral character; it was a malignancy that lay outside the substance abuser's control. Alcoholism had traditionally been viewed as a deliberate transgression against the social code or, in the community I grew up in, a sin. Now it was being repackaged into something closer to melanoma or lupus.

By this point in my life, I knew quite a bit about alcohol. I'd been drinking since I was fifteen, sometimes too much, sometimes too often. I never for a moment thought I would end up like my father, but by my middle thirties I was still working at a backwater job, making little headway as a writer, and I was starting to wonder if alcohol might be part of the problem. Unlike my father, who turned belligerent when he drank, I turned passive. I didn't want to fight with people when I was drinking; I was content to sit and watch sports. But in the long run, alcohol was having the same effect on both of us: We were not achieving any of the things we had hoped to achieve when we were young.

One day, I decided to attend a support group for the children of alcoholics. It scared me speechless. The other people in the group were hard drinkers, which I was not. They got up in the morning and thought about alcohol, which I did not. They'd ruined marriages and lost jobs and wrecked automobiles because of alcohol, which I had not. All the same, I liked a drink or two when I came home from work. Sometimes, more than two. Did this mean I was doomed to end up like them?

One night Francesca announced that she was pregnant for the second time. We soon found out that she was carrying a boy. My drinking days were over. It would be nice to think that I made a solemn vow to never put my son through what I'd been through as a child; but why then had I not stopped drinking when my daughter was born, two years earlier? No, it was more a case of fatigue with alcohol as a substance, a rationalization, a topic, a word. For thirty-five years, alcohol had been at the center of every conversation my family engaged in, and now I wanted that conversation to end. I didn't want to drink alcohol, think about alcohol, talk about alcohol. I wanted alcohol—as a beverage, a theme, a backdrop, a depressant, a leitmotif, an excuse, a casus belli—out of my life forever. I stopped drinking the day I found out that my wife was carrying a boy. I never drank again.

A few months later, perhaps not coincidentally, my career took off. Articles I wrote appeared in rapid succession in *The Wall Street Journal*, *The New Republic*, *The New York Times*. Doors that had been shut now swung open. One such door was the "My Turn" column in *Newsweek*. "My Turn" was designed as a forum for nonprofessionals, a sounding board for voices that did not resemble those of the solid, reliable, but uninspiring members of the staff. Because I was still technically considered a layman at the time, and because good essays were hard to come by, *Newsweek* was happy to purchase my wares. My first column was a tongue-in-cheek defense of bean counters, whose numbers included my wife: Francesca, a chartered accountant, had led a life that was far more interesting than that of most of the people I knew, because she was, in fact, far more interesting than most people.

The second column, "Too Late to Say 'I'm Sorry,'" was an all-out assault on alcoholics in general, and my father in particular. It recounted the beatings, the terror, the rationalizations, the halfhearted handshake. It was uncompromising and vicious, taking direct aim at AA and its army of smarmy self-congratulators. Since I had struggled with the same predisposition toward alcoholism that my father had inherited from his father, and that his father had inherited from his father, and that everyone named McNulty or Monaghan or O'Rourke had supposedly inherited from some male progenitor in our engaging but accursed ethnic group, I knew that reinventing alcoholism as a medical condition was despicable. Physiologically, alcohol was not an especially addictive drug; it was certainly much less addictive than cocaine or, for that matter, nicotine. Everyone who put a glass of liquor to his lips knew exactly what he was doing; it was not like coming down with malaria because you'd strayed into the wrong jungle.

While it was true that hard-core alkies might suffer from delirium tremens and need to be hospitalized for a few days after trying to conquer their addiction, this was not the case with the vast majority of alcoholics, who merely used liquor as a socially sanctioned medication enabling them to pretend that they were not the people they so obviously were. It was certainly not true of my father; as with most alcoholics, his nocturnal bacchanalias did not prevent him from getting up bright and early the following morning, suffering no physiological effects more serious than a headache or a bad case of the heaves. He never once got so drunk that it deprived him of the physical ability to hit us the next day. The Aquarian Age approach to alcoholism suited him to a tee: First you beat your kids, then you blamed on it on your metabolism.

Because I had pulled the plug on liquor forever in a relatively short period of time, I had little patience or sympathy for alcoholics. Others felt the same way. The day the *Newsweek* column appeared, I received a string of phone calls from children of alcoholics. The calls kept coming all day, always from women. Their stories ran much the same: Their fathers had beaten them. Their boyfriends had raped them. Their boyfriends had beaten them. Their fathers had raped them. Then, years later, as if on cue, the unexpected call came from out of nowhere: "Margie, you probably don't remember me, but I did some terrible things to you when we were together. And now I just want to say I'm sorry." "Betsy, I know that I hurt you . . ." "Louise, I know that when we were together . . ."

Several weeks after the "My Turn" column ran, a UPS truck pulled up outside my house and a large box was deposited on my porch. The box contained hundreds of letters and packages responding to the column, forwarded by *Newsweek*. Unlike the callers, the letter writers were apoplectic. By a margin of nine to one—I counted—they condemned me for writing the story. They said I had hate in my heart. They deplored my callous refusal to forgive. They quoted scripture in the way that believers always quote scripture to nonbelievers, as if an argument were closed simply because Saint Paul had once written a letter to the Corinthians about it.

Some of the packages included Bibles, missals, religious tracts, pamphlets, creating the impression that an incompetent Christian publishing house had inadvertently sent a single misbegotten atheist enough inspirational reading material to convert an entire heathen Zip Code. Virtually all of the letter writers were recovering alcoholics, who were unanimous in their belief that the refusal to forgive usurped the power of the Lord, that withholding forgiveness upset the natural order of the universe. It was clear from my exegesis of these unsolicited materials that the only thing a drunk enjoyed more than talking about his sobriety was writing about his sobriety.

I did not write the *Newsweek* essay in order to be cruel to my father. I wrote it because I knew that it was a story others would appreciate, because it was the best story I would ever have an opportunity to recount in a nine-hundred-word format, and because it was the only story that ever really mattered to me. None of us knew where my father was living when the piece appeared, nor did any of us have any real expectations that he would ever read it. One report had him yet again settling in with his younger sister Rosemary behind the Venetian blinds that never opened. Another indicated that he was out in the suburbs somewhere. Recently, he had been spotted in Philadelphia's historic district. No, he was sharing an apartment with a mysterious jewelry dealer who later turned up dead. There were occasional sightings at Old Saint Joseph's Church, where he was said to be attending mass every morning. Or perhaps it was Saint Mary's, where Commodore Barry, the father of the U.S. Navy, and Jackie Kennedy's wayward father, Black Jack Bouvier, were buried. The grapevine also served notice that he had fleetingly returned to a truly awful neighborhood in North Philadelphia where he had spent a few years as a boy, but that he was now living on the third story of a building on the stretch of Vine Street known as Skid Row. He was out there somewhere, hither or yon. He had gone walkabout, and would for all intents and purposes drop off the face of the earth for the next decade.

Seven years after the *Newsweek* essay appeared, I made a mordant, amateurish film called *Twelve Steps to Death*. Its central character was a stone-hearted police officer investigating a murder in which all the suspects were alkies, cokeheads, junkies, credit-card addicts, porkers, chocoholics, sex addicts. Into it I channeled all my contempt for twelve-step programs, built up over the course of a lifetime. Some people thought I was being gratuitously mean at the time, playing the substance-abuse joke for laughs, but there was nothing gratuitous about it.

We finished shooting the movie on a Sunday night. The next day, Francesca and I had plans to take our two children on a vacation in Ontario. When I returned to the house Sunday evening, my wife had not yet begun packing. She'd been keeping something from me until the film was in the can. Now she broke the news: She'd received a call from one of my sisters, announcing that my father had been admitted to Pennsylvania Hospital in downtown Philadelphia, suffering from cancerous nodes on his lungs. He had, so she gathered, been living in a nearby flophouse and had begun to suffer breathing pains. He had always had the most exquisite taste in flophouses, for even though the building itself was a stinking dive with crummy lighting, a fetid bath-room, doors that would not lock, and a clientele consisting entirely of the living dead, it was right around the corner from Independence Hall, one of the most beautiful buildings in America. It was also within easy walking distance of several of the finest teaching hospitals in the United States.

We canceled the trip to Canada, and the next morning I took a train down to Philadelphia to check on my father's health. This time, he had stepped in clover; if you were a cancer victim recuperating from malig-nant nodes on the lungs, this was a swell place to do it. Pennsylvania Hospital is an ingratiating, Federal-era redbrick building on one of those leafy cobblestone streets that give Old Philadelphia all the charm that New Philadelphia lacks. My father was surprised when I sidled into his room that morning, as well he should have been. It had been a while.

"I never thought I'd see *you* down here, buddy," he said.

"I'm full of surprises."

"You sure are."

"I sure am."

We chatted affably, in the fashion of convivial men, as if we were a normal father and a normal son; as if I hadn't moved 130 miles north just to get away from him; as if he weren't living in a vermin-infested hellhole; as if the last forty-four years hadn't happened. I checked on his medical condition and learned that the operation had been a success. He would have to stop smoking, of course, but otherwise his health wasn't all that bad, considering that he'd been drinking since he was thirteen and smoking since he was ten and had last done any physical exercise the year the Reds crossed the Yalu.

The doctors said he would be free to leave within a few days, provided he had someplace to go. We discussed his options, such as they were. Then I did what I always did in situations such as this; I pulled out my checkbook and made a problem go away. There was never any possibility of my wife and I taking my father into our home in suburban New York; I did not want to expose my children to him on a regular basis and then have to explain why we had to throw him out, or why he had disappeared and taken several of the appliances with him. Besides, he loved Philadelphia, where all his memories were. On the other hand, I couldn't simply fork over a substantial sum of money to get him settled somewhere, because any spare cash would prove an insurmountable temptation that would send him hurtling back into the nearest saloon. So we put our heads together and figured out precisely how many of his expenses would be covered by Social Security and how much he would need from our end to maintain a decent standard of living. It wasn't really much of a discussion; it was more like an edict.

"You can't go back to Seventh Street, Dad," I explained. "You'll die there. The smell alone will kill you."

"The two nice fellows who run the candy store downstairs said they'd let me stay rent-free if I painted the hallway . . ." he volunteered.

"You don't know how to paint, Dad. You never did. Neither do I. And people who run flophouses aren't nice fellows."

"I won't be able to get an apartment, Joe," he confessed. "I bolted out on the last one and beat the landlord out of a month's rent, and I never paid the gas and electric . . ."

"This whole town is filled with people who haven't paid their gas and electric bills, Dad. We'll take care of it."

"I bolted on the apartment before that . . ."

"We'll take care of that, too."

I told my father that I was willing to pay his electric bills and his gas bills, but that he must find himself a decent apartment in a sensible neighborhood where the rest of us wouldn't have to worry about him getting knifed in the back by crackheads. The flophouse was a glorified holding tank, with primitive, almost aleatory heating. If he went back there, he would die alone, and no one would know he was dead for weeks. I had a strong personal interest in avoiding this sort of Grand Guignol finale. If he was going to die, let him die respectably. Let him die the way other people died.

Eventually, he agreed to do as I asked. He would patch things up with the utility companies. He would straighten things out with his landlord. I wrote him a check for $500. Why I thought he would have a bank account or an I.D. or any mechanism for cashing a check that size is beyond me; I had long since lost track of the idiosyncrasies of the underclass. I walked to an ATM and returned with a few hundred dollars in cash. Now the look I knew only too well surged onto his face.

"I don't deserve this," he said, making a clumsy effort to clasp me in his arms. "You kids are so good to me, and I've never done anything to deserve it."

I stiffened, as I always stiffened when he essayed one of his clumsy embraces. These gestures were parodies of normal expressions of affection; in the field of emotion, we were both rank amateurs. Viewed from a distance, we must have looked like feuding capos engaging in ceremonial rites of feigned amity, gestures alien to men who had never mastered the techniques needed to make their feelings visually intelligible.

"This isn't going to be the Walton Family Christmas, Dad," I said, lacerating him with the offhanded malice that had by this point become my livelihood. The hugging abruptly ceased.

A few weeks later, we visited him in his new apartment. Philadelphia had lost a third of its population over the previous twenty years, so finding inexpensive lodgings in a relatively safe neighborhood presented no major problem. The one-bedroom unit was furnished in the Lacedaemonian fashion he favored: a folding table in the kitchen, a bed, a cot, some plastic lawn chairs. There was also a cheap clock radio but no TV. As usual, he had a good supply of books on hand: mysteries, religious tracts, a well-thumbed copy of *A Tale of Two Cities.*

To let him know we were coming, we had to send a postcard, as he had no phone. We did not tell my mother or sisters about this flying visit, because they would worry that he would be inspired to reinsinuate himself into their lives as well. The night we arrived, he had set up a folding table in the kitchen on which were arrayed what he always referred to as "nice" lunch meats and kaiser rolls and Tastykakes for the children. From time immemorial, the word "nice" had constituted the highest praise he could offer, signifying that the lunch meats were "fresh" rather than "prepackaged" and consisted of mouthwatering slices of turkey and roast beef rather than generic baloney or pressed ham. We ate with him that day and chatted amiably. We reminisced. We tried to remember who played Sydney Carton in the film version of *A Tale of Two Cities*. The children, eleven and eight, amused themselves with the stuffed animals he had bought for them. They tried their best to be affectionate, though, frankly, they must have found the whole thing baffling. If this was their grandfather, why didn't anyone want to see him? Why didn't he ever come visit us? Why didn't he have a television? And who was Madame Defarge?

We stayed for perhaps an hour. Then it was time to go. It was obvious from the look on my father's face that he was crushed by this information.

"I thought you could stay longer," he said, all the air gone out of the balloon. "Maybe have another sandwich."

We could not stay any longer. Visiting time was over. We knew that if we stayed long enough, he would exhume the same old arguments and start the same old fights. To avoid this, we trotted out an assortment of pretexts for leaving. We'd promised to take the kids to the movies. I-95 was murder after sundown. A storm was brewing. What more did he expect? Our pilgrimage to his doorstep was an act of charity, not an obligation. He had no claim on our generosity or friendship, much less our time. We were prepared to come, but we were not prepared to stay.

On the table sat a plastic respirator he was supposed to use several times a day in order to strengthen his lungs. Right next to it sat a carton of off-brand cigarettes, the dirt-cheap, generic version of the filterless

Pall Malls he had been puffing on since he was knee-high to a grasshopper. My wife chided him for continuing to smoke, gently pointing out that it was counterproductive for a seventy-year-old cancer survivor to do rigorous breathing exercises every two hours if he was only going to crack open a fresh pack of coffin nails. But my father had always been a perverse and self-destructive man, and we both knew that the endgame was at hand.

One balmy evening in December 1997, I received an unexpected phone call from my father's downstairs neighbor. My father was desperately ill and had been rushed to a nearby hospital. A month earlier, he had begun complaining about severe back pain. John, who lived in the unit below him, had been coping with spinal problems for years and had volunteered to share his powerful painkillers. This buddy-system self-medicating program had been going on for about six weeks. By this point, my father's torment had become excruciating. As it became clear that his affliction was more than garden-variety back pain, John begged for permission to call the family. My father said he would never speak to him again if he did. He did not want to inconvenience anyone; he had inconvenienced us enough.

John, who finally broke down and phoned the emergency medical service, was the last in a long series of confederates, admirers, and minions who had fallen under my father's potent spell over the years. In the final twelve months of his life, he had been living in a bland four-unit apartment building in a reputable working-class district of northeast Philadelphia. It was his second tour of duty there. One of his neighbors was a divorced young woman with two small children whom he often babysat when she needed to go out shopping. The children adored him. There was also a likable, well-preserved widow roughly my mother's age living directly across the path. She, too, found him to be good company. John, his closest friend in the building, was a divorced man the same age as me. He had a droll sense of humor, a huge collection of baseball cards that proved endlessly fascinating to my son, a copious supply of painkillers, and enormous affection for my father. Thus, it became clear that Dad had created a parallel universe populated by a substitute family, with a stand-in wife, an alternate son and daughter, and a matching set of surrogate grandkids, all of whom thought he was a prince among men. This masterpiece of vicarious parenting showcased my father at his most extravagantly ironic: He who saved other families, his own he could not save.

The fondness his neighbors felt toward my father was profound, genuine, and evident to the naked eye; they could not imagine why he had been cast out into the darkness by his wife and children. They may have seen him a wee bit tipsy on those few occasions when he fell off the wagon, but it is unlikely that they ever saw him reeling drunk. They certainly never witnessed one of his frothing rages, when he would start threatening people and smashing windows and demanding that the Warren Commission reconvene. They dreaded the moment this most engaging of men would disappear from their lives, as he had on a previous occasion, because once he was gone, his special brand of magic would disappear, and this magic could not be replaced.

After John called, I had a brutally straightforward conversation with a doctor at the hospital where my father was being treated. The physician, who knew my identity via a common friend, did not mince words: The patient was dying. He had cancer of the spine, the throat, the lungs, assorted other organs. Whatever the oncologists—dissemblers of the first order—might tell me over the next few days during our consultations about how long my father had to live, the verdict was already in. It might be months; it might be weeks; but this was the last roundup.

When informed that my father would soon be no more, I did not react with the reflexive horror one normally associates with such a disclosure. Instead, I experienced an odd mixture of curiosity and relief. Curiosity because I knew that my father, so long dead to me in my heart, would now be dead to me as a medical fact, making me wonder what it would feel like when he had officially left the stage. Relief because his being hustled off to a hospital from which he would never reemerge was probably the only way he could avoid a sordid demise on Skid Row. For years, I had expected the middle-of-the-night phone call telling me that he had been found with his throat slit ear to ear, long one of the most plausible scenarios for his departure from this vale of tears. Death by cancer was better than death by misadventure. We had reached the end of a long, hard road, but if he shuffled off this mortal coil now, while under professional supervision in a clean, well-lighted place, he would at least die in a state of grace: reconciled to his Church, partially reconciled to his son and one daughter, relatively clean, relatively sober. If he continued to live, he would almost certainly go AWOL and perish in a gin mill, a drunk tank, a flophouse, or a gutter. A proper demise was infinitely preferable; once he was gone, we could all stop worrying about him and, even better, stop thinking about him. For forty years, he had taken up all the emotional space in our lives; it was time for a fresh leading man. From the logistical point of view, it also made my life much easier: Death, I would sometimes remark afterward, was the only way I could keep an eye on him. It was a callous thing to say, but it was true. This was not love; this was surveillance.

When I learned that my father was on the way out, I dropped everything I was working on and headed down to Philadelphia. He had chosen a convenient moment to die: That winter was a placid time in my life, as I had literally just finished writing a book and had no pressing obligations weighing on me. Unlike my sisters, two of whom lived in Philadelphia, the third 120 miles west in Harrisburg, I did not have a job I needed to go to every day, so I was the one best positioned to chaperone our father off the planet, to make the proper arrangements, to sign the relevant documents. For the next few weeks, I tried to spend as much time at the hospital as possible, often remaining on-site for twelve hours at a time. The first few days, as I had been warned the night I learned of my father's illness, the medical staff went through the customary charade of sugarcoating the gravity of his illness. It was boilerplate oncological etiquette: The doctors, males, made sure I was never present when they dropped by for a visit; the nurses, females all, were angels of mercy. Though it was obvious that there was no chance of his surviving the myriad strains of cancer shredding his organs, it was impossible to persuade any of the specialists to provide even a ballpark estimate of how long he had to live. Six months was a possibility. Three months seemed more likely. He could last as long as a year; he could be gone in a matter of weeks. It was impossible to say, they assured me, even though he already had cancer in his throat, lungs, spine, and liver. But I recognized these people for the seasoned liars they were. The truth was, a few weeks were all he had left. The scent of death was already in the room.

The earth moves when a parent dies. But it starts to move earlier. A strange type of shock descends upon us when we realize that those who brought us into the world have reached the end of the line, making it impossible for us to think straight. One day I would run out and buy him thirteen paperback mysteries, enough reading material to last for weeks. But the very same day I would call my sisters to say that he was sinking fast, and if they had any desire to see him before he went, they should make it quick. There was, perhaps, a part of me that wanted to believe that as long as I still felt comfortable enough to wander off hospital grounds and scarf down a cheesesteak or take in a movie, he was not in any imminent danger of dying. Or perhaps by behaving in such cavalier fashion, I was encouraging him to believe that he was not nearly as sick as he was. Be that as it may, I made that call to my sisters.

My father and I did a great deal of talking in the next eight days, always avoiding serious topics. We chatted about why he hated professional football (he thought it was rigged) and professional basketball (the players were all bums). We talked about the legendary 0–0 tie that Notre Dame and Army had played at Yankee Stadium in 1946. We talked about Billy Conn's heroic but disastrous decision to go for the knockout against Joe Louis in their famous title fight; way ahead on points, Conn merely needed to stay out of harm's way the final three rounds and the heavyweight crown would be his. Instead he went for the kill, and Louis knocked him out.

"Why couldn't you let me have the title for six months?" Conn supposedly asked Louis many years later.

"You couldn't hold the title for three rounds," came the reply. "What makes you think you could have held it for six months?"

It was one of my father's favorite stories; the other was when Phillies Hall-of-Famer Robin Roberts was asked toward the end of his career why he had never developed a pickoff move in his youth. To which Roberts replied, "When I was young, there wasn't anybody on base to pick off." My father had worked as a peanut vendor at Connie Mack Stadium in 1950, the year Roberts led the Whiz Kids to their first World Series in thirty-five years. Needless to say, the Yankees wiped the floor with them in the Fall Classic, four games to none. This happened just two weeks before I was born; the Phils would not win another pennant for thirty years, by which point my father, like many old-timers, had given up on baseball. In this sense, my birth came either far too early or ever so slightly too late.

We traded many stories of this nature. I asked if it was true that Frank Rizzo, while still a cop on the beat down on Erie Avenue, had perfected the art of bouncing his nightstick off the pavement and making it ricochet between a fleeing man's legs, breaking one or more of them in the process.

"So they say," he replied. "They used to call him the Cisco Kid."

At the end of each day I would leave the hospital and visit my mother or one of my sisters, who lived nearby. My mother stopped by the hospital a couple of times toward the end, more because of me than because of him. Perhaps she thought I would view it as small of her if she did not at least pop in to say goodbye. Their meetings were oddly formal and ritualistic, as if they had convened in a law office to settle a patent-infringement case. My parents spoke to each other in the way that elderly strangers conversed; they reminisced about a generic past they shared because of their age, not because of their marriage. My father had always insisted that he had never stopped loving my mother, an asser-tion she found either deceitful or irrelevant. In any event, the sentiment was not reciprocated.

Throughout these visits, as he tried to engage her in conversation, my mother sat in a chair on the far side of the room, emitting an arctic civil-ity. He talked to her like a husband; she talked to him like a neighbor. It reminded me of the time I had taken her to a South Street restaurant of no great distinction five years earlier. She had expressed an interest in visiting the bar and grill because of its classic Irish name, Bridget Foy's, admittedly not the sort of enticement that would induce most epicures to make a beeline for the establishment. Later, working our way back toward Reading Terminal train station, we collided with an older gent emerging from the subway.

"Hi," I said to the man.

"Hey, buddy, what are you doing here?" he replied.

"Who's that?" asked my mother, standing at my side, locked in that ethereal, trancelike state she had entered decades earlier, when the world failed her, a state from which she never fully reemerged.

"Well, you were married to him for thirty years, Mom," I said.

My youngest sister, Mary Ann, would join me every day at my father's bedside, but my two other sisters, one a year older, one three years younger, wanted nothing to do with him. Eileen, a health industry executive out in Harrisburg, visited just once; Ree, who worked for the Internal Revenue Service a mile up the road, never. He was, in their eyes, beyond redemption. There was a common fear among us that he might yet pull off a Houdini-like escape, that he might miraculously cheat death and hang on for a few more years, bringing fresh misery to us all, since one of us might be forced to take him in. Nix to that, was my older sisters' attitude: If he cheated death, let him cheat it elsewhere. Children are not born with their hearts hardened in this fashion, not even Irish-Catholic children. They have to be taught by professionals.

I was hardly surprised by my sisters' refusal to visit my father in his final days, as my own motives in this autumnal rescue operation were suspect. Over the past three years, my father and I had jerry-built a relationship of sorts, but it was never rooted in affection. It was more like the stillness at Appomattox, with both combatants exhausted by a war one of them had started, then wished he hadn't, but each had needlessly prolonged. Prosperous, successful, and happy, I saw no reason to be cruel to my ancient enemy. My feelings toward him, however, derived not from love or respect or even pity but from a sense of noblesse oblige. It was not merely that I could afford to be generous to a vanquished adversary; it would have seemed tactless to do otherwise. This was more like a civic obligation; I was not so much a son as an escort.

Ultimately, my attitude toward him was rooted in the sense of Christian duty I had learned as a child, for even after I stopped believing in God, I did not stop believing in Christ, who said that we were obliged to feed the poor, not to like them. I was determined to be at my father's side when the end came, not because he deserved it or would appreciate the gesture but because having a bad father does not give anyone the right to be a bad son. One night, when I was walking out the door to return to

Philadelphia during those final days, my ten-year-old son wandered out into the hallway to say goodbye.

"You're taking good care of your father, aren't you?" he asked.

"Yes," I replied. "Take notes."

My father had his own reasons for cultivating our tenuous liaison over those last couple of years: My wife and I had the scratch to bail him out of a jam. To his credit, he never asked for large sums of money, turning down any amount greater than $250 because being flush would only lead him into temptation. Yet I was more than a steady source of petty cash to him; my way of life intrigued him. His attitude toward me was rooted in a sense of wonder. He was fascinated by my ability to make my way in the world, not only as a writer but as a husband and a father. He seemed amazed that anyone genetically linked to him could possibly amount to anything. He saw the hand of God at work here, not his own.

Puzzled by my success, not entirely sure what I did for a living, he would carry around clippings of articles I had written and show them to friends at AA meetings. Yet on the few occasions when he would introduce me to his neighbors or fellow alkies, he did not speak in the lovingly proprietary way most fathers speak about their sons. Instead, his tone suggested that I was some personable chap he had crossed paths with a few years back, and that against all odds we had somehow managed to stay in touch. Once he even asked me why I had never changed my name.

"Why would I change my name?"

"Well . . . because you might not want to be associated with me."

"It's my name. Anyhow, it's not like you're famous or something."

"I know, but I thought you might not want people to know that I was your father."

"Well, you thought wrong. I like my name. And you are my father."

People who saw us together could not decode our relationship. If this really was your son, how come he never invited you home for Thanksgiving or Christmas dinner? How come you saw him only a couple of times a year and almost never brought along his grandchildren? To an outsider, like my father's landlords, the two Yuppies who ran a prissy candy shoppe on the ground floor and a repellent flophouse on the second, our relationship must have seemed incomprehensible. It was an indisputable fact that I was his son; it was right there in the court records. But there was no way to tell from the way we behaved around one another that we were related. Seeing us together, it would have been easy to mistake me for an industrious census taker gathering data on my appointed rounds and him for one of my accommodating clients. We never gave the impression that we were chums, pals, family.

There is no universally accepted protocol for dying. Some people become alarmingly chatty and forthright as the end draws near. Others clam up entirely in the presence of the Grim Reaper. Some people want to make amends. Others would like to get a few things off their chest. Deathbed confessions are by no means rare. But this is not how my father chose to make his exit. Whenever I was in his room, we would maintain the fiction that he had merely stopped by for a routine checkup. We did not discuss cancer, death, the Last Rites, absolution, or getting his affairs in order. We acted as if this whole thing was a tempest in a teapot, a kerfuffle that would soon blow over. Of course, I could have begun grilling him about unexplained family mysteries, but that would have been a clear signal to him that he was dying. He did not want to believe this; who would? So we pretended that everything was shipshape and never got around to reckoning our accounts and closing the books. He never asked why I wrote that *Newsweek* article. I never asked why he went out of his way to supply such copious material for the essay. He never asked if I was really trying to kill myself that torrid August night. I didn't ask how his little sister died. He didn't ask when I realized that I did not want to be a priest. I didn't ask when he realized that he would never be a monk. He didn't ask if any of us had ever loved him. I didn't ask if he had ever loved us.

Afterward, I wished I had pinned him down on what really happened with the military police when he was arrested after going AWOL and what horrors befell him in the military prison in Georgia where he spent three years after being convicted of desertion. Perhaps I should have used that time to find out why he had been shot as a teenager (I had long since ceased to believe in the ricocheting-bullet explanation), how my mother's brother Henry had died, what circumstances had turned my father's brother Johnny into a career criminal. I would have liked to learn why my father married a woman who did not love him—and never tried terribly hard to disguise the fact—and why the two of them even bothered to have children in the first place. I would have also liked to know what pleasure could possibly be derived from beating children. Did making us worthless make him feel less worthless? Or had he perhaps not noticed that we were unhappy? Hadn't a family-wide rash of suicide attempts and nervous breakdowns and seventeen-year-olds bolting off to New York twenty-four hours after graduating from high school been a tip-off that all was not well? But these subjects were never discussed, because we had never established any effective mechanism for communicating with each other and had a hard time getting the conversational ball rolling. The emotions we had relied on in our dealings for the past five decades were hatred, resentment, condescension, distrust. There was no possibility of a full debriefing or a chimes-at-midnight heart-to-heart now. We were like battered warships that desperately sought to engage but could never maneuver close enough to get the grappling hooks secured.

We did discuss the war years. My father had been out of the country just once, when he was shipped to New Caledonia during the Second World War. New Caledonia was a French colony in the South Pacific, populated by people who were, in his words, as black as the ace of spades. There were still a few Japanese hostiles on the island when he arrived, but not many; the colony had little strategic importance, and the infantry was merely there to mop up. My father loved New Caledonia; throughout his life, he would make references to those years before suddenly dropping the subject, fearing perhaps that it might lead to unsettling questions about his dishonorable discharge and imprisonment. He was not unlike Fletcher Christian and his shipmates in *Mutiny on the Bounty*. He, like they, had fallen hopelessly in love with a tropical paradise, where he was liberated from all responsibility and found himself surrounded by affable, nonthreatening aboriginals. Then he fell ill, perhaps with malaria, and was forcibly recalled from this personal Eden. My father would have made a better life for himself had he never returned from the South Pacific. It was, I believe, the only place he was ever truly happy.

As his life wound down, I avoided all but the most statutory physical contact and any attempt to simulate emotions we did not, in fact, possess. Late in my childhood, my father had developed the habit of hugging his children and telling them that he loved them. He may have learned this from watching television; there was a good deal of choreographed paternal affection in programs of the era. These gestures we found both repulsive and inappropriate, an invasion of privacy, a charade. I am not sure he was ever aware of this. An unreciprocated embrace, the glacial resistance one feels when clasping another human being who does not clasp back, is almost impossible to go undetected. When I was small and defenseless, he had used his arms to beat me. He could not redefine their function now. The statute of limitations on parental affection had long since run out; if you didn't show your kids that you loved them when they were young, it was too late to do it when you were old. I didn't mind my father hugging my kids, because he'd never beaten them with his belt buckle, or abandoned them in a blizzard, or left them alone in a housing project gnawing uncooked spaghetti at midnight while he was out in a taproom getting soused. But I didn't want him hugging me. The nerve endings he was trying to reach had been dead for thirty-five years.

As per my policy for the previous quarter-century, I was keeping my distance, physically, emotionally, even verbally. I was not going to blame him, harass him, badger him, cross-examine him. I was taking the high road. The father I had feared and loathed and wished to see incarcerated or incinerated or flattened by a tractor-trailer had vanished, his place now taken by a harmless, defanged old man. He had not wrecked my life; he had merely wrecked my childhood. And for this he had paid the price. I would rather have suffered any amount of physical abuse as a child than be an adult so reviled by his own children that they wouldn't even come to see him before he died. As he lay there in that Philadelphia hospital, being eaten alive by cancer, it crossed my mind that the God he had long professed to love so deeply was finally evening up the score for a lifetime of transgressions. All his life, my father would rattle on about the lonely passion of Christ Crucified; now he had a chance to find out exactly what it felt like to be Jesus that Friday afternoon on Golgotha when His so-called friends ran away and left Him to face the Romans all by Himself. I did not enjoy watching my father in the throes of agony; I merely felt that his torments did not seem inappropriate. He had done bad things to God's children, and now God was doing bad things to him.

The second and last time my mother visited the hospital was the afternoon my sister Mary Ann and I stopped by the funeral home to arrange for his burial. For some reason, Mom insisted on tagging along. We selected a cheap casket, a cheap funeral service, and the cheapest means of disposing of the remains: cremation. When it came time to discuss what should appear on the mass card at his funeral, my mother piped up, "Memento Mori," which was her favorite prayer, not his. She even recited a few lines: "Out of the depths I have cried out to you, Lord; Lord, hear my prayer." The funeral director then asked how the survivors should be listed in the newspaper obituary notice.

"Survived by wife Agnes," I ventured, but my mother shook her head.

"I'm sorry, but I don't want to be listed in the obituary."

The funeral director and I exchanged glances. My heavens, this was personal. "Survived by daughter Agnes Marie . . ."

Again, my mother shook her head.

"Survived by son Joseph . . ."

Here she registered no objection.

"Survived by daughter Eileen Patricia . . ."

Another shake of the head.

"Survived by daughter Mary Ann . . ."

As Mary Ann was in situ, fully capable of speaking for herself, my mother could not scotch that suggestion. Later on, out in the car, she explained why she chose not to be identified in his obituary. Catholics, of course, were forbidden to divorce, much less remarry. But my mother had never even taken the step of obtaining a legal separation. "I didn't do it to be mean," she explained, "but since we were never legally separated, I'm worried that I might get stuck with all his bills." Afterward, my youngest sister and I discussed printing up an invoice from Mulligan's Tavern designed to look fifty years old, which would read:

```
December 8, 1997
Dear Mrs. Queenan:

Re: Unpaid Beverages on December 8, 1947
Four Tom Collins
Three Manhattans
Eight Depth Charges

With interest, that comes to $32,853. Payable by
check or money order.

Sincerely, The Mulligans
```

But we never did. My mother had a wonderful sense of humor, but a prank like that might have killed her. Later that day, I asked my youngest sister if she hated our father. "No," she replied.

"Why not?" I asked.

"Because hatred is a useless emotion."

The day after our trip to the funeral home, the hospital made the absurd announcement that my father was ready for discharge and could medicate himself at home until the situation deteriorated to such a point that it would be necessary to readmit him to the hospital. I responded to this lunacy by giving his doctor an earful. When this accomplished nothing, I booked a room in an assisted-care facility a few miles up the road and arranged for an ambulance to pick us up the following morning.

This proved unnecessary. When I arrived at the hospital on Saturday morning, my father had fallen prey to pneumonia and at least one other malady. Dying of cancer, he had been cleared for release; incapacitated by pneumonia, he was strictly forbidden to leave the premises. It was like telling a leper not to sleep in front of an electric fan for fear he might catch a chill. Grudgingly, the doctors accepted the indisputable evidence that he was in intense pain and started in with the morphine drip the next day. We were on the killing floor now. My father began to nod off. When I left him that Saturday night, he was dozing. The next morning he lapsed into a deep sleep that may have been a coma. That was it; he was finished; the deathwatch had begun. There was never any formal send-off; we never said goodbye. I do not remember the last words we exchanged. I probably told him to take care of himself, which was as close to affection as I could get. He probably said to be careful riding the subway, as not even the specter of death could deter a pasty-faced Philadelphian from getting in one last dig at the city's anathematized metropolitan transport system. But for all I know, he may have asked for a firmer pillow or a package of Tastykakes. It does not matter. He was a worn-out old man, and it was time for him to go to sleep.

My father remained in this placid, comalike state for the rest of the week. Every day when I arrived, I was told by the nurses that his condition was "stable," that this euthanasia in everything but name had not yet run its course. I would hang around for a while, studying him intently, monitoring his irregular respiratory pattern, sometimes convinced that he had stopped breathing. I was determined to be there when the end came, if not physically on the premises, at least nearby, in the city of his birth.

Meanwhile, back in New York, one of my best friends was winding up a round-the-world trip he had awarded himself as a fiftieth-birthday present. He had started his adventure all the way out in the Cotswolds, in the west of England, then traveled to Sydney, Hawaii, Victoria, and now he had finally arrived in New York. He had been at my house for a few days and was planning to fly home to England on Sunday. John was married to one of my wife's oldest friends and lived in a sixteenth-century manor house with a cabal of anti-establishment holdouts who were only just starting to realize that Margaret Thatcher had killed off the sixties for good. There was a tiny chapel in the backyard that had survived the depredations of Henry VIII because it was privately owned, not part of the monastic system, and was still in use by local Catholics. John belonged to a world I could never have entered had I not met my wife. He would very much like to see me before he returned home, and I would very much like to see him. With my father in a serene vegetative state but the end not yet officially in sight, I decided it was safe to sneak back home for a day to see John and my family.

Friday morning, John and I rose bright and early and headed into Manhattan. New York is never more beguiling than when people not born there get to serve as tour guides. It reminds them that Gotham, like Bach, is a one-off; that, as a friend who grew up in the rural South before moving to Brooklyn once observed, "After you've seen New York, it's *all* Podunk." Friday, December 19, was an unseasonably gorgeous December day, and John and I had a swell time. We managed to squeeze in Central Park, the Museum of Modern Art, Rockefeller Center, the Staten Island Ferry, a stroll across the Brooklyn Bridge, dinner in Chinatown, cheesecake and cappuccino at Ferraro's in Little Italy. It was the Glenn Dreibelbis Circuit, with a few new wrinkles. Topping it off was a chance for John to visit Madison Square Garden for the first time in his life; as luck would have it, a sassy British fighter named Prince Naseem Hamed was topping the card that night.

We bought our tickets, guffawed a bit as the hapless up-and-comers in the prelims flailed about, marveled at the raucous crowd. There were the usual hard-core fight fans, many of them Hispanic, plus a liberal sprinkling of those homegrown old-timers in grimy fedoras who have always given the fight game a special air of romance, not so much because they are especially knowledgeable about boxing but because they know how to wear a fedora. There was also an enormous contingent of stereotypically repellent English hooligans: hog-faced lager louts who had flown over from London to take in the fight and perhaps start a few of their own. Just before the talented but excessively operatic Prince Naseem climbed into the ring, I ducked out to a phone booth to check on my father's condition.

"He won't make it through the night," the nurse who answered the phone informed me.

"But I was told that his condition was stable."

"I don't know who told you that," she replied, "but he won't make it through the night."

"This is his son, Joe," I now informed her. "Could you do me a favor and go in and tell him that I'm coming?"

"He's in a coma," she replied.

"Then he won't mind you telling him."

I returned to my seat, told John that I had to leave, then hustled downstairs from the Garden to Penn Station. The next train leaving for Philadelphia was at 8:05. I was on it. I jumped off at Trenton and grabbed the local train to Holmesburg Station, a few blocks from my little sister's house, a few blocks from the prison where my uncle Johnny had spent so much of his life, one day volunteering for the medical experiments that would eventually kill him. We rushed off to the hospital, took the elevator to the third floor, tumbled into the corridor. We were met by two nurses. We were too late.

My father had breathed his last at 8:05, just as I was getting on the train at Penn Station. Subconsciously, I must have expected this, knowing that a red-letter day like the one John and I had just experienced could not possibly come without a price. As I had always feared, he would die alone. It was typical, and there was no reason to be surprised: He had never given me a break while he was living; he certainly wasn't going to do me any favors when he died.

My sister and I wept a bit, she more than I. We could not help noticing how small and shriveled up he had become. It was hard to believe that someone so frail could have terrorized us for so long. It was a terrible shame, I observed, that he had to be cremated, as we, neither as a family nor as a nation, would soon look again on the likes of his fabulous World War II–era tattoos. My father had crude markings on each of his biceps, one an arrow transfixing a heart beneath the words LOVE, EILEEN, the other a somewhat jaunty anchor. Eileen was my younger sister's name, but this was not the Eileen in question. It was always a source of confusion and embarrassment whenever we went to the beach and he took off his shirt. They were primitive tattoos; they looked like someone named Shanghai or Three-Fingers Brown had sedated him, carved ugly designs into his arm with a trenching tool, poured a vat of blue ink into the holes, then sewed up the whole mess with hemp. I suspect that he got the tattoos in San Francisco the night before he shipped out for the South Pacific in 1943, ten years before my middle sister was born. None of us ever found out who Eileen was. Probably some Frisco floozie.

"We ought to get these things surgically detached and sent to the Smithsonian," I suggested, only half in jest. If it was true, as we were told in catechism class, that the body was the temple of the Lord, then my father had not treated this temple with the respect it deserved. If nothing else, our discussion of the tattoos' artistic merits lightened the mood.

After that, we covered his face with a sheet.

"Don't take any wooden nickels," my sister said in parting. Then I called my mother and told her that her husband was dead. Her response is written in my heart. "It's always something," she said.

"He did have his good qualities."

So my mother would often remark after he was gone. It was true. As my father's death approached I made a laundry list of the things I admired about him. The list was surprisingly long. He was the type of man who bantered effortlessly with strangers, an art not all men possess, and certainly not men of my generation, whose idea of conversing with tradespeople or counter help is glib condescension. He was not afraid to visit rough neighborhoods, because he believed that neighborhoods never stopped belonging to the people who had grown up in them; that the old haunts were sacred, and in some way beautiful, no matter how ravaged they might seem to the naked eye.

He truly loved Philadelphia, a city that is not especially easy to love. He knew where John Barry was buried, where Benjamin Franklin was interred. He would take you there if you liked, then lead you to the pew where Betsy Ross sat every Sunday in Old Christ Church. He could tell you the history of Roman Catholicism in Federal-era Philadelphia, or the causes of the Civil War, and was reasonably conversant with the circumstances surrounding the disintegration of the Roman Empire. He may not have known who Tacitus was, but he was no stranger to the name Tiberius. He knew where Birnam Wood was and why Macbeth feared its arrival in Dunsinane. He could explain why Henry Plantagenet had ordered his henchmen to murder Thomas à Becket. He could tell you why no one was terribly broken up when Oliver Cromwell died. He could tell you the same about Crassus, Marie Antoinette, Joe McCarthy. In late-twentieth-century America, such acumen was astounding.

Many of his traits were bequeathed to me, though not all would agree that these traits were desirable. He had a hair-trigger temper. He did not vacillate when making judgments about people, and once he decided that he hated you, he hated you for good. He maintained a fierce devotion to unpopular theories, even when he suspected that they were no longer tenable. He mispronounced the words "theater" and "nuclear," and seemed to derive considerable pleasure from doing so. He had nothing but disdain for anything that could be categorized as "rah-rah": fraternities, Ivy League tailgaters, anyone who opened his yap about the regatta. He did not dislike rich people, only rich people who pretended they were not; he had no patience with instigators, organizers, and Maoists, convinced that the unscrubbed card-carrying radical in the FREE MUMIA tee shirt was almost certainly the son of the third most sought-after obstetrician in Bryn Mawr. He suspected that anyone who waxed poetic about the old neighborhood in Kensington or Brewerytown or South Philly had probably grown up in Cherry Hill, New Jersey. He also believed that middle-class people who impersonated working-class people should be prosecuted, just like anyone who tried to pass himself off as a doctor or a cop. It was one subject on which we were always in complete agreement, even though my own escape from the proletariat was the greatest achievement of my life. I, like him, could never stomach faux proles, with their nebulous economic underpinnings and suspicious genealogies, creeps who acted as if choreographed goatishness was the salient feature of the blue-collar experience. Just because I wanted out of the working class didn't mean I had invited anyone else in.

For the last twelve months of his life, my father lived in a one-bedroom apartment in a glamour-free but safe working-class neighborhood in Philadelphia. It was the prototypical Quaker City community, where tattered Eagles banners rippled from every flagpole; where the streets teemed with husky young women sporting big hair, their mammoth thighs shoehorned into stonewashed jeans, every last one of them hawking their merchandise in skintight Philadelphia Flyers jackets. It was the kind of community where no block was complete without a funeral home named McGivney's or McGuire's or McGettigan's. It was at one of these establishments that we held the funeral service. Fifteen people attended. There were no eulogies, no reveries, no affirmations, no wisecracks. People were there to mourn and weep, not to try out new material. The priest said what he had to say, and that was that. At one point in the service, my father's downstairs neighbor John, his accomplice in pain management, began to cry inconsolably, to the point that I had to turn around and hug him. Jesus Christ Almighty, I thought at the time; this was my father's funeral; I was the one who should be weeping, yet here I was, consoling the inconsolable. Yet in a way, this situation seemed neither inappropriate nor unexpected. After all, John had enjoyed a better relationship with my father than I did.

After the service and a brief farewell luncheon, my wife and I took the children back to John's apartment. While she was chatting and the kids were admiring his baseball cards, I drifted upstairs to take one last gander at my father's final dwelling place. One thing I found particularly admirable was the way he had prepared for death by getting rid of everything he did not need. His living quarters were spartan even by Spartan standards: a bed, a chifforobe, a folding table in the kitchen, a tape player. He had lived the last few years of his life without a television, a modus vivendi everyone should aspire to. There were plenty of paperback books scattered about: Agatha Christie, Bruce Catton, Taylor Caldwell, Erle Stanley Gardner. That was about the extent of it. This was a place of refuge, the safe house of a gypsy who could get himself packed and out the door in five minutes flat. At the end of his life, my father had turned his apartment into a monk's cell. After all these years, he had finally turned himself into the Trappist he had always dreamed of becoming.

When I rifled through the three plastic bags that contained all his worldly possessions, I felt a burst of pity: A man ought to have more to show for his life than the contents of three Hefty bags. But the more I thought about it, the more I came to believe that this was the way all of us should go to meet our maker. Strip down to the bare essentials. Take what you need and leave the rest. Get ready for the Judgment Day.

In Mike Leigh's film *Vera Drake,* a somewhat daft working-class woman risks everything by performing clumsy, amateur abortions on poor girls who have gotten themselves in the family way and are in no position to bring a child into the world. When the long arm of the law finally clamps down on her, the viewer expects her coarse, not especially bright son-in-law to react with horror at her crimes. Instead, he exonerates her, defending her impoverished clients as well. "If you can't feed them, you can't love them," he says.

This is a lovely sentiment, and it works to perfection on-screen. But it isn't true. By all rights, it *shouldn't* be possible to love children if you can't feed them. But all sorts of people do. Throughout my youth, I was surrounded by poor children whose parents adored them. They were white, black, Latino, Native American. For life's castoffs such as them, having children they loved and who loved them back made all the deprivation and humiliation bearable. They had nothing in the world other than their children, but that was enough, for when the world turned dark, their children banished the darkness.

After my father died, I briefly enshrined him in an afterglow of myth, extolling his sparkling sense of humor, his multitudinous idiosyncrasies, his nomadic lifestyle. I applauded the fact that at the end of his life he had constructed a parallel family and had managed to die in a state of grace, a feat I had long viewed as unattainable. I was even amused when I found out that his brother Johnny had not in fact sent a memorable letter to his siblings announcing that he was going to Kentucky and not coming back, the way we had always been told, but had dragged out the remainder of his short life in the suburbs of Philadelphia, breathing his last fourteen years earlier. I was equally amused when I learned that the house on Henry Avenue where we used to shovel snow was not the house Grace Kelly had grown up in; Dad had made it all up, perhaps to impress me, perhaps because he honestly believed it. He was a rogue to the last; he certainly had his moments; he was truly the life of the party. But the afterglow of affection did not last. Three years after he died, December 19 passed without my noticing it. The nostalgic period had ended. My father was dead, and I did not miss him.

Epilogue

When my daughter was accepted to Harvard in 2001, the first words out of my mouth were "Well, that settles it. You're definitely smarter than I am." This was said in a spirit of mirth, but there was a serious undercurrent. My daughter's acceptance was a triumph not only for her, not only for me and my wife, and by extension our parents, but most especially for my grandparents, intrepid strangers I never knew, who had gathered up their belongings in rural Ireland, booked passage to a distant land, and started a new life. They did this because they had heard that the streets were paved with gold, and were not going to be told otherwise. Bridget's triumph was something everyone could share in, even the long dead, for their childlike theories about the paving materials used in American roadwork had now been proven correct. They, more than anyone else, were the ones responsible for my daughter's good fortune. This was why her name was Bridget, not Britney; why my son, Gordon, was named after an RAF wing commander who killed Nazis, not somebody named Skyler, who didn't. I wanted my kids to know where they came from; I didn't want them to think they had dropped out of the skies.

My father never once derived this kind of joy from the achievements of his children. Not until he was at the very brink of death did he realize that children are jewels, and the only jewels worth having; that the radiance they give off reflects back on those who breathed life into them in the first place. My life has been an attempt to fit this man into some kind of context where he is not merely a villain. This has not been easy. He never gave me the opportunity to love him; the closest I ever got was pity. One of the signal events in my youth, which made me feel sorry for myself at the time, years later made me feel an eerie, gut-wrenching compassion for him instead. The event was the night my uncle Jim came over with that set of jim-dandy American Flyer trains, and my father sent me out to the store, and by the time I returned, he had destroyed the engine, rendering the train set useless. I was enraged at the time; I thought no one in the world could be less fortunate than me. But this was not true. I would grow up, I would earn scads of money, I would buy electric trains for my own son, thereby putting the past to rest forever.

But what was it like to be Joe Queenan Sr. that Sunday evening? What was it like to go through life always being the man who forgot to remove the electric trains from the soon-to-be flooded cellar, the man who, when given a chance to redeem himself with another set of trains, sent them flying off the track as well? What was it like to be the man who looks into his children's eyes and sees fear where there should be affection, hatred where there should be love? What was it like to be the man who was damned if he did and damned if he didn't?

My life has ceaselessly been brightened by men who were more than prepared to fill the role of surrogate father. But I never wanted a surrogate father; I wanted the real thing. I did not get my wish, nor did he, for whatever he wanted in a son, I was not it. In the end, I pity my father for all he missed out on. He never got to take his grandchildren to the zoo. He never got to buy his grandson a hot dog at a ball game. He never got to take his granddaughter to see *Cinderella* or *The Nutcracker*. He never got to have his grandchildren sit on his lap and scratch his beard and beg him to tell them a ghost story. He never got to have his own children visit his home, gather around the fireplace, seek his counsel, mourn his passing.

When a father dies, it is customary to forage through stored memories and conjure up an image that casts him in the most attractive light. If you are lucky, the memory can be so powerful that it supplants, eclipses, or eradicates all others. Here is my memory. The autumn before my father died, I took the commuter local down to Philadelphia to visit him, with my son in tow. I could not reach him by phone; I did not know his address; he had again gone walkabout. But his movements were easy to track; I knew all his old stomping grounds. We found him in a fast-food joint right down the street from his favorite flophouse, one block west of Independence Hall. The restaurant, he maintained, brewed coffee of unimaginable piquancy, though this, like so many of his assertions, had no basis in fact. He was surprised to see us, ashamed that he had again flown the coop. Just as he used to drag me along to prisons and tenebrous inner sanctums where unfulfilled old men were dying, I was dragging my son along to a council of war where I would read my father the riot act. Our sons were our confederates, our partners in crime. We shielded them from some of the unpleasant truths about life but not from all of them. We made it impossible for them to avoid growing up early.

As my son gamboled about in the park across the street from Independence Hall, I told my father, once again, that I would pay his electric bills and his gas bills and pony up for the rent he had run out on. But I insisted that he return to the apartment he had recently bolted from up in Frankford. The flophouse was a hellhole, full stop. It was no place for a sick old man. Beaten down by my hectoring, he agreed to do as I asked. He would patch things up with the landlord and the utility companies. But to do so, he would need a little cash. Once again, we would be visiting the ATM.

My son, for whom my father was more a figure of myth than a real-life creature made of flesh and blood, was ten at the time, a frisky and adventurous age, so the three of us strolled over to the Delaware River to visit a World War II–era submarine that had been turned into a museum. Gordon clambered aboard, merrily scooting through the sub's tiny compartments; I banged my head against the ceiling several times; my father wondered how on earth it was possible for men to function in these floating tombs, indeed, to have volunteered for submarine duty at all. He served up the chilling information that 75 percent of U-boat crewmen ended up in Davy Jones's locker. I was always amazed that he knew such things. Working-class people were supposed to be ignorant. Or hadn't he heard?

Afterward, the three of us took a walk down South Street. My father, who knew the history of the city inside out, was enthralled by the transformation this street had undergone in recent years, when it gradually morphed from a borderline slum into a gaudy bohemian district, the Quaker City's answer to New York's St. Mark's Place. The streets were filled with head shops and tattoo emporiums and Middle Eastern restaurants and used-record stores. It was not the sort of neighborhood where one would expect to find a man in his seventies, but my father had always loved the bright lights and effortlessly rubbed shoulders with the newly tattooed and the freshly pierced without feeling the least bit threatened or outclassed. He possessed that enviable obliviousness that is so common in the elderly; if the streets are crackling with a year-round Mardi Gras ambience, this is where they want to be. Old people don't care about fashion or verifying that everything is up-to-date in Kansas City. The only thing old people want out of life is to breathe another breath and see another sunset.

My son asked if we could stop for pizza. My father, never fond of what he anachronistically referred to as "tomato pies," ordered a meatball sandwich and a cup of coffee. I did the same. The spry young Mexican behind the counter explained that the establishment did not sell coffee but that he would be more than happy to run across the street and get some. We said this was not necessary, but the man insisted, so off he went. I never ceased to marvel at these occurrences, at my poorly dressed, poorly shod father's ability to induce complete strangers to run errands for him, as if he were the last surviving member of the Fujimoro Shogunate on an overnight trip to South Philly. It was a trick I wished he had taught me.

We sat there, talking about beloved old ballplayers, about long-dead singers, about legendarily crooked local politicians. All the while, we munched on our sandwiches. My father mentioned the latest travails of a man who presently headed the City Council and would soon be mayor, whose brother owed thousands of dollars in parking tickets written up for a hot dog stand that had been illegally parked outside Temple University for decades. The scofflaw brother, to the surprise of no one in the Delaware Valley, was a state senator. It was vintage Quaker City lore; the clowns might change, but the clownishness didn't. We were happy, I recall; we were happy like the times we would go out on his pretzel truck and range across the south Jersey countryside and he would buy me a hamburger with French fries and a vanilla milkshake and proudly introduce me to all his customers as the brightest student in my class, the apple of his eye, the well-beloved son in whom he was well pleased.

Once again, we were a team, and today we had my own little boy riding shotgun.

Now that my father is gone and I think back to that afternoon, I regret that there were not more days like that, joyful interludes when a wise old grandfather shuffled around the harbor with his grandson, regaling him with improbable tales of high adventure in the South Pacific. But this was not to be. I once heard a violinist make the seemingly indefensible assertion that there were passages in Schoenberg's music that were as beautiful as anything in Brahms or Mozart but that you had to listen carefully, because there weren't many and they wouldn't last. So it was here. I had taken my son to Philadelphia on a school holiday, and we had spent four hours with my father. It was the only day the three of us would ever spend in one another's company, the only time the three generations of men would be alone together. It was a nippy afternoon, if memory serves correctly, but the sun was shining, the food was delightful, the rancor had subsided, and there was hope in the offing. I was in my forty-sixth year, my father in his seventy-first. It was the second Monday in November. It was Armistice Day.

Acknowledgments

This book owes its existence to the unceasing support of Elise Blackwell, Hella Winston, Rob McQuilkin, and Rick Kot. I am indebted to my sister Mary Ann for help in researching my family's history, to Mike Prendergast and Chris Wogan for supplying information about Cardinal Dougherty High School, and to Mike Walsh for his generous assistance in retracing my steps at the Maryknoll Junior Seminary. Tom Donahue, Rob Weiss, Chris Taylor, and Richie Giardinelli were invaluable in resolving assorted mysteries involving the Quaker City. I am very grateful to Laura Tisdel, Francesca Belanger, Paul Buckley, Sharon Gonzalez, Ann Day, and Sonya Cheuse at Viking, and to designer Erin Schnell. A special debt of thanks is due to my son, Gordon, who fact-checked the manuscript, and to my daughter, Bridget, who acted as a sounding board throughout the four years I worked on this project.

Finally, without the unflagging encouragement and patience of my wife, Francesca, this book would never have come into being.